Transformations

Transformations
Art and the City

Edited by Elizabeth M. Grierson

intellect Bristol, UK / Chicago, USA

First published in the UK in 2017 by
Intellect, The Mill, Parnall Road, Fishponds, Bristol, BS16 3JG, UK

First published in the USA in 2017 by
Intellect, The University of Chicago Press, 1427 E. 60th Street,
Chicago, IL 60637, USA

A catalogue record for this book is available from the British Library.

Copy-editor: MPS Technologies
Cover designer: Lucy McArthur
Production manager: Jelena Stanovnik, Matthew Greenfield and
    Naomi Curston
Typesetting: Contentra Technologies

Print ISBN: 978-1-78320-772-5
ePDF ISBN: 978-1-78320-773-2
ePUB ISBN: 978-1-78320-774-9

This work has been developed and published in collaboration with AMPS
(Architecture, Media, Politics, Society).

Printed and bound by Hobbs, UK

Sponsored by CAST Research Centre for Art Society and Transformations
RMIT University Melbourne Australia.

This is part of the Mediated Cities series.
ISSN: 2058-9409
Series editor: Graham Cairns, AMPS

This is a peer-reviewed publication.

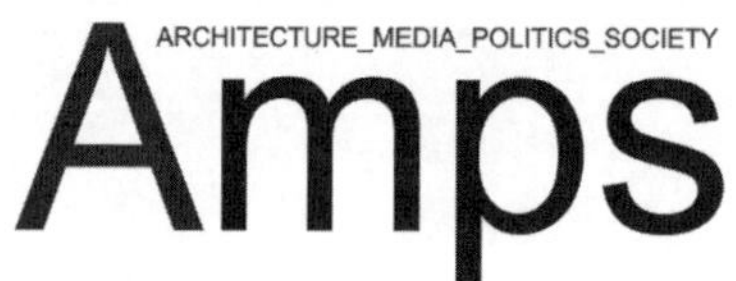

Contents

Foreword

This anthology emerged from a very special symposium that brought together leading arts practitioners, academics and stakeholders from industry and government to grapple with pressing issues in the public and urban realm. Its driving questions were framed around the notion of transformation, the operation of changing—by rotation, mapping, mutation— from one configuration or expression into another. Transformation can be radical or incremental, it can be sudden or gradual, but (as most definitions tell us) it will eventually result in a marked change of appearance, usually (according to the more optimistic texts) for the better.

This is an ambitious claim and the contributors to this highly stimulating volume rise to the task in hand. They do so largely, though not uniquely, through the multi-focal lens of creative practices. Many of the chapters also embrace trans- and inter-disciplinary thinking, exploring the urban through a diverse set of interests—arts, media, education, policy, business, science, engineering, cartography, law. The result is a stimulating cocktail of enquiry that offers fresh insight alongside rigorous critique.

Focusing on the roles of creative and aesthetic practice, this new study offers innovative insights into contemporary debates and the current dynamics of our urban domain. By problematizing the dominant rhetoric, the anthology offers a fresh critique of our over-furnished cities, explores the essential role of socially engaged practices and invites a reappraisal of the current fascination with place-making. Contributors take to task the easy diction of space, place and the urban; through some excellent analyses they contest the familiar—and possibly overused—ideas that permeate the discourse of 'public art', a term now so overused as to have lost much of its traction.

It is the right moment to offer up this critique. This timely anthology, originating from Australia but drawing on global case studies and examples, highlights a refreshing array of projects and positions through the lens of differentiated and material practices. Taking 'the city' as an extensive field of enquiry, it adopts a five-part structure to lend thematic shape to the book, allowing the very notion of difference to form its own organizing strategy.

Sixty years ago, in 'The Natural History of Urbanization' Lewis Mumford warned that 'the blind forces of urbanisation, flowing along the lines of least resistance, show no aptitude for creating an urban and industrial pattern that will be stable, self-sustaining and self-renewing'. However bleak this prognosis and however real its dystopian vision, this volume demonstrates a willingness to bring together artists, art historians, philosophers, architects, political geographers, cultural theorists, urbanists, and media practitioners and writers to address the concerns of globalization and the environment, and to grapple—with wit, innovation and creative insight—with the twenty-first-century conditions and concerns of urban space, the public realm and the human condition.

Professor Paul Gough
Pro-Vice Chancellor and Vice-President
RMIT University Melbourne

Acknowledgements

The editor would like to thank Intellect Ltd., UK for accepting this book into the Mediated Cities series. Thanks are due also to the anonymous reviewers of the manuscript for their practical and helpful comments.

Grateful thanks to Paul Gough for dedicating his time to provide a Foreword for the book. And a special thank you to all the contributing authors for their scholarly and readable texts, and, during the editing stages, for their attention to detail and coherence.

Thanks are due to the Research Centre for Art, Society and Transformations (CAST) at RMIT University for supporting this publication.

Acknowledgement is given to those artists, photographers and institutions who gave permission for images to be reproduced in these pages.

Finally, the editor and authors acknowledge the Traditional Custodians of the lands on which we work and live, and extend respect to all Aboriginal and Torres Strait Islander peoples in Australia, and to the *tangata whenua* of Aotearoa New Zealand. We pay our respects to their Elders past and present.

Introduction: Situating trans-formations

Elizabeth M. Grierson

Situating Trans-formations

This book investigates *trans-formations* in an urban context. It raises enquiry about cities, the ways we live in them, engage with them and react to them. *It asks what it may mean to form and transform the places we inhabit.* Is transformation something that just happens in the collective processes of daily lives? Or do we set out to transform urban environments with active intent? How may aesthetic practices play a part to activate or transform city inhabitants and spaces; and likewise, to what extent do cities, their inhabitants and regulatory technologies effect practices?

The impetus for this book project came from a symposium on art and city transformations held by the Research Centre for Art, Society and Transformations (CAST) at RMIT University, Melbourne in 2014. That event brought together a wide range of disciplinary perspectives—arts, media, communications, education, policy, business, science, engineering, geography, cartography, law—to address issues of change and transformation in and of the city. Stimulating debates around discourses arose. It became clear that the time was right to grasp the ideas in ferment, to extend the research and to widen the audience for this important topic.

Trans- acts as a crucial sign in thematizing this book: *trans*-formations, *trans*-positions, *trans*-locations, *trans*-figurations, *trans*itions, *trans*cripts, *trans*lations, all suggesting a movement across, lending spatial and temporal dimensions to place. As art, design and architecture form objects in their spatial dynamics, so they also trans-pose those same dynamics. Between formation and trans-position lies a productive site of transformation.

The signs of transformation are situating discourses 'as practices obeying certain rules' (Foucault 1994: 138). The collection acts as a discourse of the city—the book as a discourse founded in discursivity with all its differential formations; it does not stand 'as a sign of something else' (Foucault 1994: 138).

Discursive practices encompass the various works, objects, ideas, languages, regulations or laws that determine a particular meaning—embedded in institutions of society—at any given time and place. The discourse as presented here 'does not seek another, better-hidden discourse' (Foucault 1994: 139). It is what it is: a construction of discursive practices that comprise its evidential findings.

Questions of Power and Politics

Some key questions arose from the symposium. What roles do the arts and aesthetics, creative practices and poetics play in this discourse? How may we understand the city of the twenty-first century through an aesthetic lens—and what possibilities exist for transformative action? The collection gives opportunity to consider the relations of power and politics in on-the-ground practices. What does it mean to have an informed public realm? Where and how shall we find it? Where shall the emphases lie?

Arising from the globalized, neo-liberal state, and 'economization' of public space, questions constitute a terrain in which debate finds fertile ground. In the global world of today, the neo-liberal project of urban planning and progress seduces every pursuit with its demands for efficient use-value of public resources. It certainly seduces the ordained institutions of society—education, health, housing, transport, policing, law and justice—to adopt an instrumentalized form of agency in the 'technologies of governmentality'—as in Foucault's 1998 conceptualization of the play of power in dominant and marginalized discourses.

If one approaches questions and problems of a city through *difference*, and places in thoughtful relief the issues and problems urban inhabitants face in everyday lives, also through difference, then one may widen the scope of approach beyond an instrumentalized economization of urban space. One may extend the enquiry to a more nuanced understanding not only of 'the urban' and what it means to have an informed public realm, but also of the human subject—as in Socrates' mission: 'in teaching people to occupy themselves with themselves, he teaches them to occupy themselves with the city' (Foucault 1998: 20).

In paying attention to the urban conditions of those both in and out of global influence, it seems inescapable that the workings of power and politics must underpin the discussions in this collection. What are the politics of urban renewal in a global world of uneven economic distribution and power relations—or city renewal in the face of environmental disaster? There is always the question of distribution of resources, inequality of voice, questions of rights and obligations, and the ever-present tensions between collective goals and private interests—even as the analyses of transformative practices emerge through the lens of art and aesthetics.

Difference as an Organizing Strategy

Curiosity and enthusiasm for *difference* as an organizing strategy for theory and practice fed the desire to bring this collection together. The politics of difference held particular sway in my archive of philosophical enquiry and this politic underscored an abiding interest in the way difference intervenes in normalized patterns. So I was keen to activate this terrain by including chapters that might address aesthetic ways of negotiating normative hegemonies in and of the city. Thus via *difference* as an organizing strategy the overall aim is to open enquiry, on the city, to a *more nuanced* understanding of 'city-ness' through the philosophies and practices of art, aesthetics, education, justice and the human subject. Difference, considered thus, is an epistemological process: it deals with knowledge formations. It is also ontological in that the human subject is always implicated in questions of ethics and justice that underpin citizenship and community engagement. And with reference to Foucault, difference is also a genealogical process as it identifies traces of meaning in the archaeologies of knowledge (Foucault 1994).

When applied to the city as a field of enquiry, the human subject in all its differential formations deserves attention: in the ways people live in a city, the ways people imagine a city, the ways people articulate and inform a city, the ways people resource a city and 'the mapping of transformations' of a city (Foucault 1994: 138). This approach to the city and its subjects, through *archaeologies of difference,* provides the inspiration and organizing strategy for the collection.

Let us imagine the potential for transformations of the city as a responsive cultural and aesthetic space; and the potential for the city to be a just, restorative and informed space. With urban place defining the twenty-first century, cities as economic hubs are informing the way we think about the global world. This collection affirms the role of creative and aesthetic practices in this process. Aware of plays of power in the ground of urban governance, the writers turn to aesthetic projects in public space to investigate apt potentials for the politics of artistic practice (Mouffe 2013).

Sites of resistance may bring new social transformations to the fore. 'Resistance upsets the hegemony of political consensus, which—however unstable—consolidates the interest of élites by normalising their interests into a common sense culture' (Grierson and Engels-Schwarzpaul 2004: 6). Perhaps upsetting the hegemony, or at least bringing it to attention, is what sustains this collection. In their quest to engage with the city, the writers contribute aesthetic projects on art and activism, policy and planning, discovery and mapping, community resilience, disaster response, restorative justice, listening to the city, enacting pedagogy and writing a poetics. Calling on a range of different philosophical, theoretical and practical positions, it could be said therefore that the writers are writing—and reading—a city through difference.

The City-State

Today's global world continues to be characterized by an aggregate of nation-states meeting at multiple global intersections, either by chance or design, and negotiating positions like Janus with an eye on their local/global political interests. Cities are part of this matrix. The ideal 'city-state' of Plato's design in *The Republic* (*c.*380 BCE, 1959) has, over the centuries, morphed in shape, character and constitution. Beyond idealist dispositions, Foucault shows how change occurs via 'the vicissitudes of history' overcoming any originary formations (Foucault 1977, cited in Bouchard 1996: 144). Rejecting explanations of historical change as naturally progressive and productive of betterment, Foucault 'asserts the radical contingency of discourses in their historical context' (Olssen 2006, cited in Grierson 2006: 68). Foucault's method of analysis, following Nietzsche, seeks to excavate a critical history in order to enlighten the present. Through aesthetic practices the writers in this collection draw attention to this critical history, on the plane of the present, while acknowledging past norms and imagining future practices.

Cities morph and change according to their modes of governance. Socrates (*The Republic,* Book VIII) speaks of four constitutional systems for the city-state: timocracy, oligarchy, democracy and tyranny. In his dialogues, Socrates contends that a city's social structure and government will pass through each system as it works towards decay. Beyond the city-state of Ancient Greece, and with the rise of the nation-state, democracy has been in ascendance with 'tyranny', as per Socrates, always waiting in the wings. Today in the global world, much political activism concerns itself with calls for 'global democracy' in international relations, law and social justice, with the distribution of political decision-making and power edging beyond the nation-state (Kuyper 2016). Where does this leave the local voices?

In the post-2001 world, in the light of shifts in global power, refugee crises and disastrous effects of natural disasters, 'we might heed a question asked by Tom Nairn (2005: 249): "What is it that we should be addressing today?"' (Grierson 2006: 66). The authors in this book show the relevance of this question via a local lens by focusing on aesthetic or vernacular practices in today's city-state. In the spaces between the local and global, there exists a fecund site for wide investigation. Cultural theorist, Homi Bhabha defined the emerging conceptual spaces between subject interests and positions (including 'race, gender, generation, institutional location, geopolitical locale') as the 'interstices—the overlap and displacement of domains of difference [in which] the intersubjective and collective experience of *nationness,* community interest, or cultural value are negotiated' (Bhabha 1995: 1–2).

Cities may be considered in these terms, where negotiations of difference reverberate at the interstices and perhaps it is there that the crucible of creative action may fire. But if the creative quotient of cities is cast as a product of the economy, and cities operate as economic hubs driven by market forces impacted by the fluid movement of capital and power on a global level, then where does the relevance of artists and other creative workers lie in the local sphere? Is there room for aesthetic practices to intervene in dominant discourses and situate a transformative voice?

Functional Complementarity

If, to follow Foucault, cities and their inhabitants respond to 'modes of production' in a 'functional complementarity' (Foucault 1994: 50), then where does this show itself? Where are cities re-coded? In the western world of the eighteenth to nineteenth centuries, agrarian societies drifted to the urban in hope of better living and work conditions. Artists and writers responded with images and tales of disappearing rural life. Cities grew exponentially as old manufacturing sites became transfigured by new technologies. Soon the industrial turned to the post-industrial state. In the later twentieth-century, urban renewal became widespread; gentrification in the name of cultural regeneration incurred realignment of resources. The entertainment industry, street culture, public art projects and community events were seen as entreprenuerial and aligned with 'urban good', while urban poverty was spreading commensurably across the Global South.[1]

Then came the internet with its potential to re-code the transactions of public space.[2] In cyberspace, new communities form, economic transactions become instantaneous, global investment determines fiscal compulsions and international trade-deals populate political agendas. Today, digital innovation and informational technologies expand at exponential speed as new economies wean out the old. While this might offer extraordinary opportunities for economic growth for some, it means inevitable destitution for others. It is here that Foucault scrutinizes institutional and social discourses to show how some practices dominate and others are marginalized, and how change occurs at points of rupture (Foucault 1994). He shows through his method of *genealogy* (from Nietzsche) how discursive processes interrupt the normative ideal of stable identities: and it is at these points of rupture that artists or cultural workers may exercise their transformative dynamics.

Public Realm

This collection focuses on the public realm. A genealogy of public space shows how practices reconfigure in concert with changing technologies of power and production. With focus on the functional complementarity of peaceful coexistence, some sovereign states of Europe started to come together post-World War II, and by 1993, the policy of 'four freedoms'— movement of goods, services, people and finance—united 28 sovereign nations of Europe in a free-market zone, with 19 nations forming a common Monetary Union in 1999. New rules and norms of governmentality authorized power relations between the wealthiest and poorer nations. Economic management formed the basis of political conversation as cities prospered or fell on the social scaffolding of finance: the public realm soon transforming into chaos with the banking failures of the Global Financial Crisis. An informed public realm can change overnight to a fraught space of social and political ferment.

Presently, the Asia-Pacific is signing trade-deals with the People's Republic of China, heralded as part of 'the new Great Game, where nations large and small are deepening old military ties and forging new ones across the Asia-Pacific' (Garnaut 2014: 4)—Australia's Free Trade Agreement (FTA) with China entered into force in 2015; New Zealand having secured its FTA in 2008; and in 2016, negotiations by both nations were under way for FTAs with India. But where do these bi-lateral deals leave the voice of local citizens and community already withstanding a public realm impacted by global interests? Cultural or creative workers need to keep their finger on the pulse to ensure they are part of any action-for-change, and not marginalized, or worse, excluded. There is, of course, a ready politic to all of this. Artists, planners, designers and other creative workers can assert alternative ways to engage with a dominant, economic and political telos. Not afraid to speak through practice, they may etch an 'otherwise' strategy of meaning-making into an over-economized urban space. This is where creative workers have the capacity to contribute actively to an informed public realm.

Take public art, for example; no longer the emphasis on art as edifice to draw attention to heroic configurations of the *polis* where the teleological input of a paternalistic state replicates its normative values with civic power and pride. At local levels cultural workers readily grapple with the challenges of registering new forms of urban vitality and civic enterprise. Thus, as a city becomes a site of 'radical democracy' (Mouffe 1992), alternatives to the economic telos may emerge. Then an 'otherwise' construction of the city is born.

Themes and Chapters

Seeking this otherwise construction of the city, the book highlights diverse projects and positions through a range of material practices. It is organized in five sections, with each section adding its differentiated voice to the whole. This approach does not demand a teleological structure with a logical point of departure working to an end point in a predictable line of progressive argument. The writers are putting their imaginative energies to work as they grapple with issues of significance for the city and its inhabitants. The chapters work in discursive fashion to the final chapter on poetics, which amplifies the undecidability of the city, as it opens city DNA to the possibility of a poetic fusion. The editing strategy in bringing the collection together is to work through difference, chapter by chapter, as a discursive whole.

In summary, the book starts with the section 'Mapped City' having three chapters that consider mapping as a crucial device for making a city recognizable in time and space. In the second section, 'Contested City', writers take different perspectives on the ways in which controversy or disputes may be noticed and negotiated. In the third section, 'Pedagogical City', the emphasis is on how to write and read the city, how to see the city as pedagogical space, which may proffer an informing process to further thinking and action. In the fourth section, 'Temporal City', the writers reveal the differentiated spaces that a city gives rise to, in time. The final section, 'Creative City', offers a way to investigate creativity in operation through acoustic encounters, curational re-engagements and a poetics of practice generating an emergent state.

Through these five thematic groupings, the reader encounters difference in action. Each theme gives form to imaginative projects. Each chapter grapples with urban-based significances, or critically engages questions of urban growth or identity, or attends to public space and pedagogy, ethics or aesthetics, justice and its other, all working towards an understanding of the political economies of changing urban ecologies.

Section I: Mapped City

The theme of 'Mapped City' concerns itself with ways of mapping to navigate, articulate and narrate a city. In Chapter 1, 'Reading the Mapped City', William Cartwright considers the way maps construct a city. With Melbourne as the selected location for this research, Cartwright gives attention to the grid-like formations that characterize the city. In designing and producing maps, cartographers compile data using the available measurement technologies of their time; they construct base maps using mathematical underpinnings, and embellish with symbology the elements in a cityscape. Cartwright shows how city maps may be read as narratives of habitation, and how the city may be envisaged other than by a linear history. With his international reputation as a scholar in cartography, Cartwright is well placed to bring a cartographic expertise to the reading of a city, and through this, the genealogies and present traces of a city like Melbourne become apparent.

Maggie McCormick, in Chapter 2, 'Carto-City Revisited: Unmapping urbaness', argues for the critical role of creative mapping in recording changing perceptions of a city and urban self. By tracing from city to urbaness, and from mapping to unmapping, McCormick posits that another practice of recording and remapping urban experience is emerging out of transformative relationships between urban and cartographic space. It is argued that while Google maps and GPS systems dominate today's urban cartography, invaluable lessons may be learnt from earlier practices. In doing so, there is enhancement of the capacity to record contemporary space of the urban—often mediated by digital screens. While citing several contemporary examples, the key focus is on the transformative practice of an international project, 'SkypeLab: Transcontinental faces and spaces'.

Jodi Newcombe, in Chapter 3, presents a project in which a city is mapped by the art project itself. 'Sensing Sydney: An experiment in public art of the smart eco-city' tells the story of *Building Run,* a public art commission emerging from *Sensing Sydney*, a 2013 pilot project in partnership between Melbourne-based environmental arts organization, Carbon Arts, and the City of Sydney. The aim of *Sensing Sydney* was to explore ways in which public art, using environmental data, can increase public participation towards a more sustainable city. Central to the vision of *Sensing Sydney* are notions of the 'participatory society' and the 'smart citizen'. In the call for public art submissions, the challenge for artists was to work through the medium of public art, open data and participation, to engage actively with environmental sustainability. Project partners included the corporate sector, along with government and arts stakeholders, to bring a complex and sometimes competing set of values to the table. The city is mapped by and through these disparate perspectives.

Section II: Contested City

Cities are inherently contested spaces. According to Foucault, in the rules and norms of governance of populations lie the politics of power and production, 'and it is through these processes and their effects on the individual that governmentality operates' (Grierson and Engels-Schwarzpaul 2004: 1). Working against the grain of institutionalized rules and norms, cultural workers employ their micro-politics in a bid for change.

The four chapters in Section II engage contested positions of the city. Clare McCracken and Roger Nelson in Chapter 4, 'Travels and Tapestries: Possibilities for creative exchange in Melbourne and Phnom Penh', address collaborative exchanges between Melbourne and Phnom Penh in their quest for congruence and rapport between cultures and communities. Through these exchanges, the authors recount a number of recent projects, with a focus on experiences of less-visible communities in Cambodia. By way of a counterpoint to the work in Cambodia, they give an account of a slow-moving excursion as *flâneur* perambulating through the streets of Melbourne. The excursion draws attention to the politics of gendered space. With micro-politics coming to the fore, the chapter argues for reflexive and creative relationships based in dialogue and an ethic of attentiveness through 'locality-specific' actions and narratives.

In Chapter 5, 'Art as Enterprise' Grace McQuilten investigates the economic and social entanglement of contemporary art as enterprise. Here we see Foucault's 'functional complementarity' in action. McQuilten addresses a business venture by artists, Jon Rubin and Dawn Weleski, *Conflict Kitchen*: a pop-up restaurant in Pittsburgh, USA serving food from countries with which the United States has been engaged in military conflict. *Conflict Kitchen* opens a critical discussion on global politics, ideology, and warfare. This raises questions about the role of art in both affirming and challenging the bio-cultural sphere of politics. Questions lead to consideration of a more explicitly critical engagement with enterprise in *Return* by Iraqi-US artist, Michael Rakowitz, which focuses on the importation and sale of Iraqi dates—the first commodities marked 'Product of Iraq' to be sold in the United States since the lifting of the trade embargo at the end of Iran-Iraq war in 2003. McQuilten addresses the question of whether art can engage effectively, and critically, with systems and structures of enterprise in an increasingly commercialized socio-political landscape.

Further political and social contestations are investigated in Chapter 6, 'Recipe for Homefullness', where Keely Macarow addresses the housing market in Australia. With the majority of housing stock in the private market, and most Australians owning their own home or renting another privately owned house, Macarow argues for change as Australian cities grow rapidly in the twenty-first century. She examines how creative practitioners may work to influence ways of meeting the need for innovative and affordable housing projects. Through this investigation, she presents the work of artists, architects and designers from Australia, Sweden, Denmark and the United Kingdom, who have collaborated on activist projects to imagine and invent new models for housing. By investigating what constitutes 'home' and 'community', these projects contest the normative view of housing in urban society.

Contestation involves interrogation of city safety in the final chapter of this group: 'Interrogating Space: The *Urban Laboratory*' by Fiona Hillary and Geoff Hogg. The authors address the contested spaces of Hosier and Rutledge Lanes, notable street-art sites in the central business district of Melbourne. The interrogation is based on a 12-month, practice-based research project commissioned by the City of Melbourne. The *Urban Laboratory* project responded to the City Council's plan to increase surveillance by installing closed circuit television cameras in Hosier and Rutledge Lanes with the aim of reducing street crime in the area. The community reacted strongly against this proposal. The *Urban Laboratory* was one of a number of responses designed to investigate and explore alternative solutions to issues of safety in public space.

Section III: Pedagogical City

What of the city as pedagogical space? If pedagogy—meaning, from Ancient Greek, 'to lead a child'—concerns teaching, then how may the city lead us into understanding and knowledge? By 'writing the city', the prism turns to locate these possibilities: from site-writing in 'transparadiso'; to writing aesthetics and alterity in therapeutic justice; to writing mosaics in urban disaster zones.

Firstly, in Chapter 8, 'Writing transparadiso', Jane Rendell writes across (*trans-*) and beside (*para-*) the different facets of the works of an architect-trained artist, Barbara Holub, and an architect/urban designer, Paul Rajakovics, both based in Vienna. In a third space, with a multi-vocal approach, Rendell places her own voice (text) alongside (beside) the others in a parallel, rather than explanatory relationship of attitudes to urbanism; and D. W. Winnicott, André Green and Félix Guattari enter the conversations with their concepts of 'transitional space and transversality'. By this methodology, there is a movement, always horizontal, on epistemological thresholds of 'writing' urban space and the human subject.

In Chapter 9, 'Raising Alterity: Working towards a just city', Elizabeth M. Grierson asks how aesthetics may play a part in 'raising alterity' for a just city. Grierson argues for recognition of difference by raising alterity to a viable position in the exercise of justice. The raising of alterity demands the recognition, consolidation and legitimation of discursive differentials of difference. Aesthetics plays its activating part here. Place and identity come together through the axis of justice writ large, a 'Therapeutic Jurisprudence' approach in particular. Engaging the lenses of Levinas on alterity, and Lyotard on legitimation of difference, the discussion activates aesthetic/justice relations by working through a series of narratives of transformation. Each works as a micro-narrative evidencing a Therapeutic Jurisprudence approach to law and justice. The focus is on Koori (Aboriginal) justice in Australia, with specific attention to the State of Victoria, and youth justice in New Zealand, particularly the marae-based, Rangatahi Court system. Alterity speaks of pedagogy within and beyond the normative liberal legacy—therein lies the capacity for a just city. Where alterity finds voice, there transforming powers of subjectivity may supervene as one works towards a just city.

Finally, in Chapter 10, 'Fragments, Lyotard and Earthquakes: A mosaic of memory and broken pieces' Kirsten Locke and Sarah Yates bring a focus to pedagogical possibilities of art in an urban disaster zone. The writers explore the responses of a group of children following the September 2010, and February 2011, Christchurch earthquakes. The project was undertaken over two years, by children from a small school in New Zealand. It sought a way of memorializing the events in a way that was appropriate and meaningful to the community. Alongside images relating directly to the earthquakes, the art form of a mosaic consisted of images and symbols that drew on the hopes and dreams of a school community refusing to be defined by the disaster. The chapter 'writes' the mosaic by positioning fragments of speech spoken by the children, placed in relation to ideas about memory, affect and the sublime, through Immanuel Kant and Jean-François Lyotard. The chapter explores the mosaic as constituted by the literal and metaphorical 'broken pieces' of the city of Christchurch in ways that confer pedagogic value to the city through children's creation of a public artspace.

Section IV: Temporal City

The theme of 'Temporal City' profiles three projects: one in the sub-urban; the second in the outer city; and a third in the centre of a dislocated city. The section begins with Chapter 11, 'Feature 13: Suburban terrain vague' by Anthony McInneny. The author investigates the notion of 'terrain vague' (from Ignasi de Solà-Morales Rubió) by considering literal and functional situations, in site-specific art, through the temporal nature of performance and digital video art. McInneny's focus is the 'suburban city', and the non-urban public spaces of metropolitan Melbourne. In particular he examines the genealogies of the site of a historic building, now demolished, re-appropriating it to maintain its emptiness. Temporality is manifest in the urban estrangement. Sites of emptiness operate as a network endemic to post-industrial cities, and specific urban place, with a past evidenced by the residue of its formation. 'Feature 13' situates, in its temporary and temporal states, the unmarked suburban site of a demolished historic building to highlight the temporalities of art and city.

Chapter 12, by Ashley Perry, 'Beyond the Tarmac: Temporality and the roadside art of Melbourne', examines site-specific, public, artworks situated within the geography of two extensive motorways: the EastLink Tollway and the Peninsula Link Freeway, on the South Eastern edges of metropolitan Melbourne. The chapter investigates the spatial, temporal and aesthetic characteristics suggested by the strategically placed, roadside artworks. Perry focuses on the ways in which two prominent artworks are transforming the physical spaces and the temporal experiences of 'drive time'. He argues that transformation becomes possible through the establishment of an array of relational, affective and momentary attachments assembled and enacted between motorists and roadside objects. Overall, Perry seeks to demonstrate how site-specific public art may produce a transformative effect on both the geographies of outer Melbourne and the motorists who travel through these semi-private landscapes.

In 'Walking the Post-Quake City: (Re)making place in Ōtautahi Christchurch', Chapter 13, Barbara Garrie considers how to navigate and inhabit a post-disaster city. Garrie selects two art projects, which document and imaginatively perform, through processes of walking, the experience of post-quake Christchurch, New Zealand. The projects are Tim Veling's photographic, *Orientation* (2011); and Chris Cottrell and Susie Pratt's audio guide, *With Fluidity* (2015). Both focus on the central city: specifically the city cordon, and the Ōtākaro Avon River, which winds its way through the urban zone. These features represent boundaries marking the city's transforming limits or frontiers. They start to operate as indicators of contestation in the city rebuild, as they magnify urban discontent with political responses to earthquake damage and city reconstruction. In the entanglements of time and space characterizing present-day Christchurch, the chapter draws attention to difficulties of transitional renewal and transformation in light of trauma and destruction.

Section V: Creative City

Is the city inherently creative? Or has the adoption of the creative industries' mantra subsumed the potential for aesthetic discourse by manoeuvring the notion of creativity into a normalized market economy? This section evidences creative city strategies in three chapters that bring on-the-ground transformations to the fore—one through acoustics; another through curating; and a third through poetics.

In Chapter 14, 'Listening to the City', Kristen Sharp explores how contemporary sound art projects from the Asia-Pacific region respond to the protean nature of cities, generating new and unexpected encounters with place. *The Library by Soundpocket* and *Stereopublic* draw attention to acoustic and embodied encounters with place. Through their method of online digital delivery, they open new understandings and awareness of the physical, symbolic and social attributes of a city. From this, the city emerges as a multifaceted and diverse place, a global space, in which the local is no longer understood as a bounded entity; rather it comprises fluid relations. These digital sound art projects move across online/offline spaces to become '*trans*located'. Through this process, they mediate how place and cities are experienced and understood aesthetically and socially; and in this way they become transformative.

Tammy Wong Hulbert in Chapter 15, 'Applying the Creative City: Curating art in urban spaces' contemplates the transformative power of re-imagining the city as a creative space. She considers an alternative model of exhibition practice of 'curating the city' as a methodology for applying creative city concepts. Currently, city inhabitants may experience a range of art in public space practices, diverse in the way they are formed; but there is potential to open the creative city concept to a wider agenda. Hulbert argues for an alternative model of publicly based exhibition practices by re-imagining urban space as a site for expressing, exploring and interpreting artistic intentions and interactions. Her writing centres on the historical city as a site for artistic engagement in the public realm, and curating as a method of re-imbuing the sacred in urban society. Ultimately she argues that the curated city presents an accessible and democratic model of exhibition practice responsive to twenty-first-century urban living.

Finally, in Chapter 16, 'The Poetic City: Old songs left beneath the arches' Nicholas Lyon Gresson investigates the notion of an inherently poetic city. Gresson problematizes the rhetoric of stabilized identities from the past being shifted to a comparative index of the present. His focus on walking the city brings him to consider the *flâneur* of Baudelaire and mid-nineteenth-century Paris living the alterity of change. He claims that the poetic is transformative when it refuses idealized formations and puts into relief the present now-ness of life—suggesting that the transformative poetic lies outside of teleological progression. By writing the city, Gresson finds the city's resonating tactics in the here and now. In conversation with the poetic city, his poetic voice is not one to concretize viewpoints or reinvest the norm with edifices of truth. From his own poetic imagery, Gresson engages with an intrinsically poetic city through the everyday tactics of walking to conjure the living transformations of it all.

Conclusion

Writers in this collection, from Australia, New Zealand and the United Kingdom interrogate, highlight and grapple with twenty-first-century urban conditions. They variously show how vistas of transformation may be manifested in, and through, practices characterized by aesthetic and/or transitional qualities.

The writers' critical and poetic engagements, with their notions of transformation in urban spaces, capably highlight art, design, aesthetic, cartographic and poetic practices in conceptual and material contexts. If there is any congruence discernible between the writers, it is the acceptance of difference in encountering city spaces. Each writer is laying claim to a more nuanced and informed public realm where aesthetic approaches to environmental conditions or oppositional politics may find thought-provoking traction. Each chapter, in its difference, adds to the whole. Ultimately, the collection arrests our attention to present-day dynamics of city transformations. In a rich tapestry of discursive strands, the writers illuminate the differentiated formations of a city in an urban epoch.

References

Bhabha, H. K. (1995), *The Location of Culture*, London: Routledge.

Bouchard, D. F. (ed.) (1996), *Michel Foucault, Language, Counter-memory, Practice: Selected essays and interviews*, Ithaca: Cornell University Press.

Foucault, M. (1998), *Technologies of the Self: A seminar with Michel Foucault*, L. H. Martin, H. Gutman and P. Hutton (eds), Amherst: University of Massachusetts Press.

——— (1994), *The Archaeology of Knowledge*, (trans. A. M. Sheridan Smith), London: Routledge. (First published in French 1969.)

Garnaut, J. (2014), 'Welcome to the new great game', *The Age*, 18 November.

Grierson, E. M. (2006), 'Between Empires: Globalization and knowledge', *ACCESS: Critical perspectives on communications, cultural and policy studies*, 25: 2, pp. 66–77.

Grierson, E. M. and Engels-Schwarzpaul, T. (2004), 'Internationalism, Education and Governmentality: Critical perspectives', *ACCESS: Critical perspectives on communications, cultural and policy studies*, 23: 2, pp. 1–11.

Grierson, E. and Sharp, K. (eds) (2013), *Re-Imagining the City: Art, globalization and urban spaces*, Bristol: Intellect Books.

Kuyper, J. (2016), 'Global Democracy', in Edward N. Zalta (ed.), *The Stanford Encyclopedia of Philosophy* (Spring 2016 ed.), http://plato.stanford.edu/archives/spr2016/entries/global-democracy/. Accessed 22 April 2016.

Mouffe, C. (2013), *Agonistics: Thinking the world politically*, London: Verso.

—— (ed.) (1992), *Dimensions of Radical Democracy: Pluralism, citizenship, community*, London: Verso.

Plato (1959), *The Republic*, (trans. and edited by H. D. P. Lee), Middlesex: Penguin Books. (First appeared in Greek c. 380 BCE.)

Notes

1 For discussion of 'Global South' see Kevin Murray, 'The Visible Hand: An urban accord for outsourced craft' in *Re-Imagining the City: Art, globalization and urban spaces* (Grierson and Sharp 2013).

2 For the way 'the urban' is contested through the advent of cyberspace and mobile media, see Larissa Hjorth, 'The Place of the Urban: Intersections between mobile and game cultures' in *Re-Imagining the City: Art, globalization and urban spaces* (Grierson and Sharp 2013).

Section I

Mapped City

Chapter 1

Reading the Mapped City

William Cartwright

Introduction

Maps are used by readers to locate information and by cartographers to represent geography. They show three-space + time. They also provide geographic narratives of place and space. They can show what is here now, what was once here, and what could be here in the future. It could be said that they allow one to travel in time, to better comprehend what a certain landscape once was or what, considering certain constraints and projected developments, it could be like in the future.

When considering maps of a city, the topic of this contribution, maps can provide a rich resource to historians and the layperson alike. They can provide snapshots when viewed individually, or a narrative when 'read' in a chronological sequence.

The focus here is the City of Melbourne, Australia. It is now a city of some 4 million+ inhabitants, and growing. The narrative that will be explored is a historical one: how maps can illustrate the establishment of a town and how certain planned developments nurtured its growth into a city.

Four maps have been selected for this discussion, around which a narrative of the city will be built. The maps are:

- 'Map shewing the site of Melbourne and the position of the huts & buildings previous to the foundation of the township by Sir Richard Bourke in 1837', Robert Russell;
- 'Plan of the city of Melbourne embracing Collingwood, South Melbourne and Sandridge, shewing part of Richmond, Prahran & St. Kilda, compiled under the direction of Thomas Ham, 1854';
- Melbourne and Metropolitan Board of Works (MMBW) Survey Field Book 678 and associated Detail Plan 1368, 1908; and
- Railways and tramways map of Melbourne and suburbs: showing railways, cable tramways, electric tramways. Collins Book Depot, 1920s.

They were selected to provide a chronological story about the early development of the city and its infrastructure. As well, they depict aspects of Melbourne from different perspectives: establishing the town; growing; consolidating; connecting.

This chapter develops a narrative of Melbourne from these maps by addressing these aspects of the city.

Melbourne

Melbourne was proclaimed a town in March 1837, named after Lord Melbourne, the British Prime Minister at the time (Museum Victoria 2015; Boyce 2015). Its founding is linked to John Batman, John Wedge and John Pascoe Fawkner. Batman and his business partner Wedge formed the Port Phillip Association in order to develop their interests in this southern part of the Colony of New South Wales, which had been established as a Colony under the *New South Wales Act 1823* (Imp).

In 1835, Batman, Wedge and Fawkner arrived in the Port Phillip District, as known then by Europeans. Even though Batman had signed a treaty with the Woi wurrung and Boon wurrung people (Broome 2008) for 500,000 acres on Port Phillip Bay in May 1835, it was Fawkner's party that arrived first, in August that year from Van Diemen's land (now known as Tasmania), while Batman and Wedge arrived, also from Van Diemen's land, to start their settlement on 2 September. However, who actually founded the town first is still a point of debate (State Library of Victoria 2015a).

Batman and Fawkner established their settlements in different locations. Batman's location for the town was where Port Melbourne is currently located. Fawkner's party settled in roughly the area where the current city grid is—on the northern bank of the Yarra River (State Library of Victoria 2015a) (*Birrarung* in the Wurrunjeri language; Eidelson 1997).

However, the settlers were deemed to be trespassers by the Government of New South Wales, and Batman's deed was declared null and void. At this time the Governor of New South Wales was vested with authority for legal, economic and social life throughout the Colony. The Sydney-based government dispatched Captain William Lonsdale to Port Phillip in September 1836 to govern the area. Formal land alienation (from the Crown to individuals) soon began. By 1838 there were 177 settlers in the area. This number grew to 23,000 by 1851, when Victoria was established with governance and legal status as a Colony separate from the Colony of New South Wales. (Victoria and New South Wales were established legally as separate states by parliamentary enactment of the Australian Constitution, 1900; from 1900 Australia was a Federation of states, territories and a central government.)

Surveying and Mapping the Port Phillip District

The first surveys of the District to determine its suitability for settlement were undertaken in 1803—by Charles Grimes (1772–1858) (State Library of Victoria 2015b; Currey 2002). Grimes reported that Port Phillip was unsuitable for settlement (Australian Dictionary of Biography 1966). This followed Matthew Flinders' detailed survey of the bay and the surrounding country in the ship *The Investigator* in April 1802 (State Library of Victoria 2015b).

Detailed mapping of the settlement was conducted under the direction of Robert Russell (1808–1900). His map (Figure 1) shows the position of the central area of the settlement and the general landscape surrounding it.

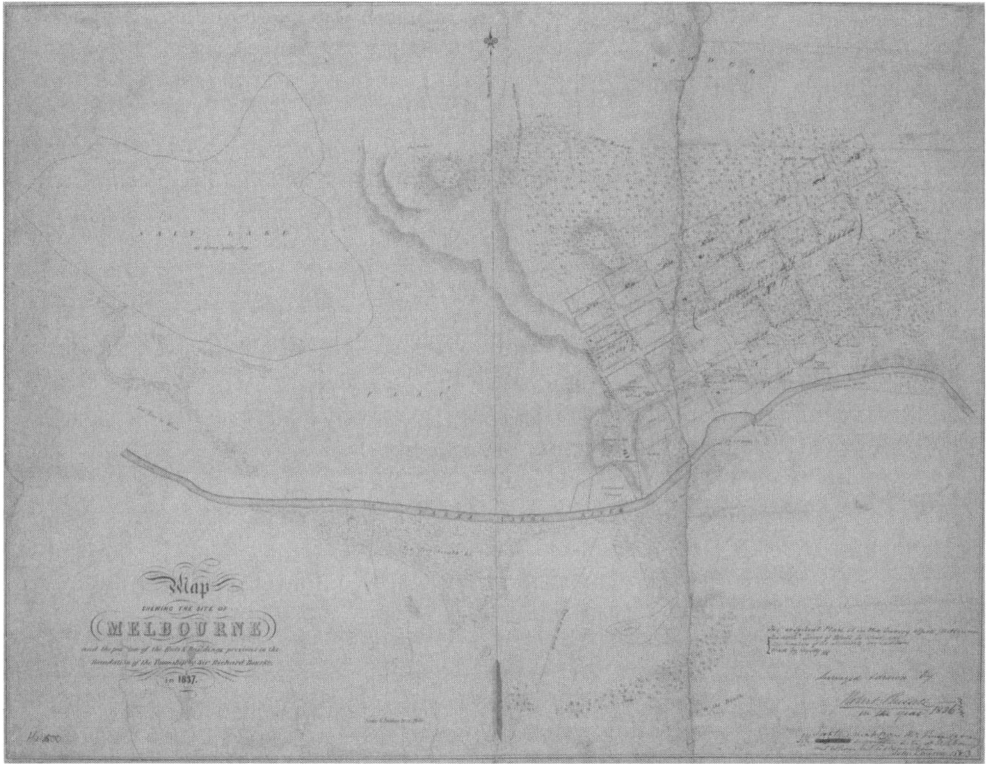

Figure 1: Map shewing the site of Melbourne and the position of the huts & buildings previous to the foundation of the township by Sir Richard Bourke in 1837. Surveyed & drawn by Robert Russell.

Source: State Library of Victoria. Out of Copyright. Persistent link: http://handle.slv.vic.gov.au/10381/74744

This work is out of copyright. No copyright restrictions apply.

Interestingly, similar to the debate about who actually founded Melbourne—the John Batman and John Wedge's Port Phillip Association or John Pascoe Fawkner—there is a continuing debate about who came up with the original layout of the grid for Melbourne. Even though Russell's map showed the central street grid, Russell is not generally attributed to this key feature of Melbourne. Rather, it is attributed to surveyor Robert Hoddle (1794–1881) and Governor Bourke. In March 1837, Bourke appointed Hoddle as senior surveyor, ahead of Russell, even though Russell had been undertaking work in the Port Phillip District since 1836 (McVicker 2010).

Russell, while not claiming to have actually laid out the grid, did suggest that it was he who developed the concept, as depicted in his map of 1837 (Figure 1). About this he wrote the following to the Editor of the Melbourne newspaper, *The Argus*, in 1881:

Sir,—Permit me to correct a small mistake in your narrative of this date concerning the late Mr. Robert Hoddle. You state that, 'Messers. Darke, D'Arcy, and Russell, at one time were hard at work defining the outlines, fixing the boundaries, and marking the corners of the streets' of Melbourne. This is a thorough fiction. I never defined, fixed, or marked one outline, boundary, or corner of the incipient city. It is true I accompanied Mr. Hoddle on horseback when he started from Batman's-hill, and began his round to his starting-point, but I was merely a looker-on. That I was the first 'surveyor in charge' at Port Phillip; that I was superseded, as I then thought and still think, unfairly; and that Mr. Hoddle drew his lines of street on the plan of my survey, drawn by Mr D'Arcy, under my instructions, prior to Mr. Hoddle's arrival, and which may still be seen at the surveyor-general's office, are facts much more to the purpose.—I am, &c. ROBERT RUSSELL East Melbourne, Oct. 29.

Hoddle and Bourke disagreed over the width of the streets, but Hoddle won the day and streets were laid out 99 feet wide, rather than Bourke's preferred 66 feet wide. However, Hoddle compromised on the width of the little streets, which were laid out to a width of 33 feet wide. Hoddle's map for the layout of Melbourne was drawn by superimposing his grid over Russell's earlier map (Scurfield n.d.).

Robert Hoddle became the first Surveyor-General of the new colony of Victoria, when it was established in 1851 (McVicker 2010). This role gave him responsibility for determining land grants for new settlers in Victoria. Robert Russell continued his career as an artist, architect and surveyor (Preston 1967).

Reading Russell's Map

Russell's map tells the story of the early settlement. It shows the central grid that is particular to this town that grew into a city. It is evident from viewing Russell's map that the layout of the grid ignored existing buildings and land ownership as well as the physical geography of the site. Looking at the grid in particular, it can be seen that the formal layout of the town completely ignored the settlement infrastructure. Any buildings that happened to be in the path of planned new streets would simply have to be removed! Ignoring the physical geography led to the constant flooding of some streets, like Elizabeth Street which was positioned on a natural watercourse (most recently inundated by a flash flood in 1972; Blainey and Foley 2005). And, the width of the little streets caused later social and environmental problems (State Library of Victoria 2015c). These narrow streets became strewn with garbage and were deemed to be places to be avoided by the more 'respectable' members of the city's population.

As well as the grid, Russell's map showed the general topography and vegetation at and nearby the settlement. What can be seen are the Yarra River, Batman's Hill and swamps to the south of the settlement.

But the map includes other stories. It provides evidence to support the argument about who settled first—Fawkner's house is marked on the map, but the map does not go far enough to the South West to show the Batman settlement at present-day Port Melbourne. It shows how future plans for transportation of the city, and the desire by citizens of the city to have the railway running into the heart of the city, demanded that a primary feature of the terrain—Batman's Hill—be removed altogether to provide a steady gradient for trains to continue from what is the current-day Southern Cross Station to today's Flinders Street Station.

However, perhaps the most poignant story from this map is that it is a reminder of how Russell's idea for the grid to be laid parallel to the Yarra River, a source of fresh water and a conduit for trade, was somewhat pushed aside by Hoddle. It was Russell who first represented the grid on his map, but it is Hoddle who is generally regarded as the 'father' of Melbourne's grid. Russell's grid remains in the physical geography of Melbourne, where it was placed graphically on his map of 1837.

Growth

With the growth of the settlement into town then city, the Crown, in principle deemed it necessary to alienate and then have land occupied after survey (Dalrymple et al. 2003). In order to do this systematically, the land was surveyed, cadastral plans produced (demarcating the lots to be sold, and later noting the subsequent purchaser) and the land sold at auction. Cadastral systems in Australia register the legal ownership of ownership texturally and graphically (Dalrymple et al. 2003). The cadastral map (or plan) is used to delineate land parcels and land ownership graphically.

The first land sales in Melbourne, authorised by Governor Bourke and conducted by Robert Hoddle were conducted in 1 June 1837. Three city blocks were sold (City of Melbourne 2015). Soon thereafter, as demand for places in the city increased, similar auctions were held to alienate land.

The cadastral map shown in Figure 2 illustrates the expansion of the city in the 1850s: Hotham (later re-named North Melbourne in 1877 [Carrol 2008], East Melbourne), Emerald (later re-named South Melbourne when city status was attained in 1883 [Priestly 2008]); and Sandridge (later re-named Port Melbourne in 1884 [City of Port Phillip 20n.d.]). North Melbourne and East Melbourne were later incorporated into the City of Melbourne, with South Melbourne and Port Melbourne operating for some time as separate cities, until their incorporation into the City of Port Phillip.

Looking firstly at the south-west corner of the map, at Sandridge, located on Hobsons Bay. Here, the first auctions of land took place in 1850 (Dryrenfurth 2008). The map shows that Sandridge was bounded by a rail line, to the west, providing a direct link to the railway station in the city (now Flinders Street Station) with the 'Railway Pier', and a shallow 'large and noxious saltwater lagoon' (Dryrenfurth 2008) to the east. (The lagoon was slowly filled-in, and completely reclaimed by 1929. This area now comprises the aptly-named 'Lagoon Reserve' [Wikipedia 2015b]. Sandridge is linked to the city by both the rail and the 'Sandridge and South Melbourne Road', which leads to a crossing of the Yarra River via the Princes Bridge built in 1845 [Priestly 2008].) Victoria's first railway was built in Melbourne in 1854.

Moving clockwise takes us to North Melbourne and Parkside (now Parkville). North Melbourne became the most densely populated part of the city during the 1880s land boom (Carrol 2008). The 1880s was a time of economic boom fuelled by the wealth from the goldfields and the wool industry. In 1880 the grand Royal Exhibition Building was built in Carlton Gardens to host the 1880 World Fair and by 1901 the building became the site of the Australian Federation's first parliament. North Melbourne comprises wide roads, the city's 'Flag Staff' (the site of today's Flagstaff Gardens), a 'Burial Ground' reserve (Melbourne's original cemetery and now the Queen Victoria Market) and a 'cattle yard' and a 'Benevolent Asylum'. In Parkside 100 acres is marked as 'Site-Granted for University' and a site is set-aside for a 'Fever Hospital'.

Then, moving clockwise on the map to East Melbourne: Robert Hoddle surveyed East Melbourne in 1839–40. Land sales were first held in East Melbourne between 1852–54 and then again in 1858. Later surveys being done in 1859, laying-out parks and squares between residential streets. As well, reserves were established for the future Parliament House and government buildings, Fitzroy Gardens and the Treasury Gardens (Murdoch 2008). The map shows these as 'Fitzroy Square' and the site of the present Parliament House is named the 'Legislative Assembly Hall'. Moving south of Victoria Street, and north of the Yarra River, a 'Cricket Ground' (the site of the present-day Melbourne Cricket Ground) sits in the middle of the 'Government paddock'. The map also shows the original course of the Yarra River before it was 'moved' further north to accommodate the expansion of the Botanic Gardens, marked on the map as being in Prahran, South Yarra having not yet been named as a separate suburb.

Then to South Melbourne, linked to the city by 'Sandridge and South Melbourne Road' and Princes Bridge (Priestly 2008). Individual plots of land, assigned for or already alienated are shown, as are reserves. The 'Reserve for Orphan School' is the site of the former City of Emerald Town hall. Today's St Kilda Road, the land between South Melbourne and the 'St Kilda Brighton and Gt. Arthurs Seat Road' (3 chains wide!) is set-aside for 'City Park Lands'; today, unfortunately, this proposed site for parklands is completely built-over. Today's Toorak Road was called then 'Gardners Creek Road'. One interesting notation on the 'Sandridge and South Melbourne Road' shows the existence of a 'Toll Road', pre-dating Melbourne's current 'City Link' toll road system (which is quite near-by) by 150 years or so.

The story of this map reveals an account of the expansion of the city and development of the early suburbs, which expanded in all of the directions of the compass. The cardinal points determined the naming of these early suburbs. The alignment of major roads and the extension of the town to the north and east abandoned the link to the banks of the Yarra River and were laid-out to accord with magnetic north. This would have sped-up early surveys, which used compasses extensively for determining azimuth. The map also reflects the desire of the city leaders to design and demark the city in a most formal manner, mimicking the English town as this was done. Generous acreages were assigned to parklands and formal gardens, albeit assignations that were depleted quite dramatically when the plans for parkland to the southwest of today's St Kilda Road are considered.

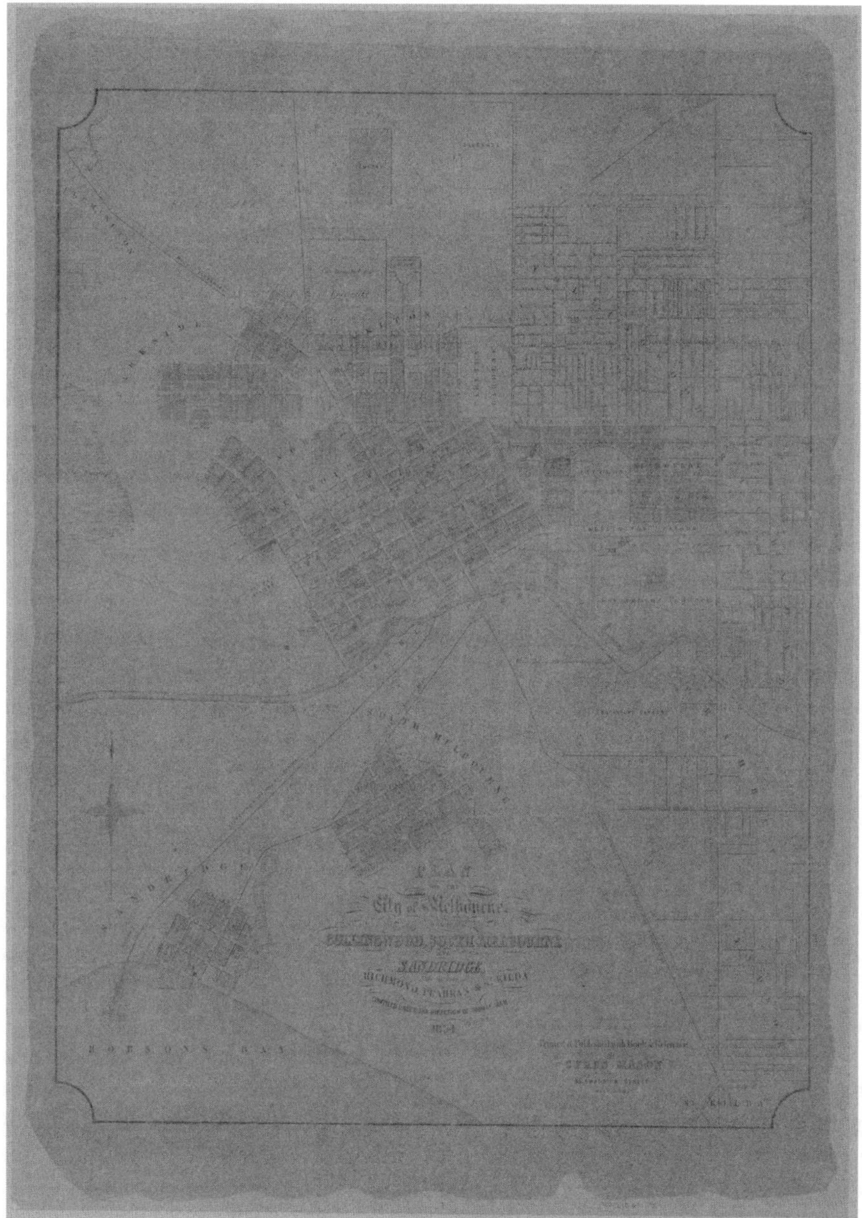

Figure 2: Plan of the city of Melbourne embracing Collingwood, South Melbourne and Sandridge, shewing part of Richmond, Prahran & St. Kilda, 1854. Compiled under the direction of Thomas Ham, Melbourne: Cyrus Mason.

Source: State Library of Victoria. Persistent link: http://handle.slv.vic.gov.au/10381/114840

This work is out of copyright. No copyright restrictions apply.

But, the map most effectively provides a narrative of the grand plans for the city, built around the grid and planned suburbs comprising grand boulevards, wide residential streets, assignations of land for future civic buildings and demarked locations for sporting events, education and public facilities.

Servicing the City

As the city grew, there was a need to ensure the proper management of fresh water, drainage. In 1853 the Government formed the Board of Commissioners of Sewers and Water Supply to provide fresh water, delivered by gravity, from the Yan Yean Reservoir, some 20 miles to the north. Melbourne received the first piped water from Yan Yean Reservoir in 1857. This was deemed to be overdue due to the rapid growth of the city (Dunstan 2008). The Board also managed the laying of reticulation pipes in the city. The Board was abolished in 1860 and replaced by the Board of Land and Works. Later, in 1891, with the need to consolidate management of sewers and water supply for the expanding city and its suburbs, the MMBW was established (Ritchie 1934). In the decade of 1880 to 1890 the population had grown 280,000 to 490,000—an era later known as 'Marvellous Melbourne' (Davison 1981) for all its urban construction profiling the best of its arts and architecture.

In order to effectively carry out its remit, the MMBW formed its own Survey Division, with the responsibility of mapping greater Melbourne's buildings, drainage and sewers. They were used to design and develop sewer reticulation (State Library of Victoria 2015d). Associated with the need to better understand the topography and the built environment of the city for the design and building of the reticulation system, information was collected in the field. MMBW surveyors were sent into the field to map the landscape and existing buildings. Processional surveying practices provided the means for the planning of water reticulation and sewage pipes that could effectively supply drinking water and remove waste, respectively, using, in most cases, only gravity. Surveyors in the field measured and then drew detailed representations of their efforts in field books (Figure 3a). These records were then used as the basis for producing the first series of detailed plans and subsequent amendments as new works were undertaken.

This formal mapping of the city was done in a regulated manner, and the results of the mapping undertaken by the Survey Division were the essential tools of hydrological engineers for developing the city's underground infrastructure. The first series of maps were produced in 1894, and continued until 1952. The series mapping continued until the third series in 1985 (The University of Melbourne 2015). The MMBW Survey Division provided over 100 years of detailed mapping of the city.

An example page from a surveyor's field book and an extract from a detailed plan, produced by surveyors and cartographers from the Survey Division are shown in Figures 3a and 3b.

The surveyor's fieldnotes were the annotations recording measurements taken in the field. They show the results of precision surveys undertaken to record all built features.

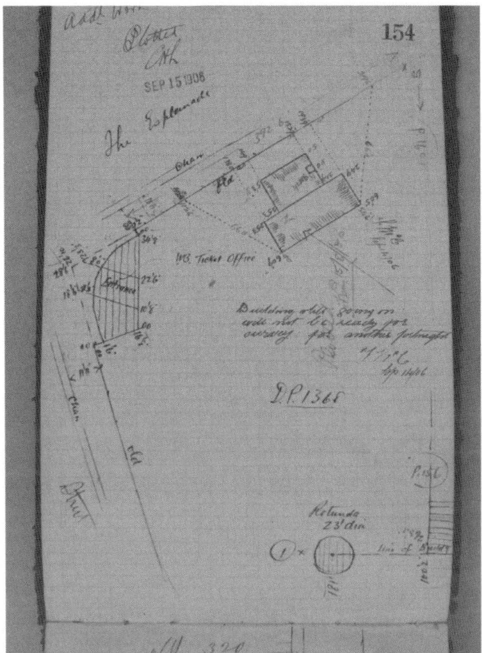

Figure 3a: MMBW Survey Field Book 678, p. 154 from VPRS 8600/P1, unit 39, 1908.

Source: Public Records Office, Victoria. http://prov. vic.gov.au/wp-content/uploads/2012/12/Luna-2-Dreamworld_sml.jpg

This work is out of copyright. No copyright restrictions apply.

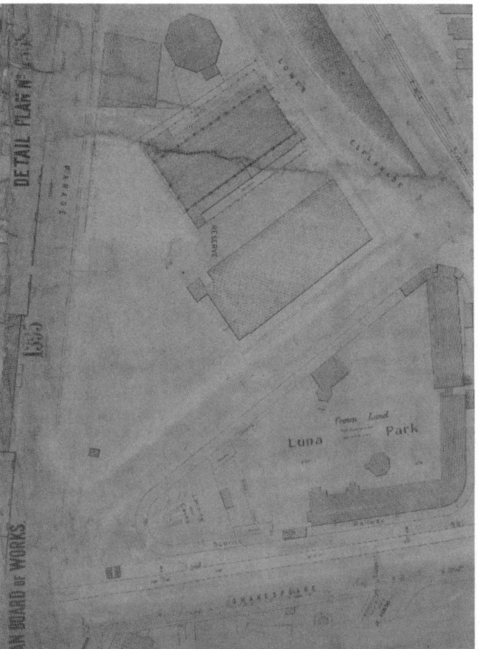

Figure 3b: MMBW Detail Plan 1368 from VPRS 8601/ P1, Detailed Base Plans [DP] 40' =1' Numeric, unit 28, ca. 1953.

Source: Public Records Office, Victoria. http://prov.vic.gov. au/wp-content/uploads/2012/12/Luna-1-Map_sml.jpg

This work is out of copyright. No copyright restrictions apply.

The field-book page in Figure 3a shows the information recorded about a new building constructed on the former Dreamland site (now present-day Luna Park). The entrance, a rotunda and the ticket office are clearly marked.

The subsequent map (Figure 3b) illustrates the roads, drainage, buildings and information about the uses of various buildings. Detailed notes from the surveyors' fieldnotes would be used as a source of information to enable changes and additions in the landscape to be faithfully represented. This extract of the map shows (the re-named) Luna Park, the Palais Theatre, Palais de Dance and the Swirl Building. This site, while containing remnants of these buildings, is currently the subject of much debate in Melbourne about what best to do with the land, with much of it being a gravel car park (Lucas 2015).

The fieldnotes and maps show the story of a city in transition. The growth of the city demands reticulated water and sewage systems. The fieldnotes illustrate the many changes happening in the city and in its suburbs. The map provides a snapshot of part of the metropolis: its infrastructure, buildings and centres for activities, like the leisure area of St. Kilda.

Connecting the City

As the city grew, also did its public transportation network. The city established its first railway line 20 years after it was founded (Wikipedia 2014). Australia's first railway line was built between Flinders Street Station and Sandridge (now Port Melbourne). Opening on 12 September 1854 (Department of Infrastructure and Regional Development, Government of Australia 2014), it linked Melbourne's main port of the time with the growing central business area. The Melbourne and Hobson's Bay Railway Company, formed in 1853, operated the line (Wikipedia 2014). Other forms of transport were the cable car, electric trams and omnibuses. The development of public transport, as a general rule, spread radially from the Central Business District. However, there was a development of other connecting services, using the various forms of transport available.

Trams have been part of Melbourne since 1884, when a horse-drawn tram-line opened in Fairfield. The cable car tram system opened soon thereafter, in 1885, operated by the Melbourne Tramway and Omnibus Company (Hoadley 2015). The network grew to be one of the largest in the world, with 75 kilometres of double track. This was the direct result of the Melbourne Tramway & Omnibus Company Act 1883 (Wikipedia 2015a). By 1940 there was an abandonment of all cable and horse tram-lines, or they were converted to either electric tram or bus operation. The cable car system operated for 55 years (Hoadley 2015).

The first electric tram ran from Box Hill Railway Station to Doncaster, in 1889. But, what is seen to be the first 'serious' electric trams was in evidence in 1906 with the North Melbourne Electric Tramway and Lighting Company. The company extended the network from the cable car network. Lines were built for travel to Essendon (Wikipedia 2015). The Victorian Railways (VR) also undertook the building of an electric tramway from Brighton to St Kilda Beach Railway Station: a line later extended to Sandringham. The VR electric tram-lines closed in 1959 (Hoadley 2015) and were replaced by rail lines.

The Brighton to St Kilda Beach electric tramway was owned by Thomas Bent, at one time Premier of the State of Victoria, Minister for Transport and, always, land speculator. He was appointed Commissioner for Works and Railways in the O'Loghlen government (1881–1883) and, in this role, extended the existing Melbourne to Caulfield railway line to Cheltenham. He owned extensive landholdings in the area through which the extended rail line passed. This increased the value of his landholdings in the Brighton and Bentleigh (named after Bent) area (Jones 2003; Wikipedia 2015c). Bent became Premier of Victoria in 1904 when William Irvine stepped down from this position to go into federal politics (apparently after a dispute with Bent). But, as well as becoming Premier, Bent also took the positions of Minister for the Treasury and the Minister for Railways. He used his ministerial position to effect the passing of the Railways Special Applications Act (No 1948) on 30 November 1904, followed on the same day by the St Kilda and Brighton Electric Street Railway Act (No 1956). Subsequently, this allowed the construction of the tramway, further enhancing the value of his real estate holdings (Glass 1993).

1919 saw the formation of the Melbourne and Metropolitan Tramways Board (MMTB) to manage Melbourne's cable trams, six of the seven electric tramway companies and the last horse tram. In 1983, the MMTB was dissolved into the Metropolitan Transit Authority.

This element of the story of Melbourne is told in the map shown in Figure 4. The 'Railways & tramways map of Melbourne and suburbs: showing railways, cable tramways, electric tramways' was published in the 1920s by the Collins Book Depot, then a major Melbourne bookseller and publisher. The map complemented the 'official' maps of the time from the Victorian Railways and the Melbourne and Metropolitan Tramways Board.

What does the map show?

The line running due south from the centre of the city shows the Port Melbourne railway line. And, the Williamstown railway line heads west, over the Maribyrnong River, then south to Hobsons Bay. The Williamstown railway line was opened in 1859, just five years after the Port Melbourne railway line. It connected Williamstown and, subsequently, Geelong, the State of Victoria's second biggest city, to the new Spencer Street Railway Station (Wikipedia 2014). Then railway lines developed further from the centre, associated with the 1880 'Land Boom' in Victoria. The advancement of the rail system continued, with lines pushing into some suburbs. The lines on the map show this push into the suburbs, with rail lines radiating from Flinders Street Station. The availability of suburban railways generated much commercial development around railway stations and the opening of new suburbs.

An Inner Circle railway line was established in 1888 and the Outer Circle in 1890 (Danno 2014). However, the circle lines proved not to be economic. The circle lines were soon closed—the Outer Circle in 1897 and the Inner Circle closed the following century, in 1948 (Danno 2014). The Inner Circle can be seen as the 'complete' circle on the map, while the Outer Circle is incomplete, with the line running between Deepdene and Ashburton stations. Remnants of these circle lines can still be seen in the suburbs once served by the railway, with the former railway land now parklands or walking/cycling paths and the railway stations put to other uses. Danno (2014) has called the Inner and Outer Circle lines Melbourne's 'Phantom Railways'.

Reading the map provides a unique historical overview of the development of Melbourne's public transportation system. The black lines illustrate the extent of the suburban train system: basically, radiating outwards from the city centre, and complemented by the inner and outer circle lines. This is the first chapter in the development of Melbourne's public transportation system. The red lines show the extent of cable tramways in the central areas and inner suburbs of the city. They serviced Melbourne's early suburbs. Then, moving a little away from the inner areas of the city, the green lines mark the coming of electric tramways, operated initially by individual trusts and later the MMTB.

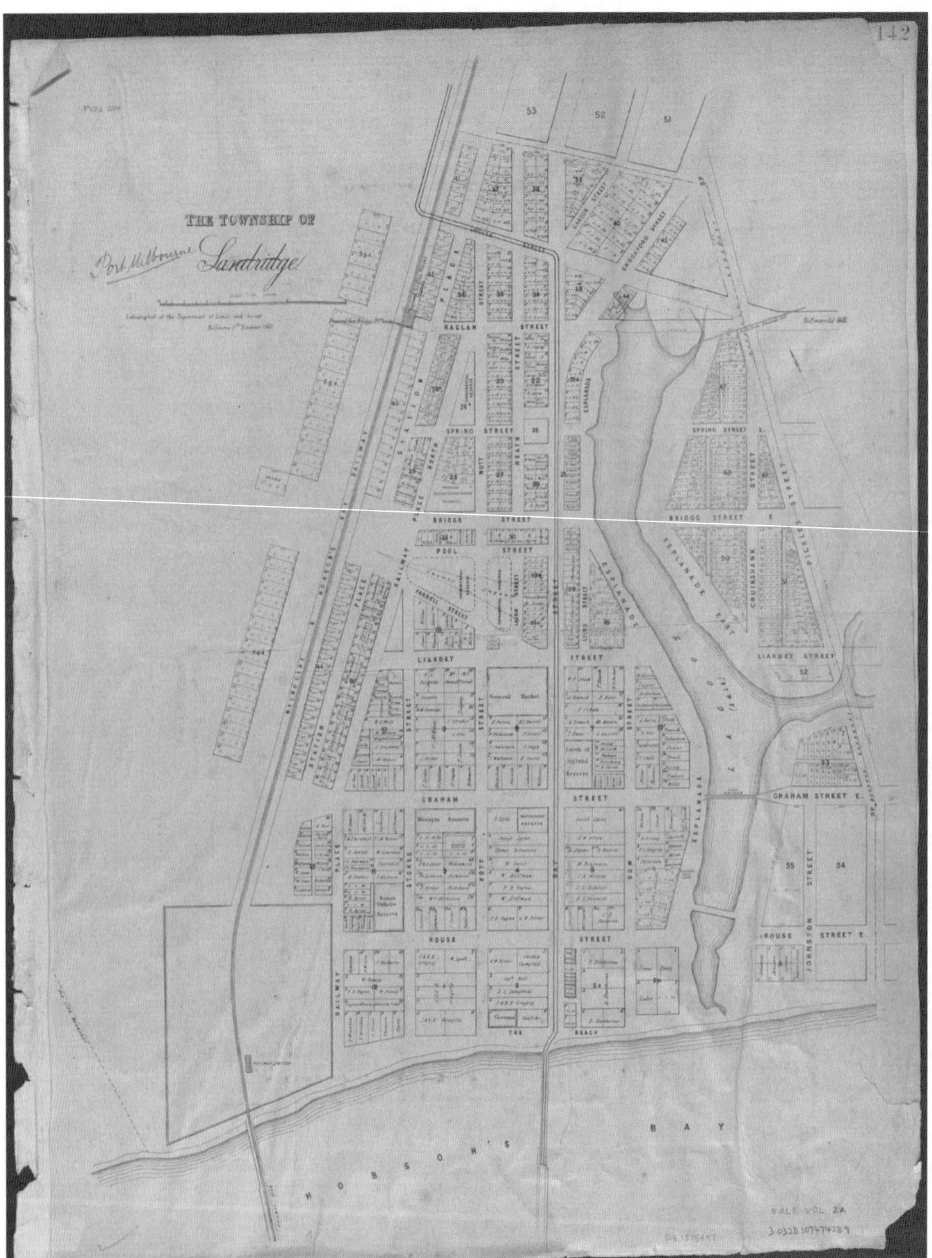

Figure 4: Railways & tramways map of Melbourne and suburbs: showing railways, cable tramways, electric tramways, 1920s, Collins Book Depot.

Source: State Library of Victoria. Persistent link: http://handle.slv.vic.gov.au/10381/163261

This work is out of copyright. No copyright restrictions apply.

The map illustrates the reach, the diversity of transportation modes and the interconnections that existed. Citizens are provided with the means to be part of the city, and partake in all that it offers, irrespective of whether they live 'in close' or in the developing suburbs. The 'Web' of the public transportation is the conduit for making the city 'work' and ensuring that almost every part of the city is accessible to all.

Reading the map also shows Melbourne's growth to the east and south-east, modest growth in the north and little development to the west. This was the pattern until quite recently, when new land developments in Melbourne's western suburbs began to move the geographical centre of Greater Melbourne to the west.

Reading the Mapped City

Reading the four examples of cartographic products provided in this article illustrate the establishment and growth of a city. The narrative of the city begins with the selection of a site that affords potable water and access to transportation via the river. Fawkner's selection of where to locate his settlement becomes the very focus of the future city, and not Batman's Port Phillip Association's site, which was located at present-day Port Melbourne. The grid is the very basis for laying out the city. Aligned at its southern border with the Yarra River, as defined by Robert Russell (but 'officially' surveyed and marked by Robert Hoddle), it becomes the starting point for the formal, planned extension of the settlement. There is a pre-determination of the growth of the suburbs, in that cadastral maps were published to show the planned city, with the provision for future civic buildings, residential streets, parklands and reserves. The first two maps are the narrative of this.

Once the city is established, the need to formally plan and construct water reticulation services and sewage systems becomes obvious. With the formation of water and sewerage authorities, the planning and implementation of city-wide installation begins. The need for accurate surveys and mapping results in the rich geographic records of surveyors' fieldnotes and city plans. Detailed records of the subterranean labyrinth of pipes and the above-ground infrastructure and buildings depict a growing city, and the maps of the city's transportation system reflect how the city becomes consolidated and its citizens connected. We read the maps and visualize a city determined to provide its citizens with the resources and facilities needed in a modern city.

Conclusion

The maps discussed in this chapter allow readers to visualize the development of the city. Four maps were chosen to illustrate the establishment, growth and consolidation of the city.

Robert Russell's map of 1837 depicts the early settlement of Melbourne and the establishment of the grid, the central city core that still exists today. The cadastral map reflects the growth of the city and the establishment of its initial suburbs. The MMBW map and fieldnotes record (in great detail) infrastructure development in the early 1900s. And, the Railways and Tramways map (1920s) shows the establishment of and expansion of the city's suburban public transportation network.

The maps are historical records of the geography of the city and illustrations of the plans implemented by city leaders to develop the city and its suburbs. They show the historic settlement/town/city, the contemporary city at the time the map was published and the envisioned future city.

The maps record European settlement and expansion. Importantly, they reveal how the actual production of these maps did dictate how the city grew.

References

Australian Dictionary of Biography (1966), Volume 1, Melbourne: Melbourne University Press, <http://adb.anu.edu.au/biography/grimes-charles-2129>. Accessed 4 August 2015.

Blainey, G. and Foley, S. (2005), *Reflections: 150 years of* The Age, Milsons Point: Doubleday Australia Pty Ltd., pp. 178–179.

Boyce, J. (2015), *1835: The founding of Melbourne & the conquest of Australia,* Carlton: Black Ink.

Broome, R. (2008), 'Aboriginal Melbourne: Melbourne, the city past and present', <http://www.emelbourne.net.au/biogs/EM00029b.htm>. Accessed 13 August 2015.

Carrol, B. (2008), 'North Melbourne: Melbourne, the city past and present', <http://www.emelbourne.net.au/biogs/EM01064b.htm>. Accessed 25 August 2015.

City of Melbourne (2015), 'Settlement to City', <https://www.melbourne.vic.gov.au/AboutMelbourne/History/Pages/SettlementtoCity.aspx>. Accessed 25 August 2015.

Currey, J. (2002), *A Journal of Grimes' Survey: The Cumberland in Port Phillip January–February 1803*, Malvern, Vic.: Banks Society Publications.

Dalrymple, K., Williamson, I. P. and Wallace, J. (2003), 'Cadastral Systems within Australia', *The Australian Surveyor,* 48: 1, pp. 37–49.

Danno (2014), 'Beside the Yarra: Melbourne's phantom railways', <http://marvmelb.blogspot.com/2014/04/melbournes-phantom-railways.html>. Accessed 16 June 2014.

Davison, G. (1981), *The Rise and Fall of Marvellous Melbourne*, Melbourne: Melbourne University Press.

Department of Infrastructure and Regional Development, Government of Australia (2014), 'History of Rail in Australia', <http://www.infrastructure.gov.au/rail/trains/history.aspx>. Accessed 16 June 2014.

Department of Transport, Planning and Local Infrastructure, Victoria (n.d.), 'Administering Victoria's Water Supply', Victorian Water Supply Heritage Study, Volume 1: Thematic environmental history', <http://www.dtpli.vic.gov.au/__data/assets/pdf_file/0004/218335/Vic_Water_Supply_study_Vol1_partB.pdf >. Accessed 4 August 2015.

Dryrenfurth, N. (2008), 'Port Melbourne: Melbourne, the city past and present', <http://www.emelbourne.net.au/biogs/EM01401b.htm>. Accessed 4 August 2015.

Dunstan, D. (2008), 'Greater Melbourne Movement', School of Historical & Philosophical Studies, The University of Melbourne, <http://www.emelbourne.net.au/biogs/EM00669b.htm>. Accessed 3 August 2015.

Eidelson, M. (1997), *The Melbourne Dreaming: A guide to the aboriginal places of Melbourne*, Canberra: Aboriginal Studies Press.

Glass, M. (1993), *Tommy Bent 'Bent by Name, Bent by Nature'*, Melbourne: Melbourne University Press.

Hoadley, D. (2015), 'Melbourne's Tram History, Trams of Australia', <http://www.railpage.org.au/tram/melbhist.html>. Accessed 3 August 2015.

Jones, R. (2003), 'Bent by Name, Bent by Nature', <http://www.hawthorntramdepot.org.au/papers/bent.htm#note1>. Accessed 26 August 2015.

Lucas, C. (2015), 'St Kilda Triangle: 16 years, $9 million down the drain, zero result', *The Age*, 9 March 2015, <http://www.theage.com.au/victoria/st-kilda-triangle-16-years-9-million-down-the-drain-zero-result-20150309-13z3dw.html>. Accessed 5 August 2015.

McVicker, N. (2010), 'EARLY SETTLEMENT: Mudgee's greatest myth: Who designed Mudgee?' <http://www.mudgeehistory.com.au/earlysettlement/robert_hoddle_myth_p8.html>. Accessed 3 August 2015.

Murdoch, W. (2008), 'East Melbourne, Melbourne, the City Past and Present', <http://www.emelbourne.net.au/biogs/EM00496b.htm>. Accessed 3 August 2015.

Museum Victoria (2015), 'The Founding of Melbourne, 1835', <http://museumvictoria.com.au/collections/themes/6775/the-founding-of-melbourne-1835>. Accessed 3 August 2015.

Preston, H. (1967), 'Russell, Robert (1808–1900)', *Australian Dictionary of Biography*, Volume 2, Melbourne: Melbourne University Press.

Priestley, S. (2008), 'East Melbourne, Melbourne, the City Past and Present', <http://www.emelbourne.net.au/biogs/EM01401b.htm>. Accessed 3 August 2015.

Public Records Office, Victoria (2012), 'Australia's Pleasure Land: Luna Park and other amusements at St Kilda', <http://prov.vic.gov.au/blog-news/australias-pleasure-land-luna-park-and-other-amusements-at-st-kilda>. Accessed 12 December 2014.

Ritchie, E. G. (1934), 'Melbourne's Water Supply Undertaking', *Journal of Institution of Engineers Australia*, 6, pp. 379–382, <http://www.consuleng.com.au/IE%20Aust%201934%20-%209%20Melb%20Water%20Supply.pdf>. Accessed 5 August 2015.

Scurfield, J. (n.d.), 'e-Melbourne Maps and Mapping', <http://www.emelbourne.net.au/biogs/EM00897b.htm>. Accessed 5 August 2015.

State Library of Victoria (2015a), 'Melbourne's Founders', <http://ergo.slv.vic.gov.au/explore-history/colonial-melbourne/pioneers/melbournes-founders>. Accessed 8 August 2015.

———— (2015b), 'Victoria's Early History, 1803–1851', <http://guides.slv.vic.gov.au/Victoriasearlyhistory/earlysurveys>. Accessed 8 August 2015.

———— (2015c), 'Melbourne City Grid', <http://ergo.slv.vic.gov.au/explore-history/colonial-melbourne/everyday-life/melbourne-city-grid>. Accessed 8 August 2015.

———— (2015d), 'How to Read the MMBW 40ft to the Inch Detail Plans', <http://guides.slv.vic.gov.au/c.php?g=245242&p=1633279>. Accessed 8 August 2015.

The University of Melbourne (2015), 'Rare and Historical Maps', <http://www.lib.unimelb.edu.au/collections/maps/map-historical.html>. Accessed 25 August 2015.

Wikipedia (2015a), 'Trams in Melbourne', <https://en.wikipedia.org/wiki/Trams_in_Melbourne>. Accessed 8 August 2015.

—— (2015b), 'Port Melbourne, Victoria', <https://en.wikipedia.org/wiki/Port_Melbourne,_Victoria>. Accessed 8 August 2015.

—— (2015c), 'Thomas Bent', <https://en.wikipedia.org/wiki/Thomas_Bent>. Accessed 25 August 2015.

—— (2014), 'Railways in Melbourne', <http://en.wikipedia.org/wiki/Railways_in_Melbourne>. Accessed 16 June 2014.

Chapter 2

Carto-City Revisited: Unmapping urbaness

Maggie McCormick

Introduction: Carto-City revisited

Carto-City is the title of Denis Cosgrove's chapter in *Else/Where: Mapping—New Cartographies of Networks and Territories* (Cosgrove 2006). Cosgrove concludes with the statement, 'Urban space and cartographic space remain inseparable; as each is transformed, their relationship alters' (Cosgrove 2006: 157). The chapter begins at this point to consider the concept of 'city' today and how this concept and reality is a far cry from the space in which cartography was born.

The experiential and perceptual shift from city to urban, paralleled by ubiquitous technology, has transformed the relationship between urban space and its mapping. An understanding of what is meant by 'city' has been transformed into a shared and experiential mindscape of urban consciousness or 'urbaness' (McCormick 2009). Equally the cartographic process has been transformed by the ephemeral space it maps, that is, a space of urbaness mediated by digital screens. It is argued that while the city is undergoing its own transitions, art practice and mapping practices are realigning and transforming increasingly into an 'unmapping' practice that is neither art nor cartography, but rather an alternative recording or remapping of contemporary urban experience and perception. Many valuable and lost aspects of earlier cartographic practice are being revisited in different ways. This time the mapping practice occurs through active interventions into the transforming space from which the practice has arisen. Combined with technological approaches these interventions have the capacity to embody and enhance, in a more fulsome way, the recording of the urban experience and perception of what a twenty-first-century city is becoming or has become.

Urban Space: The city transformed

The often-quoted question posed by Lewis Mumford in the 1930s, 'What is a City?' is today a far more complex question. While Mumford's view of the city as 'a theatre of social action' (1937) recognized the city as more than a constructed, physical space, he could not have envisioned the complex action and interaction of urban networks that is experienced by today's societies. Mumford's thinking was framed at a time when the idea of the individual modern city was emerging. The idea of the 'Megalopolis' or urban cluster (Gottmann 1961) that linked geographically connected cities such as BosWash (Boston and Washington) was yet to come. Later this concept was extended to connected urban spaces such as those of the Pearl River Delta in China, reflecting in part a changing emphasis in urban research from expanding cities of Europe to those of Asia. This in itself reflects the rapid growth in urbanization across the planet. The text 'World = City' appears on the back cover of *Mutations: Harvard project on the city* (2001). This project undertaken by Rem Koolhaas set out to explore contemporary interpretations of the city in relation to 'what used to be the city' (Koolhaas et al. 2001: 19) by focusing on understanding the city well beyond its concrete manifestations. James Donald (2000), in discussing the 'immaterial city' talks about the city as a state of mind, and references back to Georg Simmel's 1903 essay, 'The Metropolis and Mental Life' that explored the state of the city of Berlin around the turn of the century. As Simmel had observed, an increased movement of people to the city intensified Berlin's rhythm. His concern was with over stimulation. Adding to Simmel's observations Donald considers the impact of emerging flows of information through the mass circulation of newspapers. Here, we see early impacts of urbanization and what would become digitalization, which was soon transforming the city into 'a category of experience' (Donald 2000: 49) of multi-layered stimulation well beyond Simmel's concerns.

Mumford's recognition of the experience of the city phenomenon and the impact of social action is significant in thinking about how 'being urban' is understood today. As over 50 per cent of the world's population will soon share a digitally connected urban mindset, we now understand social urban experience within the framework of such concepts as time/space compression (Harvey 1989), space of flows (Castells 1996), liquid times (Bauman 2007) and telesthesia (Wark 2012). Shaped by these contexts that shrink time and space, cities have transformed into sites of 'cityness' (Sassen 2005) and intersections of 'exacerbated difference' (Koolhaas et al. 2001: 21) that constantly recreate the other. While Sassen as social and economic analyst on globalization and Koolhaas as architect and urban critic are referring to how the individual city is transforming, each is also well aware of the connections between cities and the impact of flows and compressions. Sassen is credited with coining the term 'Global City' in the early 1990s based on her observation of movements between New York, London and Tokyo. It is an example of Wark's telesthesia where information and ideas move faster than people or things between spaces 'to bring what is distant near, and make what is distant a site of action' (Wark 2012: 207). Cities today are connected in unprecedented ways as they grow and merge to create new urban realities. In the early 1960s, Marshall McLuhan described what he observed as a collective identity emerging out of pervasive electronic media with the oxymoron 'Global Village'. This was devised as 'a term where the modifier and the noun don't belong together'; that 'we lose sight of the strangeness of these terms speaks to an acclimatization' to what was once perceived as a paradoxical space (Wark 2012: 27).

While discussions on the city and its increasing paradoxes have enlivened academic discourse for some time, concepts that bring the city into closer alignment with urban mind space than to geographical space have been entering public consciousness since the start of the twenty-first century. Take, for example, the front cover of *Newsweek* magazine featuring an image of a woman wearing a t-shirt that reads 'I ♥ NY-LON', with the article headline of 'A tale of one city. Living, working and playing in New York and London' (2002). As Sassen observed, the flight between these two cities is one of the world's most heavily used connection routes, so it is not surprising to find that New York and London might have more in common with each other than with other cities in the United States of America or the United Kingdom. For some, the journey between is as much the city as the two cities themselves. Airline flight route maps are visual recordings of urban transience reflecting contemporary states of mind. If we ask Mumford's question again—'What is a city?'—answers may be found in this mind space, the space of 'urbaness' (McCormick 2009: 30).

What is urbaness? In earlier writing (2009) I define urbaness as a specific state of urban consciousness shaped by transience between, and compression of, space, time and difference, where all are perceived as the norm. Forms of urban consciousness are as old as cities themselves with concepts of transience and compression embedded in the trains, cars and planes that increasingly diminished the distances between and within cities and people. The difference is now the speed at which this takes place. Instantaneous satellite connection means we can be simultaneously in many places and time zones. Urban experience is both seen and unseen within a cacophony of layered, fragmented, transient alignments across multiple screens. What is also different is 'understanding of the increased mind mobility' (McCormick 2013a: 117). The concept that one is 'born urban, born transient' (McCormick 2009: 17) in both body and mind is arguably now a contemporary life experience.

The urban rhythm created by transience is not new to the understanding of what is a city. Cosgrove, for example, in his discussion of early city maps of the 1500s talks about how the rhythms of each city were embodied in the cartographic methodology (2006: 153). Central to urbaness though is the concept of urban arrhythm. This is a term used by Henri Lefebvre in writing about the city from the perspective of Rhythmanalysis (2004). Lefebvre used Paris as his model. At the time Lefebvre identified arrhythmia as a conflict between or among two or more rhythms that he saw as a negative, but he also observed that the rhythm became clearer at the point at which rhythms break down (Lefebvre 2004: 16).

Today's experience of urbaness, where accelerated global rhythms continuously clash at the points of contact, relates conceptually to Lefebvre's idea of moments when change takes place. Ben Highmore (2005) recognizes the value of Lefebvre's analysis in more fully understanding the shaping urban experience. He extends and applies Rhythmanalysis to several other individual cityscapes. Highmore observes that rhythm is 'a vital aspect of cities and all texts concerned with figuring the city' (2005: 141) and further observes that it is 'the measure of dynamic relationships' (2005: 9). My interest lies in the nature of that dynamic relationship in regard to contemporary urban consciousness. In earlier writing (McCormick 2013a, 2009) I moved the focus from rhythm to arrhythm, arguing that this reflects more fully the nature of current day urbaness: a position posed here. Arrhythm is brought about by transience between difference and the compression of difference via digital interfaces. It becomes the prism through which urban consciousness is experienced and understood, and this prism shapes how 'city' is conceptualized. Further, it transforms the perspective of the mapmaker and consequently the map itself.

Cartographic Space: The map transformed

City mapping dates back to the first human settlements such as the Bedolina and Giadighe petroglyphs at Valcamonica (2500 BC) and wall painting at Çatal Hüyük (6200 BC) (Turnbull 1989: 13). These graphic systems lie somewhere between art and science, drawing and cartography; and they lay the foundation of cartography's journey into future concepts of what a city is or might be. Later in the growth of world cities like London, it takes until the 1930s for the publication of Phyllis Pearsall's A-Z London Street Directory. For the first time some 23,000 roads, streets and lanes in London were recorded by walking the city. While Pearsall was certainly not of the *flâneur* or *dérive* model of mapping the city, through walking, as her intentions were grounded in practicalities not poetics, there is, in each mapping mode, recognition of the value of experiential mapping in understanding and recording a city.

Walter Benjamin in his unfinished work on Paris, the 'Arcades Project' (1927–1940), drew on the poetry of Charles Baudelaire to bring to the forefront the concept of strolling as an urban observer or mapper by immersing oneself in the city's rhythm. In the 1950s and 1960s the International Situationists and the concept of the *dérive* introduced rapidity, chance and unexpected encounters into the experiential knowing of the city, thus paving the way for numerous approaches within psychogeography. Guy Debord's 1957 cartographic work, *Guide Psychogeographique De Paris,* mapped the atmospheric connections of Paris that link separate neighbourhoods in people's minds, by splitting up the city of Paris into sections linked by arrows. Debord recorded the city as a fragmented and transitory experience that has emerged into everyday urban experience. Now digital screens mediate such experience.

Today's urban cartography is dominated by screens such as GIS (geographic information systems) designed to capture, analyse and present all manner of spatial or geographical data resulting in Google Maps and GPS global positioning systems offering real-time navigation. While these systems can deliver us incredibly accurate geographical information, engage with concepts of transience and connectedness, and even interpret urban data based on cultural as well as spatial perceptions, there continues to be a gap in their capacity to fully map the nature of contemporary urban culture. Such mapping devices deliver to us not only mapped urban space in minute detail, but at the same time they map us, the map-reader. A great deal has been written about maps, mapmakers and power (Cosgrove 1999; Monmonier 1996; Wood and Fels 1992), and while much of contemporary mapping is dominated by global companies as mapmaker and, as such, power maker, this situation is not central to the present discussion. The map is never neutral. While negative aspects of the mapmaker's position of power are often central to discussions, the interest lies here in the power of the creative mapmaker and creative mapping methodologies to enhance digital capacities in cartography to more fully embody the recording of the city of the twenty-first century.

Aspects of earlier mapping methodologies such as those employed by Georg Braun and Frans Hogenberg in the first comprehensive city atlas, the *Civitas Orbis Terrarum* (1572) as a companion to Abraham Ortelius's world atlas, *Theatrum Orbis Terrarum* (1570), holds some clues. Cosgrove (2006: 153) points out that there had been earlier city atlases (Hartmann Schedel, *Cronical*, 1493, and Sebastian Münster, *Cosmographica*, 1544), but these did not set out to illustrate every known major world city, as did Braun and Hogenberg, nor to make these cities accessible to the viewer within their private reading room. Ironically, an urban mind space was already in train as the viewer turned from one map to the next throughout the urban space of the atlas pages. The word *civitas*, while referring here to 'city', has its roots in Latin as the social body of the 'cives', citizens, bound by the rights and duties of law. In the case of the *Civitas Orbis Terrarum* the maps focus on the civic and cultural pride of particular cities by being decorated with images of those people considered to be important. A similar approach can be seen in Ming Dynasty scrolls in China that depict the Forbidden City, again with images of its important citizens. In addition, Forbidden City maps often recorded an envisioned city, how one hoped the city to be remembered, despite the fact that the cartographers of the time were well able to map a physical likeness (Shatzman Steinhardt 1998).

Art and science have always shared a capacity to imagine. The Chinese imagined Beijing and China as the centre of the world. In the fifteenth century, the Yongle Emperor (reigned 1402–1424) relocated China's capital to Beijing and commenced work on the Forbidden City. Mapping of the time shows the Forbidden City, surrounded by a series of walls moving outwards, to the city, to China and to the final outer-zones inhabited by those considered to be cultural barbarians. Medieval Europe's T-O maps did much the same by marking Jerusalem as the centre of the known world. While more scientific approaches to cartography began to dominate after the Medieval period, imagination and what is often referred to as 'creative mapping' has a very important role to play in mapping the complexity of today's urbaness.

A contemporary atlas, the *AMO Atlas* developed by OMA Office for Metropolitan Architecture (Koolhaas 2004), is not a far cry from the city patterns and rhythms of *Civitas Orbis Terrarum* depicted through its often bird's eye view and inclusion of citizen portraits in its mapping devices. The *AMO Atlas* aims to snap shot the world in transition, which it accomplishes through visualizing data to record physical and non-physical, interconnected, global information and trends that link cities across the world. From McDonald's outlets to Chinatowns, the *AMO Atlas* records diverse urban connections from commercial expansion to cultural dispersions. In recording Right Wing Think Tanks and Left Wing Action Tanks, photographic portraits play an important part in the visualizing of data. Segments of city maps across Europe are drawn together in one graphic diagram, simultaneously mapping and unmapping. The difference between the *Civitas Orbis Terrarum* and the *AMO Atlas* lies in the recording of the multiplicity of physical and digital mind-links between contemporary cities brought about by the globalization of the planet and facilitated by advances in technologies. While Braun and Hogenberg could well have identified with the cartographer as both scientist and artist, they could not have envisaged such an urban state or comprehended the concept of art 'unmapping' science.

Unmapping Mapping

Increasingly, 'the relationship between maps and art has swung around' towards what 'art can tell us about maps' (Harmon 2009: 9) and the space being mapped. *Unmapping the World* was part of the Experimenta International Design Biennial in 2013 in Portugal where mapping methodology was explored through art practice. The project was located in the Tropical Research Institute in Lisbon, the site of the main cartographic association in Portugal in the nineteenth century. Scientists at the time were set the task of mapping the 'new' worlds, but left unrecorded the effect of these colonial times.

Unmapping the World took the approach of introducing an alternative methodology by posing the proposition that a more accurate map of the times was embedded in the blanks that were left in the maps rather than in the content of detailed scientific charts. This fluid investigatory practice resulted in a cartography that 'doesn't draw borders, but opens them up in the mind' (De Vet and Coelho 2013). Art here decodes codes, declassifies classifications and in the process challenges traditional cartographic power structures through unmapping.

This project addresses mind space, albeit within a historical framework, and presents a methodology for recording such space. While not investigating digital space specifically, it explores layers of meaning across temporal and spatial perceptions. A similar process can be seen in MelBeiVien that formed part of the doctoral thesis, 'The Transient City: mapping urban consciousness through contemporary art practice' (McCormick 2009). Urban space perception was identified and recorded through combining subway maps from Melbourne, Beijing and Vienna, as a metaphorical cartography of personal urban experience at the time—born in Melbourne, residing in Beijing and curating in Vienna. MelBeiVien was exhibited in the 798 Art District in Beijing, itself symptomatic of urban flows and collisions. The works unmapped formal city maps by transforming them from geographically directional works to expressions of urban perception that, while personal, reflected wider experience.

Contemporary art practice is increasingly an unmapping process. Artists employ crawling (William Pope. L, *The Great White Way: 22 miles, 5 years, 1 street*, 2002), melting and leaking (Francis Alys, *The Leak*, 1995, *Paradox of Praxis* 1, 1997), lighting (Olifur Eliasson, *Daylight Map*, 2005), tattooing (Qin Ga, *Walking Visual Display*, 2002), transiting (Yin Xiuzhen, *Portable City*, 2007, commenced in 2001) among a myriad of other unmapping methodologies. Many have been compiled and recorded by Kathryn Harmon (2009, 2004). While some owe allegiance to mapping in its more traditional form, all reflect the impact of the urban and digital state of mind expressed through the 'public turn' (McCormick 2012) in contemporary art practice where 'mapping' becomes an active and interactive performative process that intertwines physical space, mind space and urban identity. Qin Ga's body mapping, for example, on one hand maps the route of the 6000 mile, Long March in China (1934–1936), recording the physical and mental pain of the experience through his own pain by undertaking the trek and having the route tattooed on his back along the way. On the other hand, Qin Ga is himself urban, an artist who lives and works in Beijing, China. He has a specific history, but is also an artist of his times, as seen in his art practice and mapping methodology that is performative and immersive, reflecting the complex layers of the subject matter.

Yin Xiuzhen's mapping in Portable City expands beyond China as a huge world map crisscrossed with colliding strings connecting world cities. The interconnection points of the strings create a density of entanglement that make it impossible to distinguish the starting and finishing points. In front of the map several suitcases sit. These have arrived by air with the artist, and have travelled with the artist direct from the airport carousel to the exhibition space. Yin Xiuzhen uses people's old clothes from cities she has visited and sews them into reconstructions of city buildings that sit within the suitcases. These works are 'a form deriving from cultural globalization, as well as a sort of collision in a 'third space' between the global and the local, revealing to us the results of communication' (Yin 2007: 290). Like Qin Ga, Yin Xiuzhen's practice maps transience as it compresses space through action. Both are engaging in a global discourse, a recording that engages them physically while also reflecting on an urban state of mind, that is, a connectedness through collective urban experience. In these examples the cartographic form is transformed again into a process of unmapping while remapping. These practices critique and pose questions about the urban unseen, while their transformative actions contribute to an understanding of experience and perception of what being urban may mean in a contemporary context.

Unmapping to Remap: Cartography of urbaness

Mapping records but also intervenes and shapes urban cartography somewhere between 'creating and recording the city' (Cosgrove 2006: 149). As the map and the city have changed, so too has the relationship between them to embody an overlapping space where this unmapping practice takes place.

The *SkypeLab: Transcontinental faces and spaces* project, led by Eichinger and McCormick, (with Yonglei Ma in China in 2015), commenced in 2014 and is ongoing. It draws on an interdisciplinary research methodology that connects cities across the contiguous space of continents. SkypeLab is a project that records urban perception mediated by digital screens. Data is collected first through drawing via the Skype screen and then by reflection leading to visual and written interpretations of this material. To date German, Australian and Chinese artists, who had not met previously, have been paired up to undertake Blind Contour Drawing sessions via Skype over periods of several months. The technique favours the senses over the analytical. While Blind Contour Drawing was originally conceived as an innovative drawing teaching technique (Nicolaîdes 1941; Edwards 1979), in SkypeLab it is transformed into a research tool for investigating the urban ephemera mediated by digital screens. While in more traditional cartography contour lines indicate the shape of the earth's surface, here contour lines record the feeling of sitting either side of a screen with a complete stranger. The two people, unknown to each other, look directly at each other while drawing, at much closer distances than the usual physical encounter and yet separated by long distances. Here perception is transformed as it responds to paradox through frozen moments and fluidity, distance and nearness, connection and disconnection, hand and brain, light and dark, clarity and loss of detail, confidence and awkwardness, limitation and possibility amidst a myriad of other apparent contradictions. Paradoxical fragments become everyday framing of how knowledge is formed, and how perceptions are created and experience recorded. Drawing via the 'Skype screen interface reinforces the idea that when we draw we mirror ourselves as much as the other and in the process we redefine ourselves' (McCormick 2013b: 74) as mapmaker and the map itself.

SkypeLab's roots lie in its forerunner *Skypetrait: Transcontinental faces* (Eichinger and McCormick 2013), which was undertaken using a similar laboratory-style methodology. While Skypetrait focused on mapping interpretation through the face on the screen, SkypeLab focuses on all aspects of the experience. A range of senses come into the recordings that are related to sight, but also to sound and touch, and to what is seen, but also unseen. This can be observed in the artistic outcomes of SkypeLab's Visuelle Bibliothek in Shanghai in 2015 at the German Consulate General in cooperation with the Goethe-Institut in China. Among the participating artists, examples include Fanding Sun who visually records strange sounds that she hears while on Skype, sounds that seem to emit from the technology itself. Grace Leone draws the sound of her German partner walking through a market, transforming this into a Braille line—sound that can be touched. Touch is also the focus of Javiera Advis who records the missing element, the equivalent of the blank space on a map. Giordano Biondi takes a similar position to that in *Unmapping the World* (2013) by focusing on the elements of the screen that usually go unexplored—the things that are half seen through pixilation or by being cut off or distorted by the screen. Similarly Riza Manalo's work unmaps by focusing on erasure as an act of creation and recording the ephemeral nature of online encounters. Clare McCracken literally removes line and pixilation from the screen to cross-stitch with embroidery thread over many hours to record the cultural gaps, collisions and memories contained in the line of the thread. Each of these processes unmaps in order to remap.

Conclusion: Unmapping urbaness

Cosgrove's Carto-City emphasized the inextirpable interconnection between cities and their cartography as does the argument presented in this chapter, but in the process the premise is extended. This chapter poses SkypeLab, along with a number of other contemporary art practices, as active, performative and interactive processes that intertwine physical space, mind space and urban identity, to record urbaness through the act of unmapping. In the process urban cartography is remapped. Through its experimental approach within digital space, SkypeLab poses and exposes questions arising out of the practice about the space itself. It asks: How do the layers, reflections and fragmentations of seeing and encountering each other via digital screens inform our urban perceptions? From this crucial question, SkypeLab aims to continue to pose questions that arise from the research labs. Labs include a major exhibition in Reutlingen, Germany, at the Städtische Galerie, and a publication (Eichinger and McCormick 2016), and continuous screen presence at www.skypelab.org and at ARTE Creative TV (France/Germany). Leading up to the next stage of SkypeLab in its fourth continent in South America, an international workshop, in Rio de Janeiro (2015)[1] explored SkypeLab's remapping processes within a body of ephemeral cartography. SkypeLab, along with the other art/cartography urban interventions discussed in this chapter, contributes valuable knowledge to an understanding of new conceptual territory within a profoundly changing urbanscape that reflects the inseparable relationship between urban space and cartographic space and the unmapping of urbaness.

References

Bauman, Z. (2007), *Liquid Times: Living in an age of uncertainty*, Cambridge, UK: Polity Press.

Benjamin, W. (1999), *Arcades Project*, (trans. H. Eiland and K. McLaughlin), Cambridge and London: Belknap Press, Harvard University Press.

Castells, M. (1996), *The Rise of the Network Society*, Cambridge: Blackwell Publishers.

Cosgrove, D. (2006), 'Carto-City', in J. Abrams and P. Hall (eds), *Else/Where: Mapping—New cartographies of networks and territories*, Minneapolis: University of Minnesota Design Institute, pp. 148–157.

——— (1999), *Mappings*, London: Reaktion.

Debord, G. (1957), *Guide Psychogeographique de Paris* map, Lecointre, D. and Drouet, D. <http://www.lecointredrouet.com/liste.php?PersNum=1784>. Accessed 17 May 2015.

De Vet, A. and Coelho, N. (Curators), (9 November–22 December, 2013), *Unmapping the World*, Experimenta International Design Biennial, Portugal: Palacio dos Condes da Calheta, <http://www.bureaudevet.be/projects/unmapping-the-world/>. Accessed 17 April 2015.

Donald, J. (2000), 'The Immaterial City: Representation, imagination and media technologies', in G. Bridge and S. Watson (eds), *A Companion to the City*, Malden: Blackwell Publishers.

Edwards, B. (1979), *Drawing on the Right Side of the Brain*, Los Angeles: J.P. Tarcher.

Eichinger, H. and McCormick, M. (2016), *SkypeLab: Transcontinental faces and spaces*, Bielefeld, Germany: Kerber Publishing.

——— (2013), *Skypetrait: Transcontinental faces*, Reutlingen, Germany: City of Reutlingen.

Gottmann, J. (1961), *Megalopolis: The urbanized northeastern seaboard of the United States*, New York: Twentieth Century Fund.

Harmon, K. (2009), *The Map as Art: Contemporary artists explore cartography*, New York: Princeton Architectural Press.

——— (2004), *You Are Here: Personal geographies and other maps of the imagination*, New York: Princeton Architectural Press.

Hartley, S. (2001), *Mrs P's Journey: The remarkable story of the woman who created the A-Z map*, London: Simon & Schuster.

Harvey, D. (1989), *The Condition of Post Modernity: An inquiry into the origins of cultural change*, Oxford: Blackwell.

Highmore, B. (2005), *Cityscapes: Cultural readings in the material and symbolic city*, Houndmills, Basingstoke, Hampshire and New York: Palgrave Macmillan.

Koolhaas, R. (ed.) (2004), Content, Köln: Taschen.

Koolhaas, R., Boeri, S., Kwinter, S. and Tazi, N. (2001), *Mutations: Harvard Project on the City*, Bordeaux and Barcelona: Arc en réve centre d'architecture.

Lefebvre, H. (2004), *Rhythmanalysis: Space, time and everyday life,* (trans. S. Elden and G. Moore), London and New York: Continuum. (First published in French 1991.)

McCormick, M. (2013a), 'The Transient City: The city as urbaness', in E. Grierson and K. Sharp (eds), *Re-Imagining the City: Art, globalization and urban spaces,* Chicago: Intellect, The University of Chicago Press.

——— (2013b), 'Skypetrait: Portraits of urbaness', in H. Eichinger and M. McCormick (eds), *Skypetrait: Transcontinental faces,* Reutlingen: City of Reutlingen.

——— (2012), 'Urban Practice and the Public Turn', *Asia Pacific Journal of Arts and Cultural Management,* Melbourne: The University of Melbourne, pp. 3–13.

——— (2009), 'The Transient City; Mapping urban consciousness through contemporary art practice', unpublished PhD thesis, Melbourne: The University of Melbourne.

——— (2007), 'Suitcases, Maps, Wolves and Glass Walls: Mapping urban consciousness and gender asymmetry in contemporary art', UNESCO Observatory, *Multi Disciplinary Research in the Arts: e-journal, 1: 1,* <http://education.unimelb.edu.au/about_us/specialist_areas/arts_education/ melbourne_unesco_observatory_of_arts_education/the_e-journal/volume_1_issue_1> and <http://education.unimelb.edu.au/__data/assets/pdf_file/0004/1105735/suitcases.pdf>. Accessed 14 March 2015.

Monmonier, M. (1996), *How to Lie with Maps,* Chicago: University of Chicago Press.

Mumford, L. ([1937] 2011), 'What is a City?', in R. LeGates and F. Stout (eds), *The City Reader,* 5th ed., Abingdon, Oxon: Routledge, pp. 91–95.

Nicolaîdes, K. (1941), *The Natural Way to Draw: A working plan for art study,* Boston: Houghton Miffin Co.

Qin, G. (2002), 'Long March' and 'Miniature Long March', in J. Lu (curator), *Long March: A walking visual display,* New York and Beijing: Long March Foundation.

Sassen, S. (2005), 'Cityness in the Urban Age', *Urban Age Bulletin,* 2 Autumn, pp. 1–3, <http:// www.intelligentagent.com/ME/Saskia_Sassen_2005>.<Cityness_In_The_Urban_Age-Bulletin2.pdf>. Accessed 14 March 2015.

——— (1991), *The Global City: New York, London, Tokyo,* Princeton: Princeton University Press.

Shatzmann Steinhart, N. (1998), 'Mapping the Chinese City', in D. Buisseret (ed.), *Envisioning the City: Six studies in urban cartography,* The Kenneth Nebenzahl, Jr. Lectures in the History of Cartography, Chicago: University of Chicago Press.

Simmel, G. ([1903] 2004), 'The Metropolis and Mental Life', in Jenks, C., *Urban Culture: Critical concepts in literary and cultural studies,* vol. 1, London, New York: Routledge, pp. 349–361, https://equella.rmit.edu.au/rmit/file/56e319ea-0b87-e43e-2e07-dbefb8109294/1/3125900 9998860.pdf>. Accessed 17 May 2015.

Turnbull, D. (1989), *Maps Are Territories: Science as an atlas,* Geelong, Victoria, Australia: Deakin University Press.

Wark, M. (2012), *Telesthesia: Communication, culture & class*, Cambridge and Malden: Polity Press.

Wood, D. and Fels, J. (1992), *The Power of Maps*, Cooper Hewitt Museum, The Smithsonian Institution's National Museum of Design, New York: Guilford Press.

Yin, X. (2007), 'Portable City', in B. Feng (ed.), *China Now*, Vienna: Sammlung Essl.

Note

1　Mapping Ephemeralities/Ephemeral Mapping workshop at the International Cartographic Association Conference, Commission on Art and Cartography, in collaboration with the Commission on Maps and Society. University of the State of Rio De Janeiro, September 2015.

Chapter 3

Sensing Sydney: An experiment in public art of the smart eco-city

Jodi Newcombe

Introduction

A new breed of environmental artist collaborating with science, technology and the built form is delivering powerfully engaging, urban interfaces. Realized with the help of diverse stakeholders from government agencies and industry to scientists and the general public, these interfaces demonstrate new models for the management of air quality, water and energy use, among other sustainability concerns of cities. Examples of large-scale, artist-led urban environmental interventions include *Living Light* (air quality) in Seoul, Korea by The Living, *Particle Falls* (air quality) by Andrea Polli, *Amphibious Architecture* (water quality) in New York City by Natalie Jeremijenko, and *Nuage Vert/Green Cloud* (energy use) in Helsinki and Paris by HeHe.

Together these creative urban interfaces employ sensor technology, mesh networks, micro-computing, mobile phone technology and online platforms to build connection both literally and figuratively between natural and social systems. The unique tactics and strategies of artists set these interfaces apart from more standard smart city proposals or data visualization efforts that fail to capture the public's imagination or neglect to foster political agency. As creative experiments in civic engagement and interdisciplinary practice, these works have been pushing boundaries both in terms of public art production and the open government movement.

This chapter tells the story of *Building Run*, a public art commission that emerged from an umbrella project called *Sensing Sydney*, a 2013 pilot project in partnership between Melbourne-based environmental arts organization, Carbon Arts and the City of Sydney. The aim of *Sensing Sydney* was to explore ways in which public art, developed from environmental data, can increase participation of the public in the making of a more sustainable city. Central to the vision of *Sensing Sydney* were notions of the 'participatory society' and the 'smart citizen'.

The marriage between public art and open data was first trialled through a four-day, City Data Slam, which was held as part of the International Symposium of Electronic Arts 2013. The Data Slam invited ten leading Australian and international artists to develop public art concepts around key sustainability challenges, with access to experts and a range of data sets. The City Data Slam is not discussed further here, but is detailed in Carbon Arts (2012a).

Sensing Sydney culminated with the production of *Building Run*, a public art project conceived by artist Keith Deverell, which was won through a national competition. A video-art installation employing near real-time, building energy data to showcase and encourage energy efficiency, *Building Run* was a unique industry, government and arts collaboration, involving additional partners Investa Office, Deutsche Bank and Buildings Alive. The installation was positioned in an office tower foyer within Sydney's central business district under the umbrella of the city's Art&About public art festival (September–October 2013).

As a pilot project, *Sensing Sydney* aimed to test the contribution that artists can make to the shaping of an urban sustainability agenda using the tools of open data and open government. It forms part of practice-led, Doctor of Philosophy research by the author titled, 'Re-designing interfaces between nature, the public and policy: The role of the creative producer', which takes as its subject the work of Carbon Arts. Positioning Carbon Arts as a creative producer or strategic designer of socially and politically engaged art projects, the research scopes the potential for this role to facilitate new pathways for participation in the governance of environmental concerns within cities.

This chapter begins by framing the aims of *Sensing Sydney* in relation to the literature and experience of similar initiatives. A fuller description of the *Building Run* commission and its outcomes follows, including results from surveys with participants and the public evaluating their experience of the project. The chapter closes with some conclusions regarding the project's intended and unintended outcomes, with a view to informing the pursuit of similar initiatives in the future.

Politics of Participation in the Smart City: How to be a smart citizen

One of the dominant trends shaping cities in the twenty-first century is an ever-present information layer, which accompanies the widespread adoption of mobile or ubiquitous computing, sensor technology, surveillance and GPS capability. Often termed the 'smart city' this merging of physical and virtual space promises both greater management capabilities for city governments, and also greater participation in governance by citizens (Crang and Graham 2007; Vande Moere and Hill 2012; Foth 2009; Greenfield 2013; Townsend 2013). These promises emerge as two competing political agendas, one advocating an orderly top-down control and the other a messier, bottom-up democracy.

Critics of the top-down, smart city agenda peddled by many IT companies[1] suggest that their emphasis on efficiency and optimization hide a questionable political ideology and a certain naïveté about how thriving cities actually function (de Waal 2014; Greenfield 2013; Hollands 2008; Townsend 2013). In reaction to this corporate vision of a techno-utopia with its authoritarian overtones, an opposing vision has emerged—that of the *smart citizen* (Haque 2012; Hill 2012; Hemment and Townsend 2013). While the call for an uprising of the smart citizen is centred on the enabling abilities of a particular set of tools and technologies, its proponents share a set of broader concerns with the many 'right to the city' movements emerging around the world, which are responding to the dehumanizing effects of global capitalism (Harvey 2012).

Mobile media and sensor technology may be used to encourage a variety of forms of bottom-up, public participation in city governance, not all of which deliver more democratic outcomes. In his analysis of applications of mobile media and sensor technology employed by city governments to engender public participation, Iveson (2011) identifies three strategies of governance that these tools can serve: *control, responsibilization* and *politicization*. Each of these represents a different vision of what constitutes a good citizen in the context of the smart city.

A strategy of *control* is associated with an authoritarian form of governance deploying, for example, surveillance technology to identify and contain anti-social behaviour. *Politicization* on the other hand is a governance strategy that encourages dissidence, debate and dialogue and works to disrupt the existing norms and rules of citizenship through a politics of agonism. As a political theory, agonism favours an approach to democracy that sees ongoing dissensus and contestation of power as intrinsic to its nature (Mouffe 2000). While a strategy of *responsibilization* offers a greater level of participation by offering citizens the tools to mobilize and take responsibility for their own selves or communities, it can also represent a rolling-back of government and the enlisting of citizens in the service of policing existing norms or rules.

The notion of the smart citizen claiming new rights to the city is closest to Iveson's strategy of *politicization*. The smart citizen resists being seen as part of the city government's optimization problem, being measured and managed through behaviour change programs, and is actively engaged through a form of participatory, self-organizing governance. The combination of technologies and techniques deployed for *politicization* work to interrupt everyday routines and the fabric of the urban environment. This notion is sympathetic to de Certeau's conception of the 'multitude of tactics' employed by citizens to re-appropriate space and form a 'network of anti-discipline' that works counter to the city's technocratic structures (de Certeau 1984).

While examples abound of how citizens are creatively expressing agency and mobilizing to affect change in their cities through the use of ubiquitous computing and open data (Foth et al. 2011; Foth 2009; Hemment and Townsend 2013), these efforts can appear dwarfed by the scale of the technocratic smart city agenda. Greenfield sees this as an urgent challenge for intellectual production and asks:

> How might we leverage the potential of the data-gathering, analysis and visualisation tools to improve a community's sense of the challenges, risks and opportunities facing it, and support it in the aim of autonomous self-governance?
>
> (Greenfield 2013: n.p.)

Sensing Sydney looked to artists to rise to this challenge. Lefebvre saw a revolution emerging from the collective creation of a myriad of *heterotopia*—or liminal social spaces of possibility where citizens can seek meaning—as a counter to the effects of modern urbanization and the dangers of a unifying utopic vision (Harvey 2012). Why and how might artists be well positioned to invent these spaces and create new possibilities for the smart citizen?

Enter the Artist: Creative practices for reclaiming the smart, sustainable city

Within emerging, contemporary art and design practice, there is a tendency towards interdisciplinary modes of working,[2] including the mixing of art and design themselves to form 'design-art', as well as various collaborations between art, science and technology that come under the banner of 'sci-art' or 'art-science'. Combining these trends with others, such as a move away from representational modes of traditional art practice towards collaborative, participatory and site-specific modes of production that generate a relational aesthetics, a distinctive ontology of art emerges (Kester 2011; Bourriaud 2002; Kwon 2002; Bishop 2012). When it comes to an art that engages with sustainability as a focus for action, this convergence of practices offers a timely opportunity for the production of new knowledge in relation to solving society's most wicked problems (Born and Barry 2010).

Not all artists see themselves as problem-solvers. Viewing artistic practice through an instrumental lens, where art is valued not just for its cultural output, but also for a stated social benefit, has been the subject of controversy for decades if not centuries. The implicit compromises involved in engaging with forms of cultural resistance outside the cultural sphere are seen by some as threats to art's self-image as a removed commentator on society (Bishop 2012; Jelinek 2013; Bourriaud 2002). Yet many eco-artists actively seek this engagement with society, and in doing so start to blur the disciplinary boundaries with collaborators in design, science and even urban planning, challenging what is art and what is 'not-art' (Jelinek 2013). Weintraub (2012) suggests that this artistic movement, if not recognized as art, might constitute a 'mass defection from the world of art'. Alternatively, it might represent the new avant-garde.

To address this question, we turn to consider emerging agenda-led, interdisciplinary practices in contemporary art and design. Projects like Natalie Jeremijenko's *Amphibious Architecture* and Andrea Polli's *Particle Falls* provide examples of this distinct ontology of art. Seeking to make a contribution to urban environmental concerns such as water ecology and air pollution, respectively, they draw on expertise in science, engineering, social media and ubiquitous computing to create what can be described as both works of design and works of art. Importantly, in terms of informing *Sensing Sydney* and the challenge of shaping the smart city or smart citizen, these projects deploy sensor networks, open data and ubiquitous computing as a powerful means for affecting public engagement through a social interface with invisible natural phenomena.

Amphibious Architecture consists of an array of buoys fitted with water quality sensors, LED lights and a fish sensor, providing a floating interface with river ecology through changing colour, movement and the broadcast of information to mobile phones (through an invitation to text a fish). Similarly *Particle Falls* deploys an air quality sensor, a napthalometer capable of detecting local particulate matter pollution, to drive a spectacular laser light display in the centre of San Jose that transforms a building façade into a dynamic indicator of environmental health risk (this information can also be picked up on a mobile phone app).

Beyond offering innovative and situated eco-visualizations[3] to the public, these projects are involved in a political process. *Particle Falls* grew out of efforts to influence the US EPA to make air quality and environmental health data more public and available as streaming data in real time. This means readings are updated and broadcast every second (interview with the artist 2011). By collaborating with Air Now, a project of the EPA to standardize and open to the public all the US-based air quality information, Polli was able to offer the data to the AirNOW data aggregator and contribute to efforts to generate a standard format or API for releasing additional air quality data. In her contextualization of *Particle Falls*, Polli also raises the opportunity for the work to inform city residents' attitudes towards a planned public works project, such as the light-rail system that would dramatically cut air pollution in downtown San Jose.

With *Amphibious Architecture* the interplay between data sets on water quality and fish presence positions the audience to make connections and hypothesis about the river's health. The audience participates in the interpretation of the installation as an interface to the river, a process that has the potential to expand their political agency. The logic is that audiences will respond to their newly befriended urban cohabitants by advocating for better aquatic living conditions. According to Benjamin and Yang (2011), participants did indeed engage with the work onsite, sending an average of three text messages per person.

From a design perspective both artworks can be perceived as works of strategic design, after Dan Hill's *Dark Matter and Trojan Horses: A Strategic Design Vocabulary* (2012). Viewed through this lens the artist becomes a strategic designer using 'matter' (an artwork) as a vehicle to re-shape cultures of public decision-making at institutional and individual levels, or what Hill refers to as 'meta' (the context). Brain and Newcombe (2015) map Hill's strategic design vocabulary to an agenda-led public art practice, noting how artworks, such as *Amphibious Architecture*, operate like a Trojan horse housing the seeds of multiple strategic outcomes in the innocuous guise of entertainment. The artwork reaches beyond its cultural value to shape the world; it contains 'hidden agendas', strategically couched in an artistic endeavour that by its nature offers alternative ways of seeing and perceiving.

From a conceptual art perspective, the two examples fall into the category of relational aesthetics, where the emphasis is not on the fabrication of an object, but rather on the fabrication of new relationships, such as the creation of communities, encounters and collaborations (Bourriaud 2002; Kester 2011). The relationships, as created in *Particle Falls* and *Amphibious Architecture,* are not limited to the social realm. They connect human and non-human entities through the networking power of smart city systems. They do this in a way that seeks to both question and engage existing power bases, taking aim at both government agencies charged with environmental management and individual citizens with the power to contribute collectively to environmental improvements.

A collaborative process with science, engineering and technology is essential for maintaining the integrity of such works, including any claims they make for shifting the status quo—in this case in relation to environmental sustainability. In the tradition of art-science collaborations, both artworks can be conceived as public experiments, after Born and Barry (2010). They go beyond providing information or understanding of science to an abstract public; they invite the public to participate in knowledge production. In doing so, they augment the resources of science and forge relations between new knowledge. This set of practices shares a common feature with conceptual art through its commitment to an entirely distinctive ontology of art, which, in itself, is concerned with conducting political and social experiments.

The Making of Building Run: Process, participation and outcomes

A major outcome of *Sensing Sydney* was to see a public art concept centred around engaging the public on an environmental challenge through a novel use or representation of data. To make this possible a partnership was forged with the City of Sydney's pre-eminent public art festival, Art&About Sydney. The festival allocated funds and space in their program for the *Sensing Sydney* commission, which was advertised widely and open to Australian and international artists to apply. Selected by a panel, the commission was awarded to artist Keith Deverell for his concept, *Building Run,* which through the medium of video art proposed to stage a daily race between different buildings based on their energy consumption data. To return to the strategic design vocabulary, the 'matter' (the designed object consisting of the Building Run installation) sought to influence the 'meta' context, in this case the complex set of decisions across a range of actors that determines the energy consumption of a building.

The theme for Art&About in 2013 was 'art in unusual spaces', which aligned well with the final decision to stage the work in the foyer of a corporate office tower at Deutsche Bank Place in Sydney's central business district. Positioning the work there, within one of the buildings participating in *Building Run*'s race, was also a strategic decision to augment opportunities for feedback between office workers, implicated in the energy performance of buildings, and the installation. Vande Moere and Hill (2012) attest that situating data visualization efforts within the environment to which they respond, rather than presenting them remotely on the Internet, can 'facilitate bringing about a new understanding of complex local issues'.

In its final guise, *Building Run* presented as an installation of five video screens housed within a structure incorporating a stage, a racetrack and a series of hurdles (see Figures 1 and 2), framing the artwork as an ongoing sporting event. A different runner appears on each of the five screens representing a different building in the race.[4] Four of the buildings are corporate towers and one is a public building operated by the City Council. All five are distinguished by previous efforts to improve their energy efficiency through a variety of investments in equipment and management. Data transmitted from the building management systems (BMS) every 15 minutes provides information on each building's energy consumption and directly determines the level of exertion of the corresponding runner on-screen.

Immersing oneself in the installation, it becomes possible to read the artwork at various levels. At a broad level, the energy-pulse of the city is legible as one witnesses the arc of the runners' speed throughout the day—slow at the start, furious in the middle and slow towards the end, mirroring the movement of people and the intensity of their work habits. More specifically, the artwork is designed to allow the tracking of the daily performance of

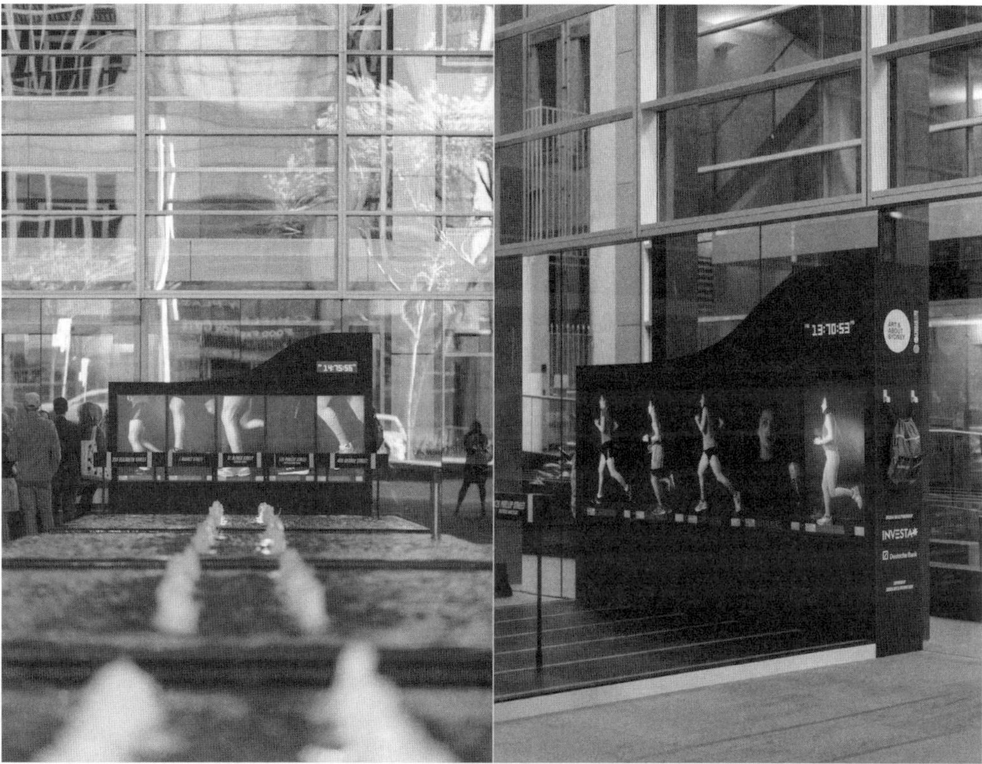

Figures 1 and 2: *Building Run* in situ. Images: Josh Hill Photography, 2013.

individual runners relative to each other and to their own personal best (PB) performance, inviting building tenants to identify and interact with the work, ideally feeding a curiosity about why different buildings do better on different days.

The artist's strategies, together with the interwoven efforts of the project partners to facilitate, promote and guide desired interactions with *Building Run*, are explored next. This includes how the artist worked collaboratively to design an interface with the public, the challenges of balancing cultural production with a range of agendas from the corporate to the civic minded and the outcomes as experienced by the range of participants and audiences. Data to inform this discussion was gathered through a series of ten in-depth interviews with project partners and a short survey with the general public.

Collaboration: A resilient ecology of stakeholders

Through pre-existing partnerships and relationships, Carbon Arts and City of Sydney were able to bring additional partners to the project in order to realize its full potential. These partners—Investa Office, Deutsche Bank and Buildings Alive—shared to a large extent the vision for the project and contributed significant additional resources to enable its execution at the appropriate scale. In-kind contributions, including the provision of expertise regarding sustainable buildings, the hosting of the artwork, brokering of relationships with participating buildings, building tenant engagement and energy data analysis, were as important as the financial contributions made.

Interviews with the project partners revealed that there was a general perception by all partners that they were investing in an experiment; that art was going to provide something unique and different that was worth exploring. That said, it is clear from these conversations that each organization had different motivations and expectations about what the project might reveal or advance for their own organization. These prospects range from the artwork's ability to market the brand or services of a business in an innovative way to its potential to engage staff or tenants in improving the energy efficiency of their operations. Table 1 maps these expectations and their contributing roles.

Table 1: Partner expectations and roles

Partner (about)	Aims/Expectations	Role*
City of Sydney (the local government authority for central Sydney and surrounds)	Getting the public on board with the City's sustainable 2030 vision, delivering engaging public art	Co-project management and design with Carbon Arts; PR and media engagement; brokering of relationships
Investa Office (one of Australia's largest listed owners and managers of office real estate, a branch of Investa Property)	Showcasing a portfolio of high performing green buildings managed by Investa Reaching out to tenants to undertake further energy efficiency measures Promoting Investa's sustainability services offering and strengths	Providing four of the five buildings to participate; brokering the relationship with Deutsche Bank to host the work; running associated educational and engagement programs/events within the buildings; assisting with design of the project; contributing to promotional efforts
Deutsche Bank (a leading, global financial services provider)	Demonstrating the power of contemporary art and environmental leadership, two priorities of the business	Hosting the work in their building foyer; engaging their staff; contributing to promotional efforts
Buildings Alive (provides technical information and analysis to help optimize the performance of buildings)	Showcasing sophisticated real-time data feedback systems and marketing the business offering of Buildings Alive	Providing the data and the back-end capability of the artwork; supporting the artist to design the interface and communication

*City of Sydney, Deutsche Bank and Investa Office all provided significant funds to realize the project, in addition to an in-kind provision of services.

Ideally for the success of projects like *Building Run,* which require a diverse set of skills and partnerships, a symbiotic relationship emerges between participants and the project, whereby each sees a benefit for their contribution. As long as these expected returns on investment are not conflicting, a 'resilient ecology of stakeholders' emerges, which is capable of maintaining the project through a mutually beneficial exchange.

Managing and understanding partner expectations and demonstrating achievement of these becomes a challenge for the creative producer, Carbon Arts, in seeking to deliver successful, complex projects. This job is made difficult by the inherent intangibility of some benefits accrued as well as the sometimes conflicting nature of expectations. For example, in the design process for *Building Run* concerns by the partners about the public image of the buildings and the related organizations meant that the celebration of a winner was avoided in favour of presenting each runner as racing against their own personal best. This typifies the type of constraint placed on artistic freedom that can result from partnerships where marketing and promotion is an associated aim.

Balancing Art and Design, Information and Affect

Building Run is the product of both art and design, bringing together as the commission required, a political agenda with a cultural outcome. Deverell, an artist, designer and programmer, worked closely with a team of technical experts from data partner, Buildings Alive, to interpret, receive and program the data in order to create a video-art interface. Other partners, such as Investa Office and City of Sydney, provided access to building managers, building statistics and energy efficiency expertise to inform more broadly the development of the runners as characters and the connection between data and energy efficiency improvements. Deverell's challenge was to translate this dense body of data and knowledge into an elegant platform for engaging the public. To do this he employed a range of artistic and design strategies.

Weintraub (2012) identifies and defines a range of strategies used by eco-artists in their work; these include procedures to visualize, metaphorize, dramatize, celebrate, perturb, activate and investigate. With *Building Run,* Deverell employs a number of these. At its heart the artwork is a visualization of energy use that works to celebrate the achievements of those working to improve the performance of buildings. By humanizing buildings—giving them familiar gestures, movements and expressions—Deverell translates an otherwise alien, intangible world into one that we can experience through a physical, bodily connection. Using the metaphor of sport he exploits our hunger for spectacle and love of competition by reframing the conversation about energy efficiency and sustainability in the language of athletics.

Video art itself offers its own aesthetic language, which Deverell exploits to blur the boundaries between reality and fiction, the literal and the poetic. As a strategy, this ambiguity encourages the viewer to ask questions and to appreciate the experience of the work at multiple levels. *Building Run* also works to activate for the 'purpose of energising the audience to take an action or motivating people to reform behaviours' (Weintraub 2012). Finally, humour and satire sit just beneath the surface, as *Building Run* gently pokes fun at Sydney's obsession with running and the body beautiful, as well as the notion of the rat race.

Together these strategies offer an alternative narrative and pathway towards engaging with the subject material of sustainability, again akin to a strategic design process of using 'matter' to shape 'meta'. A news story that ran on ABC TV about the artwork, titled 'Power Run', provided a rare opportunity to address a broad audience with a positive and uniquely framed message on energy efficiency. However, for the building tenants and the general public encountering the artwork, these artistic strategies do the work of affecting and engaging people in order that they might connect directly to the informational content of the work.

The relationship between engagement, affect and information is explored in Fritsch and Brynskov (2011) in relation to the design of urban interfaces intended to stir debate and reflection. They find the level of audience engagement is dictated partly by the amount of information provided and the means by which it is delivered; too much information and people do not engage, too little and the engagement is meaningless. They propose a scale of interactivity (see Figure 3), ranging from least to most, against which the level of information can be adjusted accordingly. The more static an interface, the less information can be transmitted, but as the interface or artwork becomes more dynamic, interactive or participatory the greater the chances of informing the audience and shaping the 'meta' context.

The design challenge for *Building Run* was therefore how to transmit the information about the energy performance of participating buildings in ways that reflected the artwork's position on the scale of interactivity. For the installation itself, a series of design interventions were pursued to augment the video art. These included the introduction of hurdles to indicate which screen represented which building, the provision of dynamic graphic icons at the bottom of each screen displaying each runners' statistics of progress (see Figure 1), and a clock at the top of the installation. Beyond the artwork a number of additional engagement strategies were deployed by project partners, such as hosting artist talks and networking events around the artwork, sending out educational emails to building staff and providing information and updates on screens throughout all the participating buildings.

For most experiencing *Building Run*, the artwork was dynamic, but not interactive. Because the energy data used to drive the installation was only for base building,[5] rather than tenancy specific energy use, there was no opportunity for office workers to influence the outcomes of the race. However, for a small subset of people—the building managers— the artwork was interactive and participatory. Their actions directly determined whether or

---

static → dynamic → reactive → interactive → participatory → communicative

---

Figure 3: Scale of interactivity (from Fritsch and Brynskov 2011).

not their building would achieve a personal best from one day to the next and ostensibly win the race. As the evaluation shows, this already informed group of participants embraced *Building Run* like a game and spent far more time than most interacting with it.

Evaluation: Outcomes and limitations

There were four distinct groups participating in *Building Run*: (1) the general public; (2) tenants of the buildings participating in the race; (3) the building managers for those buildings; and (4) those partners involved directly in making the project. All were interviewed to inform an evaluation of the project, namely how was it received and how did outcomes measure up to expectations.

Building tenants/general public

A small, intercept survey conducted in the foyer revealed a mixed view of the artwork by office workers. For some, attraction to the artwork was a matter of taste. For many, presence of the artwork did not challenge them to change their patterns of behaviour in the foyer and move beyond, for example buying a coffee, to spending time with the artwork in order to find out what it was about.

On the other hand, observations collected by the concierge, revealed a strong curiosity about the work by tenants in the first couple of weeks of its showing. Over ten people a day asked the concierge about the work, what it meant, how it worked and who was winning. The overwhelming response was 'interesting'. There was a desire expressed by many to understand the mechanics behind the work (a glimpse into the functioning of the smart city) and receive updates on performance in the race.

Investa Office reported that presentations about the artwork in the office activated a subset of employees who identified with art and/or sustainability. These staff brought enthusiasm to the project expressing pride that the company was putting on display these shared values. In this way, projects like *Building Run* can be important contributors to employee satisfaction and employee retention.

Building managers

All of the buildings competing in *Building Run*, with one exception, achieved significant levels of improvement in energy efficiency over the period of the work's showing. Calculated as a percentage improvement over the predicted performance of each building, based on historical records and prevailing conditions such as weather, the results paint a picture of continual improvement. Gains in energy efficiency ranged from less than one per cent

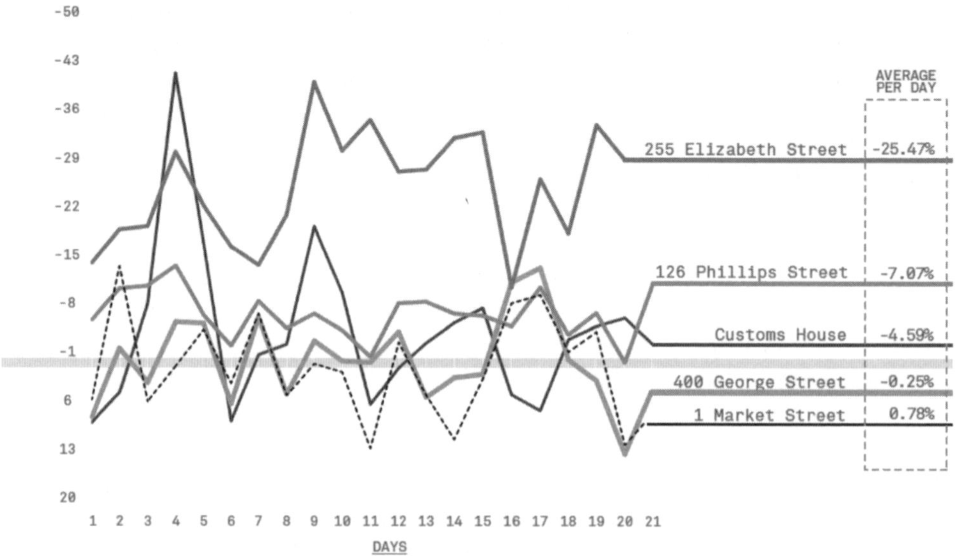

Graph 1: Percentage (%) Energy Savings over and above Personal Best & average saving per day.

improvement over the period (calculated as an average improvement per day) to over a 25 per cent improvement (see Graph 1).

The building managers, who were effectively those pulling the levers behind the artwork and affecting the performance of the runners, reported feeling the spotlight. That the competition was not an overt one between the buildings meant for the most part that this increased attention on the role of building managers was felt as a positive one. Bringing a mostly hidden, and potentially underappreciated, role to the fore gave greater emphasis to the hard work that goes into making tenants comfortable and buildings efficient in their use of energy.

Partners

As an artwork, *Building Run* satisfied the demands of the City of Sydney Arts & Culture branch for its public art program, as well as those of Deutsche Bank, a major global collector of contemporary art, awarding it two very different and significant ticks of approval from a critical art perspective.

As a vehicle for incentivizing other buildings to get on board with energy efficiency, data sharing and management, stakeholders involved in *Building Run* have noted some success. The City of Sydney, in particular, found that the artwork offered opportunities to have meaningful conversations with partners in the sector, which allowed them to make progress in addressing energy efficiency challenges collaboratively. All of these efforts assist in moving us closer to energy efficiency gains.

The act of bringing the artwork to the building involved coordination between different sides of Investa Office's business, as well as between tenants in the building. These often-new connections served to cement relationships that are instrumental to driving a sustainability agenda, which by its nature requires collaboration. For example, the launch party was the first time many of the tenants of Deutsche Bank Place had met, an important first step towards Investa and City of Sydney's vision for creating vertical communities in office towers that will affect positive change.

Building Run led to improved relationships between businesses or between a business and its staff, or led to the development of new relationships. For a business like Investa Office, where leasing contracts are financially significant and core to business, any effort that will increase the likelihood of a tenant's contract renewal is a worthy investment. Deutsche Bank's partnership with *Building Run,* and praise for its outcomes, point to an ongoing commitment to its tenancy, and to the sustainability benefits offered by Investa Office's building management.

The ability of Buildings Alive to secure new clients based on the demonstration of its systems through *Building Run* remains to be seen. However, the artwork, even after its decommissioning, offers an ongoing opportunity to market the achievements of the partners in bringing it about. Investa and Deutsche Bank's joint promotional video on *Building Run*, developed post-exhibition, is testament to the power of the arts to bring a new angle to existing businesses and relationships.

Conclusions: Art of the smart eco-citizen

Building Run broke new ground artistically in Australia, and arguably at a global level, with its innovative use of energy data to drive a near-real-time system based on energy performance. Merging the domains of video art and data visualization through his poetic use of visual language, hyper-real video footage and manipulation of speed, Deverell achieved a number of firsts. The ambitious nature of the project, particularly given the time and system constraints, put all partners to the test, but eventually paid off, reaping dividends, both tangible and intangible, in exchange for the risks taken.

Building Run stands as an example of a new ontology of art described at the outset of this chapter as an art practice that, like the eco-art movement, is concerned with shaping the world. It is interdisciplinary and collaborative by nature, combining the skills and strategies of art, design and science, and importantly, one that works with the tools of the smart city— ubiquitous computing, open data and sensor systems—to create unique urban interfaces between social and natural systems.

This chapter has argued that the significance of this mode of art production is its ability to contribute towards a more democratic and participatory engagement of citizens in the making of the smart city, in particular in harnessing technology to facilitate collective management of environmental resources. A set of strategies used by contemporary artists and designers can combine to offer spaces of innovation and contestation, where the work of governance is shared and aired.

If this is the promise of the 'art of the smart eco-city', then it is clear that *Building Run* is only part way towards achieving that vision. The limitations discussed above offer some insight into how this pilot project might be improved in order to move in a more participatory and agonistic direction. Because *Building Run* was only able to employ data from the energy use of the buildings' common areas, the building managers responsible for these areas were the only ones able to influence the outcome of the race. Allowing tenants to be able to influence the system in the same way, by connecting tenancy-specific data to the artwork, would introduce greater participation and opportunities for learning, as the collective energy-saving efforts of individual office workers impact upon the outcomes of the race. Making this data feedback loop possible in real time would also introduce possibilities for dramatization of energy use reductions, driving further engagement.

Access to real-time tenancy data is a significant barrier created by a complex set of technical, regulatory and organizational hurdles that stem from privacy concerns, the incompatibility of different technology platforms within a building and the structure of the energy market. If a project like *Building Run* is going to do the work of strategic design, using an artwork to influence such 'meta' concerns (Hill 2012), it will need the long-term buy-in and commitment of a number of stakeholders, requiring as described earlier a resilient ecology of stakeholders and a committed creative producer or strategic designer driving a process of iteration. Already *Building Run* has been taken up by the City of Melbourne with Investa Office and Buildings Alive in 2015. For this iteration a number of new communication and engagement strategies were introduced, reflecting upon lessons learned in Sydney, such as a more direct engagement of building managers in event-style performances.

As we saw with *Building Run* and with *Particle Falls*, there are opportunities for the *process* of art-making itself to shift cultures of decision-making within project partner organizations. The benefits accrued to the partners, in terms of shifting internal practices, forging new relationships and providing platforms for conversation, can be significant and play out in ways that affect change felt by the general public. We might understand these artworks as 'powerful symbols and motivations for a small, but influential audience consisting of the bureaucrats, the politicians and the city government themselves' (Brain and Newcombe 2015).

Perhaps the larger challenge is reconciling *Building Run*'s politics of engagement. If the smart citizen resists being seen as part of the city government's optimization problem and resists being measured and managed through behaviour change programs, then he or she will also resist being coerced into reducing energy use by a set of government and corporate partners. To encourage truly participatory, self-organizing governance might require letting go of goals altogether, potentially a controversial proposition given what we know about climate change. Letting go of intended outcomes might present a riskier proposition for potential funding and knowledge partners, or it might create a truly innovative platform that reflects well on those supporting it, both in terms of experiments in governance and employee engagement.

How might *Building Run* be redesigned as a more 'politicized' form of engagement, after Iveson (2011); or as a public experiment where citizens are engaged in the production of knowledge through an equal partnership between art and science, after Born and Barry (2010)? Arguably, the case studies presented earlier also have to further move in this direction. Both *Amphibious Architecture* and *Particle Falls* offer dynamic interfaces with environmental quality in the city with some invitations for interaction, but participation, as with *Building Run*, is limited to those people involved in creating the project or the systems that sit behind them. With *Building Run* we discovered that the main participants—the people who have agency to influence the outcomes of the race and address the 'meta' context through their actions—were the building managers. The artwork was a successful interface for this small, but influential group to shape the city.

In *Building Run*, a number of different stakeholders are brought together, with the notion that such partnerships held together by a set of complementary agendas (motivated by both public and private benefits) can create a space for artists to play a productive role in shaping the city. At the centre of this network of relationships is a creative producer, in this case Carbon Arts, steering the artwork towards achieving the project's 'hidden agendas' of awareness raising and action on energy consumption. The success of future iterations of *Building Run*, and similar projects, may depend upon the ability of this creative producer to operate like a strategic designer, working over various iterations of project design and building long-term partnerships to increase art's ability to shape a culture of sustainability.

References

Barry, A., Born, G. and Weszkalnys, G. (2008), 'Logics of Interdisciplinarity', *Economy and Society*, 37: 1, pp. 20–49.

Benjamin, D. and Yang, S. (2001), 'Amphibious Envelopes', in M. Shepard (ed.), *Sentient City: Ubiquitous computing, architecture, and the future of urban space*, New York City and Cambridge: MIT Press, pp. 49-53.

Bishop, C. (2012), *Artificial Hells: Participatory art and the politics of spectatorship*, London and Brooklyn: Verso Books.

Born, G. and Barry, A. (2010), 'ART-SCIENCE', *Journal of Cultural Economy*, 3: 1 (March), pp. 103–119.

Bourriaud, N. (2002), *Relational Aesthetics,* (trans. S. Pleasance and F. Woods), Paris: Les presses du reel. (First published in French 1998.)

Brain, T. and Newcombe, J. (2015), 'Exploring Environmental Stewardship through Data-driven Practices', in F. Marchese (ed.), *Media Art and the Urban Environment—Engendering public engagement with urban ecology*, Switzerland: Springer International Publishing, pp. 47–61.

Carbon Arts (2012a), *City Data Slam: Sensing Sydney Report I*, Report to the City of Sydney, <http://carbonarts.org/wp-content/uploads/2013/05/CITY_DATA_SLAM_REPORT_web_MD.pdf>. Accessed 25 August 2015.

———— (2012b), *Building Run: Sensing Sydney Report II*, Report to the City of Sydney, <http://carbonarts.org/wp-content/uploads/2013/07/BUILDING_RUN_REPORT_web.pdf>. Accessed 25 August 2015.

Certeau, M. de (1984), *The Practice of Everyday Life,* 3rd ed., Berkeley: University of California Press. (First published in French 1980.)

Crang, M. and Graham, S. (2007), 'Sentient cities: Ambient intelligence and the politics of urban space', *Information, Communication & Society*, 10: 6, pp. 789–817.

de Waal, M. (2014), *The City as Interface | How new media are changing the city.* Rotterdam: nai010 Publishers.

DiSalvo, C. (2012), *Adversarial Design*, Cambridge: MIT Press.

Foth, M. (ed.) (2009), *Handbook of Research on Urban Informatics: The practice and promise of the real-time city*, Information Science Reference, Hershey, Pennsylvania: IGI Global.

Foth, M., Forlano, L., Satchell, C. and Gibbs, M. (eds) (2011), *From Social Butterfly to Engaged Citizen: Urban informatics, social media, ubiquitous computing, and mobile technology to support citizen engagement*, Cambridge, Massachussets: MIT Press.

Fritsch, J. and Brynskov, M. (2011), 'Between Experience, Affect, and Information: Experimental urban media in the climate change debate', in M. Foth, L. Forlano, M. Gibbs and C. Satchell (eds), *From Social Butterfly to Engaged Citizen: Urban informatics, social media, ubiquitous computing, and mobile technology to support citizen engagement,* Cambridge: MIT Press, pp. 115–135.

Greenfield, A. (2013), *Against the Smart City (The City Is Here for You to Use)*, New York City: Do Projects.

Harvey, D. (2012), *Rebel Cities: From the right to the city to the urban revolution*, New York: Verso.

Haque, U. (2012), 'What is a City that It would be "Smart"?', *City in a Box*, 34, pp. 140–142, <http://volumeproject.org/blog/2012/12/21/volume34city inabox/>. Accessed 25 August 2015.

Hemment, D. and Townsend, A. (2013), *Smart Citizens.* Manchester: FutureEverything, <http://futureeverything.org/wp-content/ uploads/2014/03/smartcitizens.pdf.>. Accessed 26 August 2015.

Hill, D. (2012), *Dark Matter and Trojan Horses: A strategic design vocabulary*, London and Moscow: Strelka Press, <http://www.strelka.com/en/press/books/dark-matter-and-trojan-horses-a-strategic-design-vocabulary>. Accessed 26 August 2015.

Hollands, R. G. (2008), 'Will the Real Smart City Please Stand Up?', *City* 12: 3, pp. 303–320.

Holmes, T. G. (2007), 'Eco-visualization: Combining art and technology to reduce energy consumption', Proceedings of the *6th ACM SIGCHI Conference on Creativity and Cognition,* ACM, New York, NY, USA, pp. 153–162.

Iveson, K. (2011), 'Mobile Media and the Strategies of Urban Citizenship: Control, responsibilization, politicization', in M. Foth, L. Forlano, M. Gibbs and C. Satchell (eds), *From Social Butterfly to Engaged Citizen: Urban informatics, social media, ubiquitous computing, and mobile technology to support citizen engagement,* Cambridge: MIT Press, pp. 55–70.

Jelinek, A. (2013), *This Is Not Art: Activism and other 'not-art'*, New York: I.B. Tauris.

Kester, G. H. (2011), *The One and the Many: Contemporary collaborative art in a global context*, Durham: Duke University Press.

Kwon, M. (2002), *One Place after Another: Site-specific art and locational identity*, Cambridge: MIT Press.

Mouffe, C. (2000), 'Deliberative Democracy of Agonistic Pluralism?', *Social Research*, 66: 3, pp. 745–758.

Townsend, A. M. (2013), *Smart Cities: Big data, civic hackers, and the quest for a new Utopia*, New York and London: W.W. Norton & Company.

Vande Moere, A. and Hill, D. (2012), 'Designing for the Situated and Public of Urban Data', *Journal of Urban Technology*, 19: 2, pp. 25–46.

Weintraub, L. (2012), *To Life! Eco Art in Pursuit of a Sustainable Planet*, Berkeley: University of California Press.

Notes

1 Greenfield (2013) offers a detailed account of the marketing strategies of IT companies in regard to smart cities.

2 Interdisciplinary is taken here after Barry et al. (2008) as a generic term that covers the spectrum from multidisciplinary to transdisciplinary practices.

3 Defined by Holmes (2007) as 'a set of novel approaches to display the real-time consumption statistics of key environmental resources for the goal of promoting ecological literacy'.

4 The runner is actually the same actress filmed in different running attire, which was carefully selected to represent the character or 'personality' of each of the buildings (see Carbon Arts 2012b for details on how the character assessments were drawn from building statistics).

5 This includes electricity consumption for HVAC, lift operation, common area lighting and other common area uses of electricity, such as electronic screens and a water feature.

Section II

Contested City

Chapter 4

Travels and Tapestries: Possibilities for creative exchange in Melbourne and Phnom Penh

Clare McCracken and Roger Nelson

Travels Close to Home

November 2013, Melbourne: Clare McCracken as Beth McGarey

On an overcast day in late-Spring 2013, artist Clare McCracken walks, slowly, around the forecourt of Federation Square, Melbourne.[1] She carries an oddly decorated walking cane, seemingly without need to lean on it for support. Federation Square is one of central Melbourne's most popular landmarks, known for its distinctive, deconstructionist architecture of fractal forms, and organic shades and textures, its mixed-use public and semi-public spaces, and broadly appealing cultural programming. McCracken is wearing a tortoise shell on her back, sculpted elaborately from papier maché and painted in glossy acrylic; also a primly buttoned silk shirt and quilted satin slippers, both of regal maroon hue; and a tidy cravat sporting a functioning compass-brooch at its heart. She squints intently at her surroundings, through large eyeglasses; her hair held back in a tight bun. The artist-as-tortoise is performing the fictional character of Beth McGarey: a diehard fan of Charles Baudelaire, Walter Benjamin and the *flâneur* (stroller). This woman—McGarey, that is, but perhaps also McCracken—is unabashedly entranced by tales of nineteenth-century dandies and their slow perambulations up and down French boulevards and arcades, accompanied by pet tortoises on leashes to set the pace. In this performance, as the fictional McGarey, the artist McCracken describes herself as 'a woman who has transformed herself—part dandy, part tortoise—to become a contemporary "botanist" of Melbourne's sidewalks' (see Figure 1).

November 2014, Phnom Penh: Sok Chanrado's *Sound Wave*

As the afternoon sunlight begins to soften and the tide of traffic thickens, Phnom Penh-based artist and film-maker, Sok Chanrado embarks on a journey through the city-centre's main roads, many of them wide and straight boulevards planned under French colonial rule.[2] Sok is travelling on a simple, steel-framed bicycle adorned with a large metal megaphone-style loudspeaker, around half-a-metre in diameter. The speaker is of a kind commonly used at weddings, ceremonies and other public gatherings, and the technology is recognizably familiar to most people in the city. Every few hundred metres, Sok pulls over to the side of the road asking strangers he happens to meet to tell him their thoughts on the issues of the day. Mostly motorcycle taxi drivers, street food-hawkers and other lower-income workers, these men and women voice their concerns and opinions into a small audio-recording device. As

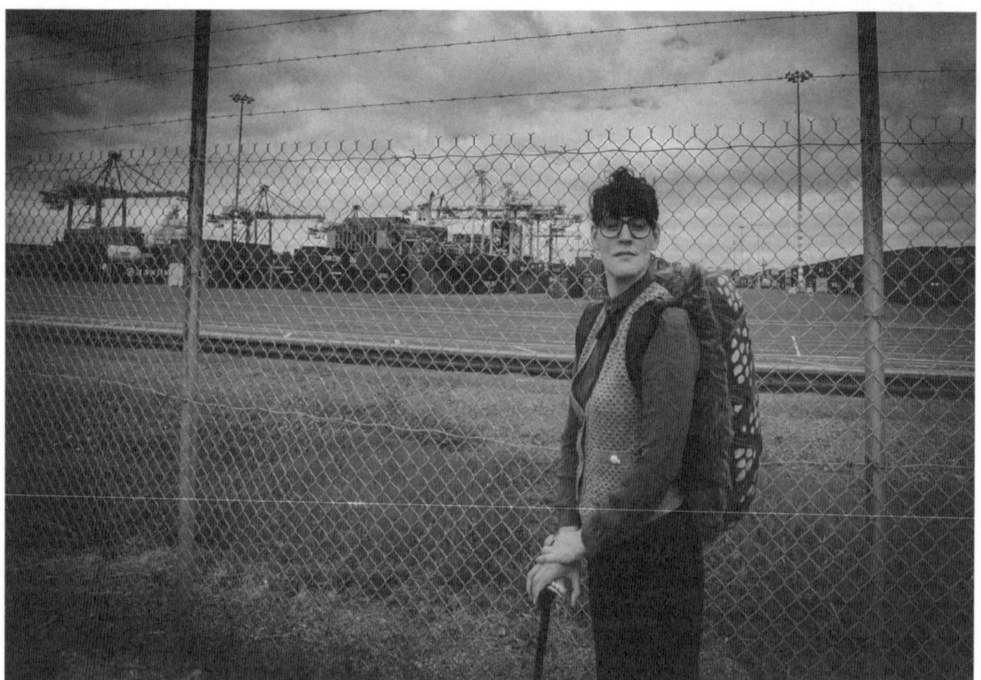

Figure 1: Clare McCracken performing as Beth McGarey, Melbourne Ports, Melbourne, 2013. Image: Andrew Ferris.

part of the invitation, Sok demonstrates how the technology works; some people refuse, but most are keen to participate.[3] After having their say, Sok rides off and, with the participants' verbal permission, broadcasts these recordings through his loudspeaker, clearly audible to the massing crowds of cyclists and motorcyclists around him in the dense peak-hour traffic. The artist describes this performance (and its single-channel video documentation) as 'a way of thinking about the media, and the hot news that ordinary people really want to share' (personal communication)[4] (see Figure 2). Titled *Sound Wave,* the work emerges from the artist's six-week residency at Sa Sa Art Projects, an experimental space located in Phnom Penh's 'White Building'. This is an iconic neighbourhood of artists and mostly lower-income Cambodians, renowned for its distinctively dilapidated, tropical, modernist architecture, and its diverse and closely knit community of residents. The White Building is also Sok's home.

Introducing Possibilities

This chapter centres on the notion of exchange within artists' practices, and on a series of creative exchanges between Clare McCracken and the creative community in Phnom Penh's White Building neighbourhood. This includes artist and educator Khvay Samnang and Sok Chanrado, both based in Phnom Penh. The White Building community first

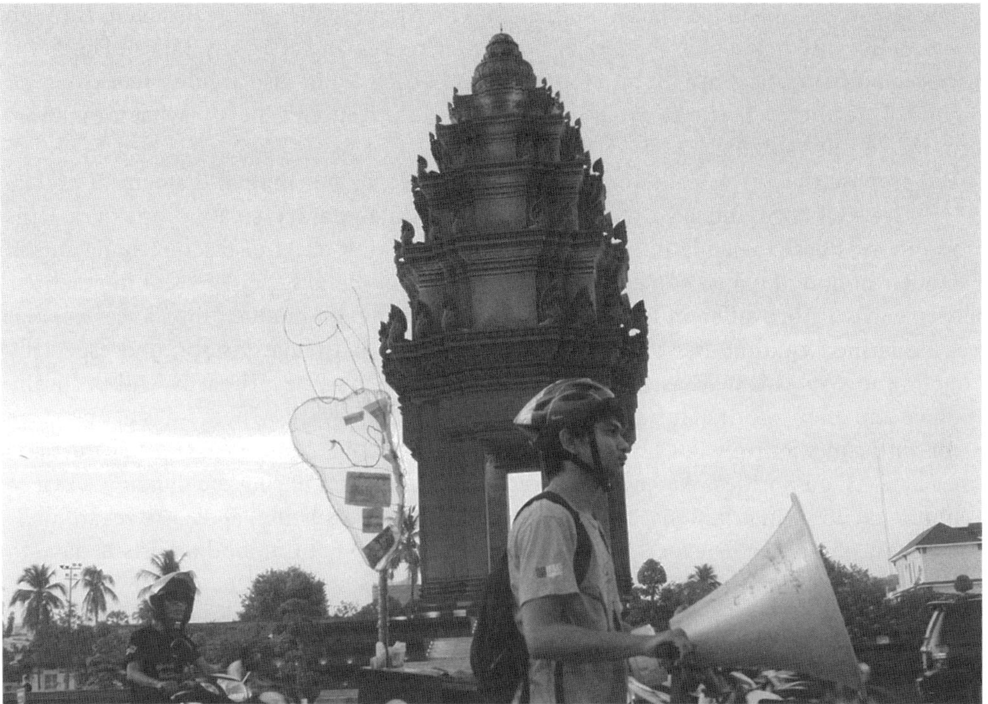

Figure 2: Sok Chanrado performing *Sound Wave,* Phnom Penh, 2013. Image: Blu Simon Wasem.

met McCracken in 2012, when she was visiting her colleague and friend Roger Nelson, a curator and researcher based in Phnom Penh. McCracken was welcomed in a series of informal gatherings, and also in the more structured setting of an artist's talk hosted by Sa Sa Art Projects. After McCracken's return to Melbourne, their conversations continued in various online formats, as well as through Nelson's mediation. In 2014, McCracken returned to Phnom Penh for a month-long residency at Sa Sa Art Projects, during which time her research-based practice focused on the White Building and its surrounding community. The experience transformed her practice in ways that continued after her return to Melbourne, and in various projects undertaken in other locations including Shanghai and Reutlingen. Her residency also had effects on the artists in and around the White Building, which Nelson continued to observe in her absence. This was a complex and multidirectional exchange, taking numerous forms, and based in an ethic of mutual respect and openness.

In a critically engaged reflection on a number of recent projects by McCracken, as well as shorter introductions to works by Khvay and Sok, this chapter takes as its particular focus works that explore the experiences, needs, desires and ideas of less-visible sectors and communities. For artists in Phnom Penh, such sectors have included predominantly those with lower incomes and those comprising creative communities. For McCracken, these less visible sectors have included mainly women, the elderly, migrants and the disabled. Through an evaluative discussion of exchanges between McCracken and artists in Phnom Penh, this discussion offers critical insight into the practices of each, while also arguing reflexively for a mode of creative exchange based in mutual dialogue and attentiveness to what the authors term the 'locality-specific'.

We propose that an orientation to the locality-specific and mutual dialogue is crucial to creative exchange and also to the analysis of contemporary creative practices. This proposition is based equally in a mistrust of the flattening effect of discourses reliant on a singular notion of global contemporaneity, and in first-hand experiences of interactions between artists from different locations that are decidedly *not* mutual. Imbalances of what may be termed cultural as well as financial capital are particularly stark, and especially troubling in contexts such as Cambodia, where artists operate primarily within locally initiated and often informal infrastructures of horizontal networks. These ways of operating occur with comparatively low levels of funding, and without support from government or other national authorities. We have observed such imbalances during the dynamic of visits to Phnom Penh by international artists, who (implicitly or explicitly) appear to regard their role as that of teacher or expert, without recognition of what Cambodian artists have to offer to visitors and others in return. Also, observed are similar dynamics in numerous and typically very short-term visits by international curators, especially those conducting research for biennales or other large-scale and well-funded museum exhibitions. This chapter posits a counterpoint to this mode of interaction that we regard as being, often, not only unethical, but also uninteresting, and frequently unsuited to meaningful creative exchange in the fullest sense of the term.

We write in cognizance not only of the prevailing imbalance of power in artistic interactions in this context, but also awareness of the political exchange of unknown numbers of refugees seeking asylum in Australia, coerced instead into settling in Cambodia. In return, the Cambodian government has accepted a donation from the Australian government of tens of millions of dollars, widely understood by many Cambodians to be a thinly veiled form of bribe. In addition to being widely covered in the media in both countries, as well as internationally, the manoeuvring of the two governments has been criticized strongly by the United Nations High Commission for Refugees, who finds the conditions that the Australian government provides for refugees to be 'harmful' and the Cambodian agreement to be 'a worrying departure from international norms' (UNHCR 2014). Our response comes not only from reasoned concern, but also a visceral feeling of disgust. As Australian citizens we see the international government action as a dirty deal. Notwithstanding, we recognize that Melbourne and Phnom Penh are both cities that have been shaped by historical movements of people and extensive interactions between many nationalities and creeds. This includes many people whose relocation was motivated not only by desire, but also by need, and often by dire necessity.

As non-Indigenous Australians engaged in this research, we are both keenly aware of our own status in Australia as descendants of uninvited aliens. Nelson writes also as a migrant himself in Cambodia, and as the grandson of a refugee. Faced with a seemingly insurmountable collusion of government action on refugees by Australian and Cambodian government, both widely perceived to be morally and politically corrupt at the time of writing, we strive for a different ethic of practice. Our dedication is to participate in modes of creative exchange based in an ethic of fairness and mutual respect. Such efforts from the micro levels of practice may lack power to effect significant change in the face of macro levels of international governance. However, as artists we proceed in a spirit of hope for the world-making (albeit and regrettably, not world-changing) potentialities of smaller-scale communities united in collaborative creative activity.

This chapter takes its title from two recurrent motifs shared in the practices of the artists discussed here. Firstly, *travels*—at a deliberately slow pace, with poetically resonant 'props', and around carefully chosen and hermeneutically charged localities—are an important mode of research and practice in a number of performances and other projects by Khvay, Sok and McCracken, and other artists and students gathered around Sa Sa Art Projects and the White Building community of artists. And secondly, the sewing of *tapestries* is a recreational pastime for lower-income women working in this neighbourhood and throughout Phnom Penh. This pastime rose sharply in popularity between McCracken's two visits in 2012 and 2014. The noticeable and rapid rise of this creative activity as a popular form of entertainment is revealing of larger social and economic shifts. Such shifts are usually rendered in anonymous statistics, yet here they are visualized in a personal and relatable form. Put simply, shopkeepers could not afford the expense of purchasing embroidery materials until they reached a certain level of economic security. Tapestries formed the basis of a new project for McCracken, in which she too takes up stitching as a meaningful pastime.

Co-authored by researchers who are also practitioners—and who write from both perspectives, not only unavoidably but also with critical intent—the discussion is interspersed here with selected excerpts from a dialogue between the co-authors. This process is intended to foreground the primacy of collaborative, creative practice in our research methodologies. This innovative and experimental format reflects the chapter's discursive and interdisciplinary approach. McCracken's personal reflections on her own practice, as well as Nelson's presentation of observations from four years of participant-observation and archival research with artists in Cambodia, allows the artists' first-person voices to be foregrounded, in dialogue with the critical literature in which McCracken's work is contextualized. Sok's and Khvay's works are discussed through a focus on first-hand observations of performances, and detailed analyses of video documentation. The decision to privilege this mode of analysis is informed in part by Nora A. Taylor's endorsement of ethnography as a vital tool in Southeast Asian contemporary art histories (Taylor 2011). Moreover, Nelson has published elsewhere an essay that offers a reading of contemporary Cambodian performance practices in light of regional and international critical and scholarly discourses (Nelson 2014). The authors are mindful that whereas McCracken is able to speak for herself in this chapter, in this format Sok and Khvay are not. All of these factors motivate our decision to frame McCracken's work in light of a critical literature, allowing Sok and Khvay's work to be introduced to readers in a context rooted in the works' locality.

The authors propose the concept of locality-specific practice both as a descriptor of existing work by artists, Khvay, Sok, McCracken and others, and as an argument for reflexive and culturally mindful modes of practice. Thus, the following discussion can be understood both as an examination of artistic contestations of urban space, and as engaged interventions in the discursive space around such practices. This approach is posited in light of the complex, contested, historical and contemporary relationship between Cambodia and Australia.

A Dialogue Between Us: 'Locality-specific'

NELSON: *I remember when you first came here. Sa Sa Art Projects invited you to give an artist's talk, and I impressed on you what a rare honour this was: few visitors are considered worthy of the community's endorsement and attention in this way; few are considered relevant. This is not because the community is ungenerous or not open—far from it, as you know—but because the White Building is such a site of exoticizing objectification, of uninvited guests who pay no respect to the people living and working there, that there is a sense of fatigue with foreign artists, a wariness and need to ensure their intentions are fair and their motives are mutual. The community is very attentive to its own needs as a locality.*

You decided to talk about those parts of your practice that are named as 'public art' in Australian contexts. Already by then—this was 2012—the distinction between work made for and installed in public spaces and work made in a studio, perhaps to be exhibited in a gallery, was a distinction that felt artificial for you: too dichotomous, maybe. Revealing more of the attitudes of institutions and funding bodies than of the nature of your practice itself. Am I describing this right?

MCCRACKEN: Absolutely. While participatory art, in particular, has really gained visibility in recent years, many Australian institutions continue to draw a line between the two parts of my practice. I think this distinction also has a lot to do with my background. Much of my practice is informed not only by my fine arts training but also by my broader humanities education. It often feels as if this is greeted with a kind of mistrust.

NELSON: *I remember also that the notion of 'public space' did not quite translate in the Cambodian context. Not for linguistic reasons, but rather for cultural ones: Phnom Penh is occupied in ways that are of course very distinct from Melbourne.*

For me, there was one conversation that arose out of that day that has recurred, again and again, here and elsewhere. It's about the ways in which your practice, and the practices of Khvay Samnang, and Sok Chanrado, and so many other people here too, even if they aren't called 'public art' per se, are so engaged with the spaces of the city: spaces and their inhabitants, of course. Am I remembering right that this was how we first started to think in terms of the 'locality-specific'? As a way to bring out the importance of both place and people in these practices, yet without disavowing the works' ability to speak to and connect with publics far from home?

MCCRACKEN: Yes, in 2013 you presented a lecture to the 'Art in Public Space' Masters students about contemporary art in Cambodia, with a focus on artists producing work in and around the White Building. I continued to refer to that lecture for the rest of the semester, as the Cambodian examples were such eloquent examples of works being intrinsically linked to their time and geographic space: they were truly 'locality-specific.' Many of our students knew little about Cambodia, and most were too young to remember the images of the war-torn country that flooded Western media during the 1980s; however, they were all profoundly affected by the works. The artists' performances, the documentation of those performances, and the ways in which the public interacted with them, meant that complex locally-specific politics were not just comprehensible to these far-removed student audiences, but also deeply affecting.

Sok Chanrado's *Sound Wave* and Khvay Samnang's *Samnang Cow Taxi*

The White Building is the point of origin in both Sok's *Sound Wave* (2014), and Khvay's *Samnang Cow Taxi in the White Building* (2011) (see Figure 3). The videos documenting both performances, establishes within a matter of seconds the artists' intimate familiarity and friendliness with the neighbourhood and its residents. The swift evocation of a sense of closeness with this locality sets the tone for both works, which invites us as viewers to follow along on a humble but poetic journey. It is significant that both works take the form of a slow physical travel through space as a method of engaging in open-ended exchange and dialogue; this approach resonates with McCracken's practice in unexpected and overlapping ways.

The opening scene of the *Sound Wave* video shows the small but busy street that runs in front of the White Building. Sok has lived in the area for his entire life, and is known to all the men and women selling snacks and drinks along this thoroughfare. In the simply-shot and roughly-edited video, this is demonstrated effectively when we see these shopkeepers address the artist fondly by name as they chat with him about his strangely decorated bicycle. Viewing the raw-feeling footage of this quick but meaningful interaction, the viewer also feels warmly

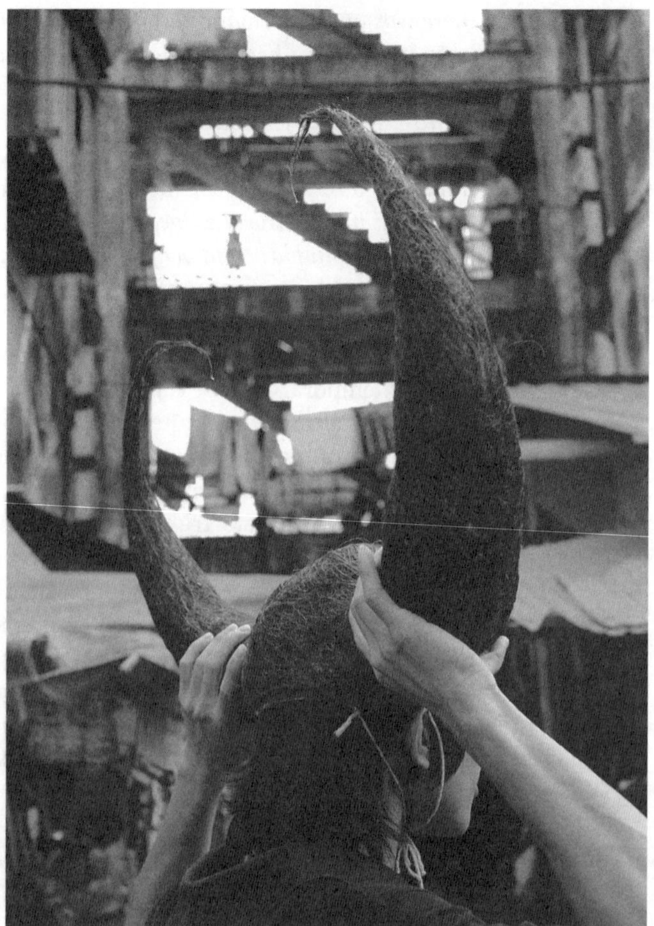

Figure 3: Khvay Samnang performing *Samnang Cow Taxi in the White Building*, Phnom Penh, 2011. Image: Vandy Rattana.

towards this young man; as he first pushes and then rides his bicycle away, the camera follows him, and the voiceover (and English subtitles) explains briefly where Sok is travelling to. All this happens within less than a minute: an economic opening sequence that efficiently yet compellingly draws in the viewers, initiating a feeling of dialogue, as we watch footage of the artist engaging in other kinds of face-to-face exchange within the performance itself.

Khvay's video also opens to the artist standing in the small street in front of the White Building. Amidst a cacophonous burst of everyday sounds—chatter, traffic, wind and market-sellers—Khvay is adjusting the fit of a pair of oversized horns he is wearing; shopkeepers look on as they go about their daily tasks, and smile with what appears to be both amusement and familiarity. *Samnang Cow Taxi in the White Building* is a performance in which the artist carried several individuals into and out of the White Building, on his back, while wearing the distinctive horns. The video documentation follows the artist as he carries two people into the structure, and up its elegant (if dilapidated) staircase, as well as carrying one person out of the building. For viewers, the work offers a quirky, but revealing, introduction to this locality: the distinctive modernist architecture and its countless improvised alterations and additions, the busy and crowded environment of residents and workers, and importantly the friendly, open and close-knit nature of the community.

But for all the participants, already familiar with the White Building, Khvay's work functions not as an introduction, but rather as a celebration of the community's value. By literally carrying people in and out of the neighbourhood, the artist is also symbolically broadening the 'path' between the White Building and the surrounding city. Long stigmatized for its visually evident state of disrepair, the community's unique history and value as a gathering place for artists was, at the time, little-known elsewhere in Phnom Penh. Indeed, this was a primary factor motivating Khvay—and fellow members of a collective of artists, Stiev Selapak[5]—to establish Phnom Penh's only artist-run space within the White Building. Called Sa Sa Art Projects, the space opened in 2010; *Samnang Cow Taxi in the White Building* is one of several works Khvay made around that time, in which the artist uses his own practice to build and strengthen his own, as well as his collective's and his audience's understanding of, and links with, the locality and community.

It is telling that both Sok and Khvay choose the form of a physical travel through geographic space in order to enact an interpersonal exchange between the artists and their community. Neither artist is dressed as a tortoise, yet both move slowly, powered only by their own bodies; it is clear to all involved that these artists are not tourists dropping in for a brief moment, but rather they are locals engaging with their own locality. Both use props made from readily available materials from everyday experiences, not from art contexts—materials familiar to the people they encounter. Sok's loudspeaker and recording device are comprehensible immediately, even to older Cambodians, whose understandings of new digital technologies may be limited. Khvay's horns are fabricated from human hair collected at road-side barbers in Phnom Penh; micro-businesses that for the artist are emblematic of the intimate scale of the city's streets and spaces.

Clare McCracken as Beth McGarey

Meanwhile in Melbourne, McCracken-as-McGarey—artist-as-tortoise—shuffled across the undulating surface of Federation Square in the Spring of 2013. As she moved, she became increasingly aware of a growing crowd on the steps to the Square's main point of entrance. This was nothing unusual, as Federation Square is a common meeting ground, the starting point of many marches and protests, and a favourite place to sit, watch and be watched on a sunny day. However, McCracken had observed over the last couple of days, all those in one particular group were wearing white T-shirts with iron-on transfers of the faces of loved ones across their chests. As she approached, many of the group members asked McCracken the same questions as others whom she had spoken with during the performance:

Why are you walking so slowly? Why are you wearing a shell? Who are you?
But also: *Aren't you afraid walking on your own, young woman?*

McCracken answered these questions in the character of McGarey, slowly and deliberately, at the pace of a tortoise. The nature of the exchange—its slowness and unpredictability—was integral to the performance.

One at a time, the artist handed her interlocutors a small book documenting the 100 kilometres of her slow walking around Melbourne, ostensibly dressed as McGarey, the woman-as-tortoise, who must travel with the support of a cane. Using hand-drawn and digital illustrations, fragments of text, found objects and landscape photography, the book maps the journeys from Federation Square to the Melbourne International Airport, as well as to the city's seaport, and 30 kilometres upstream along the gently flowing Yarra River—all sites of exchange, places for the movement of people and things. The book was a gift from a strange woman to these women strangers, an object that is small, but that aspires to a kind of beauty in its oddity.

On this day, however, McCracken encountered a different kind of interest from this particular group of strangers. 'Thanks a lot', said Lee, a woman with bright hair and a big smile. 'I will keep this as a reminder that our city *can* be safe for women, in public, anyway'. As the group turned to leave the Square, one of Lee's friends held up a hand-made placard: 'Australian Families Affected by Murder'. This text was printed also on the reverse of their T-shirts, in explanation of the iron-on transfer portraits adorning the front sides. McCracken-as-McGarey waved goodbye to Lee, the woman with the bright hair and big smile, a woman who had lost her sister to domestic violence.

McCracken's chance encounter with this quiet yet affecting group of demonstrators was a singular illustration of the ability of an artist's performance in public space to engage with publics that might otherwise have remained invisible to her. In this sense, engagement is not a didactic act of the artist assuming to enlighten her chosen publics, but rather of the artist being humbled and enlightened by those publics who choose to engage with her: in short, a creative exchange. But while the conversation with Lee, the woman whose sister had been murdered, was one that arose by chance, in fact the questions of women's inhabitation of public spaces and the (real and perceived) safety of public spaces for women were already on McCracken's mind while she was developing this performance. These were among the most pressing issues of the day in Melbourne—what Sok Chanrado might term 'hot news'—discussed in official media sources and in unofficial forums, online and offline alike.

In response to the violent death of 17-year-old, school student, Masa Vukotic who was fatally attacked in daylight in a park in Doncaster (a Melbourne suburb), a senior member of the homicide division of the State of Victoria's police force stated on national radio (ABC

Radio National 2015) that the incident had highlighted concerns for the personal safety of women in public space. He suggested that women should try, as much as possible, to use public spaces only in the company of others (Calligeros 2015).

In *Mobilities*, sociologist John Urry argues that power relations determine when and where different social groups walk (Urry 2008: 69). As Haussmann's Paris was constructed, and sophisticated networks of paved walking paths were assembled in a city for the first time, wealthy men quickly became the prevailing users. In nineteenth-century Paris the footpath was not a place for 'respectable women', and for working-class women it was full of risks 'especially from the gaze of male flâneurs' (Urry 2008: 69). While the actual safety of many public walking paths has improved for men and women since that time, victim-blaming statements highlight a prevailing gender divide in the ways Australian authorities see women inhabiting and using public space.

Typically, a higher proportion of violent acts against men occur in public spaces, whereas for women, violence occurs most commonly in the home and at the hands of a current or former male partner (Australian Institute of Criminology 2015). Research by Kirsten Day, an urban design and behaviour specialist, suggests that popular and officially sanctioned attitudes around women's perceived vulnerability in public spaces have more to do with entrenched divides between genders than with statistics of actual bodily safety. Day proposes that the hegemonic perception of men as strong and independent compared to women, who are characterized as defenceless and in need of protection, is foundational to common understandings of the relative safety of public spaces for men and for women in contemporary western cities (Day 2001).

Twenty-first century attitudes about the gendered uses of public space have antecedents in legal and social discourses from a century earlier. In the introduction to *A Room of One's Own*, Virginia Woolf describes in detail an afternoon where she used the act of walking through public space as a way of working through complex ideas. Just as she finds herself on the precipice of a discovery, she is interrupted by a gardener who rushes forward to point out that she had strolled absentmindedly from the path onto a section of grass set aside for male academics (Woolf 2000: 6). Most cities tend not to, officially or legally, regulate and restrict the mobility of women in the present as they did in the past. Yet Day's research into attitudes about safety and the aforementioned comments by a police inspector serve to illuminate the ways in which many cities continue, culturally and socially, to restrict women's movement by entrenched gender divides.

McCracken's dandy-tortoise performance grew out of a research project around community safety in a central Melbourne laneway, Hosier Lane, best known for its colourful graffiti wall-murals that have become a prominent tourist attraction over the past decade. Designed initially to research women's sense of safety in that locality, the dandy-tortoise project evolved after the widely publicized death, in 2012, of Jill Meagher, a 29-year-old Irish woman living in inner-city Melbourne. Kidnapped, raped and murdered on her way home at 3.00am, Meagher's case consumed the city, prompting immediate action and debate about CCTV, the parole system and women's safety in public space. For McCracken, and for many others who live in and love Melbourne, the rhetoric around CCTV and the parole system drowned out the more important discussion the city needed to have: of women's right to equal habitation of the city's public spaces, in particular its footpaths. Such a conversation would necessarily be coupled with a close analysis of the ways in which law enforcement authorities, politicians, the media and the community at large situate violent crimes against women in public spaces. McCracken, like many other feminists in Melbourne (echoing counterparts in many other cities), considered that the language and advice offered to women by various authorities works insidiously to perpetuate the manifold ways (both deliberate and unconscious) in which women, and their families and friends, restrict their use of public space.

McCracken joined many thousands of others in a series of street demonstrations that followed Jill Meagher's death. McCracken's performance as Beth McGarey, the tortoise-loving-dandy, conceived in the aftermath of this tragedy (and thus in the shadow of its media spectacle), may be considered an articulation of resistance to those many voices telling women that public spaces are dangerous and to be avoided. The artist is mindful of the history of slow movement through city footpaths as an act of dissent. Petra Kuppers argues that the French dandies, who leashed their tortoises to walk slowly through the arcades of mid-nineteenth-century France, were performing a type of urban-based protest. Choosing to follow the pace of the tortoise with its 'stubby legs' was a subversive act, which momentarily destabilized the rhythm of the city, creating a counter rhythm, a pre-industrial rhythm (Kuppers 2003: 2). McCracken's long and lonesome walks around Melbourne as McGarey—part woman, part endangered animal—were an act of protest, playful yet pointed, the artist's way of declaring: *I am here, I am a woman, and I have a right to use public space and our footpaths in the ways that I see fit and the ways for which public space is intended.*

In *Social Acupuncture*, Daren O'Donnell suggests that artists can rebalance the *qi* of cities by finding points of social inequality and disruption—a city's 'blockages'—and using their art to generate a discourse that draws attention to, and resolves, those inequalities and imbalances (O'Donnell 2006). O'Donnell's holistic yet quirky approach resonates with McCracken's practice. By concluding her long walks with a month-long *flâneur* around Federation Square, McCracken used her arts practice to perform a kind of 'social acupuncture'. By sharing the fictional story of Beth McGarey—a woman who loves to inhabit the pavements of Melbourne and has done so for days on end—in conversations with thousands of strangers, perhaps McCracken was able to shift people's perception of women's safety in public space. Discussing, but also embodying, the possibility of a woman feeling (and being) perfectly safe while alone in public environments, McCracken-as-McGarey's engagingly oddball conversations as part of the performance sought, in part, to tease out why those people who stopped to chat had such entrenched beliefs about which gender could safely inhabit public space. It was an exchange that strove for a mutual rethinking, even enlightenment, on these ever-present and highly topical questions.

A Dialogue Between Us: Exchanging tapestries

NELSON: *I remember visiting you-as-Beth-McGarey, first in Hosier Lane and then in Federation Square, and just finding it so hilarious that you wouldn't slip out of character, you insisted on speaking in that oh-so-very-slow voice. What struck me was how quickly your appearance in those spaces shifted from being an oddity—something that stood out—to being a new commonplace, blending in with everything else: just another walking tortoise-woman.*

MCCRACKEN: The locations that I performed in definitely shifted the impact of the costume. The sites that you saw me in are both very visible locations: spaces where people come to watch or be watched. When I walked along the Yarra River, I also seemed to blend in, perhaps that is because I was walking along a popular shared-user path, where some people 'perform' by running fast, wearing designer exercise clothes and stretching. The times that people watched me, with suspicion, were when I was clearly an outsider, moving through the suburban areas on the way to the airport, or the industrial estates in that area.

NELSON: *Melbourne's city and its sprawling suburbs are localities you know intimately, from years of living and researching and working there. What was your initial feeling about shifting your practice from this familiar site to the comparatively unfamiliar White Building in Phnom Penh?*

MCCRACKEN: The ethics of working with communities and their stories are complex. When I produce site-specific works in Australia, which interrogate social issues, I spend a lot of time thinking about agency, responsibilities and outcomes. Flying from Melbourne to Phnom Penh for my month-long residency at the White Building, I was anxious about how I would negotiate these considerations in another country, especially one where I did not speak the language.

My exchange with the residents of the building began with a guided tour of the neighbourhood led by Kourn Lyna, the residency coordinator at Sa Sa Art Projects. During her tour, Lyna introduced me to many residents, students, business owners and vendors. At the end of the tour I asked Lyna to introduce me to a group of women who worked in, and ran, a nail salon in the White Building. As the Cambodian (and also several Cambodian-Vietnamese) women painted my nails, we discussed their families, their education, and—unexpectedly—an elaborate cross-stitch tapestry of a mermaid that one of them was making.

I had been in Phnom Penh two years prior to my residency. Since then the rapid transformations of the city were evident the moment I got off the plane. I soon noticed that for many women, particularly those running market stalls, an increase in income and leisure was evident in the proliferation of hobbies, most notably cross-stitch tapestries. The women of the White Building and its surrounding markets, during quiet times, lovingly stitch the tapestries, following their intricate patterns.

NELSON: *The sudden appearance of tapestries in the laps of market-sellers was something I'd noticed before you arrived, but I'd never given it much thought. I remember that my Cambodian friends and I were quite taken by your powers of observation in reading so much into something that was, for us, already quite familiar and everyday. This is a neat illustration of the special nature of what many curators and scholars term 'artistic research.' But how did your interest in this cross-stitching activity translate into your own practice?*

MCCRACKEN: In crowded markets, a cross-stich tapestry became my 'conch' of conversation, a way to work through language barriers and power dynamics. Initially I worked with the women at the White Building nail salon to learn how to cross-stitch, but gradually, I also started to use the project to start up conversations with other women. As we stitched, we covered many conversation topics. But overwhelmingly, and often, we discussed housing security. Many former high-density neighbourhoods housing Phnom Penh's lower socio-economic populations had been demolished, and residents forcibly evicted. The women of the White Building were fearful that they too would be forced to leave their home and community.

As our relationships grew, I stopped cross-stitching the patterns suggested in the tapestry kits, and started instead to stitch the shapes of recycled building materials that women and their families had added to their shops and homes in the White Building. Initially, I focused on wrought iron window grilles and terracotta air-vents. These keep the tropical air circulating, an alternative to costly air-conditioning. My stitching also started to include fragments of designs from old tiles, both from the French colonial era and the 1950s and 1960s building boom. The tapestries serve as a memento of the White Building and its community.

Conclusion

It is widely acknowledged in the twenty-first century that creative practices are more transnational and more interdisciplinary than ever before. Yet still rare are models for exchange based in an ethics of mutual respect, which value and privilege the creative possibilities inherent in cities and communities. This chapter has proposed the notion of the locality-specific by presenting a discussion of the practices of Melbourne-based artist, Clare McCracken, and Phnom Penh-based artists, Sok Chanrado and Khvay Samnang. Each artist's work, in part, champions the needs and experiences of less visible sectors of the community, and each displays an interest in the symbolic and dialogic possibilities of slow travels through the spaces of the city. These processes include making spaces for under-represented voices to be heard, and challenging the violence of gendered space.

In a context of another violence of exclusion—that of inequitable manoeuvrings on the part of both the Australian and Cambodian governments, working politically, socially and spatially to exclude the most vulnerable—this discussion has sought to illuminate the power and possibility of creative exchange. The exchange processes work on the power of inclusion, privileging the voices and spatial experiences of less-visible members of the community. In both the streets of Melbourne and the neighbourhood of Phnom Penh's White Building, the authors—writing as participants and practitioners—have drawn attention to the possibilities for artists' locality-specific actions to forge mutual dialogue, and to establish attentive, ethical and respectful relationships.

Acknowledgements

The authors thank Dr Maggie McCormick, Dr Geoff Hogg, Renee Dudfield, Kendyl Rossi, Katerina Larsen (Astrinakis), Chhum Phanith, Khvay Samnang, Kourn Lyna, Pen Sereypagna, Sok Chanrado and Vuth Lyno for conversations that have contributed to our thinking in the writing of this chapter; and the artists who generously granted permission to reproduce their work.

References

ABC Radio National (2015), *RN Breakfast with Fran Kelly*, radio program, 17 March.

Australian Institute of Criminology (2015), *Location of Homicide*, <http://www.aic.gov.au>. Accessed 15 May 2015.

——— (2009), *Homicides Resulting from Domestic Altercations Higher for Women*, <http://www.aic.gov.au>. Accessed 15 May 2015.

Calligeros, M. (2015), 'Parks Not Safe for Women, Says Homicide Boss', *The Age*, 20 March, <http://www.theage.com.au/victoria/parks-not-safe-for-women-says-homicide-squad-boss-20150320-1m2rgc.html>. Accessed 20 May 2015.

Day, K. (2001), 'Constructing Masculinity and Women's Fear in Public Space in Irvine, California', *Gender Place and Culture: A journal of feminist geography*, 8: 2, pp. 109–127.

Kuppers, P. (2003), *Disability and Contemporary Performance: Bodies on edge*, London and New York: Routledge.

Nelson, R. (2014), 'Performance is Contemporary: Performance and its documentation in visual art in Cambodia', *Udaya, Journal of Khmer Studies*, 12, pp. 95–143.

O'Donnell, D. (2006), *Social Acupuncture: A guide to suicide, performance and utopia*, Toronto: Couch House Books.

Pen, S. (2014–ongoing), *Genealogy of Bassac*, <https://genealogyofbassac.wordpress.com/>. Accessed 10 June 2015.

Taylor, N. A. (2011), 'The southeast Asian art historian as ethnographer?', *Third Text*, 25: 4 pp. 475–488.

United Nations High Commissioner for Refugees (2014), 'UNHCR Statement on Australia-Cambodia Agreement on Refugee Relocation', 26 September, <http://www.unhcr.org/542526db9.html>. Accessed 15 August 2015.

Urry, J. (2008), *Mobilities*, Cambridge: Polity Press.

Woolf, V. (2000), *A Room of One's Own*, London: Penguin Books. (First published 1928.)

Notes

1 Clare McCracken was born in 1982 in Myrtleford, Australia. She lives and works in Melbourne.

2 Khvay Samnang was born 1982 in Svay Rieng, Cambodia. He lives and works in Phnom Penh. Sok Chanrado was born 1994 in Phnom Penh, Cambodia, where he continues to live and work. In this chapter, Cambodian family names precede given names, and the authors follow the Latin spelling of Cambodian names that is used by the individuals themselves.

3 In the Australian institutional context, such a performance as part of a research project would require formal ethics approval. In Cambodia, there is no functioning system for such a process. Artists such as Sok rely on face-to-face explanations of their projects for participants; and sensitivity to the 'locality-specific' ethics of his practice. The equivalent to ethics approval is an informal process of collective agreement—between participants, the artist, peers and mentors in the community—a process met by Sok.

4 Unless otherwise noted, all quotes from Sok and Khvay Samnang are from conversations with Nelson between 2012 and 2015. Translation from Khmer to English is by Nelson.

5 Stiev Selapak is the name chosen by a collective of artists founded in 2007 in Phnom Penh. The name is often loosely translated as 'Art Rebels'.

Chapter 5

Art as Enterprise

Grace McQuilten

Introduction

This chapter explores the economic and social entanglement of contemporary art through examples of art as enterprise. Firstly, the chapter addresses a beguiling business venture by artists Jon Rubin and Dawn Weleski's called *Conflict Kitchen*, a pop-up restaurant in Pittsburgh, USA that serves food from countries with which the United States has been engaged through military conflict (see Figure 1). *Conflict Kitchen* opens up discussion and critical thinking about global politics, ideology and warfare. This ongoing venture, which started in 2010, has a seemingly conventional engagement with business and commodity exchange while simultaneously undermining the expectations of customers and audiences alike. It raises questions about the role of art in both affirming and challenging the bio-cultural sphere of politics. These questions lead to consideration of a more explicitly critical engagement with enterprise in *Return*, a project by Iraqi-US artist, Michael Rakowitz. *Return* is an enterprise involving the importation and sale of Iraqi dates, the first commodities marked 'Product of Iraq' to be sold in the United States since the lifting of the trade embargo at the end of Iran-Iraq war in 2003. Both *Conflict Kitchen* and *Return* raise the question of whether art can engage critically with the systems and structures of enterprise in an increasingly commercialized socio-political landscape.

In *A Voyage on the North Sea*, Rosalind Krauss (2000) describes contemporary art practice as 'post-media', stemming from the impact of Conceptual Art of the 1960s, whereby the differences between traditional art media such as drawing and painting had lost relevance. As a consequence, artists 'have recourse to every material support one can imagine, from pictures to words to video to readymade objects to films' (Krauss 2000: 1). This post-media practice coincided with an increasing commodification of artistic experience where all materials, media and even aspects of the art market itself become homogenized. In this context, Krauss argues, 'every material support, including the site itself—whether art magazine, dealer's fair booth, or museum gallery—will now be leveled' (Krauss 2000: 15). Perhaps as a result of this homogenization, the field of contemporary art practice now extends not only to materials and processes, but also to economic form, as exemplified by artists such as Rubin, Waleski and Rakowitz using overt forms of business as artistic media.

What explains this positioning of the artist as entrepreneur? Political and social theorists from the 1970s onwards have argued repeatedly that the possibility of an external position

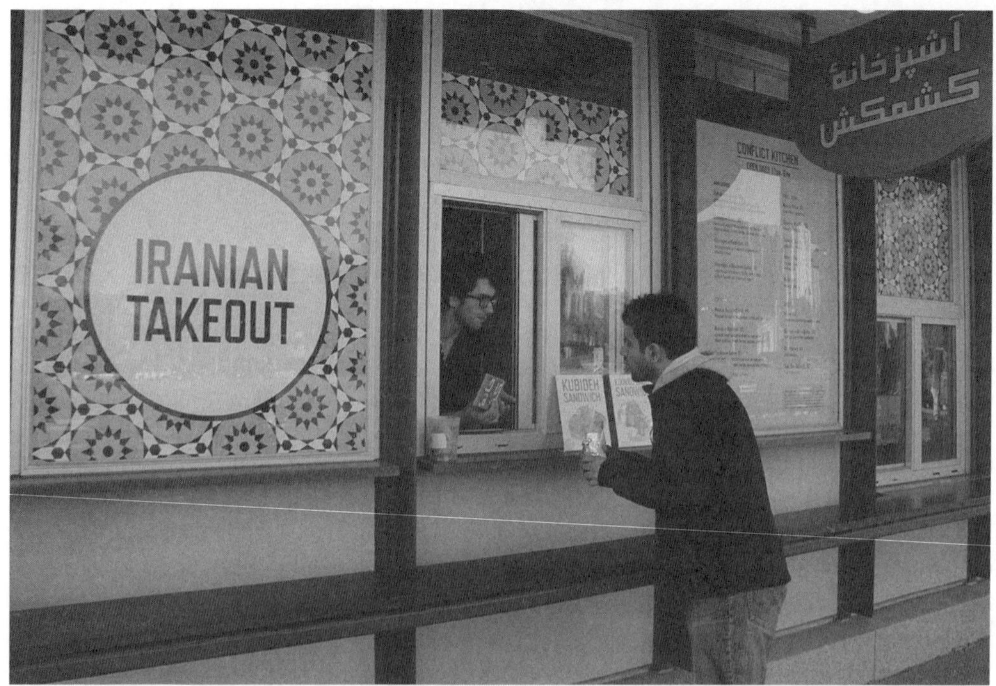

Figure 1: *Conflict Kitchen*, Pittsburgh, USA, 2013. Image: Jon Rubin and Dawn Weleski, 2015.

from which to reflect critically upon and challenge the inequalities produced by advanced capitalism has all but disappeared. Rather, forms of resistance and social transformation are now occurring within the institutions and mechanisms of production, consumption and exchange. The most effective form this resistance might take is the subject of differing critical viewpoints, with thinkers such as Gilles Deleuze, Félix Guattari, Michael Hardt, Antonio Negri and Paul Virno advocating a radical critique of contemporary capitalism through the generation of new forms of collectivity. On the other hand, political theorists Ernesto Laclau and Chantal Mouffe argue for organized action within the institutions of representative politics (Deleuze and Guattari 2004; Hardt and Negri 2000; Virno 2007; Laclau 2011; Mouffe 2013). In *Agonistics: Rethinking the world politically*, Mouffe writes: 'I advocate a strategy of "engagement with." Such a strategy includes a multiplicity of counter-hegemonic moves aiming at a profound transformation, not a desertion, of existing institutions' (Mouffe 2013: xvi). The idea of 'engagement with' is an important framework within which to understand the emerging phenomenon of art as enterprise, connected also to the rise of socially engaged practices in contemporary art (Davis 2013).

Social practice is a loose and wide-ranging development in art that has been informed by the work of various curators, theorists and practitioners including the likes of Nicolas Bourriaud and his seminal text *Relational Aesthetics*; Grant Kester's work on dialogic and collaborative art; Nato Thompson's work on art-activism and Miwon Kwon's work on site-specific art in different community and cultural contexts (Bourriaud 2002; Kester 2011; Kwon 2002; Thompson 2012). Bourriaud was hugely influential in the early millennium for championing the work of artists who facilitate social connection through their work, such as Rirkrit Tirivanija, known for preparing and sharing meals to celebrate the concept of hospitality in galleries, using food as a vehicle to create a convivial relationship between audience and artist (Bourriaud 2002).

The turn towards social practice broadly expresses a renewed political optimism in art, along with a rejection of commodity culture in the commercial art market. However, this kind of work has also been accused of disguising social problems, through presenting an appearance of social cohesion within the limited context of the art gallery. The positive experiences that occur within the gallery hide the difficulties of human relations outside of the gallery, where money, class, race, sexuality, location, education and experience all play a part in how we interact, what opportunities we have and the extent to which we are able to experience social connection. This is the basis of Claire Bishop's critique of relational aesthetics. She argues instead that 'a democratic society is one in which relations of conflict are sustained, not erased' (Bishop 2004: 66). Furthermore, the presumption that socially engaged art presents an alternative to the commercial aspects of the art market is hard to maintain when taking into account the rise of social marketing in business. Social practice may simply present a new way for the art market to expand its marketing reach and attain a competitive edge, by reaching contemporary audiences who are already transacting via social networks.

Any account of socially engaged art, in this context, also needs to explore the economic dimension of specific works and practices. It needs to ask the question of whether these artworks simply re-present and thereby affirm what already is taking place in dominant economic and political systems, or rather do they provoke, challenge and transform these structures? It is in this light that the idea of art as enterprise takes on a critical potential, as a means to engage with, expose and potentially transform business structures in the context of a consumer-driven world. *Conflict Kitchen* and *Return* are artworks that bring together transparent entrepreneurship with the political and social intentions of relational-art. By so doing, they help to identify both the risks and potential opportunities available to art as a critical enterprise.

Conflict Kitchen

Artists Jon Rubin and Dawn Weleski's *Conflict Kitchen* is a pop-up restaurant in Pittsburgh, USA that serves food from countries with which the United States is engaged through military conflict. *Conflict Kitchen* opens up a space of discussion and critical thinking about global politics, ideology and warfare, describing itself as 'a take-out restaurant that only serves cuisine from countries with which the United States government is in conflict'

(Roberts 2011). Here, in evidence is the idea of conflict coming together with the idea of hospitality in an overtly political manifestation. The idea of the event as artwork is to bring people together through 'the lens of culture and food' in order to allow discussion that would otherwise not happen, and to draw attention to the nature of conflict and the motivations of both political and cultural forces that drive and dispel conflict (Maher 2013). *Conflict Kitchen* has had numerous iterations since starting in 2010, each operating for several months to highlight one particular country, which so far has included Afghanistan, North Korea, Cuba, Iran and Venezuela.

As an event, *Conflict Kitchen* engages directly with the economic structure of business; it is an ongoing trading entity, rather than a project, exhibition or gallery experience. The vehicle of business has the ability to reach new and different audiences to those usually frequenting galleries, with the potential to speak to a more diverse community base. It also offers a range of ways to engage audiences, from the production of food to financial transactions to consumption. Restaurant customers participate actively in the work in a number of ways: firstly, by stopping at the restaurant; secondly, by choosing to purchase an item from the menu; thirdly by paying for it; and finally, through the experience of unwrapping and consuming the meal. Each dish at *Conflict Kitchen* is wrapped in specially designed, brightly coloured paper that highlights political conflict by featuring blocks of text that reflect the viewpoints of people from countries with which the United States is in conflict. The customers therefore get more than they bargained for, with the transaction involving both an exchange of money and an exchange of viewpoints. Rubin notes, 'I'm interested in how you can engage someone in a work (of art) when they don't' even know it's a work' (Roberts 2011).

This commercial transaction raises a set of new questions, however, relating to the participation of audiences. Is it only those with disposable incomes who are able to participate in the work? What is the relative diversity of those public members who *do* choose to participate? Does the transaction reduce complex political differences to an act of consumption?

The Iranian take-out restaurant, *Kubideh Kitchen* first operated in 2012 and subsequently re-appeared in 2013, responding to renewed political tensions between the United States and Iran. *Kubideh Kitchen*, as the name suggests, served food popular in Iran, focusing on the feature dish of kubideh: spiced meat in freshly baked barbari bread, served with onion, mint, and basil. Each kubideh was individually wrapped in custom-designed paper printed with quotations from Iranians on subjects ranging from Persian poetry to the current political turmoil and perspectives on Iran's potential, and actual, conflicts with the United States. In one example of the wrapping paper, an Iranian is quoted on the topic of nuclear power:

> I don't think a nuclear capable Iran is a threat to the U.S. or any country in the world. This is how the events are presented in the mainstream media as a scare tactic to make Americans live in fear and to justify any action against Iran for the American people. I

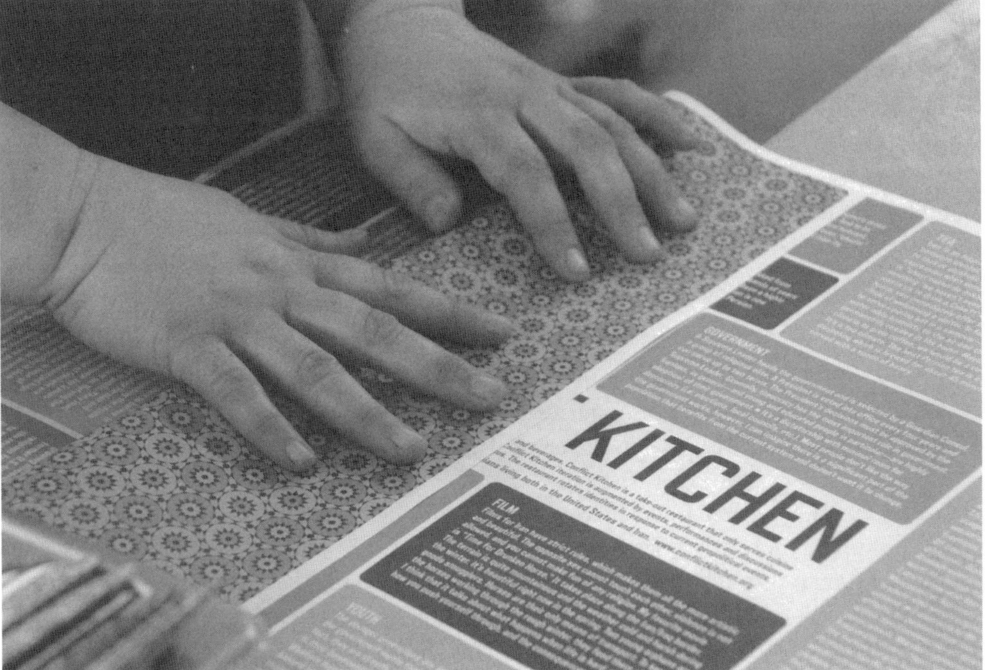

Figure 2: Food wraps that contain quotations from Iranians on politics and culture for Kubideh Kitchen, 2013. Image: Jon Rubin and Dawn Weleski, 2015.

don't know whether Iran is developing nuclear power for weapons or for energy. I am very concerned that the U.S. may go to war with Iran, which would be beneficial for both governments. The U.S. would benefit from the war profit and the Iranian government would benefit by stabilizing its position among its own dissatisfied population.

(Conflict Kitchen 2015)

Here we see the dissemination of a viewpoint openly dissenting from the messages expressed by both the USA Government and mainstream media, and yet a viewpoint that is not one-sided; rather it shows openness to critique of both sides of the Iran-USA conflict (see Figure 2).

Throughout the run of *Kubideh Kitchen*, the artists along with staff of the kitchen facilitated widespread public discussion about Iranian culture and politics, extending the commercial and transactional aspects of the enterprise to a range of community activities and events. This included, for example, a live Skype meal between Tehran and Pittsburgh described as 'an inter-continental dinner party' (Conflict Kitchen 2015). Here citizens from both sides of the conflict were brought together to exchange ideas in a way that reached very different audiences in both countries. Perhaps as a result of these non-commercial ancillary activities, *Conflict Kitchen* has attracted worldwide media attention. Of particular note is television news coverage by

Al Jazeera that was broadcast internationally in 2012. This coverage served to extend the reach of the project beyond discourse in the United States and to influence international perceptions of the United States. *Al Jazeera* reporter Mohammad Almee reported:

> This experimental and humble idea could seem like a commercial ploy to ensure commercial income for the restaurant, but it nevertheless succeeded in provoking debate about the cultures of people that the US Targets with hostility, and also about the real causes of this hostility.
>
> (Almee 2012)

Despite the enterprise's explicit focus on 'conflict', however, it appears instead to have facilitated mostly positive, peace-building dialogue. This is particularly evident in campaign materials used to support a Kickstarter crowd-funding campaign for a new iteration of *Conflict Kitchen*. In the campaign materials, various customers provide testimonials for the positive outcomes of the enterprise. One customer suggests it makes them feel as if they are 'working together to save the planet', where another describes 'It's a delicious way to learn about becoming more human', and yet another suggests the venture provides 'an alternative to the bogeyman through eats' (Kickstarter 2010). These affirmations attest to the positive effect the project might be having on audiences; however, it is harder to gauge its impact in terms of the lived complexity of international conflict.

In response to *Conflict Kitchen's* Afghan iteration in 2011, USA-Afghan artist Aman Mojadidi commented, 'it does seem a bit naïve in that it attempts to give a view of what Afghans think [...] Ultimately this is a precarious endeavor since the opinions can, and will, vary widely. And just because it comes from an Afghan, doesn't make it true, such as the romantic notion of self-sufficiency before the wars' (Roberts 2011). Here, Mojadidi highlights the problems inherent to politically engaged art in a western context. Art runs the risk of appearing tokenistic, and assuaging middle-class guilt rather than activating political dissent. Mojadidi's reflection points to various critiques of the way contemporary art is being asked increasingly to solve social problems through the lens of social practice. The demand for art to have a social impact can lend itself to *serving* institutional demands, rather than challenging social structures (Rancière 2009).

In the case of *Conflict Kitchen*, it is important to note that food and culinary exchange is being used increasingly as a tool for diplomacy around the world—from the White House to British-Indian international relations (Dasgupta 2012). *Conflict Kitchen* inadvertently mirrors these institutional tools, as evident for example when Rubin describes a customer by saying to him, 'I saw you on Al Jazeera, and it changed the way I thought about Americans' (Stromberg 2013). The question is whether the enterprise ultimately presents an image of American *tolerance* by enacting, even performing, self-critical debate, or whether it exposes political difference. Rancière (2009) argues in 'The Ethical Turn of Aesthetics and Politics' that prevailing humanitarian sentiments stymie real political action and social change, by privileging, instead, social 'consensus'. This consensus, he argues, results in a condition where differences 'disappear in the law of a global situation' and politics 'disappear in the indistinctness of ethics' (Rancière 2009: 120). The influence of this ethical turn in art, he suggests, is the prevalence of artworks that focus on recuperation, either by forming social bonds between participants, or by bearing witness to catastrophe. Recuperative artworks eradicate the potential for politics, which he suggests relies upon division, difference, ambiguity, precarity and, most importantly, dissensus.

The question of *Conflict Kitchen*'s impact in social terms, therefore, depends less on the ability of the enterprise to generate positive reactions from audiences locally and abroad, and more on its ability to maintain internal contradictions and tensions—for example, the extent to which it fails to promote consensus; the extent to which the business challenges its transactional, commercial basis; the ways in which it might celebrate dysfunction over conventional measures of success. In the case of *Conflict Kitchen*, the enterprise could be seen arguably to serve the diplomatic agenda of softening the public face of US international relations, making the US public appear to be open to difference and self-critique on a cultural level, while political action continues in the same course.

This is the basis of Slavoj Žižek's analysis of contemporary consumer culture in terms of a 'false enlightenment' where the appearance of a critical attitude serves to disguise the continuation of dominant ideologies (Žižek 1989). For philosophers Gilles Deleuze and Félix Guattari, the most powerful way that art can create societal change is by introducing an element of natural dysfunction into production. They write, 'The artist is the master of objects; he puts before us shattered, burned, broken-down objects' (Deleuze and Guattari 2004). In this way, they open up the possibility that art can radically transform capitalist society, not through means of representation, but through a dysfunctional *engagement with* the means of production.

Return

This idea of dysfunction more explicitly informs artist Michael Rakowitz's engagement with the market in his 2006 work *Return*, which saw the establishment of a storefront in New York City (see Figure 3). The store contained a double-edged functionality; the first part entailed the free shipping of goods from the United States to Iraq, reversing the usual commodity-exchange process by 'gifting' the cost of shipping to customers. In the process, it exposed the economic and cultural barriers to 'free trade' between the United States and countries with which it has been in ideological conflict. It pointed to the social and cultural impact of economic policy—highlighting the human challenges faced by expatriate communities wanting to maintain material connections with families and friends in Iraq.

The second function of the store was to sell imported dates from Iraq, and in so doing to provide the first 'Product of Iraq' labelled, consumer good in the United States since the lifting of the trade embargo with Iraq in 2003. Rakowitz explains, 'We wanted to sign

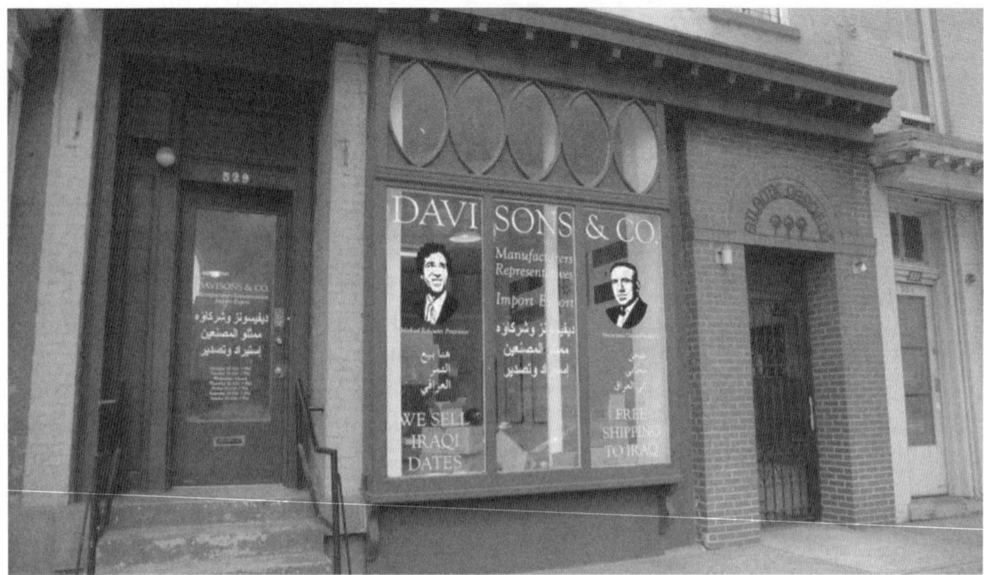

Figure 3: Michael Rakowitz, *Return*, October to December, 2006. Davisons & Co. Import/export company, 529 Atlantic Avenue Brooklyn, NY. Image: Courtesy Lombard-Freid Projects, New York.

the first deal to bring in Iraqi dates clearly labelled as such, in what we believed would be the first such transaction in over thirty years. Nothing labelled "Product of Iraq" had hit American store shelves since the beginning of the Iran-Iraq war' (Johnson 2007: 15). The artist's interest in importing dates stemmed from his father's migrant journey. Rakowitz's father was an Iraqi Jew who migrated to the United States in 1946 and subsequently established an import/export business called Davisons & Co. His father also taught the artist the traditional method of making date syrup.

The store was opened with the support of Creative Time in New York with a lease that commenced in September and operated for three months. During this time, the artist documented the trials and tribulations of trying to import the dates from Iraq, and reported the story to customers in store. The importing process was long and convoluted and involved his Iraqi counterparts travelling across the country, getting stuck at borders, the product being destroyed, exorbitant shipping costs, unexpected flights and a host of other hurdles. As a result, the Iraqi dates were unavailable in store until the last two weeks of its trading life. When the Iraqi dates did arrive, the supply was so scarce that the artist was only able to provide small rations to customers for the price of US$8.00. The struggle for the dates' export from Iraq and travel to the United States became a metaphor for human migration and the complexity of traversing our global political landscape. Rakowitz described the dates, for example, as 'surrogates for people waiting at the border' (Johnson 2007: 16).

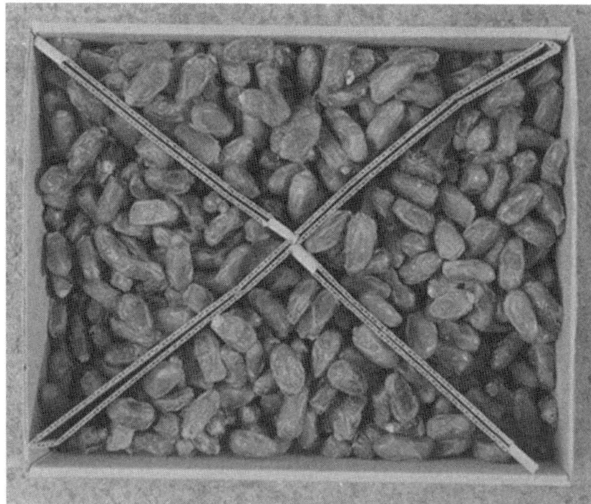

Figure 4: Michael Rakowitz, *Return*, October to December, 2006.
Image: Courtesy Lombard-Freid Projects, New York.

In the meantime, however, customers were able to purchase Californian dates and talk to the artist about his difficulties in attempting to do business with a country with which the United States has been in deep ideological conflict. In this way, the *Return* storefront publically undermined the proud declarations of free trade and equal enterprise opportunity espoused by American politicians and entrepreneurs alike. The presence of Californian dates also pointed to historical trade routes between the Middle East and the United States. Dates produced in California originate from seeds imported from Iraq. The artist explains, 'Our dates are from Iraqi seed. So it's the enemy within' (Johnson 2007: 14).

The *Return* storefront was for all intents and purposes a commercial failure. The imported dates were unavailable for purchase for the majority of the store's existence; when they arrived they were of a poor quality and the low quantities inflated the consumer price. The artist lost more money than he generated in revenue and the whole enterprise drew to a close after three months. It was precisely through these failures and the project's dysfunction that *Return* exposed the true complexity of trade and economic flows in the contemporary global context. State powers and ideology still play a significant role in determining the shape and structure of business, and art events, despite the appearance of global mobility and increasing multiculturalism worldwide.

In comparison with *Conflict Kitchen*, *Return* presented a more typical 'art' experience (see Figure 4). *Return* was thoughtful, stylized and aesthetically formal engagement with the processes of trade and commodity exchange. The work relied on support from the arts' community, arts' funding, and the presence and personal story of the artist became central to the construction of meaning and the audience's engagement with the store. Rakowitz acknowledges this link to his personal narrative, explaining, 'I wanted this to be more than just a business transaction, however. The project inevitably became personally meaningful, since I am half Iraqi' (Johnson 2007: 15). *Return* was not a fully-fledged enterprise and its exchanges were strategically mapped out. This enabled a much stronger critique of the market and a more explicit embrace of dysfunctional production. For critic, Sofia Hernandez Chong Cuy, the project was effective by precisely this undermining of its business mandate. She writes, 'Representation and deceit—as in, "a store that is not a store"—are part of encountering and discovering the work' (Cuy 2009: 88). This is echoed in Rakowitz's own description of the enterprise in terms of 'bad business'. He explains, 'So it's not cost-effective to import Iraqi goods. It's bad business, and that's what got my started on this project' (Johnson 2007: 13).

While 'bad business' may seem to be more effective as an artistic strategy in terms of generating critique than the affirmative business model of *Conflict Kitchen*, *Return* was nevertheless limited in its capacity to change the systems it was engaging with. This limitation was compounded by the fact that it was a durational work, limited to its three-month tenure. It is in this light that *Conflict Kitchen*, while certainly more ambiguous in its critique of economic systems, proved to have a longer lasting and potentially further-reaching impact. By reorienting the structures of business towards generating debate and productive social antagonism, and maintaining this complex position day-in, day-out over several years of trade, the enterprise impacted upon and changed the structures of both business and art while reaching a wide, varied and at times unsuspecting audience. The question that remains is the extent to which it can maintain this structural tension over time, and the extent to which its success in both cultural and economic terms might serve broader ideological and political interests.

Conclusion

In conclusion, both *Conflict Kitchen* and *Return* demonstrate a nuanced and critical engagement with the systems of commerce. Practices of art as enterprise have emerged in recognition of the economic forces that influence artistic production, providing greater agency for artists in the production and reception of their work.

In the context of a commercially driven global landscape, where all kinds of artistic practice are entwined with systems of funding and expectations of both commercial and institutional outcomes, the opportunity for art to retain space for critique is rapidly eroding. In this context, a position either inside or outside of commercial culture is of less importance than the degree to which artists can retain space for critical thinking and artistic freedom amid multiple institutional and economic demands.

References

Almee, M. (2012), 'Conflict Kitchen', *Al Jazeera News*, May 4.
Bishop, C. (2004), 'Antagonism and Relational Aesthetics', *October*, 110, p. 66.

Bourriaud, N. (2002), *Relational Aesthetics,* (trans. S. Pleasance and F. Woods), Paris: Les presses du reel. (First published in French 1998.)

Conflict Kitchen (2015), *Conflict Kitchen,* <http://conflictkitchen.org>. Accessed 10 March 2015.

Cuy, S. (2009), 'Storytelling', *Afterall: A Journal of Art, Context and Enquiry*, 21, pp. 80–82.

Dasgupta, R. (2012), 'Foreign Policy of Food: India is a laggard in deploying cuisine in diplomacy', *The Economic Times*, August 13.

Davis, B. (2013), 'A Critique of Social Practice Art: What does it mean to be a political artist?' *International Socialist Review*, 90: July, <http://isreview.org/issue/90/critique-social-practice-art>. Accessed 15 June 2015.

Deleuze, G. and Guattari, F. (2004), *Anti-Oedipus: Capitalism and schizophrenia*, London and New York: Continuum.

Hardt, M. and Negri, A. (2000), *Empire*, Cambridge and London: Harvard University Press.

Johnson, L. (2007), 'Enemy Kitchen: An interview with Michael Rakowitz', *Gastronomica: The Journal of Critical Food Studies*, 7: 3, pp. 11–18.

Kester, G. (2011), *The One and the Many: Contemporary collaborative art in a global context*, Durham: Duke University Press.

Kickstarter (2010), 'Conflict Kitchen', <https://www.kickstarter.com/projects/1859717557/conflict-kitchen>. Accessed 8 March 2015.

Krauss, R. (2000), *A Voyage on the North Sea: Art in the age of the post-medium condition*, London: Thames & Hudson.

Kwon, M. (2002), *One Place After Another: Site-specific art and locational identity*, Cambridge: MIT Press.

Laclau, E. (2011), *Politics and Ideology in Marxist Theory: Capitalism—fascism—populism*, London and New York: Verso.

Maher, H. (2013), 'Changing American Perspectives of US Adversaries, One Dish at a Time', *Yale Global Online*, May 16.

Mouffe, C. (2013), *Agonistics: Rethinking the world politically*, London and New York: Verso.

Rancière, J. (2009), *Aesthetics and Its Discontents*, Cambridge and Malden: Polity Press.

Roberts, N. (2011), 'Promoting Cross-cultural Understanding through Food and Art', *The Christian Science Monitor*, February 28.

Stromberg, J. (2013), 'Global Food Fight', *Smithsonian*, 44: 6, p. 16.

Thompson, N. (ed.) (2012), *Living as Form: Socially engaged art from 1991–2011*, New York and Cambridge: Creative Time Books and MIT Press.

Virno, P. (2007), *Multitude Between Innovation and Negation,* (trans. James Cascaito), Cambridge and London: Semiotext(e). (First published in Italian 2007.)

Žižek, S. (1989), *The Sublime Object of Ideology*, London and New York: Verso.

Chapter 6

Recipe for Homefullness

Keely Macarow

My Confession

I commence this chapter with a confession: I have an obsession with housing. I have taken hundreds of photos of houses, apartment blocks, units, shacks, co-housing quarters, nursing homes, public and private housing in Australia and Sweden. The photos document privately owned, public and social housing. My focus has been on taking photographs of a range of housing in areas throughout two cities, Melbourne and Stockholm, to gain a sense of the diversity in Swedish and Australian housing and to consider the commonalities and differences in housing across these two cities.

In my country of residence, governments and media mark the purchase of a home as the defining outcome of adulthood. However, I am a serial renter. I have lived in Victorian terrace houses, art deco apartments, artist studios, warehouses, council flats, Edwardian houses, apartments above shops and weatherboard cottages in Melbourne, London and Sydney. As the prices of housing soars, my capacity to build a deposit for a permanent home diminishes. I am certainly not the only person that faces inequities in housing markets in Australia or other OECD countries. However, my concern is with current housing options and our future housing needs. I use my story to reveal the narrative we collectively share about housing.

Australian Housing

In Australia, the majority of Australian housing stock is tied up in the private market, with most Australians owning their own home or renting someone else's house. There are currently very few options in housing in Australian cities aside from the private market, with expensive housing vastly outweighing social and affordable housing stock. For instance, the 2011 Australian Census revealed that 67 per cent of Australia's 7,760,322 private dwellings were occupied by owners of the property (whether outright or through a mortgage), while 29.6 per cent of private dwellings were rented (Australian Bureau of Statistics 2012). The peak Australian housing organization, National Shelter reported: 'In 2015, there were 403,767 social housing dwellings in Australia' (National Shelter 2016: 7). Thus, Australian social housing stock is small compared to the amount of homes that are privately owned. This demonstrates that Australia is overwhelmingly a nation of private home-owners.

In the discussion paper, 'Transforming Housing: Affordable housing for all', Carolyn Whitzman, Clare Newton and Alexander Sheko estimate that Australia will require 6.5 million new dwellings to coincide with a massive spike in population, which is predicted to reach around 36 million people in 2050 (Whitzman, Newton and Sheko 2015).[1] This suggests that there will be a substantial rise in the population of major Australian cities over the next 30 years. However, the population of Melbourne is already increasing rapidly, with projections that greater Melbourne's population will reach a population of 8 million people by 2050 (Australian Bureau of Statistics 2015) and between 9 and 12.1 million in 2061 (Australian Bureau of Statistics 2013) as a result of current trends in births, deaths and migration. This steep rise in population is an increase from the recorded 4,440,300 people in greater Melbourne in 2014 (Australian Bureau of Statistics 2015a) and will require a massive expansion in housing, transport, education, healthcare, energy, cultural and recreation services, infrastructure and utilities.

Like Sydney, Melbourne currently has an over-heated housing market with escalating prices. Both cities are two of the most expensive cities in the world in which to live and their housing is among the world's most unaffordable. In fact, Australian housing is viewed as 'severely unaffordable' with Sydney and Melbourne ranked the third and ninth least affordable out of 378 housing markets across the United States, Canada, Ireland, the United Kingdom, Australia, New Zealand, Singapore, China and Japan (Cox and Pavletich 2015).

If these predictions are accurate and Australian cities such as Melbourne increase to double or triple their current population in the next 35 years, tremendous vision, planning and action will be required to ensure that the future population's housing needs are met. Otherwise, if the appropriate resources are not developed to meet the needs of this growing city, housing disadvantage will be prevalent in Melbourne.

2050

2050, when Melbourne reaches its predicted 8 million population, is not far away. To give some perspective: I was 15 years old in 1980 and my son is now 17. My mother is 85 and I will be 85 in 2050. These comparisons bring relative times and dates closer to home. 1980 was a significant year for art, music and cinema. Mike Parr represented Australia at the 1980 Venice Biennale, John Landis' film, *The Blues Brothers* premiered and Joy Division's *Love Will Tear us Apart* was released by Factory records: pivotal cultural moments in the not so distant past.

However, the focus here is with housing and there are troubling signs that current Australian governments do not want to take seriously the concerns about the rising prices of Australia housing market, much less invest in the massive new housing stock the country will require into the twenty-first century if projections play out as envisaged.[2] The emphasis has been on rising housing markets, rather than the large-scale expansion of social and affordable housing. This has meant that public discourse tends to focus on the difficulties of first-home buyers entering the housing market. Noting such difficulties as a valid preoccupation, it is not the only concern. As a result, Australian public debates have paid lip service to affordable housing, but have yet to explore diverse options in housing.

To meet the looming demands and predictions of 2050, a rapid housing response must be developed and implemented now; we already lack diverse options in affordable housing. The predicted 8 million Melbournians deserve action from government, planners and designers today to enable it to grow into a sustainable city with extensive affordable housing for all by 2050. If planning and action can be implemented with vision now, cities such as Melbourne could house its growing population in a myriad of sustainable and affordable housing options. It follows that we should work towards the imperative of affordable housing for all rather than investing in mechanisms to ensure that private housing remains the major if not only choice for most people living in Australia.

My concern is with the issues that face a city such as Melbourne if it does not rise to its housing challenge during the next three decades. However, this scenario is also faced by a number of cities around the world. Although my discussion focuses on Melbourne's predicted growth in population size, the planning and development issues it faces could be applied easily to cities elsewhere.

Responses from Artists, Architects, Urban Designers

Designing for the future may lead to a marked change in the way we organize our communities. This discussion turns now to consider the work of artists, architects and urban designers from Australia, the United Kingdom and Europe who have produced projects to imagine and invent new models for housing. I suggest that artists and designers contribute to the thinking, planning and action that have to take place to ensure that we do not have major housing disadvantage in cities such as Melbourne, Sheffield or Stockholm. This is the challenge of the artist and designer who is designing for the future today: to be engaged in the design of diverse, large-scale and sustainable options for housing infrastructure, and to ensure that such housing is affordable for renters and buyers alike.

The one certainty we have about the future is that of uncertainty. Although projections are based on current trends, unknown events could ensure that a predicted growth in population does not reach the suggested figure. However, if current projections do coalesce, we would be remiss not to confront tricky problems of today to address and respond to how we want to live in the future. I advocate for bold artistic interventions and unique design solutions to be part of this conundrum.

Studio Polpo: Sheffield

Artists and designers working with socially engaged art and participatory design provide insight into the sustainable outcomes we require to ensure there are appropriate housing options for all residents and visitors of twenty-first-century cities. Art and design is the outcome of an imagination that uses materials and tools to experiment, speculate, pose questions, challenge conventions, trawl through problems and have the courage and innovation to find solutions. Artists and designers use tools and materials to create real and virtual artefacts, which may add value, critique or change the way in which society operates.

Studio Polpo is a Sheffield-based architectural social enterprise (Studio Polpo 2015). The Studio has six directors with expertise across architecture, social enterprise, performance art, sustainable building, communal housing, urban design and landscape architecture.[3] As a not-for-profit studio it models its practice on social, environmental, economic and ethical responsibility and sustainability.

Yorkshire's city of Sheffield, in the north of England, has a population of 563,749 (Sheffield City Council 2015). It is a small town with two universities; the health, education and retail industries provide the majority of employment opportunities (Sheffield City Council 2014; Dabinett, Walshaw and Squires 2015). Studio Polpo has worked on a range of diverse projects located in Sheffield from sustainable co-housing and mobile cookery units to art projects (Studio Polpo 2015). In September 2014, Studio Polpo presented a socially engaged art event, *OPERA#1* in a disused Co-op department store in the Sheffield CBD, with the aim of encouraging discussion about unused spaces and affordable housing. For 10 days Studio Polpo inhabited the site and used recycled materials to rebuild a section of the building for domestic and communal inhabitation. During the occupation of the building, Studio Polpo hosted meals for local council officers and architects among others as a vehicle to discuss Sheffield housing.

Since this event, Studio Polpo has engaged in a dialogue with Sheffield City Council about the potential of developing housing in the Sheffield CBD. The conversation between local government and the Studio is a major achievement in a locality that does not have a history of housing in the city centre. However, the conversation may not have emerged if Studio Polpo did not inhabit the former Co-op department store as a site for discussion about affordable housing.

Studio Polpo's *OPERA#1* demonstrates how the use of vacant buildings encourages activity in city zones that would otherwise lie neglected. The project draws attention to the potential of unused or underused buildings for adaptation into temporary or permanent sites for cultural dialogue and exhibition, which is effectively what the Co-op store was transformed into over the duration of the project. *OPERA#1* demonstrates how artists and designers can shape public thinking about the use of urban space and how they may draw attention to the potential of abandoned buildings for infrastructure such as housing.

The Untitled Collective: Melbourne

The Untitled Collective was founded in Melbourne in late 2011 by a group of artists, designers, architects and housing researchers who were concerned at the lack of action on affordable housing by multiple Australian governments.[4] The Collective combines expertise in art, industrial, urban and graphic design and architecture, and research in socially engaged art, participatory design and housing. The Collective's members link housing unaffordability with housing stress and homelessness and use creative interventions to draw attention to these challenges. From 2013, the Collective included Swedish researchers and drew on commonalities and differences in housing disadvantage between Sweden and Australia, coupled with innovations in Swedish design and social housing.

The Untitled Collective's first activity was to author *Homefullness: A Manifesto for Full Housing* (Untitled Collective 2011) as a response to the 2011 Homelessness Design Challenge led by Melbourne's Design Research Institute.[5] The Untitled Collective was concerned that respondents would propose minimal capsule units similar to the 1988 mobile homeless vehicles of Polish artist, Krzystof Wodiczko. These vehicles were designed for homeless people to sleep and wash in (Hebdidge 2012). Similarly transient was *Park Bench House* (2002) by Australian architect, Sean Godsell, which transformed public seating into a bed for homeless people.[6]

While these small housing units raise awareness about the plight of homeless people, they do not propose solutions to the lack of affordable or emergency housing for cities such as New York or Melbourne, where the projects premiered. Instead, Wodiczko and Godsell's units pivot homelessness around the responsibility of the individual to adapt to minimal circumstances and minimalist housing. These design solutions do not offer the scope for homeless people to be housed in abodes that the designers would presumably find acceptable for their own occupation.

The Untitled Collective wrote the *Homefullness Manifesto* as a counterpoint to projects such as these, to 'demand the expansion of social housing options and the swift development of an expansive, sustainable and affordable rental accommodation sector, and the broad establishment of housing cooperatives' (Untitled Collective 2011). The *Homefullness Manifesto* is the guiding document and inspiration behind the Untitled Collective's writing, presentations and exhibitions. It provides an ecology of thinking and making for the Collective's projects and aspirations.

The *Homefullness Manifesto* is unflinching in its concern for those who are suffering acute housing stress and homelessness as a result of western housing markets that revolve around the perpetual escalation of housing prices. The Collective argues for an end to tax concessions such as Australia's negative gearing, which provides financial incentive for investment property owners at the expense of first home buyers (Untitled Collective 2011).

The Collective proposes expansive options in housing and advocates for a 'reduction in housing sales to stop the escalation of unaffordable housing that preclude so many people from owning their own homes' (Untitled Collective 2011). The Collective is adamant in the belief that housing is a human right and 'insist on affordable, sustainable housing for all' (Untitled Collective 2011). Housing, for the Untitled Collective, is a social ecology that facilitates community and enables wellbeing and inclusion (Untitled Collective 2011).

From 26 June to 26 July 2014, Melbourne members of the Untitled Collective (Keely Macarow, Neal Haslem, Margie McKay, Mim Whiting and Mick Douglas) exhibited *Open for Inspection* at Melbourne's West Space gallery. *Open for Inspection* featured a floor-based drawing, a single channel video projection, a lounge setting with domestic artefacts, and a clothesline with especially designed tea towels, including the *Homefullness Manifesto* (see Figure 1). The floor drawing was a one-to-one plan of a kitchen typical of those that were designed as part of the Swedish Million Homes Programme (Macarow 2015).

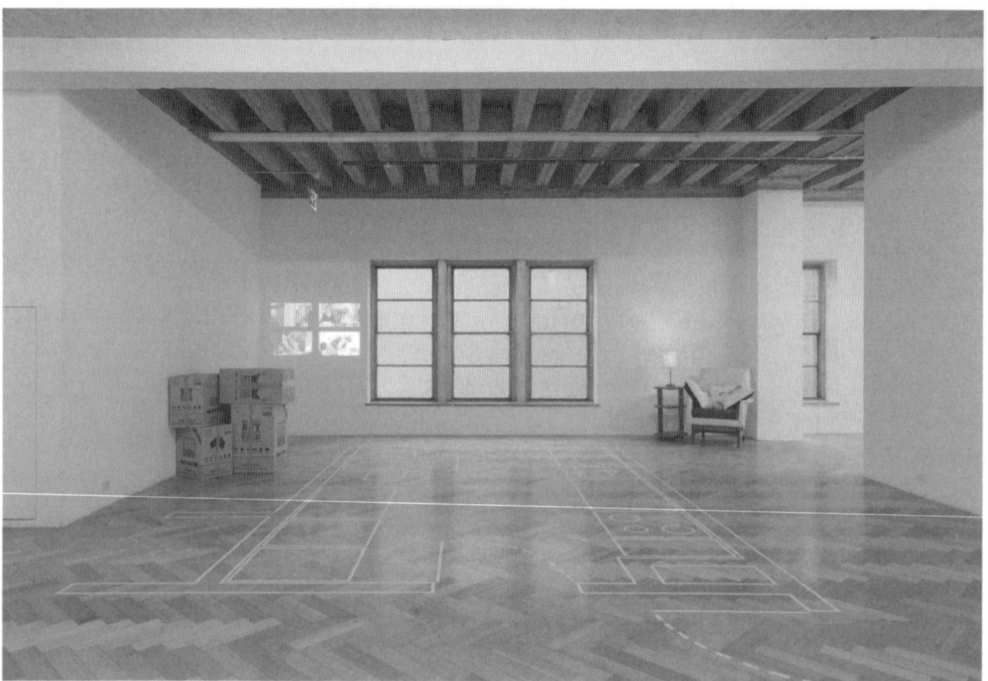

Figure 1: Untitled Collective, *Open for Inspection*, West Space, Melbourne, 2014. Image: Christo Crocker, 2014.

The Untitled Collective was inspired by this large-scale social housing program, which was designed to address a crisis in Swedish housing in the 1960s (Macarow 2015). From 1965 to 1974, a million homes (ranging from houses to large apartment blocks) were built to house Swedes (Hall and Vidén 2005; Christophers 2013). The Swedish housing programme was instituted following an act of parliament and viewed as an extension of the Swedish welfare state (Hall and Vidén 2005; Holmqvist and Magnusson Turner 2014). In contrast, Australian public housing has predominantly been the responsibility and concern of State governments, who have built high-rise and medium density public housing projects since Federation. In post-war Australia, the Commonwealth Government constructed public housing, but has been more involved in providing 'housing assistance and homelessness services' (Australian Government n.d.) since the 1970s. The stark contrast in the numbers of public and private housing stock in Australia reveals that the nation's priority has been with the continual growth of the private housing market, with Commonwealth-funded housing services dealing with the effects of housing stress and lack of affordable housing.

However, the ambitious scale of the Swedish Million Homes Programme provides compelling evidence that governments can build mass housing programs to address housing crises. In comparison, the under investment in mass housing programs in the Australian context has contributed to over-inflated housing markets across the country. If governments

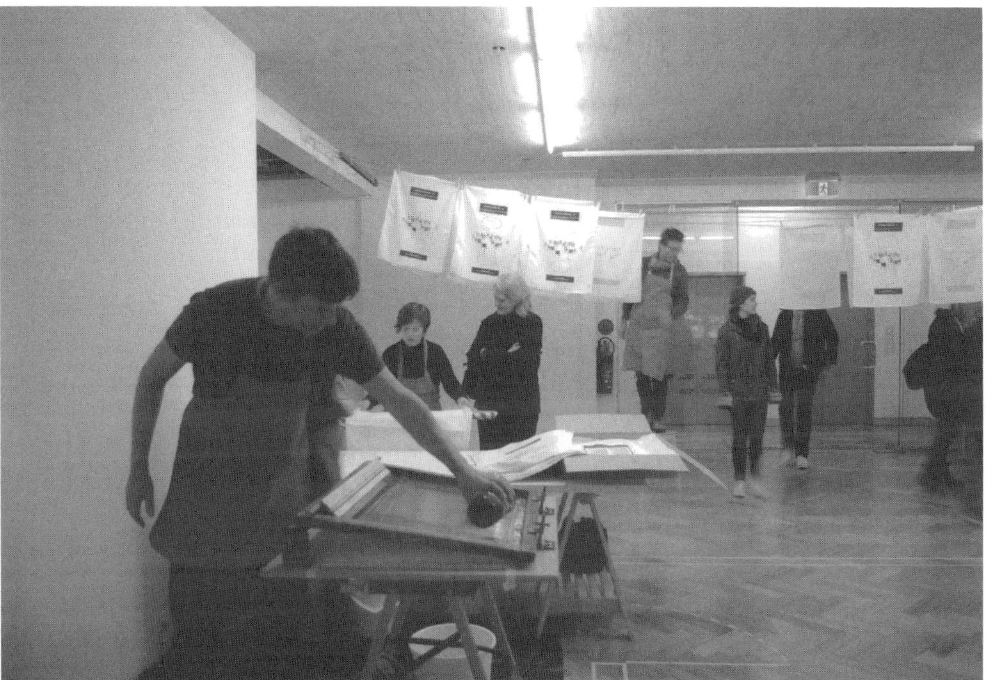

Figure 2: Untitled Collective, *Open for Inspection*, live print run, West Space, Melbourne, 2014. Image: Neal Haslem, 2014.

viewed housing services and infrastructure on a par with those services that are funded to defend the nation, the public might see funds and action flow into new, large-scale, affordable, housing developments.

Open for Inspection also included four participatory events comprising public discussions and live print runs (see Figure 2). The participatory events included an informal afternoon tea in which members of the Collective engaged in conversations with invited guests and gallery visitors. Concerns about homelessness, limited public debates about housing, social inclusion and options in housing and unaffordable prices of the private and rental housing markets emerged throughout these discussions. These themes inspired new tea towels, which were printed and hung on the clothes line installed at the entrance of the gallery. The exhibition concluded with a public House Meeting, with speakers from not-for-profit housing and homeless organizations, and an architectural practice that specializes in affordable and sustainable housing (Macarow 2015). *Open for Inspection* demonstrates how participatory art projects facilitate conversations about social concerns such as housing. More importantly, discussions generated during the project revealed that people are concerned about the rising prices of Australian homes, and are interested in broader options in housing. For this, art provides an important role in bringing a range of stakeholders together to spark and share ideas, narratives, statistics, questions and solutions.

Within Walls: Malmo and Copenhagen

Moa Liew (Malmo, Sweden) and Christel Nisbeth (Copenhagen, Denmark) are the architects behind *Within Walls*, a Swedish/Danish practice designed to be a communicative conduit between architecture and communities (Within Walls 2013). Moa and Christel use film-making, live action animation and art to explore ideas about architecture from the design of palliative care settings to people's requirements and desires for housing. In *Yndlingsbolig (Favorite Housing)* the artists embrace live action animation to show the creation of a house made of cake (Within Walls 2010). The film's narrator provides:

> Recipe on a house for four persons: Start your dream house with happiness, visions, bedroom, dining kitchen, entertainment room, children's room, a carport, hospitality, open space, a bathroom, clean lines, a summer room, a computer room, utility room, a guest room, laundry room, prestige, dining room, game room, wine cellar, space [...] Lot's of space! Depending on personal taste you could add: Sauna, study, home cinema, a pantry, hobby room, patio room, canoe shed, spa and a hunting room en suite.
>
> (Within Walls 2010)

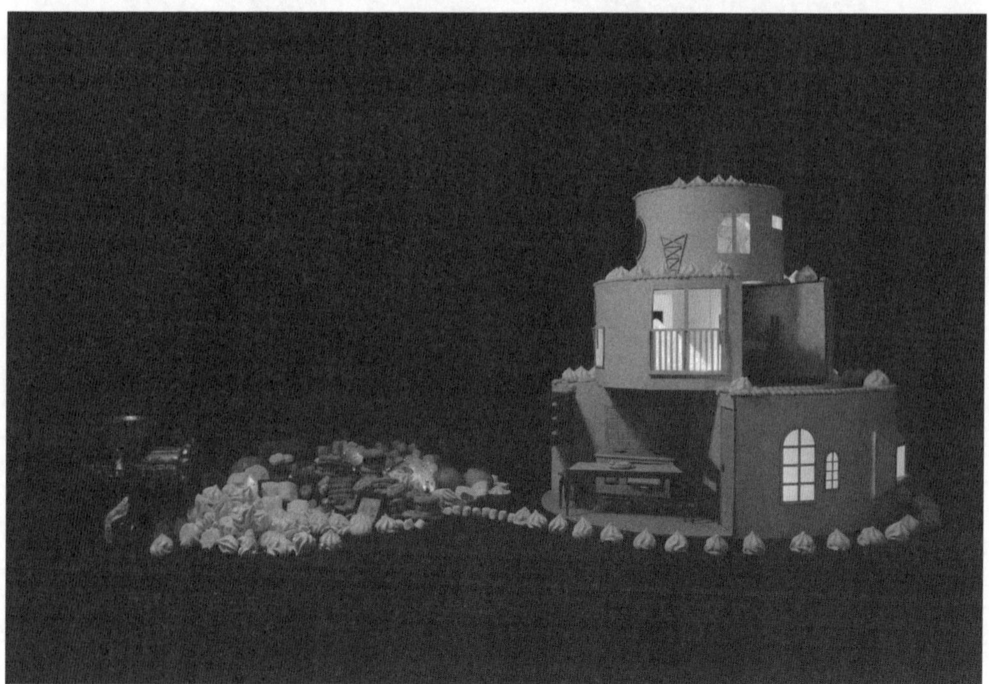

Figure 3: Within Walls, Yndlingsbolig (Favorite Housing), Moa Liew, Christel Nisbeth, Annemie Sandahl and Agnes Mohlin, Copenhagen, 2010. Stop motion animation, 3 minutes. Image: Within Walls, 2010.

The list of rooms is exhaustive. Eventually the viewer is asked, 'But why don't we just select the best?' (Within Walls 2010). The cake-house unfolds through knobs of icing, the scattering of paper and the churning of dough. We see the creation of rooms (bathroom, kitchen) and the exterior of the three-storey, tiered, circular house-cake. An assemblage of voices discuss their favourite rooms as the camera glides through the house to reveal a kitchen, a music room, a bathroom, a study: all with exquisite furnishings and stories (see Figure 3).

However, the film-makers remind viewers at the end of the film:

The best home doesn't always equal the biggest home. If you only take your favorite pieces, there will be plenty to go around.

(Within Walls 2010)

Yndlingsbolig (Favorite Housing) is a cautionary tale which reminds us that our appetite for large houses could be at the expense of housing being made available for many. The film acts as a warning to resident groups who advocate against the development of high-density housing. The 'not in my backyard' ethos of some resident groups provides challenges to the development of apartment blocks in cities such as Melbourne, which have been designed predominantly around low-level housing. For instance, the Australian preference for detached housing on suburban quarter-acre blocks has, on a whole, precluded a culture of high-density living that could house large groups of people. This must be re-considered as we plan for massive population spikes in cities such as Melbourne.

Questions about housing could be posed quite differently. What will people live in if insufficient formal housing is provided? Will informal housing settlements emerge on the edge of cities such as Melbourne if we do not move forward with expansive housing programs?

Concluding Challenges

However, for cities such as Melbourne, the time to act on housing needs is now. Larger scale housing developments have to be encouraged across cities, spanning apartment blocks, town houses and units rather than large houses, which have high-energy requirements, are expensive to maintain and do not necessarily house many people. Housing developments could contain spaces shared by residents including laundries, large dining rooms and kitchens for entertaining, vegetable gardens, courtyards and other garden features, parking for bikes, workshops to mend furniture and studios to create craft and artworks. Not all homes require these features if shared rooms and spaces such as these were built into housing developments. As a result of such planning, housing units could become smaller and community engagement and wellbeing may increase because residents are sharing resources.

The architects and artists discussed in this chapter provide us with clues for how we could respond to housing shortages in cities such as Melbourne, Sheffield, Malmo and

Copenhagen. The discussion suggests that studies ought to be undertaken to audit buildings for underused and unused spaces in order to discern suitable spaces and buildings to be adapted and transformed into affordable housing. Governments should plan for spikes in population and develop mass housing programs, with investment in large-scale social and public housing. To cope with a spiral in population growth there needs to be social, public, political and economic support for massive housing developments, which are managed by government, housing associations and housing cooperatives. We should not merely view investments in housing as financial assets. Instead we should see housing as an investment in civil society and our collective future.

References

Australian Bureau of Statistics (2016), *Population Clock*, 22 March 2016, <http://www.abs.gov.au/ausstats/abs%40.nsf/94713ad445ff1425ca25682000192af2/1647509ef7e25faaca2568a900154b63?OpenDocument>. Accessed 22 March 2016.

———— (2015), 'Capital Cities: Past, present and future', <http://www.abs.gov.au/ausstats/abs@.nsf/products/AC53A071B4B231A6CA257CAE000ECCE5?OpenDocument>. Accessed 19 May 2015.

———— (2015a), 'Estimated Resident Population(a): Greater Capital City Statistical Areas (GCCSAs)', <http://www.abs.gov.au/ausstats/abs@.nsf/mf/3218.0/>. Accessed 19 May 2015.

————(2013), 'Victoria Population Size', <http://www.abs.gov.au/ausstats/abs@.nsf/Latestproducts/3222.0Main%20Features82012%20%28base%29%20to%202101?opendocument&tabname=Summary&prodno=3222.0&issue=2012%20%28base%29%20to%202101&num=&view=>. Accessed 10 July 2015.

———— (2012), 'Census for a Brighter Future, Housing Tenure Data in the Census', <http://www.abs.gov.au/websitedbs/censushome.nsf/home/factsheetshtdc?opendocument&navpos=450>. Accessed 10 July 2015.

Australian Government (n.d.), 'Reform of the Federation White Paper. Issues Paper 2. Part One: Evolution of government involvement in housing and homelessness', <https://federation.dpmc.gov.au/part-one-evolution-government-involvement-housing-and-homelessness>. Accessed 18 March 2016.

Awan, N., Scheider, T. and Till, J. (2011), *Spatial Agency: Other ways of doing architecture*, Oxon and New York: Routledge.

Bourke, L. (2015), 'Tony Abbott stands by Joe Hockey Following "Out of Touch" Claims', *The Sydney Morning Herald*, 10 June 2015, <http://www.smh.com.au/federal-politics/political-news/tony-abbott-stands-by-joe-hockey-following-out-of-touch-claims-20150610-ghklak.html>. Accessed 31 July 2015.

Christophers, B. A. (2013), 'Monstrous Hybrid: The political economy of housing in early twenty-first century Sweden', *New Political Economy*, 18: 6, pp. 885–911.

Countrymeters (2015), 'Australian Population', <http://countrymeters.info/en/Australia>. Accessed 12 June 2015.

Cox, W. and Pavletich, H. (2015), '11th Annual Demographia International Housing Affordable Housing Survey, 2015 ed.: Data from the 3rd quarter 2014', <http://www.demographia.com/dhi.pdf>. Accessed 19 May 2015.

Dabinett, G., Walshaw, A. and Squires, S. (2015), *State of Sheffield*, p. 23, <https://www.sheffieldfirst.com/key-documents/state-of-sheffield)>. Accessed 21 July 2015.

Gorscchlüter, P. (2009), *The Fifth Floor: Ideas taking space*, Liverpool: Liverpool University Press.

Hall, T. and Vidén, S. (2005), 'The Million Homes Programme: A review of the great Swedish planning project', *Planning Perspectives*, 20: 3, pp. 301–328.

Heartney, E. (2013), *Art & Today*, London and New York: Phaidon Press Inc.

Hebdidge, D. (2012), 'The Machine Is Unheimlich: Krzysztof Wodiczko's Homeless Vehicle Project', <http://www.walkerart.org/magazine/2012/krzysztof-wodiczkos-homeless-vehicle-project>. Accessed 23 July 2015.

Holmqvist, E. and Magnusson Turner, L. (2014), 'Swedish Welfare State and Housing Markets: Under economic and political pressure', *Journal Housing and the Built Environment*, 29, pp. 237–254.

Kester, G. H. (2011), *The One and the Many: Contemporary art in a global context*, Durham and London: Duke University Press.

Kiendl, A. (2008), *Informal Architectures: Space and contemporary culture*, London: Black Dog Publishing.

Klanten, R., Hübner, M., Bieber, A., Alonzo, P. and Jansen, G. (2006), *Art & Agenda: Political art and activism*, Berlin: Gestalten.

Lefèbvre, M. and Suarez, A. (n.d.), *Social Impact Assessment of the 'Affordable Housing for Life' Project*, NSW: Macquarie University.

Macarow, K. (2015), 'What Use is a Tea Towel', in C. McIntosh (ed.), *Engaging Publics*, Auckland: Auckland Art Gallery.

Maris Youth Care (2015), 'Affordable Housing for Life', <http://www.maristyc.com.au/affordable-housing-for-life>. Accessed 31 July 2015.

McQuirk, J. (2014), *Radical Cities: Across Latin America in search of a new architecture*, London and New York: Verso.

Meers, D. and Houghton, N. (2015), 'Joe Hockey defends His 'Get a Well Paid Good Job' Comment on Sydney House Prices', *The Daily Telegraph*, 10 June 2015, <http://www.dailytelegraph.com.au/news/nsw/joe-hockey-defends-his-get-a-well-paid-job-comment-on-sydney-house-prices/story-fni0cx12-1227390897438>. Accessed 31 July 2015.

Museum Victoria (n.d.), *High Rise Housing in Melbourne: Atherton Gardens Estate, Fitzroy*, <http://museumvictoria.com.au/discoverycentre/infosheets/the-melbourne-story/high-rise-housing-in-melbourne-atherton-gardens-estate-fitzroy-/>. Accessed 31 July 2015.

National Shelter (2016), 'National Shelter Response to the Treasurer's Call for pre-Budget Submissions 2016–2017', <http://www.sheltertas.org.au/national-shelter-response-to-the-treasurers-call-for-pre-budget-submissions-2016-17/>. Accessed 18 March 2016.

Orlek, J. (2015), 'Residential Performance as Architectural Research', at *Housing A Critical Perspective* conference, Liverpool England, 8–9 April, Liverpool: Liverpool University and Liverpool John Moores University.

Parsons, M. (2015), 'A House for Today', at *Housing A Critical Perspective* conference, Liverpool England, 8–9 April, Liverpool: Liverpool University and Liverpool John Moores University.

RMIT University (2011), 'Design Challenge 2011 Homelessness', <http://www.designresearch.rmit.edu.au/programs/design-challenge-old/2011-design-challenge-homelessness>. Accessed 23 July 2015.

Sean Godsell Architects, 'Park Bench House', <http://www.seangodsell.com/park-bench-house>. Accessed 8 June 2015.

Sheffield City Council (2015), 'Sheffield Population Estimates', <https://www.sheffield.gov.uk/your-city-council/sheffield-profile/population-and-health/population-estimates.html>. Accessed 21 July 2015.

—————— (2014), 'Population and Health of Sheffield', <https://www.sheffield.gov.uk/your-city-council/sheffield-profile/population-and-health.html>. Accessed 21 July 2015.

Studio Polpo (2015), 'Studio Polpo', <http://www.studiopolpo.com/>. Accessed 23 July 2015.

Untitled Collective (2011), *Homefullness: A manifesto for full housing*, Melbourne: Untitled Collective.

Within Walls (2013), <http://withinwalls.dk/nyhjemmeside/>. Accessed 21 July 2015.

—————— (2010), *Yndlingsbolig (Favorite Housing)*, vimeo, <https://vimeo.com/109906683>. Accessed 21 July 2015.

Whitzman, C., Newton, C. and Sheko, A. (2015), 'Affordable Housing for All: Partnership options for policy, investment and demonstration projects', <https://msd.unimelb.edu.au/transforming-housing-affordable-housing-all>. Accessed 12 June 2015.

Notes

1　As of 22 March 2016, the Australian population was 24,033,732 (Australian Bureau of Statistics 2016).

2　The former Australian Prime Minister, Tony Abbott and former treasurer, Joe Hockey, garnered much media attention for their comments about rising prices of Australian housing in mid-2015 when the Prime Minister 'as a homeowner' welcomed the rise in the housing market, and the Treasurer suggested that people should 'get a good job that pays well' in order to purchase a home (Bourke 2015).

3　Studio Polpo Directors: Mark Parsons, Cristina Cerulli, Anna Holder, Jon Orlek, Stuart Thomason and Julia Udell (Studio Polpo 2015).

4　The Untitled Collective commenced in 2011 with Keely Macarow, Neal Haslem, Mick Douglas, Guy Johnson (RMIT University), Margie McKay (City of Whittlesea); Hélène Frichot (KTH, Stockholm) and Rochus Hinkel (Publisher, Stockholm), Mim Whiting (Artist, Melbourne) and Marcus Knutagard (Lund University, Sweden) joined the Collective in 2013.

5　RMIT University Design Research Institute organized annual Design Challenges to encourage designers to respond to social issues. Further information on the 2011 Homelessness Challenge: see RMIT University (2011), Design Challenge 2011 Homelessness, <http://www.designresearch.rmit.edu.au/programs/design-challenge-old/2011-design-challenge-homelessness>. Accessed 23 July 2015.

Chapter 7

Interrogating Space: The *Urban Laboratory*

Fiona Hillary and Geoff Hogg

Introduction

This chapter explores the role public art can play in interrogating public space by revealing tensions and creating a critical site for dialogue. It considers how the curation of 'live test sites' for public art practice may enrich the research capacity of artists and creative practitioners to provide innovative visions of a city through practical research.

In 2013, the City of Melbourne and RMIT University collaborated on a 12-month project, the *Urban Laboratory*, to research issues of city safety via the commissioning of public art in two inner city laneways. Five artists were commissioned in consecutive, curated engagements to exchange ideas and interrogate the site. The following discussion examines the resultant, creative works, and their provocative and transformative capacity to engage diverse communities in dialogue. The aim was to build solidarity, and to enable the extrapolation of meaning through identification of contradictions. Each of the works is considered by detailing its unique contribution to the unfolding creative discussions around changing perspectives of safety in public spaces in the inner city district of Melbourne, Australia.

The broader Melbourne metropolitan area has a population of 4.1 million, with the City of Melbourne's residential population at 100,611. An average of 805,000 people use the city every day for work, recreation and travel (City of Melbourne 2015). Hosier and Rutledge Lanes comprise a 720 square metre site between Flinders Street and Flinders Lane in the heart of the central business district. The laneways are bordered by 'the Forum', one of Melbourne's leading, live music venues; 'Movida', internationally renowned for its gastronomic delights; residential buildings; some of Melbourne's high-end fashion boutiques; and a multi-storey car park. In the middle of this site is a public health service for homeless people. It is also a notable street-art site; well known enough to be listed in the *Lonely Planet* as 'Melbourne's most celebrated laneway for street art' (Lonely Planet 2015). This site encapsulates the socio-economic breadth of the city. In her recent publication, Alison Young, specialist in art and public culture, states:

> In cities, the lines of law tend to coincide with those of cartography and timetabling, resulting in an image of the city as smooth, compartmentalized, organized around boundaries, and functional. However, such an assemblage is based in a desire to control the city's perceived unruliness and fecklessness.
>
> (Young 2014: 146)

What we know about the city, and from our exploration of safety, is that delving into the legalized landscape and individual experiences of the streets is a way to provoke, enchant, engage and explore, in order to extrapolate from individual and collective experiences.

In this context the *Urban Laboratory* was designed to investigate perceptions of safety through artistic innovation and creative risk. The investigation developed in response to the Melbourne City Council's plan to install Closed Circuit Television (CCTV) cameras in Hosier and Rutledge Lanes, a small but vibrant network of lanes in the centre of the city. The Council was responding to a perceived risk of street crime in the area, and the community was reacting strongly to the Council's proposed surveillance plan. Street artists were concerned that the installation of CCTV cameras would threaten the artists' anonymity and may be used for prosecution purposes if and when their work appeared in areas where authorities took a less tolerant approach to street art. The local residents, who formed a proactive committee Hosier Inc., embraced the street-art culture of Hosier and Rutledge Lanes and considered that the presence of CCTV cameras would shift the street-art culture away from the area.

The *Urban Laboratory* was one of a number of responses commissioned by Melbourne City Council to explore solutions to the general perceptions of a lack of community safety in the space. When speaking of community in this context, it is important to acknowledge its heterogeneity. Researchers Michelle Duffy and Judith Mair, in their publication on community events and festivals, remind us that the notion of community is complex: 'given the various forms of identification, belonging is never fixed and coherent but rather fragmented, partial and mobile' (Mair and Duffy 2014: 55). This complexity characterizes the setting of the research project.

Through the investigations by researchers, artists and creative practitioners, the project engaged with French theorist, Michel de Certeau, whose work explores the individual in the cityscape. He acknowledges that we are 'walkers' joining walkers, engaging in and observing the poetics of the city by exploring the 'contradiction between the collective mode of administration and an individual mode of reappropriation' (de Certeau 1984: 95).

The project sought to explore and engage with a positive and inclusive view of safety, and to reflect on individual experiences of the laneways. It considered not just the traditional notion of safety that invokes freedom from danger, but also the sense of safety that occurs through engagement, dialogue and site activation. In their most recent safe city strategy, the City of Melbourne places the individual in the city at the core of their vision and echoes an empowered focus on safety:

We support our community members—whatever their age, sex, physical ability, socio-economic status, sexuality or cultural background—to feel like they can be active, healthy and valued. We plan and design for our growing city, including safe, healthy and high-quality public spaces.

(City of Melbourne 2014)

Building on the work of sociologist Sophie Watson, Young suggests:

> [T]he key to a revitalized sense of belonging is to search out 'sites of magical urban encounters, hidden in the interstices of the planned and monumental, divided and segregated, or privatized and thematized, spaces that more usually capture public attention.' The experience of stumbling across a street-based artwork can provide, for its enthusiasts, exactly this sense of magical serendipity.
>
> (Young 2014: 148)

The *Urban Laboratory* was advanced to investigate how such encounters can reveal experiences of city spaces. The artists were selected for *Urban Laboratory* via direct commissioning, meeting criteria based on their previous work in the urban environment. It was critical that the commissioned artists had prior experience of working in a community context; that their work could be defined as 'socially engaged'; and that they were able to work closely with the curator/producer as active creative collaborators in order to facilitate a dialogue between artists, participants and spectators. Hosier and Rutledge Lanes became the 'test-site' for a praxiological curatorial framework where there were no predetermined outcomes; works changed and developed in response to the experience of practice, which was tested against the research structure as originally planned.

The project was designed, therefore, to unfold over time. In her recent publication *Out of time Out of place* renowned public space curator, Claire Doherty cites the work of psychosocial researcher, Lynn Froggett and her findings that artwork in the public realm can 'generate new relational forms or critical dialogue' (Doherty 2015: 16). Doherty argues for investment in temporary works alongside longer-term durational projects. The *Urban Laboratory* was deliberately curated as a durational work in two phases: an incubation phase and an iteration phase, which took place over a 12-month period. The incubation was designed to engage the commissioned artists to explore the space and reveal an experience of safety. The incubation artists were Ben Cittadini, Adrian Doyle and Clare McCracken.

The second phase, the iteration, asked newly commissioned artists, Ceri Hann and Yandell Walton to respond to the initial suite of works and the issues that had emerged during the incubation. Additionally we, as researchers, conducted 50 surveys within the space during the iteration. In addition, the research team surveyed the stakeholder group identified in discussions with Melbourne City Council. Throughout the 12-month period we met regularly with a steering committee formed by the City of Melbourne to observe, inform and critique the approaches being advanced. The membership of this committee included City of Melbourne staff, and representatives from Hosier Inc, the Salvation Army street teams, Youth projects, Victorian Police and other stakeholders as appropriate to the issues raised and discussed.

The Artworks: Incubation

> [...] ghostly voices lost in the 'scriptural economy' (de Certeau 1984: 95). Contemporary communal identity is often only a simulacrum of the identities which briefly interconnect

and leave a palimpsest of assemblage. The dispersed or fragmented nature of this assemblage is held in stasis and referred to as 'diversity'. However, a diversity, which diversifies continually, as a component in the process of fluid engagement in social spaces, cannot be maintained as the atrophied simulacrum of communal identity.

(Cittadini 2013)

In his work *Community Ghosting*, performance artist Ben Cittadini took to the laneways, inviting members of the general public to fill in survey forms to register an odour, a daydream, their positioning in the space of the city, or to make a declaration of infinity, something that would last forever. With an A-frame sign inviting the public to participate, Cittadini traversed the laneway. People engaged by revealing the climatic conditions during their daydream, where they had been throughout the day, whether they had detected an odour in the laneway, and if so, how they would rate and describe it, and even what they thought would last forever, with life, god and family featuring regularly. Cittadini used the written surveys and his interpretive observations to develop a series of diagrams, charts

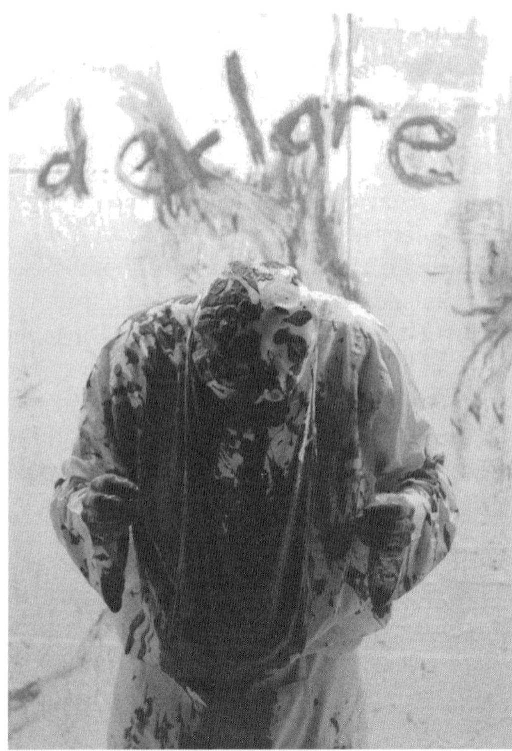

Figure 1: Ben Cittadini, *Community Ghosting*. Image: Chris Parkinson, 2013.

and tables that created an engaging reporting-back mechanism, which ultimately inspired a performative response. Cittadini proposed that we challenge the laneway by painting it. Wearing a culturally non-specific white outfit with a personal microphone Cittadini invited people to graffiti with him, to paint the space white. He had no takers, but continued chatting to the incidental passers-by via his microphone.

At sunset, a smoke machine and a fluorescent light added ambience to the space. Was it a disco? Was it a shrine? What was he creating? A sound work and a trance-like performance unfolded, reflecting the gestures of street artists, of people questioning the space, of a figure seeking enlightenment perhaps. Red paint dripped onto Cittadini from above and what one passer-by had likened to a Yoko Ono work, as it was unfolding, appeared to another passer-by to be a reflection on the killing of a young soldier on a street in the English town of Bradford that had made headlines some weeks earlier (see Figure 1).

Cittadini's work evoked a breadth of reaction that was unexpected and even insightful. A critical point was reached when a group of young people wandered into the lane mid-performance. This group was known for its destructive and aggressive effect in the laneways. With varied degrees of intoxication the group members engaged with Cittadini's work, a few of them gathered around: 'Was he famous?' Quickly word spread among the dozen or so that he could be famous? 'Was he ok? Did he need help?' Two boys stepped in and out of the performance, in a kind of choreographed response: 'Did he know how to tag?' They could show him if he wanted. Cittadini wrote on the back wall of the alcove in red paint 'I declare…': 'Was that his tag? Does he even know how to do it?' As the performance ended the group gathered together and stumbled through the lane; that night they had not threatened anyone; had not smashed anything; they were captivated and became active participants in the work. Responding to his work, Ben Cittadini wrote:

From within the threadbare pocket at the back of the Forum I imagine the ghost of spectacle appearing in a theatrical cloud of smoke to stage the terrible realities of our visual cultures: our slovenly desire for the eye to comprehend the image. I imagine a bloodied hand waving in every lens and a masked face synthesizing the fear and titillation of the transgressive other, raising the stakes of the spectacle. Paint is made flesh in the eye of the iPhone. Through the hysterical repetition of the image we are haunted by our present.

(Cittadini 2013)

The act of painting the alcove revealed the potency of re-inscription. Conjuring the ghost of spectacle the curators and artists then resolved to paint the whole laneway. Noted street artist, Adrian Doyle had been working with Dulux paints to develop his own colour, a blue that was sickly and represented to him the lack of attainability of the great Australian dream family: a quarter-acre block, house, Hills Hoist clothes line and suburban contentment. Doyle called the colour 'Empty-Nursery Blue'. He wanted to bring a fine art process of painting into a street-art context, to allow the colour to define the laneway, if only momentarily. It was also defining his identity. On a sunny Sunday morning we cordoned off the space and

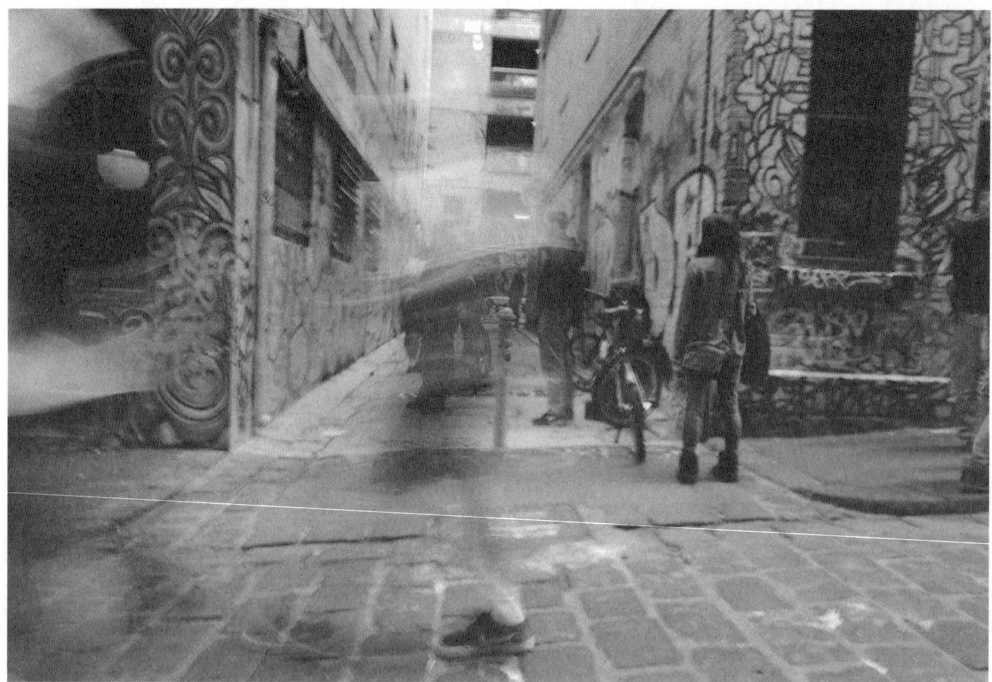

Figure 2: Adrian Doyle, *Empty Nursery Blue*. Image: Pia Johnson, 2013.

with two paint guns, multiple rollers and brushes, and a scissor lift, Doyle's work unfolded in Rutledge Lane. It was a logistical challenge, an epic marathon-like, performative, painting installation. The ground and the walls glowed to second storey level, shifting the atmosphere in the laneway. By lunchtime we received a text to say we were trending on a blog site in Bristol, an internationally significant street-art city.

People gathered at either entrance of the lane to catch a glimpse of what we were doing, to take photos and talk about what was unfolding before them (see Figure 2). As we neared the end of the lane, already we could hear the sound of paint cans being readied to make marks on the newly pristine walls. This was an incidental installation, in that it had not been promoted and we had not released any media statements in the lead-up time. What transpired over the following days and weeks was a significant debate about who has the right to paint this public space, and in what circumstances; and more often, what was this work about? A site for activating the imagination, and for activating questions of regulation and ownership, had been created well beyond the physical limits of the laneway.

[…] in addition to its material intervention, Empty Nursery Blue can be understood as an intimate exploration of the experience of place. Doyle invoked his own personal and family history with the choice of colour, immersing viewers in a space mediated through the artwork.

(Hillary and Sumartojo 2014: 208)

The temporary nature of the work also marked a point in the site's history, helping to reveal ways of understanding and inhabiting our cities, including how such places might affect our perceptions of ourselves in city spaces. Reactions to the work framed Empty Nursery Blue as part of a wider set of concepts that apply to our shared urban environment: materiality, bodily experience, time and urban change.

Every day, the laneway was filled with people curious to experience this environment for themselves and ask others about it. The project was listed by ArtsHub, Australia's foremost arts news website, as one of the top ten projects talked about that year of 2013. Blogs, face-to-face debate, media flurry, discussion and debate unfolded. It made way for Hosier Inc., the residents' committee, to push forward a proposal, in a relationship with the National Gallery of Victoria, to paint the lane black and curate street artists for the duration of *Melbourne Now*, an extensive survey of contemporary art in Melbourne (2014). This evidenced the subtle incorporation of street art into an institutionally endorsed position, shifting the laneway space from a site of illegal inscription to a gallery site for street art.

Hosier and Rutledge Lanes function as a spectacle: there, street artists work in broad daylight, with the time to develop their practice. This was very evident in Blue as people gathered to watch the installation and to comment on or re-inscribe the space afterwards. Through his work Doyle engaged young street artists and the broader community in a dialogue about the intention and form of what can now be painted in Rutledge Lane, or indeed any other urban space. As anthropologist and curator Rafael Schacter reminds us, 'Graffiti can provide proof that cities are places of public dialogue and heterogeneity'.

(Hillary and Sumartojo 2014: 214)

Doyle's work 'Empty Nursery Blue' created discussion about the laneway in multiple forums; it also created further opportunity for artistic work and a united voice within Hosier Inc. In a written response to the work, Shanti Sumartojo citing Bishop (2012: 26) addresses the impact of the work:

Exploring the space through the suite of works developed by the *Urban Laboratory* aroused public curiosity. Blue brought to the surface tensions between the disparate user groups frequenting the laneway and publicized these via word of mouth, media and social networks. The public debate provided an opportunity to explore the competing rights to the city in a live and unfolding performance of its own, invoking Bishop's argument that 'unease, discomfort or frustration, along with fear, contradiction, exhilaration and absurdity can be crucial to any work's artistic impact'.

(Hillary and Sumartojo 2014: 214)

Clare McCracken's work was the final artistic project in the incubation phase of the research. McCracken is interested in female experience of space, particularly in the male-dominated environment that in her perception characterizes many street-art sites. She investigated the public realm via a series of walks from her home in inner Melbourne, documenting the activity of the laneway with drawings. McCracken explained her sources from Charles Baudelaire, who in mid-nineteenth-century Paris 'felt the traditional arts were inadequate when it came to expressing and engaging with the complications of his rapidly industrialising city'. She explained how 'Baudelaire argued that artists should immerse themselves in the metropolis and become a botanist of the sidewalk, and that the tool for this was the character of the *flâneur*, who experienced the city by strolling through it' (McCracken 2013).

Invoking Baudelaire's *flâneur*, and Zeno's paradox of Achilles and the tortoise, McCracken's encountered the space of the city as a dandy, endangered, Australian turtle—embodying the theoretical frameworks as metaphors. Zeno's paradox assisted McCracken's performance as she asked people in the lane to help her determine the beginning and end of her walk, and then re-routed her turtle-paced performance according to this advice, investigating the critical role of the body in how we describe, measure and experience space. McCracken became a slow-moving, female figure, in a male-dominated space, engaging community members through conversation and encounter, and thereby echoing the performative nature of the space.

To explore other responses to what is safe and unsafe in the city, McCracken commissioned a taxi driver, Wazza to locate this endangered, Australian turtle. The only instruction to Wazza was that she would be in the 'least safe place' in the city. Wazza recorded his journey with an audio recorder. The recordings of his singing suggested he had found the correct day job as a taxi driver, but Wazza did not find the endangered turtle. He focused his journey around other parts of the city that he perceived to be more dangerous. Upon reflection, McCracken deduced that as a taxi driver he was viewing the world from a private space, albeit a mobile one, rather than the public space inhabited by the turtle. If this be so, it would raise more questions about how we encounter safety in the divide between public and private spaces. True to intention, McCracken's performance was specifically gendered, engaging women often seen as marginalized in street-art cultures.

Together, the incubation artists, Cittadini, Doyle and McCracken created a strong site analysis, providing a wealth of experience and material on which to base the iteration phase. Artists and researchers deliberated on the experiences to this point in a debrief/prebrief process that ushered in Ceri Hann and Yandell Walton as the artists charged with responding to the experiences of the incubation.

The Artworks: Iteration

Ceri Hann created a suite of characters representing different public roles. Armed with props Hann explored the laneways from the perspective of the characters he adopted, and through his performance he encouraged the public to ask questions. The characters engaged everyone in the laneway for the duration of each performance. One character, Safety Man, measured the health and wellbeing of the artworks. Using tweezers, stethoscope and smiley faced stickers, Hann encouraged people to question the artwork and its preservation or destruction; he explored who might be the stakeholders and how we 'brand' space. A contemporary Ned Kelly character, with a helmet constructed from discarded everyday street signs was wearing camouflage and high-visibility clothing (see Figure 3). Hann questioned the iconography of terrorism and invoked the use of 'Gesture-tech'—aerosol for the nose, a eucalyptus spray as an alternative to intoxicating aerosol paints. In an urban dance, Icon Man created some of the most aromatic works. Surveillance Man wore armour of concave security mirrors and discarded CCTV cameras, using them as a means to explore the laneway and question physical safety. Surveillance Man tested how people reacted to watching themselves reflected in the imagery of the laneway:

'What are you doing?'

'This lane reflects the city, I am just reflecting the laneway, so you can be seen to be seeing yourself in it. Do you feel safer being able to watch yourself being watched? Listening to yourself being listened to is a lot more boring. Ultimately my name is blank, but I'm sure my real crisis is an identity that is tracked by a phone that is smarter than me.'

(Hann 2013)

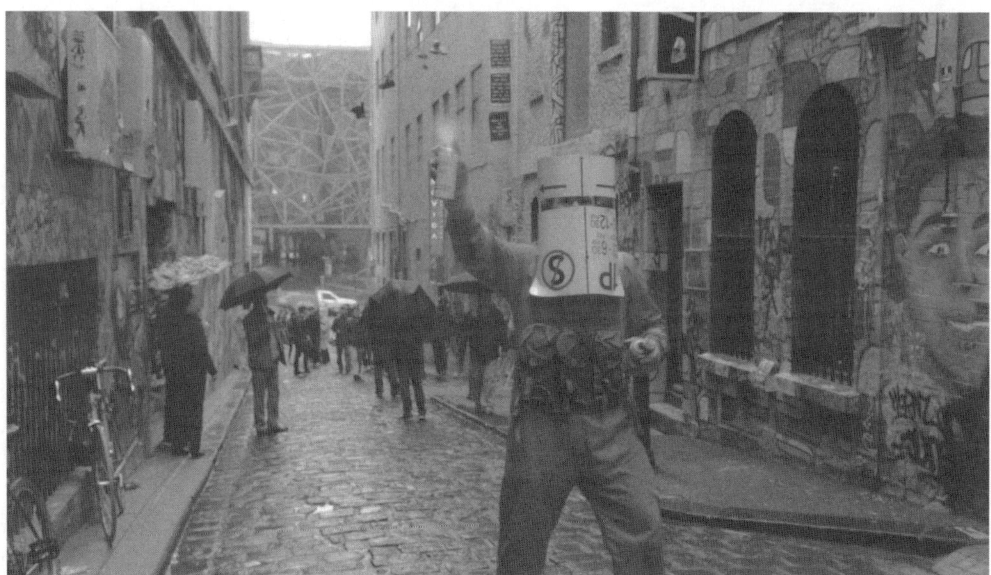

Figure 3: Ceri Hann, 'Gesture-tech'. Image: Fiona Hillary, 2013.

Surveillance Man along with Art Dealer Man became the most photographed of the works, appearing in group-tourist photos that will inevitably travel the world to inhabit a range of photo storage devices, with the potential to be reviewed well into the future. Art Dealer Man probed the worth of art and questioned the role of the public in and of the gallery in public space. Dressed in Armani attire, a chunky oversized $2 coin hanging on a gold chain around his neck, Art Dealer Man gave away tissue currency and became a blank canvas asking people to paint him with high-visibility colours. Art Dealer Man's performance concluded with him stumbling around the Lane, blinded by a white cube on his head, which represented the traditional 'gallery'. In this blinded state he walked repeatedly into the wall. This performance spoke of the shifting value of street art, focusing on its redefining as a marketable 'art form'. Through its collection by art dealers and gallerists, street art is thus shifting its very nature from an active site of social and political intervention to that of commodity.

The final work, by Yandell Walton, investigated the concept of absence and impermanence as a feature of the city. Her work, *Transition,* was a salute to the space as the artists and researchers experience it. The work captured the attention of the everyday person engaging in the laneway by creating an ethereal projection of oversized silhouetted figures onto Hosier Lane (see Figure 4). Setting up her studio in Rutledge Lane over a few weeks,

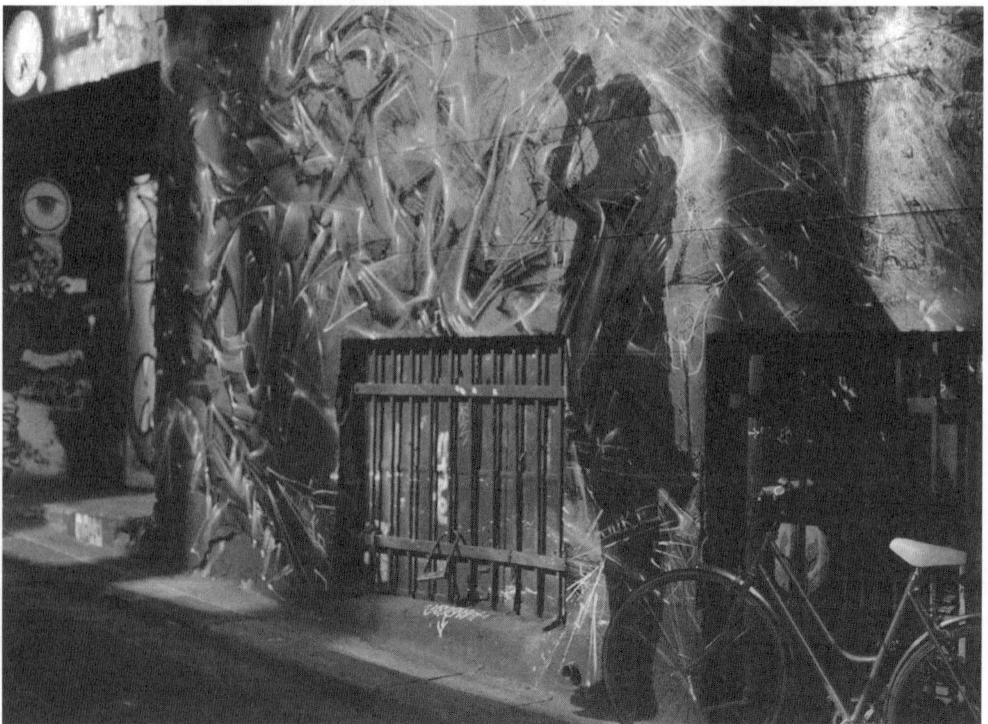

Figure 4: Yandell Walton, *Transition.* Image: Lauren Dunn, 2013.

thereby mirroring the public practice of the street artists in the laneway, Walton exposed the methodology behind her practice in a raw, open and honest manner. It was as if she were giving something to the space and the people in it, while with her lens capturing the gesture of the street artist, the movement of the tourists and the character of the space itself.

The realization of the projection piece captivated the passers-by. Watching as they explored the laneway to find out who was casting the shadows, some questioned if they were indeed their own shadows. Most then captured a photo of themselves within the work. This engagement allowed people to explore the laneway in a refreshed manner, in that it created a sense of enchantment as Bennett describes it: 'people transfixed, spellbound momentarily' then looking for the source of the projection (Bennett 2001: 5). *Transition* encouraged people to talk to each other, to ask a stranger to take a photo of them in the work. A sense of enchantment allowed people to re-imagine their presence, when they gathered, when they communicated; the space became more active, giving the general public permission to explore the environs. In doing so, there was in action the creation of a safer place.

Conclusion

So what did this durational framework and set of experiences reveal about perceptions and experiences of safety in an active and contested part of the City of Melbourne? Through embedded ethnography of onsite observations, interviews and surveys, the emergence of a series of discoveries was in evidence.

The major safety issues evident in our research pertain to the mixed use of the space, and safety, as it relates to engagement between diverse communities who occupy the area. The level of violent crime in this space documented by Victoria Police and the Salvation Army Street Teams is not, in fact, considered high when compared to other similar spaces in the city. Cittadini's work *Community Ghosting* most strikingly engaged the young people identified by residents as 'troublemakers'; the atmosphere and spontaneity of this engagement was critical. This group of young people has not been attracted to programmed events, but is more likely to engage in something different or unexpected occurring in the laneway. 'Empty Nursery Blue' forged alliances among sometimes-disparate voices, bringing to the fore points of conflict that were debated and argued in online forums and publications long after the physical events had concluded. McCracken's work predominantly engaged women, providing an opportunity to explore the translation of physical presence in public spaces. Hann playfully invited the general public to consider critical issues in shared spaces, from introducing 'Gesture-tech', a healthy alternative to aerosols, to instigating critical debate about the role of art in public spaces. Families, artists and young people became the subject of Walton's work, by engaging and reflecting on the diverse nature of user groups in the laneways.

In summary, key findings of the research focused on the diversity of the space and its user groups. The research found that acts of embracing this diversity and creating an inclusive curatorial framework are critical to the success of such projects. In evidence were ever-present issues around how inner city redevelopment impacts a space, for example the introduction of scaffolding and gantries that make buildings scalable, and the interruption to the flow and accessibility of spaces.

The research team made recommendations to the City: that Melbourne City Council implement a percentage-for-art scheme to enable future developments in the space for socially engaged art projects to effectively minimize the impact of the development itself. The impact of weather in the space deserves consideration as people use the space differently according to the time of the year. Thus we recommended seasonal programming as a way of effectively engaging the site and maximizing this use. We considered it was important to draw attention to the toxicity of aerosols and the need for community education, as there was a potential for the area to be filled with toxic fumes which have associated health risks. Furthermore, we noted the importance of fostering dialogue among universities, local government and communities to strengthen shared knowledge.

From this project, we are confident of the importance of the activation of spaces as a positive way to enhance perceptions of safety. Provocation via art practice provides a healthy platform for public debate. We recognize the heterogeneity of the category 'youth' and reflect on incidental engagement as a means of supporting young people's adoption of the space. Finally we recognize Hosier and Rutledge Lanes and their geographic placement in a key part of the city, and encourage connections within the broader cultural hub including Federation Square, Melbourne's premier open space, and its associated galleries and institutions.

Public art has long been recognized as a site of cultural reflection on and in space. It is a referenced medium for place-makers to create a sense of locality for a new development or an area experiencing renewal. It has been identified as a method to deliver or at least usher in changes in government policy. Increasingly, researchers understand and value the capacity of art in public space to shift behaviour. In their recent publication, 'Art as a means to disrupt routine use of space', Martin, Dalton and Nikolopoulou (2013) draw on research that recognizes the capacity of art to shift the way people view themselves and others in public spaces. The research available via the *Urban Laboratory* reflects three of the issues those writers identify as critical to changing both perceptions and experiences of community safety through public art. Firstly, the creation of social atmospheres encourages people to behave differently in public spaces. Secondly, art's capacity for acknowledging the sense of ambiguity makes people think differently and heightens their awareness of themselves. And thirdly is the art's capacity for playfulness and the way this enables a shift in the way people interact in the space (Martin, Dalton and Nikolopoulou 2013).

The *Urban Laboratory* research methodology provided the framework for spatial nuances to emerge. This approach also enabled reflective works to engage user groups in active consideration of the issues associated with the laneways. As Hillary and Sumartojo (2014: 216) observe: 'as laneway user groups were invited to participate in and experience a suite of incidental works, reactions to the art were part of a larger process of unpacking the multiple meanings of the space'.

The *Urban Laboratory* provided a platform via art to explore what safety meant to the user groups in Hosier Lane and Rutledge Lane. This platform was achieved by creating a live-testing ground for art practice and its participatory role as a research methodology for onsite investigation and analysis. The research from *Urban Laboratory* reveals the ways in which people approach art in public space, and the inherent characteristics and capacity of such art to make people feel safer in public space. It is not just the fact of art's presence in public space that may enhance public safety, but it is more: art facilitates a ground for engagement that challenges conventions of identity and conditions of behaviour.

References

Bennett, J. (2001), *The Enchantment of Modern Life*, Princeton: Princeton University Press.

Bishop, C. (2012), *Artificial Hells: Participatory art and the politics of spectatorship*, London: Verso.

Certeau, M. de (1984), *The Practice of Everyday Life*, (trans. S. Rendall), Berkeley: University of California Press. (First published in French 1980.)

Cittadini, B. (2013), 'Urban Laboratory Artist's Notes', *Urban Laboratory Report*, unpublished.

City of Melbourne (2015), 'City of Melbourne Profile: City of Melbourne', <http://www.melbourne.vic.gov.au/AboutMelbourne/MelbourneProfile/Pages/CityofMelbourneprofile.aspx>. Accessed 24 June 2015.

—— (2014), 'Beyond the Safe City Strategy', Melbourne: City of Melbourne.

Doherty, C. (ed.) (2015), *Out of Time, Out of Place: Public art (now)*, London: Art / Books.

Francis, J., Giles-Corti, B., Wood, L. and Knuiman, M. (2012), 'Creating Sense of Community: The role of public space', *Journal of Environmental Psychology*, 32: 4, pp. 401–409.

Hann, C. (2013), 'Urban Laboratory Artist's Notes', *Urban Laboratory Report*, unpublished.

Hillary, F. and Hogg, G. (2013), *Urban Laboratory Report*, unpublished.

Hillary, F. and Sumartojo, S. (2014), 'Empty-Nursery Blue: On atmosphere, meaning and methodology in Melbourne street art', *Public Art Dialogue*, 4: 2, pp. 201–220.

Lonely Planet (2015), 'Hosier Lane', *Lonely Planet*, <http://www.lonelyplanet.com/australia/melbourne/sights/neighbourhoods-villages/hosier-lane>. Accessed 24 June 2015.

Mair, J. and Duffy, M. (2014), '4 Festivals and Sense of Community in Places of Transition', in A. Jepson and A. Clarke (eds), *Exploring Community Festivals and Events*, London and New York: Routledge, pp. 54–65.

Martin, K., Dalton, B. and Nikolopoulou, M. (2013), 'Art as a Means to Disrupt Routine Use of Space', *Journal of Police and Criminal Psychology*, 28: 2, pp. 139–149.

McCracken, C. (2013), 'Urban Laboratory Artist's Notes', *Urban Laboratory Report*, unpublished.

Young, A. (2014), 'Cities in the City: Street art, enchantment, and the urban commons', *Law & Literature*, 26: 2, pp. 145–161.

Section III

Pedagogical City

Chapter 8

Writing transparadiso: Across and beside

Jane Rendell

Introduction

transparadiso, comprising architect-trained artist Barbara Holub and architect/urban designer Paul Rajakovics, based in Vienna, but working internationally, have, over the past 10–15 years, produced a complex assembly of artefacts and events—art installations, performance pieces, videoworks, urban interventions, master plans, design competition entries and completed works of architecture and urban design—often with other professionals, clients, planners, user groups and urban citizens.

In the text that follows, in the spirit of my site-writing practice (Rendell 2010), I attempt to write transparadiso. In so doing I pick up on many of the dominant moods and modes of their operation—two of them evident in their name that includes the prepositions: *trans*—across and *para*—beside. My intention is to write across and beside the different facets of their methodology that continually experiment with combining attitudes to urbanism held by art, architecture and planning: always critical, astute and questioning, but also playful. Acknowledging the importance of threes in understandings of transitional space and transversality in the work of D. W. Winnicott, André Green and Félix Guattari, the text is trivalent: the first two texts are placed beside or 'para' to one another, positioning the voice of a theorist/philosopher in parallel with that of a practitioner;[1] my own voice comes in as a third, writing across the space of relation between the other two. The three voices are distinct and do not attempt to define or explain each other, rather they allow for different associations and connections to be made by the reader.

Transitional Space

This potential space is at the interplay between there being nothing but me and there being objects and phenomena outside omnipotent control. [...] I have tried to draw attention to the importance both in theory and in practice of a third area, that of play which expands into creative living and into the whole cultural life of man. This third area has been contrasted with inner or personal psychic reality and with the actual world in which the individual lives and which can be objectively perceived.

(Winnicott 1967)[2]

Jemandsland 1997/2011: In 1997 Paul Rajakovics was invited by ACMA Milano to lead an architecture workshop in Gorizia (Italy) on the issue of the border. Together with his students he collected drawings of the residents of Gorizia and Nova Gorica (Slovenia) as a response to three questions on the future of the two cities. The visions turned out to be quite traumatic so that he decided to continue to work on the project, but with young people. One year later he returned with his partners (Bernd Vlay and Margarethe Müller) to Gorizia and continued the project spremembazione. *In a casting party four young Italians and four young Slovenians were invited to show their favourite places. As the final event,* spremembazione *managed to remove the border at the Piazzale della Transalpina in front of the train station. For the duration of a cross-border badminton game the video camera was placed on a pedestal replacing the fence. On 1 May 2004, the EU-border was lifted as Slovenia joined the EU. The fence in front of the train station was removed and a circle was placed there instead. Over time, flower pots were added, installing a new barrier...*

The focus of the theory of object relations created and developed by the Independent British Analysts is the unconscious relationship that exists between a subject and his/her objects, both internally and externally (Kohon 1986: 20).[3] In continuing to explore the internal world of the subject, their work can be thought of as a continuation of Sigmund Freud's research, but there are also important differences, particularly in the way that the instincts are conceptualized and the relative importance assigned to the mother and father in the development of the infant. Exploring the concept of an object relation to describe how bodily drives satisfy their need, Freud theorized the instincts as pleasure-seeking, but Ronald Fairbairn, an influential member of the Independent Group, suggested instead that they were object-seeking, that the libido is not primarily aimed at pleasure but at making relationships with others. For Melanie Klein too, objects play a decisive role in the development of a subject and can be either part-objects, like the breast, or whole-objects, like the mother. But whereas for Freud, it is the relationship with the father that retrospectively determines the relationship with the mother, for Klein, it is the experience of separation from the first object, the breast that determines all later experiences.[4]

Following on and also developing aspects of Klein's work, D. W. Winnicott introduced the idea of a transitional object, related to, but distinct from, both the external object, the mother's breast, and the internal object, the introjected breast. For Winnicott, the transitional object or the original 'not-me' possession stands for the breast or first object, but the use of symbolism implies the child's ability to make a distinction between fantasy and fact, between internal and external objects (Winnicott 1953: 89, 94; 1969: 711–716; 1991). This ability to keep inner and outer realities separate yet inter-related results in an intermediate area of experience, the 'potential space', which Winnicott claimed is retained and later in life contributes to the intensity of cultural experiences around art and religion. Winnicott discussed cultural experience as located in the 'potential space' between 'the individual and the environment (originally the object)'. In Winnicott's terms, for the baby this is the place between the 'subjective object and the object objectively perceived' (Winnicott 1967: 371).

Paramedics

In German, the word *Klinik* signifies a hospital for inpatients. The term is derived from the Greek word *klinein*, which means 'lying down'. What in English is called 'clinic' is in German designated as *Ambulatorium*, which is derived from the Latin *ambulare*, 'to walk around'.

(Danto 1998: 287–300)

On Invitation Only: *The* Indikatormobil *is a flexible tool for operations in the urban context situated between urban and artistic interventions—a tool for 'Direct Urbanism'. It offers the possibility to include tactile aspects of urban planning into urban planning and urban design transgressing conventional genres. The* Indikatormobil *operates upon request or invitation as well as taking the initiative to trace urban 'emergencies' and to develop interventions according to the specific context. Parallel to transparadiso's exhibition at the MAK, Vienna, transparadiso held a MAK nite: they invited special guests to a dinner 'on invitation only' in the main hall of the MAK. The non-invited regular visitors of the MAK nite were guided to the courtyard, where the* Indikatormobil *parked. In that very cold night the guests outside were offered a Russian soup (borschtsch) and hot wine, and they were welcomed by 'Asyl in Not', an organisation taking care of immigrants seeking asylum. A live-video-conference between the main hall of the MAK and the* Indikatormobil *in the courtyard enabled communication between the selected dinner guests inside and the other guests outside.*

Leading figures for the Austrian Social Democrats, such as Victor Adler and Otto Bauer, put forward proposals for a project of economic and social regeneration, combining culture and politics in a new way. In Vienna, where the Social Democrats had the majority between 1918 and 1934, psychoanalysis played a key role in the process of radical reform, which aimed to create an urban environment that responded to the needs of children and workers' families (Danto 1998: 287–300). In 1918, in his speech in Budapest, and in other speeches and writings, Freud had sanctioned the development of free, psychoanalytic, out-patient clinics, including the Poliklinik in Berlin, which opened in 1920, and the Ambulatorium in Vienna, which opened in 1922 (Kadyrov 2005: 467–482), to which he gave moral and financial support (Danto 1998: 287–300).

Wilhelm Reich, an Austrian 'Freudo-Marxist' and key member of the Vienna clinic in the 1920s, was radicalized by the experience, and in his subsequent work considered social conditions to have an influence on neurosis. He later aimed to make psychoanalysis more accessible by 'setting up free clinics throughout Vienna, even turning the back of a van into a mobile clinic that he would take into working class neighborhoods, dispensing therapeutic advice about emotional problems along with a political message about how sexual misery and family breakdown posed the need for socialism' (Brenner 1999). This practice of mobile psychoanalysis, where help is offered point to point from a moving vehicle, offers a psychic equivalent to the paramedic who comes to the site of the medical emergency equipped to give aid, and reminds me of Gilles Deleuze's comments concerning how theory can be used like a tool.

In a fascinating conversation between philosophers Deleuze and Michel Foucault that took place in 1972, Deleuze reveals quite directly, though certainly abstractly, how he comprehends a 'new relation between theory and practice'. Rather than understanding practice as an application of theory or as the inspiration for theory, Deleuze suggests that these 'new relationships appear more fragmentary and partial' (Foucault and Deleuze 1977: 205), and discusses their relationship in terms of what he calls 'relays': 'Practice is a set of relays from one theoretical point to another, and theory is a relay from one practice to another. No theory can develop without eventually encountering a wall, and practice is necessary for piercing this wall' (1977: 206). For Deleuze, theory is 'not for itself': 'A theory is exactly like a box of tools. […] It must be useful. It must function. And not for itself. If no one uses it, beginning with the theoretician himself (who then ceases to be a theoretician), then the theory is worthless or the moment is inappropriate' (1977: 208). Deleuze notes that in its encounter with 'obstacles, walls and blockages', theory requires transformation into another discourse, presumably practice, to 'eventually pass to a different domain' (Deleuze 1977: 206).

It is this possibility of transformation—the potential for change following the relay from theory to practice and back again—that interests me. transparadiso, like many conceptual artists before them, are practitioners highly versed in theoretical discourse, but they do not see themselves as 'theoreticians'; however, in reflecting critically upon the procedures they employ and the ideological questions raised by a close attention to methodology, to practice after conceptualism is to perform a kind of theory. The practice of transparadiso offers them a kind of theoretical 'tool kit'—arriving on site they are prepared to provide 'help' in a given situation—offering space and time for tricky issues to be aired, and inviting questions to be played out and tested in different domains. It is not the way of transparadiso to put forward immediate quick-fix solutions to long-term problems. Instead their process is more like the slow and fluctuating process of psychoanalysis with all its loops, blockages, dead-ends and detours, involving conversations that might start casually in the 'back of a van', yet provide strategies that work their way towards the future over a much longer term, sometimes with intended consequences, at other times unexpected and surprising.

Transference

The analytic object is neither internal (to the analysand or to the analyst), nor external (to either the one or the other), but is situated between the two. So it corresponds precisely to Winnicott's definition of the transitional object and to its location in the intermediate area of potential space, the space of 'overlap' demarcated by the analytic setting.

(Green 1978: 180)

Commons come to Liezen: *Liezen's town park was previously and is still today an orchard serving as a common. A pavilion was erected there that functions first of all as a storage space for large-scale tangram pieces. The pieces were sold as a limited edition of art objects and as part of a collective work of art. As they were sold, the pavilion emptied out. The proceeds went directly back to Liezen and to the local population, and were earmarked for events which took place in the pavilion. Months before the pavilion was built, transparadiso invited the public to play tangram. While people were playing, they could discuss vital topics concerning the city and its future* (see Figures 1 and 2).

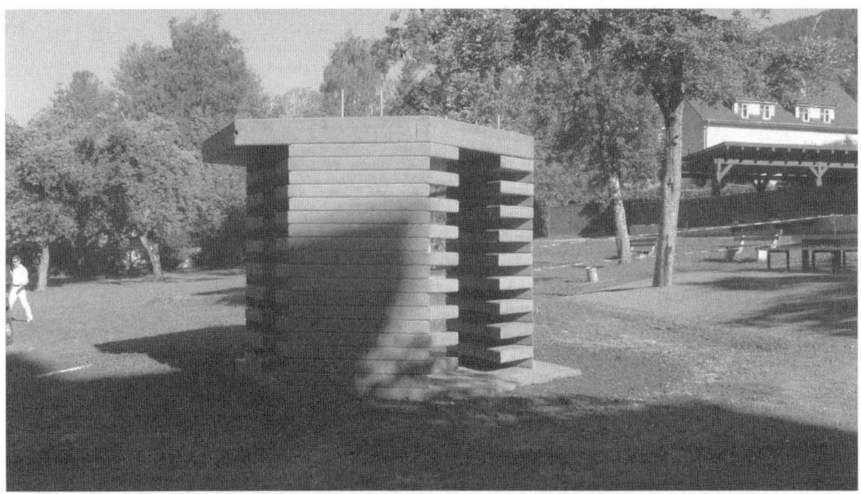

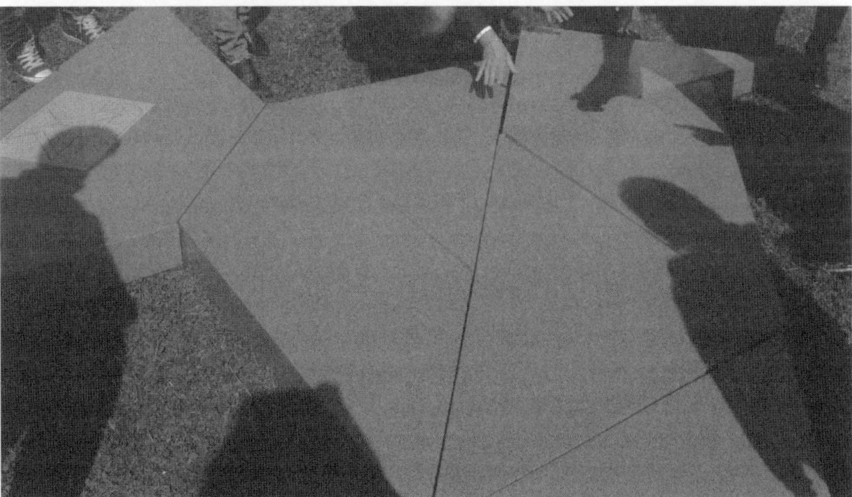

Figures 1 and 2: transparadiso, *Commons come to Liezen*, 2011. Images: transparadiso, 1992.

The 'setting' is a term used to describe the conditions within which the psychoanalytic encounter occurs. Following Freud, these conditions include 'arrangements' about time and money, as well as 'certain ceremonials' governing the physical positions of analysand (lying on a couch and speaking) and analyst (sitting behind the analysand on a chair and listening) (Freud 1958: 126, 133). Coined by Winnicott, 'as the sum of all the details of management that are more or less accepted by all psychoanalysts' (Nissin Momigliano 1992: 33–34), the term has been modified by others. In the work of José Bleger the setting comprises both the process of psychoanalysis, and the non-process or frame, which provides a set of constants, or limits, to the 'behaviours' that occur within it (Bleger 1967: 518). And in terms of its spatial configuration, Jean Laplanche considers the setting to be a double-walled tub (Laplanche 1999: 226),[5] and for André Green it is a casing or casket that holds the 'jewel' of the psychoanalytic process (Green 2005: 33).[6]

Green has drawn attention to the setting not as a static tableau, but as a psychoanalytic apparatus, not as a representation of psychic structure, but as an expression of it. For Green, the position of the consulting room between inside and outside relates to its function as a transitional space between analyst and analysand, as does its typology as a closed space that is different from both inner and outer worlds, 'The consulting room [...] is different from the outside space, and it is different, from what we can imagine, from inner space. It has a specificity of its own' (Kohon 1999: 29).[7] In Green's work the setting is a 'homologue' for what he calls the third element in analysis, the 'analytic object', which is formed through the analytic association between analyst and analysand (Green 1975: 12), at the point of interaction between transference and counter-transference, which according to Green corresponds to Winnicott's definition of the transitional object located in the intermediate area of potential space—that of play.

*Para*textuality

More than a boundary or a sealed border, the paratext is, rather, a *threshold,* or [...] a 'vestibule' that offers the world at large the possibility of either stepping inside or turning back. It is an 'undefined zone' between the inside and the outside, a zone without any hard or fast boundary on either the inward side (turned toward the text) or the outward side (turned toward the world's discourse about the text), an edge [...].

(Genette 1997a: 1–2)

Uitzicht Op!: *The public periscope* Uitzicht Op *was originally installed for the Blue House in Amsterdam-IJburg in 2009. IJburg is a series of five islands currently being constructed in the East of Amsterdam, in its final state creating a link to Almere. The pioneer spirit of gaining land from the sea was accompanied by the aim to create a high standard of living, yet being based on a conventional urban design [...]. From 2005–9 this new urban development was accompanied by the Blue House, to which Jeanne van Heeswijk invited other artists and people from various professional backgrounds to deal with the complex issues of how to construct an urban living form from scratch in a huge new urban development, addressing the shortcomings and discrepancies between vision and reality. transparadiso focused on the consequences of urban planning, especially the promise of a view of the IJmer as one of the most significant assets of this new urban development and its geographical location. But for many residents this view was a temporary privilege, because the view continuously disappeared with the completion of IJburg [...]. The periscope was made publicly accessible by the owners of a private roof terrace, for the duration of the project.*

In the early pages of *Palimpsests* in 1982, Genette redefines transtextuality as the subject of poetics (Genette 1997b: 1), and extends his system of transtextualities into a five-part schema: intertextuality—a relation of co-presence between two or more texts or (in Genette more literally than in Kristeva) the actual presence of one text within another, through, for example quotes, plagiarism, allusion; paratextuality—comprising those liminal devices and conventions, both within the book (peritext) and outside it (epitext), that mediate the book to the reader, for example, its title, subtitle, prefaces, postfaces, forewords, notes, blurbs, book covers, dust jackets; metatextuality—the transtextual relationship that links a commentary to 'the text it comments upon (without necessarily citing it)'; hypertextuality—the superimposition of a later text on an earlier one, in other words, a relationship relating text b (hypertext) to an earlier text a (hypotext); and architextuality (or architexture) (Genette 1997b: 1–7).

According to Richard Macksey, the 'topology' explored by Genette in *Paratexts* is one of the 'borderland', between the text and the 'outside' to which it relates (Macksey 1997: xiv–xv). For Macksey, Genette's notion of the paratext is neither on the interior nor on the exterior, neither container or contained, but is an undecideable space: 'it is on the threshold; and it is on this very site that we must study it, because essentially, *perhaps its being depends upon its site*' (Macksey 1997: xvii).

Transformations

Préposer: to put somebody in a position to carry out a function by giving them the means or the authority to fulfil it. The term *préposé* in French may refer to an agent or clerk, and is commonly used to refer to a postman. When messengers are commissioned to transport messages through message-bearing systems, they require some means of transport: Hermes and the myriad angels travel on wings; the postman carries his bicycle—or is it the other way around? [...] *Préposés:* They don't change in themselves, but they change everything around them, words, things and people.

(Serres 1995: 139, 140–146)[8]

Deseo Urbano: *In Valparaiso transparadiso presented* deseo urbano, *an urban game, which used the dynamics of games like 'trivial pursuit'. The public sites where the games were played (cafés, parks, restaurants, community centres) were announced in local papers, by postcards and posters. As well as these public events the game was played with the MINVU (Ministry for Housing and Urban Planning) of the 5th region of Chile. Playing the game with these diverse participants, their passion and active involvement allowed for a reconsideration of the conventional practice of urban design and opened up the possibilities of negotiation with the planning authorities. The players noted their wishes and desires on postcards, which were presented to Daniel Sepulveda, the director of the MINVU. The resulting questions and wishes served as a starting point for moving towards developing a diversified planning process.*

The figure of the angel features strongly in the intellectual project of Michel Serres. Truly transdisciplinary, Serres travels across science, literature, philosophy and art, constantly interrogating in the most poetic fashion, the nature of knowledge itself. In earlier texts this operates implicitly through the figure of the guide and the messenger. In the *Hermes* texts I–V (1969–1980) the fascination is with information theory, transport and the multiplication of messages through diverse spaces of communication (Serres 1984, 1981, 1980, 1974, 1972). Later in *The Troubadour of Knowledge* (1991), in a discussion of the passage between the exact sciences and sciences of man, Serres refers to the importance of points of exchange and conditions of passage (Serres 1997). But in a more recent publication, *Angels: A Modern Myth*, his interest in angels is far more explicit. This text is a narrative, of sorts, set up as a conversation between two characters whose lives are based around an airport—one is a pilot, the other a doctor at the airport.

Serres' interest in angels concerns their threshold condition and occupation of a passage between. But although his work also highlights the angelic condition as temporal and spatial, his real emphasis is on communication, mediation and transformation as a result of exchange. Serres suggests that there are certain places where messages from angels increase in number and intensity; he calls these 'passing places of angels'; they are spaces of transition or interchange, such as airports, places of mass transit and new technologies. Serres emphasizes the unstable nature of angels and their dual role as verbal messengers and elemental fluxes, but perhaps the most interesting thing Serres has to say about angels is that they are the personification of prepositions. Prepositions make connections between people, objects and places; some emphasize position, others focus on relations, and yet others, the directional nature of relations. Following Serres, it is possible to rethink the connections between objects, people and places in terms of transformation. Like prepositions, objects can suggest a number of different narratives about their histories and by indicating new future uses have the potential to change things around them. As gifts, in challenging capitalist notions of profit and ownership, objects also have an important role to play as mediators, bridging the private worlds of separate individuals. As toys, in encouraging play and speculation, animate objects mediate between real and imaginary, allowing for the invention of new possibilities and imaginary scenarios, often through games.

Paradox

I shall not first give a historical survey and show the development of my ideas from the theories of others, because my mind does not work that way. What happens is that I gather this and that, here and there, settle down to clinical experience, from my own theories and then last of all interest myself in looking to see where I stole what. Perhaps this is as good a method as any.

(Winnicott 1945: 137)

Sites as Set: *As one element of the larger project* Sites as Set, The Magic Panorama *with the sea as an empty centre visualises the tension between enforced development and staged standstill, typical for tourist areas like Rovinj: the coastline, the horizon of the sea and its mythical borders—Rovinj and Muca—form a circle of a magic panorama. 3 dots, A, B, C (Hypermarket/Supermarket/X-Change) set the coastline under tension: different speeds, as well as programmes of non-determined extension (CLOUDS), initiated on specific spots, generate a hyperactive beachzone, a dense parcours of enhanced use-value: together with PARA-SITE (zone for possible micro-economies) which contaminates the housing-area, the PARA-COURS builds those spaces of surplus value that undermine dominant developments without hindering their flux.*

One of the more serious failings of so-called public art has been to do precisely what Winnicott in the first quote above says that he cannot do: go directly from a to b—not 'gathering' this and that on the way and not trusting the process of 'settling down' to experience. Linear processes, which do not allow for the seemingly wasteful time of 'gathering' and 'settling down', have often produced public spaces and objects that approach problems rather directly with the aim of providing solutions and offering answers to questions. If there is such a practice as public art, and that in itself is debatable, then shouldn't public art be engaged instead in the production of restless objects and spaces, ones that provoke us, that refuse to give up their meanings easily but instead demand that we question the very formation of the problems that we are presented with as givens?

A client's brief is often driven by the need for an 'application', which might make it less usual for a designer to be encouraged to make a 'problematic' object or a design that critiques the context of an application and to take seriously the construction of critique as a reasonable design outcome. Indeed such an approach—to work against the aim of the brief, or to oppose the expressed desire of the client—might seem paradoxical if one is in the mindset of characterizing design as the provision of an artefact made to 'solve' a problem. Yet, transparadiso's practice suggests that by operating in a more critical mode, urban practitioners can create projects that put forward questions as the central tenet of the research, instead of (or sometimes as well as) solving or resolving problems, they expand the concept of the object from a singular artefact to a setting or situation that may of course include actual things, but more importantly through which it is possible to fundamentally rethink the parameters of the problem itself.

Here the role of the unrealized project becomes important. Competition entries provide important sites for working through ideas and concepts, and for questioning the parameters of a problem, and the institutions that frame and endorse such problems—in particular in architecture and planning.[9] There is a long history of architects producing their most innovative work as so-called paper architecture. Yet the relationship constructed between the imagined and real is far more complex than built and unbuilt, since some so-called paper projects hope to be built, while others set themselves up as unbuildable; as well as a third type that often uses normative representational codes, and appears to describe an intended physical construction, while in fact questioning the assumptions implicit in architectural discourse concerning what we consider appropriate and buildable. The sites of exhibition and publishing are therefore essential to the practice of urbanism in providing places to explore the critical and conceptual potential of architectural design and planning.

I have argued that such projects, which critically intervene in the sites into which they are inserted as well as the disciplinary procedures through which they operate, can be called 'critical spatial practice' (Rendell 2006, 2003: 221–233).[10] Drawing on the work of Michael de Certeau and Henri Lefebvre, I distinguish between those strategies that aim to maintain and reinforce existing social and spatial orders, and those tactics that seek to critique and question them. I extend the definition of the term 'critical', from Frankfurt School of critical theory, to encompass practice—particularly those critical practices that involved self-reflection and the desire for social change: that seek to transform rather than to only describe (Rendell 2006).

The directness that the term 'intervention' suggests might relate to the practice of 'direct urbanism', put forward by transparadiso as a third mode of urbanism, along with design and planning. Yet although transparadiso's way of working is direct in that it is a form of action on the ground, it is not a type of interruption or breakage; instead their practice is a point from which to start out, and so offers a sense of trajectory with an as-yet-undetermined potential. Not wishing to follow the most obvious and logically efficient route from A to B, transparadiso's 'desire lines' seek out and make time for the gathering of this and that, here and there, along the way, thus raising important issues concerning temporality for critical spatial practice.

Typically, critical interventions are considered to be short term, especially those that operate following the 'shock' principle of montage, where new insertions into existing sites produce immediate juxtapositions displacing dominant meanings and interrupting particular contexts, but the experience of an intervention might also be a pause from which one can draw out more subtle ambiguities over time. When instigated as part of the much longer process of urban design and planning, an apparently small situation might be taken up again, later, but in an alternative way in a new context, so connecting different temporalities—the short- and the long-term as well as all the times between—hinting at how a temporary intervention might—along the way—turn the present towards the future as well as the past.

Reflecting on the work of art-architecture, collaborative muf critic Kath Shonfield posed the following questions and observations:

> How do you develop a city-wide strategy when you are fascinated by the detail of things? And how can you make something small-scale in the here and now if you are driven by the urge to formulate strategic proposals for the future? In a sense, this conundrum has always presented itself to the architect-planner [...] It is in this context that I want to start to look at some of the implications of muf's work that could be considered a possible paradigm for the operations of the architecture-planner [...] muf's work [...] develops the particular to the general and back to the particular [...]. It is expressed in the formula d/s = DETAIL/STRATEGY.
>
> (Shonfield 2001: 14)

Shonfield's analysis of muf's working processes is absolutely spot-on, yet the tendency of the alternative urbanisms that emerged in the 1990s, especially in the UK where muf are located, was to frame such micro-macro interactions through the spatial turn, as my own term 'critical spatial practice' also indicates. However, it has become increasingly clear that the tactics and strategies—ambulant, instant, insurgent, DIY and direct—of this current phase of urbanism are highly sophisticated in their approach to time. And this is where, or perhaps I should say when, transparadiso set the tone for a nuanced exploration of the temporality of urban interventions, the need for both the fleeting event and the patience born of waiting for that proposition that might occur in a far-distant future. transparadiso's urban practice enjoys the reciprocity of micro and macro times—the moments and the mullings—and the opportunities they offer each other: where fleeting insights can be gathered, to return to Winnicott, to activate much slower evolutions, while within a long-term framework even a tiny incident can have resonance.

Transversality

> Transversality in the group is a dimension opposite and complementary to the structures that generate pyramidal hierarchisation and sterile ways of transmitting messages.
>
> Transversality is the unconscious source of action in the group, going beyond the objective laws on which it is based, carrying the group's desire.
>
> (Guattari 1984: 22)

Lichtventilator, Resonanzboden, Vogerlbad: *transparadiso were commissioned to develop a design for the extended corridor zone of the hospice in the concrete-lined trench planned for a biotope [...] A 'light fan' throws patches of light onto the floor that can be gradually altered by the individual control of the vanes as if sunlight were streaming through a canopy of leaves—and yet the object concerned is a lamp. The trench is filled with a slightly sunken Iroko parquet floor, and it is transformed into an echo chamber by bass shakers. Seating with an integrated stereo grows out of this, from where one can observe the birds in a specially conceived birdbath in the adjacent atrium. If one turns one's gaze back inside, a feint drawing is to be seen on the rear wall of the extended living room, showing the outlines of patches of light similar to those projected onto the floor.*

In both academic and arts-based contexts, the term 'interdisciplinarity' is often used interchangeably with multidisciplinarity, but I have argued that the two terms mean quite different things. In my view, multidisciplinarity describes a way of working where a number of disciplines are present but maintain their own distinct identities and ways of doing things, whereas in interdisciplinarity individuals operate between, across and at the edge of their disciplines and in so doing question the ways in which they usually work (Rendell 2006). In exploring questions of method or process that discussions of interdisciplinarity inevitably bring to the fore, Julia Kristeva has argued for the construction of 'a diagonal axis', and noted that 'interdisciplinarity is always a site where expressions of resistance are latent' (Kristeva 1997: 5–6), while Homi Bhabha has also described interdisciplinarity in psychoanalytic terms as an 'ambivalent movement between pedagogical and performative address' (Bhabha 1994: 163).[11]

It is precisely because of the presence of unconscious processes that I am a passionate advocate of interdisciplinarity; for me interdisciplinary work is difficult, not only because it is critical, ethical and political, but also because it is emotional, and as such raises issues that are material and intellectual, but also psychic. In demanding that we exchange what we know for what we do not know, and that we give up the safety of competence and specialism for the fear of inability and the associated dangers of failure, the transformational experience of interdisciplinary work produces a potentially destabilizing engagement with existing power structures, allowing the emergence of fragile and uncertain forms of new and untested experience, knowledge and understanding.

If interdisciplinarity is concerned with working between the gaps in order to question the edge of a discipline, transdisciplinarity is often described as a horizontal movement, concerned with moving across, transversally. Derived from the Latin preposition 'trans', meaning 'across, to or on the farther side of, beyond, over', the term can be used to give the sense of 'across, through, over, to or on the other side of, beyond, outside of, from one place, person, thing, or state to another'.[12] In Gary Genosko's excellent book on Félix Guattari, he describes how for Guattari, the interdisciplinarity (of 1968) was compromised; it relied too much on the disciplines between which it was located, and served to strengthen rather than question their dominance. For Guattari, it is transdisciplinarity that holds the potential of radical critique, related, in his own philosophy, to 'transversality [...] explicitly a creature of the middle' (Genosko 2002: 60), where the 'trans' is capable of transversal actions, which, in cutting across existing territories of knowledge, allows them to be experienced differently, thus providing new positions and perspectives.

Guattari, in his essay of 1964, 'The Transference', notes that 'in the transference there is virtually never any actual dual relation' (Guattari 1996: 63). He argues that dual relations are always triangular in character, noting that 'there is always in a real situation a mediating object that acts as an ambiguous support or medium' (Guattari 1996: 63). As Genosko notes, Guattari relies to a certain extent both on Winnicott's notion of the transitional object and potential space between mother and child as a third entity, but also Jacques Lacan's *object a*, as that which provokes the institution's desire. As Genosko puts it, for Guattari 'it is with the triangle and threes that micropolitics begins' (Genosko 2003: 132). According to Genosko, a key early question for Guattari concerns what becomes of transference in the institutional setting of the hospital, and it is transversality that for him provides the possibility of critiquing the 'institutional context, its constraints, organisation, practices, etc., all those things and relations which normally exist in the background' (Genosko 2002: 71).

With transparadiso we have a practice that desires to transform and is itself transformative, hoping to transform—through engagement—the situations and subjects it encounters—but not leaving the challenging task of change to others, instead also seeking to continuously transform itself in response to its own processes and products, folding ongoing self-reflection and institutional critique into the process of making urban work. transparadiso is both transdisciplinary and transversal. Moving across art, architecture and urbanism, transparadiso call into question institutional structures and the ways in which they become manifest at the crossings between different disciplinary contexts, and rather than back away from a stoppage, they turn blockages into interesting opportunities and places for imaginative play.

*Parad*ise

First there are the utopias. Utopias are sites with no real place. They are sites that have a general relation of direct or inverted analogy with the real space of society. They present society itself in a perfected form, or else society turned upside down, but in any case these utopias are fundamentally unreal spaces. [...] There are also, probably in every culture, in every civilisation, real places—places that do exist and that are formed in the very founding of society—which are something like counter-sites, a kind of effectively enacted utopia in which the real sites, all the other real sites that can be found within the culture, are simultaneously represented, contested, and inverted. Places of this kind are outside of all places, even though it may be possible to indicate their location in reality. Because these places are absolutely different from all the sites that they reflect and speak about, I shall call them, in contrast to utopias, heterotopias. I believe that between utopias and these quite other sites, these heterotopias, there might be a sort of mixed, joint experience, which would be the mirror.

(Foucault 1984)[13]

Stadt: Werk: Lehen: *An association was founded in order to realise the backbone and parallel strategy of transparadiso's concept for this new quarter: to create an urban boulevard which will offer a public life not just for this housing area but also for the adjacent areas of public housing and the whole district of Salzburg-Lehen. Therefore a special concept was developed with subsidised ground floor areas dedicated to establish public uses along the boulevard as a mixture of NGOs and community uses (Volkshochschule/adult education centre, kindergarten, studio building, café, boulder centre) and cultural institutions (Gallery of the City of Salzburg and Fotohof Gallery) (see Figures 3 and 4).*

For Michel Foucault, the sealed and self-contained world of the garden could be described as a 'heterotopia'—a place with a different ordering system. Yet unlike paradise, the 'no place' of the perfect world depicted by utopia, the unique logic of the garden also has a physical location. Paradise gardens have a spiritual rather than a pragmatic function—they are places removed from the everyday—sanctuaries often used for reflection. While the Japanese dry garden forms a symbolic analogue to nature, the rugs of the Middle East follow the sanctity of water in dry lands and depict walled gardens with dancing fountains at their centre, exemplified in the design of religious architectural complexes, such as those built in Seville, Granada and Córdoba. In the west we have tended to separate the productive use of irrigated land for farming and agriculture, from the contemplation of nature in its various romantic forms, the untamed sublime of the wild and its domesticated and more comforting picturesque equivalent.

In some traditional separations of art and architecture, similar distinctions have been made, between architecture located on the side of the functional and productive, and art positioned in the place of the decorative and contemplative. Yet the work of transparadiso does not accept these divisions and normative ordering devices; instead, they seek to produce projects that multiply the possibilities of exchange across the border between art and architecture, working on multiple scales from the single object and detail of one instance among many through to much more complex urban situations and unfolding developments. By placing the disciplines side by side and performing double and sometimes triple roles—as artist, architect, and client—transparadiso repeatedly change standpoints. With the shift in attitude that comes from adopting an unexpected position, they ask more of a discipline than one would expect. As well they demand that we face up to social issues, but not necessarily directly, sometimes instead making hidden things visible by playing situations at their own game.

* * * *

Swinging: A videowork by Barbara Holub provides me with a concluding motif, a figure or emblem that occurs and then reoccurs through transparadiso's practice: a girl swings into and away from the camera, moving back and forth, now near, then far, but always, and forever, moving *across*.

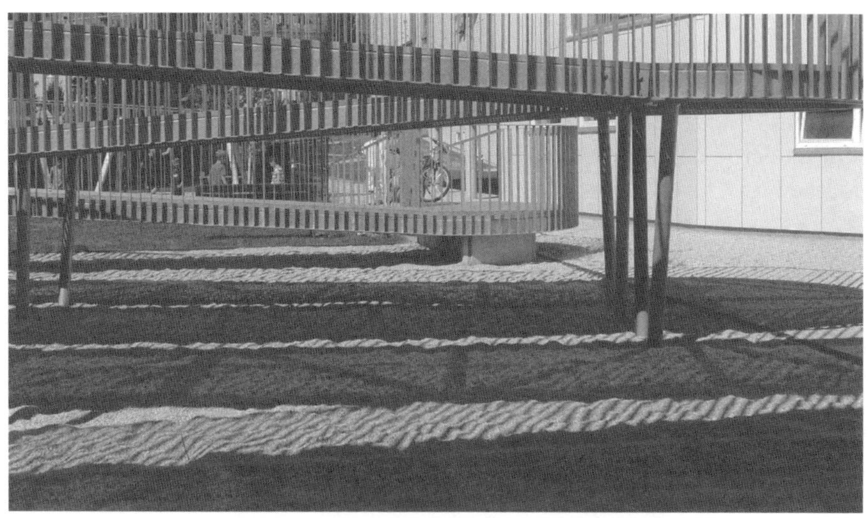

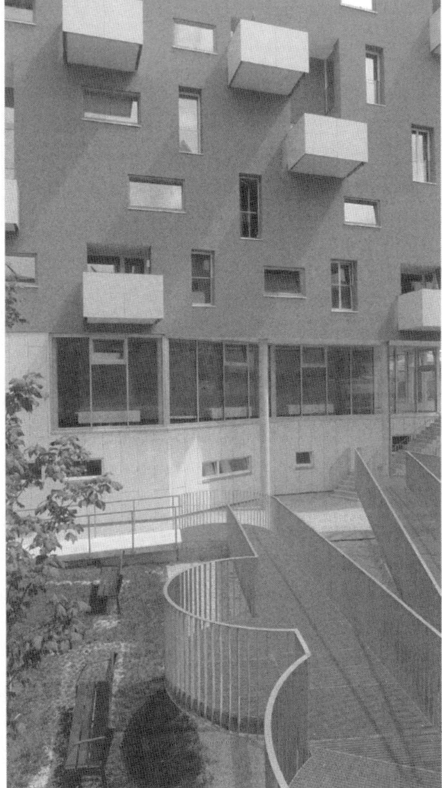

Figures 3 and 4: transparadiso, *Stadt: Werk: Lehen*, 2006–11. Images: transparadiso, 1992.

Acknowledgements

This essay was first published in transparadiso's practice monograph: Rendell, Jane (2013), 'Writing transparadiso: Across and Beside', transparadiso, *Direct Urbanism*, Nürnberg: Verlag für moderne Kunst. (German/English). Many thanks to transparadiso and to Verlag für moderne Kunst for allowing it to be republished in this collection.

References

Bhabha, H. K. (1994), *The Location of Culture*, London: Routledge.

Bleger, J. (1967), 'Psycho-Analysis of the Psycho-Analytic Frame', *The International Journal of Psycho-Analysis*, 48, pp. 511–519.

Brenner, F. (1999), 'Intrepid Thought: Psychoanalysis in the Soviet Union', International Committee of the Fourth International (ICFI), World Socialist Website, <https://www.wsws.org/en/articles/1999/06/freu-j11.html>. Accessed 2 November 2015.

Danto, E. A. (1998), 'The Ambulatorium: Freud's Free Clinic in Vienna', *The International Journal of Psycho-Analysis*, 79, pp. 287–300.

Foucault, M. (1984), 'Of Other Spaces: Utopias and heterotopias', (trans. Jay Miskowiec), *Architecture, Mouvement, Continuité*, 5, pp. 46–49, <http://web.mit.edu/allanmc/www/foucault1.pdf>. Accessed 4 November 2015. (First published in French 1967.)

Foucault, M. and Deleuze, G. (1977), 'Intellectuals and Power: A conversation between Michel Foucault and Gilles Deleuze', in Donald F. Bouchard (ed.), *Language, Counter-memory, Practice: Selected essays and interviews*, New York: Ithaca, pp. 205–217.

Freud, S. (1958), 'On Beginning the Treatment (Further Recommendations on the Technique of Psycho-Analysis I)', *The Standard Edition of the Complete Psychological Works of Sigmund Freud, Volume XII (1911–1913): The case of Schreber, papers on technique and other works*, (translated from German under the general editorship of James Strachey), London: The Hogarth Press, pp. 121–144, 126, 133. (First published in German 1913.)

Genette, G. (1997a), *Paratexts: Thresholds of interpretation*, (trans. Jane E. Lewin), Cambridge: Cambridge University Press, pp. 1–2. (First published in French 1987.)

—— (1997b), *Palimpsests: Literature in the second degree*, (trans. Channa Newman and Claude Doubinsky), Lincoln: University of Nebraska Press. (First published in French 1982.)

Genosko, G. (2002), *Félix Guattari: An aberrant introduction*, London: Continuum.

—— (2003), 'Félix Guattari', *Angelaki: Journal of the Theoretical Humanities*, 8: 1, pp. 129–140.

Green, A. (2005), *Key Ideas for a Contemporary Psychoanalysis: Misrecognition and recognition of the unconscious*, London: Routledge.

—— (1978), 'Potential Space in Psychoanalysis: The object in the setting', in Simon A. Grolnick and Leonard Barkin (eds), *Between Reality and Fantasy: Transitional objects and phenomena*, New York and London: Jason Aronson Inc., pp. 169–189.

—— (1975), 'The Analyst, Symbolization and Absence in the Analytic Setting (On Changes in Analytic Practice and Analytic Experience)—In Memory of D. W. Winnicott', *The International Journal of Psycho-Analysis*, 56, pp. 1–22.

Guattari, F. (1996), 'The Transference', in Gary Genosko (ed.), *The Guattari Reader,* Oxford: Blackwell Publishers Ltd., pp. 61–68. (First published in French 1964.)

—— (1984), 'Transversality', in Félix Guattari, *Molecular Revolution: Psychiatry and politics,* (trans. Rosemary Sheed), Harmondsworth: Penguin Books Ltd., pp. 11–23. (First published in French 1964.)

Hill, J. (1998), *The Illegal Architect,* London: Black Dog Publishing.

Kadyrov, I. M. (2005), 'Analytical Space and Work in Russia: Some remarks on past and present', *The International Journal of Psycho-Analysis,* 86, part 2, pp. 467–482.

Klein, M. (1988), 'Notes on Some Schizoid Mechanisms', in M. Klein, *Envy and Gratitude and Other Worlds 1946–1963,* London: Virago, pp. 1–24. (First published in German 1946.)

—— (1981), *Love, Guilt and Reparation and Other Works 1921–1945,* London: The Hogarth Press and the Institute of Psycho-Analysis.

Kohon, G. (ed.) (1999), *The Dead Mother: The work of André Green,* London: Routledge, published in association with the Institute of Psycho-Analysis.

—— (ed.) (1986), *The British School of Psychoanalysis: The independent tradition,* London: Free Association Books.

Kristeva, J. (1997), 'Institutional Interdisciplinarity in Theory and Practice: An interview', in Alex Coles and Alexia Defert (eds), *The Anxiety of Interdisciplinarity, De-, Dis-, Ex-,* v.2, London: Blackdog Publishing, pp. 3–21.

Laplanche, J. (1999), 'Transference: Its provocation by the analyst', *Essays on Otherness,* (trans. Luke Thurston, ed. John Fletcher), London: Routledge, pp. 214–233. (First published in French 1992.)

Macksey, R. (1997), 'Foreword', in G. Genette, *Paratexts: Thresholds of interpretation,* (trans. Jane E. Lewin), Cambridge: Cambridge University Press, pp. xi–xxii.

Mitchell, W. J. T. (1995), 'Translator Translated', (interview with cultural theorist Homi Bhabha), *Artforum,* 33: 7, pp. 80–84.

Nissin Momigliano, L. (1992), 'The Analytic Setting: A theme with variations', in *Continuity and Change in Psychoanalysis: Letters from Milan,* London and New York: Karnac Books, 1992, pp. 33–61.

Rendell, J. (2013), 'Writing transparadiso: Across and beside', transparadiso, *Direct Urbanism,* Nürnberg: Verlag für moderne Kunst (German/English).

—— (2010), *Site-Writing: The architecture of art criticism,* London: I.B. Tauris.

—— (2006), *Art and Architecture: A place between,* London: I.B. Tauris.

—— (2003), 'A Place Between Art, Architecture and Critical Theory', in *Proceedings to Place and Location,* Tallinn, Estonia, pp. 221–233.

Serres, M. (1997), *The Troubadour of Knowledge,* (trans. Sheila Faria Gloser and William Paulson), Ann Arbor: University of Michigan Press. (First published in French 1991.)

—— (1995), *Angels: A Modern Myth,* Paris: Flammarion.

—— (1984), *Hermès* Vol 1: *La Communication,* Paris: Editions de Minuit. (First published in French 1969.)

—— (1981), *Hermès* Vol 4: *La Distribution,* Paris: Editions de Minuit. (First published in French 1977.)

—— (1980), *Hermès.* Vol 5: *Le Passage du nord-ouest,* Paris: Editions de Minuit.

———— (1974), *Hermès* Vol 3: *La Traduction*, Paris: Editions de Minuit.

———— (1972), *Hermès* Vol 2: *L'Interférence*, Paris: Editions de Minuit.

Shonfield, K. (2001), 'Premature Gratification and Other Pleasures', in muf, *This Is What We Do: A muf manual*, London: Ellipsis, pp. 14–23.

Winnicott, D. W. (1991), *Playing and Reality*, London: Routledge.

———— (1969), 'The Use of an Object', *The International Journal of Psycho-Analysis*, 50, pp. 711–716.

———— (1967), 'The Location of Cultural Experience', *The International Journal of Psycho-Analysis*, 48, pp. 368–372.

———— (1953), 'Transitional Objects and Transitional Phenomena', *International Journal of Psychoanalysis*, 34, pp. 89–97.

———— (1945), 'Primitive Emotional Development', *The International Journal of Psycho-Analysis*, 26, pp. 137–143.

Notes

1 All quotes in italics come from the words of transparadiso themselves, and previously published or included in unpublished but written project descriptions.

2 Republished in Winnicott (1991).

3 The British School of Psychoanalysis consists of psychoanalysts belonging to the British Psycho-Analytical Society; within this society are three groups, the Kleinian Group, the 'B' Group (followers of Anna Freud) and the Independent Group.

4 Klein describes the early stages of childhood development in terms of different 'positions'. The paranoid schizophrenic position characterizes the child's state of one-ness with the mother, where he or she relates to part-objects such as the mother's breast, as either good or bad, satisfying or frustrating (see Klein 1988). This position is replaced by a depressive stage where in recognizing its own identity and that of the mother as a whole person, the child feels guilty for the previous aggression inflicted on the mother (see Klein 1981).

5 The French term used is 'baquet' (Laplanche 1999: 226, note).

6 The French word used is 'écrin' (Green 2005: 33, note).

7 'Dialogues with André Green', in Kohon (1999: 29).

8 Serres refers to Jacques Tati (1908–82), *Jour de Fete*, on p. 139, and then pp. 140–146.

9 See, for example, Hill (1998).

10 I first introduced the term 'critical spatial practice' in my article (2003), 'A Place Between Art, Architecture and Critical Theory', and later consolidated and developed the concept in my book (2006), *Art and Architecture: A place between*. Since that time, the same term has been taken up by individuals such as Judith Rugg in her seminars at the RIBA, London, from around 2008; Eyal Weisman to describe activities as part of the 'MA: Research Architecture' at Goldsmiths College of Art, London; and most recently by Marcus Miessen to identify the 'MA: Architecture and Critical Spatial Practice' launched in 2011 at the Städelschule, Frankfurt.

11 In an interview with English and art historian W. J. T. Mitchell, cultural critic Homi Bhabha discusses the operation of two different forms of interdisciplinarity in academic institutions

over the last 30 to 40 years. The first, which he names 'Interdisciplinarity 1', assumes that different disciplines have 'foundational truths', but that by putting 'two foundations in proximity' a 'wider base' can be created. Bhabha believes the institutions are quite comfortable with Interdisciplinarity 1, but that there is another interdisciplinary mode, which he calls 'Interdisciplinarity 2'. For Bhabha, 'Interdisciplinarity 2 is not an attempt to strengthen one foundation by drawing from another; it is a reaction to the fact that we are living at the real border of our own disciplines, where some of the fundamental ideas of our discipline are being profoundly shaken'. In his view, 'questions to do with the indeterminate, with contingency, with intertextuality, have become central—the issue of ambivalence too', and that this is 'because Interdisciplinarity 2 is fired with a desire to understand more fully, and more problematically, that it's posed at the point of our disciplines' liminality' (Bhabha in Mitchell 1995).

12 <http://oed.com/view/Entry/204575?rskey=0uUZXL&result=2-eid> and <http://oed.com/view/Entry/204575?rskey=KjaYsa&result=2&isAdvanced=false-eid>. Accessed 1 June 2012.

13 This text, entitled 'Des Espace Autres' and published by the French journal *Architecture/Mouvement/Continuité* in October, 1984, was the basis of a lecture given by Michel Foucault in March 1967. Translated from the French by Jay Miskowiec. <http://www.opa-a2a.org/dissensus/wp-content/uploads/2008/03/foucault_michel_des_spaces_autres.pdf>. Accessed 30 May 2012.

Chapter 9

Raising Alterity: Working towards a just city

Elizabeth M. Grierson

Introduction: Raising alterity

[T]he thesis common to Levinas and Lyotard [...] holds that the interests of justice can only be served by raising alterity to a high point of principle, by maximizing the range of discursive or narrative differentials, and by seeking to dislodge the cognitive phrase-regime (or the subject-centred epistemology of knowledge and truth) from its position of unwarranted pre-eminence.

(Christopher Norris 1995: 33)

This chapter brings together the apparently disparate threads of aesthetics, justice and the city. To raise alterity in the interests of justice for a just city is the transformational task here. Questions surface. The social and political may be spoken through the epistemic authority of law, but where is justice situated? Crime may be answered via the procedural authority of punishment, but where is restoration situated? How to find answers for a just city, and learn from these answers, is the task of this discussion.

In raising alterity of the human subject to 'a high point of principle' (Norris 1995: 33), a sensibility and responsibility to law and justice becomes evident; likewise accentuating law's responsibility to the human subject. The alterity of aesthetics works as pedagogy: it teaches.

Alterity is defined as 'otherness: the quality or state of being radically alien to the conscious self or a particular cultural orientation' from *alter*, Latin, meaning 'other (of two)' (Merriam Webster online). So in this discussion it is *the other* that we seek: to recognize and accept *difference* in discourses of justice. In raising *difference* into recognition before the norms of law, the aim is to recognize the 'is-ness' specific to each participant in terms of his or her story: there the *other* will find the capacity for voice.

For victims and offenders, according to principles of Therapeutic Jurisprudence punishment goes hand-in-hand with healing. For public justice to be served victims of crime need acknowledgement of harm caused; and offenders need to own responsibility for harm. A Therapeutic Jurisprudence approach to law goes some way towards meeting these obligations. Narratives of aesthetics and difference hold relevance to this approach.

In light of these preoccupations, the following discussion sustains a hermeneutic enquiry into therapeutic and restorative approaches to law and justice for a just city. It focuses on urban court settings although the principles addressed here are trans-locatable. In this discussion aesthetic practices carry specific cultural significance.

Engaging the lenses of Emmanuel Levinas on alterity (Levinas 1999; Bergo 2015), and Jean-François Lyotard on legitimating micro-narratives of difference (Lyotard 1984), the discussion activates a series of narratives to evidence the potential for transformations of individuals and community. Each narrative highlights aesthetic-justice relationships in specific settings in Australia and New Zealand; and each narrative evidences pedagogic approaches to the city and to the self. Each proposes the raising of alterity via attention to aesthetic practices in a justice setting.

A basic tenet of justice is the right to be heard; and recognizing this right is a first step in the obligations of justice. Where alterity finds voice, there transforming powers of justice may supervene.

Justice and Therapeutic Jurisprudence (TJ)

In this discussion, 'justice', the descriptor 'just', and a 'Therapeutic Jurisprudence' approach to law call for clarification. Firstly, what does 'just' mean? By definition, to be just is to be fair, equitable, unbiased, unprejudiced, open-minded, non-discriminatory and non-partisan—values that underpin the normative ethics of distributive justice. Calling forth honesty, reasonableness, truth and fairness, Justice stands firm as one of the Cardinal Virtues, depicted by writers and artists for centuries. The Cardinal Virtues from Classical Antiquity (discussed by Plato in *The Republic* Book IV) coupled with the Christian Theological Virtues (via St Augustine), and their corresponding Vices are depicted by Florentine artist, Giotto in the 1305 *Cappella della Scrovegni*, Arena Chapel. On the South Wall, Justice, steadfast on her plinth, is accompanied by Hope, Charity, Faith, Temperance, Fortitude and Prudence; and opposite them, on the North Wall, the corresponding Vices. These grisaille sequences work to pedagogic effect teaching values to the local populace—those walking the stone-paved floors of the Arena Chapel in the fourteenth-century, city-state of Padua. The aesthetic depictions offered clear lessons on the ways one *ought* to act if one is to live a good, honest, wise, courageous, temperate, pious, productive and just life—as in Socrates' *eudaimonia*, *happiness for the good life*, for living collectively in a just city.

The question of justice and happiness is addressed in the Socratic dialogues of Plato's *Republic* (c. 380 BCE, 1959). Socrates speaks of justice, its definition and workings in the political community of a city-state, and the character of the just citizen. Socrates proposes the desirability of justice: if the city is just, the individuals will be happy and just. Moving from Plato's ideal city-state (excluding women, as not citizens; artists, as dealing with illusion not reality; and poets, as writing fiction not truth), how does law take account of difference for today's just city?

Therapeutic jurisprudence (TJ) is an approach to law, and a field of legal enquiry that seeks 'to minimize law's destructive effects' (Brookbanks 2015: 3). 'Jurisprudence' is the study of law, its theories, philosophies and applications; and 'therapeutic' signifies care or healing to achieve a state of wellbeing for *all* stakeholders in today's city-state. Brookbanks explains that

TJ 'grew out of the investigations of its founders, professors Bruce Winick and David Wexler, whose early work in mental health jurisprudence led them to investigate the antitherapeutic effects that law and legal processes commonly produce' (Brookbanks n.d.: online).

Law has the potential to act as a healing agent via TJ approaches. Full respect for different languages, cultural histories and perceptions—'other' to the dominant norm—hold relevance for therapeutic approaches to law. Yet law, to achieve regularity and certainty, may overlook 'the lesson that Hume tried to instill more than 200 years ago that "ought" cannot be deduced from "is"' (Freeman 2011: 40). What is the micro-narrative of this or that person 'standing before the law'? Principles of natural law say that every person *ought* to be treated the same, but what *is* this person's language, culture, family or economic circumstances?

Society comprises cultural differences; yet law as a normative regulatory system may refuse cultural difference an authentic voice. Abnegation may have deleterious effects. However, disavowal does not always and only reside on the side of law. There is a deficit when the person before a court lacks the cultural knowledge or confidence to claim an authentic speaking position. Relevantly, New Zealand Judge Heemi Taumaunu (Ngāti Porou, Ngāi Tahu) states:

> It is a tragedy that most Māori youth who appear before the Youth Court have no knowledge of their own Māori language and have no idea of who they are and where they are from […], they exist in a vacuum, where the 'here and now' is all that matters. For these young Māori to have any sense of purpose in the future, they need to start by knowing where they have come from and who they are. It is difficult, if not impossible, for any Court to attempt to point young people in the right direction if they are without this knowledge.
>
> (Taumaunu 2012: 2)

This statement underpins the argument offered here—to find confidence in the legal system it is vital for people to have knowledge of, and respect for their own cultural and belief systems. Over the past two or three decades, TJ 'has become the descriptor of an approach to the discipline of law which, while preserving and upholding due process values, seeks to draw more "value" out of the law itself' (Brookbanks 2015: 4). The activation of aesthetics may assist in this quest—giving attention to cultural objects, images, stories, songs or rituals that have a significance to a 'user' of the justice system.

Application of a TJ approach to law encourages 'psychological wellbeing, procedural fairness, and access to justice' (Wexler 2015: xiii). In a TJ approach to criminal jurisdiction the offender is seen as subject rather than object of law, and is given voice in the process of a hearing and sentencing. While special problem-solving courts are set up to foster the TJ approach, such as indigenous courts, drug courts, mental health courts, children's court, youth and family justice courts, there is today increasing attention to 'mainstreaming' TJ in courts of general jurisdiction.

Activating Aesthetics

Justice Taumaunu's statement highlights how crucial it is to activate a participant's worldview. The proposition here is that this activation may occur through aesthetics in a solutions-focused approach. The discussion does not adopt an analytical lens on aesthetics: it is not the universal test or perception of beauty from German idealism, not disinterested judgement or taste, nor an attitude, purposive or teleological; neither is it an embodiment of the human spirit in progressive form. None of those analytical frameworks apply here.

Rather, it is aesthetics as a way of 'setting-forth' in Heidegger's terms (see Grierson 2015a), by activating stories, histories, places and times, and bringing them into a temporal relationship with other court participants and the court setting. Aesthetic stories, artworks or rituals, with particular resonance for a court participant, may enliven that person's sense of 'self'. Acknowledging and including cultural aesthetics may be a way of raising alterity—a voice from 'somewhere else' calling a person into the immediate presence of 'being there'—fully present at that place and time. When brought to a justice setting aesthetics may activate a transformative pedagogy, and understandings may grow regarding the matrix of rights and responsibilities—undeniably relevant for an individual and a just city.

At the end of his seminal text, *The Postmodern Condition*, Jean-François Lyotard urged: 'Let us wage war on totality [...] let us activate the differences' (Lyotard 1984: 82). Lyotard points to the metanarratives of western history as a culture's way of endorsing its totalizing truth claims, drowning out other languages, traditions and narratives. These metanarratives have their basis in the ethical values of reason, progress and the transcendental subject that legitimate western meaning-making—be they normative claims of knowledge, ethics or justice. Dominating metanarratives run like a river beneath the ground of western thinking and action. Their practices of re-legitimating their authority serve to de-legitimate alterity and efface difference.

Taking the term 'legitimation' from German sociologist Jürgen Habermas, whose work was concerned with a crisis of legitimation in the political realm (Bohman and Rehg 2014), Lyotard (1988, 1984) focuses on the tyranny of totalizing truth statements and processes of consensus that rest with systems of authority—obfuscating the very dominations that sustain them. Such authoritarian systems are predicated by the prioritization of rules of judgement in making appeal to the 'cognitive phrase' of logical reason. Lyotard made clear the necessity to 'maximize the range of discursive differentials [...] to avoid what he (like Foucault) regards as the "blackmail" of Enlightenment reason' (Norris 1995: 13). These authorizing systems underpin law as a system of justice, just as they drive institutional practices of education and government.

Lyotard's theories endorse the underpinning argument of this discussion that aesthetics may activate another way of legitimating meaning for the myriad of differences coalescing in the justice system. The challenge is to overcome totalizing truth claims, to find the justice of alterity, and the alterity of justice. By this micro-level activation there may be a collective effect at a macro level—and this may be beneficial for 'the just city'.

Otherness and the Law: Caring about justice in criminal jurisdiction

Part of the judicial oath is to do justice according to law, not to do law, but to do justice…
There's not much point in being a lawyer unless you care about justice.

The Honorable Marilyn Warren AC
Chief Justice of the Supreme Court of Victoria (2005)

The authorizing system of law has a history peppered with injustice aligning with histories of colonization. Today, in Australia and New Zealand there are continuing moves towards 'restoring effects' of the colonizing project, particular to Aboriginal and Māori peoples and cultures. But how may restoration manifest in the court system? There is a difference between 'the legal system as a system of norms and the legal system as a system of procedures' (Alexy, cited in Freeman 2011: 432). Procedures of law produce results, outcomes, which become norms of the legal system; and in this argument it is the procedural activities and approaches that are the focus, which in turn may change the norms of the system.

In this argument, caring about justice is about ensuring those out of power may have the necessary legal opportunity to exercise their individual rights and obligations on a par with the dominant group. Of 'restorative justice', leading proponent John Braithwaite said, 'because crime hurts, justice should heal. It follows that conversations with those who have been hurt and with those who have afflicted the harm must be central to the process' (Braithwaite 2004; Grierson 2015b).

Notwithstanding worthy sentiment, it should be noted that the term 'restorative' implies that there is something to go back to, something worthwhile to restore. Where does the potential for restoration lie? In her analysis of TJ in terms of colonized people and the law, Khylee Quince points to the 'interdependent relationship between a disrupted cultural identity, poverty and ongoing capability deprivation' as being 'complex and mutually reinforcing' (Quince 2015: 356). It is not about transforming one individual who fits the 'liberal myth of the rational individual actor with free will to choose to participate in offending behaviour' (Quince 2015: 357). Rather, it is about seeking a possible transformation or restoration within community. For Māori people, says Quince, 'This state of wellbeing is achieved through the operation of core values of communitarianism and co-operation' (Quince 2015: 357).

How do these values manifest in actual practices of the law? Group conferencing and victim-offender mediation play a significant role, but they do not necessarily dim the question of how to balance opposing forces. Following the need to emphasize community in restorative justice, the New Zealand Ministry of Justice defines restorative justice as:

[...] a process for resolving crime that focuses on redressing the harm experienced by victims, while also holding the offender to account for what they have done.

The process involves the victim and the offender coming face-to-face at a meeting called a restorative justice conference. This conference allows the victim to express how the offending has affected them, and allows all the people present to acknowledge the harm that has been caused.

(New Zealand Ministry of Justice)

The aim is to highlight shifts of emphasis in crime and punishment, from adversarialism and blame, as in traditional lawyering, to insights for responsibility, repair and reparation as in a TJ approach. The principle is for the offender to be an active and willing participant throughout, foregrounding respect for all parties. Quince refers to 'the desire to "whakahoki mauri"—to restore the life-force of the people involved; to rehabilitate their mana—their dignity, reputation and self-worth' (Quince 2015: 351). This process offers repair for the victim as much as for the offender—victims are full stakeholders in any system that is therapeutic, constructive or restorative.

The potential for transformation is present through these processes. In his work on 'journey to belonging' in criminal justice, Howard Zehr confirms that restorative justice is affirmative for both victim and offender in helping them 'transform their stories' (Zehr 2002: 29).

Transforming Stories: Sorry

It took until 2008 for the Australian Government to apologize officially and publicly to the Indigenous people of Australia, but apologize they eventually did. Why apologize? The Prime Minister of the day, Kevin Rudd, asked Parliament to reflect on the facts:

[T]hat, between 1910 and 1970, between 10 and 30 per cent of Indigenous children were forcibly taken from their mothers and fathers; that, as a result, up to 50,000 children were forcibly taken from their families; that this was the product of the deliberate, calculated policies of the state as reflected in the explicit powers given to them under statute; that this policy was taken to such extremes by some in administrative authority that the forced extractions of children of so-called 'mixed lineage' were seen as part of a broader policy of dealing with 'the problem of the Aboriginal population'.

One of the most notorious examples of this approach was from the Northern Territory Protector of Natives, who stated: 'Generally by the fifth and invariably by the sixth generation, all native characteristics of the Australian aborigine are eradicated. The problem of our half-castes'—to quote the Protector—'will quickly be eliminated by the complete disappearance of the black race, and the swift submergence of their progeny in the white' [...]

(Kevin Rudd 2008)

From the Federal Parliament, House of Representatives, Prime Minister Kevin Rudd's speech was broadcast across the nation. People gathered outside Parliament in Canberra— on Ngunnawal land—in public gatherings, before giant screens, televisions and radios, in city parks and streets, factories and offices, cafés and shops, schools and universities. A nation held its breath, everywhere, to listen to the 'Sorry Speech':

> *We apologise* for the laws and policies of successive Parliaments and governments that have inflicted profound grief, suffering and loss on these our fellow Australians. *We apologise* especially for the removal of Aboriginal and Torres Strait Islander children from their families, their communities and their country. For the pain, suffering and hurt of these stolen generations, their descendants and for their families left behind, *we say sorry*. To the mothers and the fathers, the brothers and the sisters, for the breaking up of families and communities, *we say sorry*. And for the indignity and degradation thus inflicted on a proud people and a proud culture, *we say sorry*.
>
> (Kevin Rudd 2008; emphasis added)

The apology was greeted with a wave of emotion across the nation. For so long Aboriginal parents and children of the 'Stolen Generation' had lived in pain and loss as they waited for the 'sorry' word from parliamentary leadership. 'There was, quite audibly, the exhalation of breath' from parliament's public gallery (Wright 2008).

Lending power to the formality of the occasion the Prime Minister told a personal story— of Nanna Nungala Fejo—just one story of tens of thousands of stories 'of forced separation of Aboriginal and Torres Strait Islander children from their mums and dads over the better part of a century' (Rudd 2008):[1]

> There is something terribly primal about these firsthand accounts. The pain is searing; it screams from the pages. The hurt, the humiliation, the degradation and the sheer brutality of the act of physically separating a mother from her children is a deep assault on our senses and on our most elemental humanity.
>
> (Rudd 2008)

These words were making direct appeal to the emotions of a nation as a restorative process writ large. In answer to the question, 'Why apologize?', Prime Minister Rudd recounted a story told to him by an 80-year old Aboriginal woman:

> Nanna Nungala Fejo [...] was born in the late 1920s. She remembers her earliest childhood days living with her family and her community in a bush camp just outside Tennant

Creek. She remembers the love and the warmth and the kinship of those days long ago, including traditional dancing around the camp fire at night. She loved the dancing. [...]

But then, sometime around 1932, when she was about four, she remembers the coming of the welfare men. Her family had feared that day and had dug holes in the creek bank where the children could run and hide. What they had not expected was that the white welfare men did not come alone. They brought a truck, two white men and an Aboriginal stockman on horseback cracking his stockwhip. The kids were found; they ran for their mothers, screaming, but they could not get away. They were herded and piled onto the back of the truck. Tears flowing, her mum tried clinging to the sides of the truck as her children were taken away to the Bungalow in Alice, all in the name of protection.

(Rudd 2008)

The story is palpable in its recounting of 'otherness', those cast into a dreadful alterity from which they are dragged into the confusion of a 'white man's world'. But more was to come in the name of Christianity:

A few years later, government policy changed. Now the children would be handed over to the missions to be cared for by the churches. But which church would care for them? The kids were simply told to line up in three lines. Nanna Fejo and her sisters stood in the middle line, her older brother and cousin on her left. Those on the left were told that they had become Catholics, those in the middle Methodists and those on the right Church of England. That is how the complex questions of post-reformation theology were resolved in the Australian outback in the 1930s. It was as crude as that. She and her sister were sent to a Methodist mission on Goulburn Island and then Croker Island. Her Catholic brother was sent to work at a cattle station and her cousin to a Catholic mission. [...]

Nanna Fejo never saw her mum again. After she left the mission, her brother let her know that her mum had died years before, a broken woman fretting for the children that had literally been ripped away from her.

(Rudd 2008)

Speaking to the hearts of the nation through this story, there could be no doubt about the gravity and dreadfulness of a shameful history. Here through the aesthetic art of story-telling, alterity is brought forth into the light of national consciousness, conversation and action—denial no longer possible.

Transforming Stories: Koori Court Victoria

Eight years earlier, on 29 May 2000, in the State of Victoria, the Wangaratta Court received a Deed of Apology and Commitment signed by the Chief Magistrate on behalf of the justice system of Victoria:

The Magistrates and Registrars who constitute the Magistrates' Court of Victoria apologise and express their sincere sorrow and regret for the injustices of the past suffered by the Aboriginal peoples of Australia and particularly the Aboriginal people of Victoria.

We commit ourselves to the Australian Declaration Towards Reconciliation. We promise to embrace to the best of our ability the cultural and spiritual values and sensitivities of all Aboriginal people to ensure that they, together with every other person interacting with the Magistrates' Court of Victoria, will receive equal justice according to law.

(Magistrates' Court of Victoria 2000)

This Deed of Apology, developed between the State Government and the Koori community of Victoria, provides the blueprint for Koori justice in Victoria. 'One of the major recommendations was the need for a Koori Court' (Magistrates' Court of Victoria, Guide to Specialist Courts: 32).

Unlike New Zealand where representatives of the Māori hapū groups and the Crown established the promise of a partnership under *Te Tiriti o Waitangi*, the Treaty of Waitangi (1840), the Aboriginal people in Australia had no such recognition—even though for Māori negotiating the rights and obligations under the Treaty has not been plain sailing over the past 175 years. Indigenous Australians were cast into a dreadful alterity by the advent of settlement: negotiation for partnership was never an option. British sovereignty was absolute in the dictum of *terra nullius* (the empty land), effectively annihilating recognition of over 60,000 years of human habitation in the vast continent. Over 500 different Aboriginal nations inhabited Australia—more than 750,000 people were already following their customary laws, speaking their languages, and respecting their custodial duty to Country. Centuries of disenfranchisement followed.

Today, Aboriginal people are over-represented in the criminal justice system, with over 25 per cent of total prison population in Australia being Aboriginal and Torres Strait Islanders (Australian Bureau of Statistics 2013). Re-offending is a key risk to be managed. In 2002, an amendment to the *Magistrates' Court Act 1989* (Vic) established the Koori Court to operate as a division of the Magistrates' Court of Victoria.

The Koori Court aims to increase the accountability of Koori communities, families and accused people; to reduce the number of breached court orders and recidivism; to explore sentencing alternatives prior to sentencing; to provide a culturally responsive court system; to encourage greater participation of Koori community in sentencing processes; to tailor sentencing orders to the needs of Koori offenders; and to encourage the accused to appear in court. Where statute decrees, social action—and hopefully resources—follow.

The first Koori Court opened in 2002 at Shepparton in northeast Victoria with a traditional Smoking Ceremony (Porter 2002). Today, in the State of Victoria, the Koori Court sits in the Magistrates Court in Melbourne City as well as in other cites of Victoria: Bairnsdale,

Broadmeadows, Latrobe Valley, Mildura, Shepparton, Swan Hill and Warrnambool. A Mildura-based Koori artist, a Gamilraay man, Lance Atkinson, designed a logo for the Koori Court, appropriately marking its distinctive presence for Koori justice. To be eligible for Koori Court an offender must identify as Koori; plead guilty to an offence; live within a Koori Court geographic boundary area; elect to go through the Koori Court system; and join the programs as directed by the Court. Koori Elders provide advice on cultural issues, which a Magistrate will consider in sentencing decisions (Magistrates' Court of Victoria, Guide to Specialist Courts: 33).

In keeping with the restorative and therapeutic approach to justice, the Koori courtroom is arranged as a conference facility. This is in contrast to the traditional hierarchical courtroom where the judge or magistrate sits on high and the offender stands in the dock or behind the defence lawyer, occupying the least visible position in the court. At the Koori Court the Magistrate and offender share the same space around a large oval table. Other participants take an active role: Koori Elders, Koori justice workers, the accused and his or her family, the defence lawyer, police prosecutor and community corrections officers. To mitigate risks the Court is more informal in its approach; and technical legal language is absent. The Magistrate speaks with the offender and his or her team in a problem-solving way to monitor progress or find solutions for the offender.[2]

In the Melbourne Koori Court, artworks around the walls by Aboriginal artists carry Koori stories specific to Country (ancestral land). Paintings and prints provide an aesthetic presence integrated implicitly into the business of the Court. There is opportunity here for a Magistrate to speak about the artworks, or invite an Elder to speak about them. They may signify locations where 'dreaming stories' occur. The Koori participant (offender) may find voice or confidence by knowing about, or identifying with the stories and language groups, or hearing about their kin from the Elders.

Beside the judicial bench, stands the Aboriginal flag; at its base a calabash in which lie dried gum tree leaves and ash from the Smoking Ceremony used to purify the courtroom at its inception. The ash is not merely a residue; it is an aesthetic reminder of deep cultural meanings and processes of significance to Koori. The Magistrate and Koori Elders may talk about what the Smoking Ceremony signifies, and how the courtrooms were closed to enable the smoking to take place. The Smoking Ceremony rids the area of bad spirits cleansing the place and the people who use it; healing ensues. The TJ approach to justice provides scope for this conversation to occur.

Drawing from the successful implementation of the Koori Court at the Magistrates' Court and Children's Court, a Koori Court was established by statute (*County Court Amendement [Koori Court] Act 2008*) as a Division of the County Court—now sitting at the Melbourne County Court, and at Morwell and Bairnsdale Courts in Gippsland, southeast Victoria. In keeping with the Magistrates' Koori Court, specific participation of the Koori community, Elders, Koori Court Officers and other Respected Persons marks the difference from courts of general jurisdiction (County Court of Victoria online).

The Courts of Victoria are paving the way towards possibilities of reparation not only for Koori offenders, but also for public justice. Through the Koori Court and its guiding principles for indigenous rights and responsibilities, the justice system is working assiduously towards a just city where citizens will be more aware of their rights and responsibilities.

Supreme Court of Victoria: Aesthetics and alterity in action

In 1852 an Act of Parliament in Victoria established the Supreme Court of Victoria, a setting of profound significance to Melbourne and Victoria's histories of justice. Above the Court's entrance sits the traditional bronze figure of Justice balancing the Scales of Justice on her knee (see Figure 1).

Embodying its 175-year history the setting suggests justice—and Westminster law—at its most elevated and eloquent level. On 22 May 2015, just prior to Reconciliation Week, a Koori Welcome to Country was held and a Smoking Ceremony cleansed the ground of this

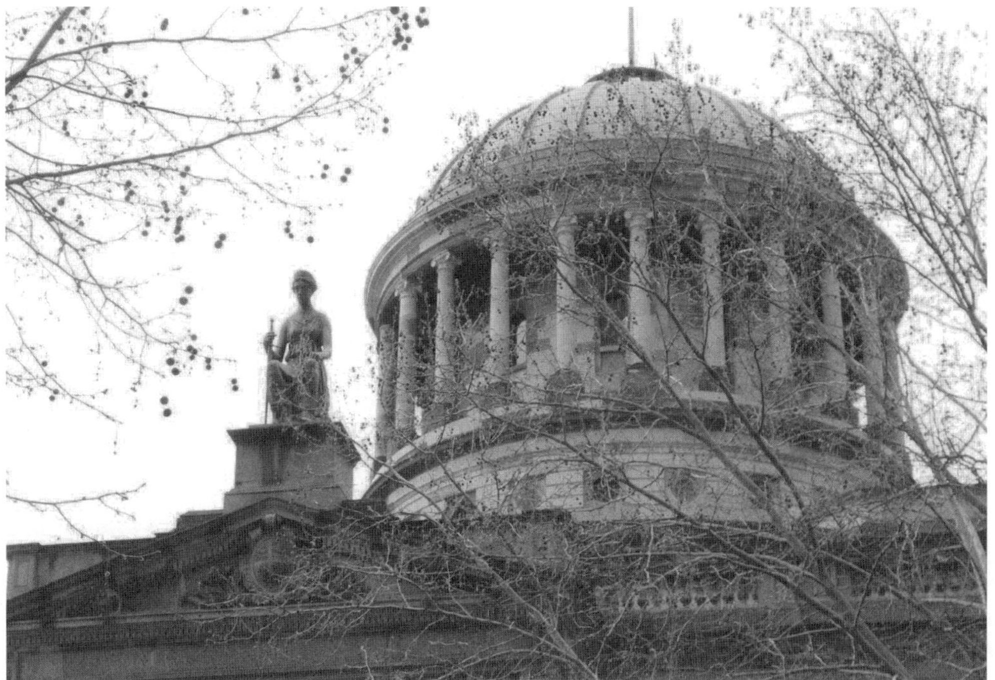

Figure 1: Figure of Justice, Supreme Court of Victoria, 210 William Street Melbourne Victoria. Image: Nicholas Gresson, 2016.

Court. Elder, Aunty Margaret Gardiner paid tribute to the Wurundjeri people, traditional custodians of the land on which the Supreme Court has stood for over 130 years:

> 'You are on Wurundjeri Country and we thank you for inviting us here today to do this first Welcome to Country,' Aunty Margaret said. She stressed the importance of working towards reconciliation and doing more to change the over-representation of Indigenous people in the justice and penal system.
>
> (Supreme Court of Victoria: 22 May 2015)

An exhibition at the Court brought together artwork by students of Worawa Aboriginal College, a Victorian College for young, female, Aboriginal students from urban, regional and remote communities of Australia. The exhibition was significant in light of the messages art may convey of what a culture values.

Not only indigenous people, but also women had been cast into alterity by the normative practices common to settler societies. In 2003 when Her Honour Chief Justice Marilyn Warren was appointed as Victoria's 11th Chief Justice, she was the first woman to occupy this elevated judicial position in any state or territory of Australia (Supreme Court 2015). Perhaps a gendered perspective brings heightened awareness of the Court's lack of recognition of 'othering' practices. Her Honour declared:

> No real offer of welcome, acceptance, acknowledgment or friendship has been given; [...] To the traditional owners I say: 'I stand here today on behalf of all the judges, associate judges, judicial registrars and staff of the Supreme Court of Victoria. I welcome and acknowledge you and I offer you our friendship'.
>
> (Marilyn Warren CJ, Supreme Court: 22 May 2015)

The raising of alterity into the light of recognition and friendship may be but one small move towards transformative justice. But in context of the Supreme Court, small is big. Institutions of society change slowly. However, for Koori people, as for Māori, 'adaptation, change and resilience is the natural way of things' (Quince 2015: 363). Stepping up to the challenge, the Supreme Court's Smoking Ceremony offers a palpable and solemn gesture to bring the otherwise silent issue of alterity to light in subsequent attitudes and practices.

Tikanga Māori: Marae-based justice

'Social, legal and cultural relationships within Māori society are both defined and governed by tikanga Maori [...] the collection of principles and practices outlining the right way to do things' (Quince 2015: 349). Where lie the transformative potentials of *tikanga Māori* (things Māori) and *taonga* (cultural treasures)? Place and aesthetics coalesce on the marae: the traditional home site of New Zealand Māori *iwi* (greater tribe, people), the place of a particular *hapū* (local or sub-tribe) and *whānau* (family group). Entering a marae ground and being welcomed at the *pōwhiri* (formal welcome) is to experience a calling to place, a calling of alterity into being—a spiritual, personal and collective experience.

Traditionally the marae occupied rural locations. Each house is named after a tribal ancestor. At Harataunga on the East Coast of the North Island, for example, she is *Rākairoa*, the female ancestress of the Ngāti Porou tribe. Renowned master carver Pakariki Harrison, whose work features significantly at Harataunga, explained that most houses in Ngāti Porou districts are named from stately women who were predominant in positions of leadership, whose stories and songs are still recorded in *waiata* (chant) and houses (Pakariki Harrison 1997, personal correspondence).[3]

With the growth of urban centres and migration of Māori from regional areas to urban centres in the 1970s, urban marae, often pan-tribal, came to mark the increasing presence of Māori communities in cities. *Hoani Waititi Marae*, opening in 1980 at Waitakere, West Auckland, became in 1985 the site of one of Auckland's earliest *kōhanga reo* (Māori language preschools). More recently, urban marae have opened in educational institutions: *Waipapa Marae* at University of Auckland; *Ngā Wai o Horotiu* at Auckland University of Technology; *Te Herenga Waka* at Victoria University in Wellington; *Te Kohinga Mārama* at University of Waikato; and *Te Kupenga o te Mataraunga* at Massey University.

At the 2015 International Therapeutic Jurisprudence conference, *Weaving Strands: Ngā Whenu Rāranga*, the visitors were welcomed onto the University of Auckland's *Waipapa Marae*, which represents all major tribes (see Figure 2). The *manuhiri* (visitors) gathered beyond *kuwaha o te marae* (gates of the marae) waiting for the *tangata whenua* (people of the land) to call them onto the sacred ground.

The welcome onto a marae ground begins with a *karanga* (sacred call): *Karanga mai, Karanga mai, Karanga mai…* Tauroa explains the *karanga* is a spiritual call across the generations of time and in this particular place (Tauroa 1991).[4] The visitors walk forward slowly in fan formation, women in front followed by the men, responding to the call of the local people (made by the women). The visitors follow the *kai whakautu*, woman who responds to the *karanga*. They move forward in silence, pausing to honour *hunga mate* (those who have died). Inside the *whare whakairo* (meeting house) traditional aesthetic practices take a central role: *te reo Māori* (the Māori language), *whakairo* (carvings), *raranga* (weaving), *harakeke* (flax weaving), *tā moko* (face tattoo), *kowhaiwhai* (painted designs, patterns), *waiata* (song, chant), *haka* (performance), *wairua* (spirit)—embodying cultural meanings. *Taonga*, 'those things of value to a person that have been handed down through the generations' (Tauroa 1991: 138) are active rather than passive repositories of the cultural and social environments that created them. Around the walls of the *wharenui* stand the ancestors, each carved with particular attributes, embodying beliefs and histories, celebrations and archives of activities and achievements, to communicate the past to those in the present. How may these protocols be relevant in the exercise of justice today?

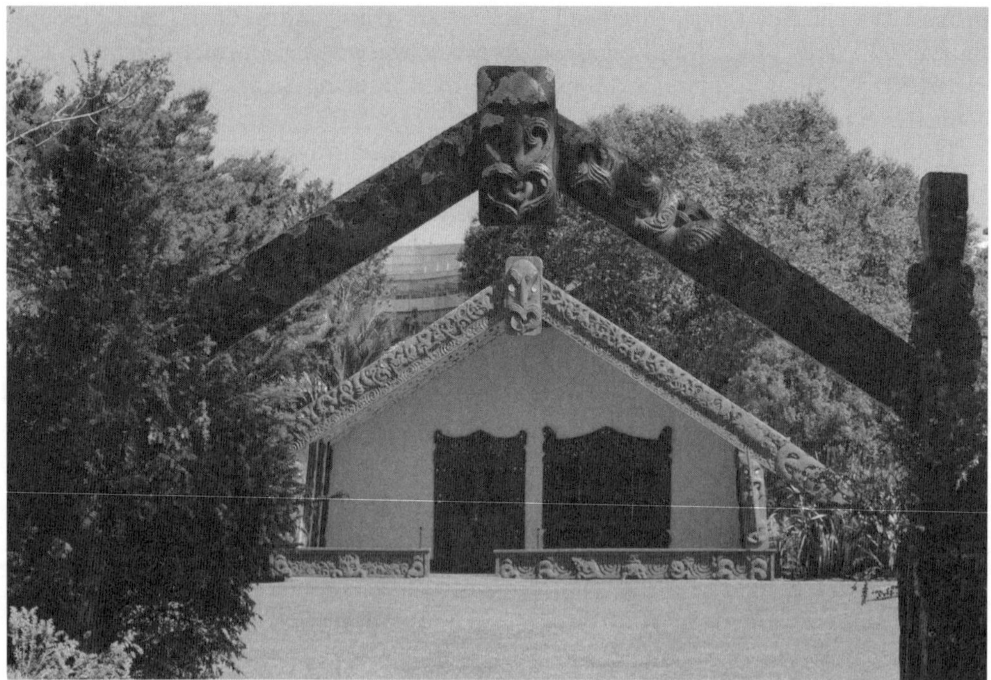

Figure 2: Waipapa Marae, The University of Auckland. Image: Nicholas Gresson, 2016.

Transforming Justice: Rangatahi Court

Aesthetics takes its place in processes of restorative justice—notable in meeting the needs of youth justice. Referencing the serious challenges of youth justice in New Zealand, Principal Youth Judge at the time, Andrew Becroft acknowledged 'the well-known and deeply challenging statistics regarding disproportionate Māori representation in the youth justice system' (Becroft 2012).

The marae-based, *Te Kooti Rangatahi Court* was inaugurated in May 2008 at *Te Poho Rawiri Marae*, Gisborne. Today there are 14 Courts. On 15 December 2015, *Kōti Rangatahi ki Tūwharetoa* was launched at *Rauhoto Marae*, Taupō, the opening hosted by Paramount Chief of Tūwharetoa, Sir Tumu Te Heuheu Tukino VIII, and attended by Chief Judge Jan-Marie Doogue and Principal Youth Court Judge Andrew Becroft, as well as a number of other Judges (*Rangatahi Court Newsletter* 2016).

Judicially led, the Rangatahi Courts differ from other courts, in that the Court hearing takes place on a marae and incorporates aesthetic processes of *te reo* (the language) and *tikanga Māori* (protocols, customs, culture) as integral to the Court process. This model of justice is open to both Māori and non-Māori. 'Young people who admit the charge(s) they are facing in the regular Youth Court can choose to have their next hearing held on the marae. Their family group conference takes place there, as does further monitoring of the offender' (Law Society of New Zealand).

The restorative justice approach aims 'to restore the well-being of victims, offenders and communities damaged by crime, and to prevent further offending' (Liebmann 2007: 25). Victim-offender mediation forms the basis of group conferencing, with a shift from traditional lawyering and court sentencing to mediation between offender and victim, and input from other stakeholders. Beyond the impersonal character of law, this approach provides a perspective that meets 'demands for voice, validation, procedural fairness, dialogue and accountability' (Brookbanks 2015: 5).

The Children, Young Persons and Their Families Act 1989 (CYPF Act) was the legislative instrument that authorized *whānau* (family) status for the first time in the youth justice system in New Zealand, and established a specific statutory framework for 'lay advocates' (CYPF Act section 327). Both legislative measures were ground-breaking, with no other counterparts anywhere in the world (Becroft 2015: 4–6). Section 5(a) of the Act provides for a child or young person's *whānau, hapū, iwi* and family group to participate, where possible, in decision making; their views should be considered in the outcome or sentencing decisions. The Court monitors the young offender's completion of the Family Group Conference (FGC) Plan for each participant. The FGC Plan is designed to 'hold the young person accountable and responsible for their offending; provide for the interests of the victims of the offending; deal with risks and needs of the young person, while [...] attempting to address the underlying causes of their offending' (*The Rangatahi Courts Newsletter* 2012: 2).[5]

There is a requirement on the young people who are appearing in the Rangatahi Court to take part in Māori protocols such as delivering a *mihi* (introduction) in Māori language. Deeply cultural is the process of voicing one's place to stand on the marae. For many, this is the first time of participating in these protocols. On the marae, oral and visual cultural forms take precedence over written. Following each speaker, the *waiata*, the role and responsibility of women, signals the quiet dispersal of history with expression of deep feelings, often in plaintive microtones. A youth advocate at Manukau, South Auckland, speaks of the profound effect of the marae-based Court on young offenders:

> The young people come in with their families, and there are also police and Child Youth and Family and other agency staff. They have a powhiri and speeches and the kai, so the atmosphere is totally different and much more relaxed than a normal court. For many of them, the marae is a completely new experience and they are a bit overwhelmed by it. But they are respectful of the marae and elders [...]
>
> (Stormie Waapu, cited in Law Society of New Zealand)

The offenders learn to deliver their *mihi*, introducing their connections to the marae and their tribal ancestors—the traditional way of establishing a birthright of bloodlines on *papatuanuku* (the land) today. Judge Gregory Hikaka (Ngā Ruahine) speaks of the value of formal *powhiri, te reo* and *waiata*, and support of the *kaumatua* and *kuia* (Elders), making the entry of the young person to *te ao Māori* (the Māori world) 'unmistakable' (Hikaka 2012: 8).

Concluding with Transformations

When customary law speaks, and Westminster law regulates, an incommensurable situation may become apparent (see Lyotard 1988). The colonial project legitimated dominant positions, the authorizing principles and systems casting 'other' voices into alterity. At colonization, western culture introduced a different legal system, and between customary law and Westminster law there lay a yawning gap. There, as Norris puts it, is a 'marked devaluation of the cognitive (or epistemic) phrase-regime, equated with the will to subsume all discourse under a single self-legitimizing rule' (Norris 1995: 13).

Normative discourses continue to be reproduced as a form of cultural hegemony—a type of 'ethnic chauvinism' as Cornell West put it (1993: 23). Restorative justice seeks to interrupt such hegemonic practices and bring cultural differences into the legal spotlight.

The Therapeutic Jurisprudence approach works with the law as a therapeutic agent. TJ conversations do not normally include aesthetics in this process. The aim of this discussion has been to show how aesthetics may play an active role in bringing to light differential interests of justice. May the workings of justice provide, then, without equivocation, this inculcation of therapeutic jurisprudence to give room for alterity and raise it to a high point of principle.

References

Australian Bureau of Statistics (2013), <http://www.abs.gov.au/ausstats/abs@.nsf/Lookup/4517.0main+features62013>. Accessed 10 August 2015.

Bohman, J. and Rehg, W., 'Jürgen Habermas', in Edward N. Zalta (ed.), *The Stanford Encyclopedia of Philosophy* (Fall 2014 ed.), <http://plato.stanford.edu/archives/fall2014/entries/habermas/>. Accessed 30 April 2016.

Becroft, A. (2015), 'The Rise and Rise of Lay Advocates in Aotearoa New Zealand', *National Youth Advocates / Lay Advocates Conference*, Auckland 13–14 July 2015, in *Court in the Act Newsletter*, Youth Court of New Zealand, 70, August, pp. 4–6.

——— (2012), *The Rangatahi Courts Newsletter*, Issue 1, June 2012, <http://www.justice.govt.nz/courts/youth>. Accessed 10 August 2015.

Bergo, B. (2015), 'Emmanuel Levinas', in Edward N. Zalta (ed.), *The Stanford Encyclopedia of Philosophy* (Summer 2015 ed.), <http://plato.stanford.edu/archives/sum2015/entries/levinas/>. Accessed 11 October 2015.

Braithwaite, J. (2004), 'Restorative Justice and De-Professionalization', *The Good Society*, 13, p. 28, <https://muse.jhu.edu/journals/good_society/v013/13.1braithwaite.html>. Accessed 10 August 2015.

Brookbanks, W. (ed.) (2015), 'Introduction', in W. Brookbanks (ed.), *Therapeutic Jurisprudence: New Zealand perspectives*, Wellington: Thomson Reuters, pp. 4–19.

———— (n.d.), 'Therapeutic Jurisprudence: A new legal paradigm', <http://www.rethinking.org.nz/assets/Newsletter_PDF/Issue_94/Warren_Brookbanks_Therapeutic_Jurisprudence.pdf>. Accessed 20 October 2015.

County Court of Victoria, County Koori Court, <https://www.countycourt.vic.gov.au/county-koori-court>. Accessed 30 April 2016.

Dearden, I. (2015), 'Mainstreaming Therapeutic Jurisprudence: A Judge's perspective', *Aotearoa Conference on Therapeutic Jurisprudence, Weaving Strands: Ngā Whenu Rāranga, 4th International Therapeutic Jurisprudence Conference*, University of Auckland, New Zealand, 3–4 September.

Freeman, M. D. A. (2011), *Lloyd's Introduction to Jurisprudence*, 8th ed., London: Sweet and Maxwell, Thomson Reuters.

Grierson, E. M. (2015a), 'Activating Aesthetics: Working with Heidegger and Bourdieu for engaged pedagogy', *Educational Philosophy and Theory incorporating ACCESS*, 47: 6, pp. 546–562.

———— (2015b), 'Restorative Justice: From adversarialism and blame to responsibility and reparation', *Aotearoa Conference on Therapeutic Jurisprudence, Weaving Strands: Ngā Whenu Rāranga, 4th International Therapeutic Jurisprudence Conference*, University of Auckland, New Zealand, 3–4 September 2015.

Hikaka, G. (2012), *The Rangatahi Courts Newsletter*, Issue 1, June, <www.youthcourt.govt.nz>. Accessed 10 August 2015.

Law Society of New Zealand, 'Te Kooti Rangatahi aims', <https://www.lawsociety.org.nz/practice-resources/commentary/law-reform-background/te-kooti-rangatahi-aims>. Accessed 30 April 2016.

Levinas, E. (1999), *Alterity and Transcendence*, (trans. Michael B. Smith), New York: Columbia University Press. (First published in French 1961.)

Liebmann, M. (2007), *Restorative Justice, How it Works*, London and Philadelphia: Jessica Kingsley Publishers.

Lyotard, J.-F. (1988), *The Differend: Phrases in dispute*, (trans. G. van den Abbeele), Oxford: Manchester University Press. (First published in French 1983.)

———— (1984), *The Postmodern Condition: A report on knowledge*, (trans. G. Bennington and B. Massumi), Minneapolis: University of Minnesota Press. (First published in French 1979.)

Magistrates' Court of Victoria, (2000), 'Deed of Apology and Commitment', 29 May Wangaratta Courthouse, Victoria.

———— (Report), 'Guide to Specialist Courts & Court Support Services'.

———— (Brochure), 'Koori Court, Information for legal representatives'.

Merriam Webster Dictionary online, <http://www.merriam-webster.com/dictionary/alterity>. Accessed 28 April 2016.

New Zealand Ministry of Justice, 'Restorative Justice', <http://www.justice.govt.nz/policy/criminal-justice/restorative-justice>. Accessed 13 October 2015.

Norris, C. (1995), 'Culture, Criticism and Communal Values: On the ethics of enquiry', in B. Adam and S. Allan (eds), *Theorizing Culture: An interdisciplinary critique after postmodernism*, London: University College London.

Plato (1959), *The Republic* (trans. and edited by H. D. P. Lee), Middlesex: Penguin Books. (First appeared in Greek c. 380 BCE.)

Porter, L. (2002), 'Dispensing Justice with Feeling', *The Age Newspaper, 1 September,* <theage. com.au>. Accessed 15 October 2015.

Quince, K. (2015), 'Therapeutic Jurisprudence and Maori', in W. Brookbanks (ed.), *Therapeutic Jurisprudence: New Zealand perspectives,* Wellington: Thomson Reuters, pp. 347–363.

The Rangatahi Courts Newsletter (2016), Issue 7: March, <www.youthcourt.govt.nz>. Accessed 2 May 2016 (2012).

—— (2012), Issue 1: June, <www.youthcourt.govt.nz>. Accessed 10 August 2015.

Rudd, K., Prime Minister (2008), Apology to the Australia's Indigenous Peoples, Parliament of Australia, House of Representative, 13 February, <http://www.australia.gov.au/about-australia/ our-country/our-people/apology-to-australias-indigenous-peoples> and <http://parlinfo.aph. gov.au/parlInfo/search/display/display.w3p;query=Id%3A%22chamber%2Fhansardr% 2F2008-02-13%2F0003%22>. Accessed 30 April 2016.

Supreme Court of Victoria, 'Judges', <http://www.supremecourt.vic.gov.au/home/about+the+ court/our+judiciary/judges/>. Accessed 15 October 2015.

—— (2015), 'Welcome to Country and Smoking Ceremony at Supreme Court', 22 May, <http:// www.supremecourt.vic.gov.au/home/contact+us/news/welcome+to+country+and+smoking +ceremony+at+supreme+court>. Accessed 15 October 2015.

Taumaunu, H. (2012), 'Rangatahi Courts in New Zealand', *The Rangatahi Courts Newsletter,* Issue 1, June.

Tauroa, H. P. (1991), *Te Marae: A guide to customs and protocol,* Auckland: Reed.

Warren, M. (2005), College of Law Victoria Graduation Speech, <http://www.austlii.edu.au/au/ journals/VicJSchol/2005/21.pdf>. Accessed 10 October 2015.

West, C. (1993), 'The New Cultural Politics of Difference', in C. McCarthy and W. Crichlow (eds), *Race, Identity and Representation in Education,* New York: Routledge, pp. 11–23.

Wexler, D. B. (2015), 'Moving Forward on Mainstreaming Therpaeutic Jurisprudence: An ongoing process to facilitate the therapeutic design and application of the law', in W. Brookbanks (ed.), *Therapeutic Jurisprudence: New Zealand perspectives,* Wellington: Thomson Reuters, pp. v–xiv.

Wright, T. (2008), 'Outburst of Emotion Echoes across the Land', *The Age Newspaper,* 14 February, <http://www.theage.com.au/news/national/australias-new-beginning/2008/02/13/ 1202760398783.html>. Accessed 30 April 2016.

Zehr, H. (2002), 'Journey to Belonging', in E. G. M. Weitekamp and H.-J. Kerner (eds), *Restorative Justice: Theoretical foundations,* Devon, UK and Portland, US: Willan Publishing, pp. 21–31.

Notes

1 'Some of these stories are graphically told in *Bringing them home,* the report commissioned in 1995 by Prime Minister Keating and received in 1997 by Prime Minister Howard' (Rudd 2008).

2 During the study for a Graduate Diploma of Legal Practice, in 2015, I undertook a work experience placement under judicial supervision of Magistrate Jelena Popovic at the Magistrates' Court of Victoria, Melbourne, and observed first-hand the workings of the Koori Court.

3 Conversations between author and Dr Pakariki Harrison, Master Carver of Rākairoa Marae, Harataunga, took place during the three-day Noho Marae visits to Rākairoa with undergraduate students when I was working as an academic at Auckland University of Technology, New Zealand.
4 Specific protocols of encounter govern the *pōwhiri* of each tribal area (Tauroa 1991).
5 The Vulnerable Children Act 2014 (NZ) amended the Children, Young Persons and Their Families Act, to provide a more child-centred approach to justice for children.

Chapter 10

Fragments, Lyotard and Earthquakes: A mosaic of memory and broken pieces

Kirsten Locke and Sarah Yates

Introduction: Writing a mosaic

This chapter explores the responses by a group of children to an art project that was undertaken by a small school in New Zealand after the September 2010 and February 2011 earthquakes in the city of Christchurch. The purpose of the project was to capture and memorialize both the collective trauma suffered by the children and wider school community, and the accompanying notions of hope and resilience that became an important dimension to the collective project of rebuilding lives and communities in the Canterbury region. Over a period of two years, the school undertook a project to build a mosaic in the corner of the school grounds. Every child in the school and every member of staff, including administrators and caretakers, contributed to the project in some form. After a ceremony that included a member of parliament laying the last tile, the mosaic was officially opened to the school and community as a space of collective commemoration that testified both to the trauma of the event of the earthquakes and the trauma-legacy that occurred in its wake.

However, the mosaic also consisted of images and symbols that clearly drew on the hopes and dreams of a school community who were refusing to be defined by the disaster. The interviews that inform this exploration were conducted a couple of months after the opening ceremony and over two years since the beginning of the project. As such, the writing of this process enters into the dialogue with the students when the actual making of the mosaic has finished, and the space itself has become absorbed into the everyday built environment of the school.

Following an ethnographic approach to interviewing that places value on the embodied relationality between the interviewer and informant (Oakley 1992), the interviews were conducted at the site of the mosaic. Selected children made the trek across a sodden playing field to talk with me about their role in the production of the mosaic. Split into four circular panels on the ground, each panel from the mosaic corresponded to a moment that was deemed significant in the narrative trajectory of the 'story' of the disaster. Placed in the centre of the circle delineated by the panels was a hexagonal chair that itself circled a planted tree, and it is here that the story was told to me by the students as we sat at, and wandered around the tiled mosaic space. One panel depicted the town, Kaiapoi, before the earthquakes. The sun is shining, there are broad smiles on the townsfolk as they go about their business, and the Kaiapoi River is gleaming in the sun. The next panel captures the major earthquake as it is happening. Houses are seen to be off kilter with falling chimneys, people are falling over, the iconic Christchurch Cathedral loses its spire, and an image of the seismograph as recorded for the Kaiapoi area, cuts dramatically across the panel. The next panel is more circumspect. There are still broken houses and not everything looks harmonious, but there is an image of a 'helping hand', and messages in Māori about keeping strong. The colour palette has shifted from the dramatic pairing of red and black of the previous panel, and once again incorporates bright colours that are found in the pre-Earthquake panel, symbolizing hope and restoration.

The final panel is the 'future-perfect' panel. It depicts Kaiapoi in a state of complete recovery. The Tuhoe boat sails triumphantly down the river. The houses are built, there are children laughing; and rather curiously, new animal forms populate the banks of the river. The river gleams in the sun and the panel depicts a version of Kaiapoi that is simultaneously rebuilt and unbroken.

This chapter presents fragments of statements taken from the interviews as the children spoke about the panels and as we strolled around the circumference of the mosaic in the bright sunshine with heat emanating from the brick tiles. The purpose is to explore the fragments of memory that appeared with the children like the shining pieces of tiles that on this day had the gleaming quality of polished jewels. While ostensibly speaking about the process of making the mosaic, through the act of talking and interacting with the artwork the children moved to topics that they associated with the memory of the earthquakes. During these sometimes-fantastic meanderings, the children spoke of their emotional experiences and memories of a time 'before' the physical-geographical and emotional ruptures of the earthquakes. They also spoke of a fearful, anxious time during the earthquakes, an altered present context, and a sometimes-hopeful articulation of a projected better future. As such, the discussion tries to honour these fragments of memories through incorporating the mosaic as 'writing apparatus' (in the Deleuzian sense of [dis]ordered structure) (Deleuze 1986), in which different pieces of dialogue and memory are placed side by side. The aim is to 'write the mosaic' by utilizing these fragments to draw a bigger picture that speaks to the discontinuities between the trauma and triumph of the children's lived experiences of a

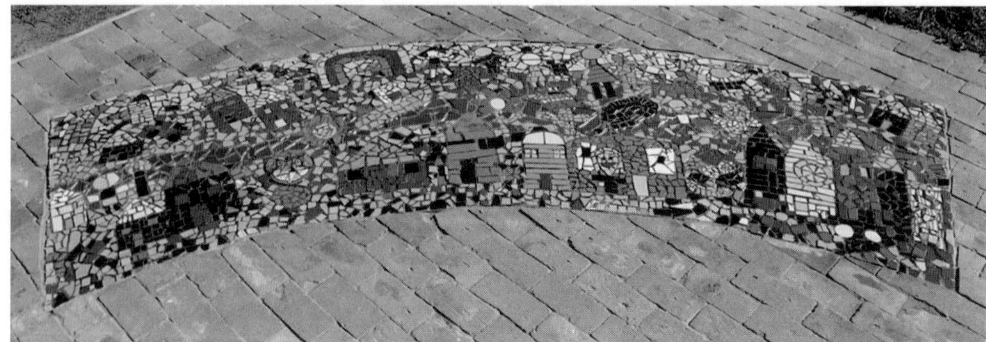

Figure 1: The final panel. Image: Carol Mutch and Sarah Yates, 2015.

significant natural disaster. This method reads the fragments of dialogue alongside the work of Jean-François Lyotard and his work on memory, the sublime and aesthetic affect.

A Sublime Rupture in the Present

And it's broken, so it can't get any more broken.

What happens to the way we interact and view the world when that world starts moving under our feet? There is a small but growing literature on post-disaster responses and the role education plays in alleviating trauma, and the cohesive role that schools play in the wider community in response to trauma (for two recent examples, see Mutch 2014a, 2014b; Mutch and Gawith 2014). The statement '*And it's broken, so it can't get any more broken*' refers to a moment in the interview with a group of children when the conversation turned to the constant aftershocks that have occurred in Christchurch since the two major

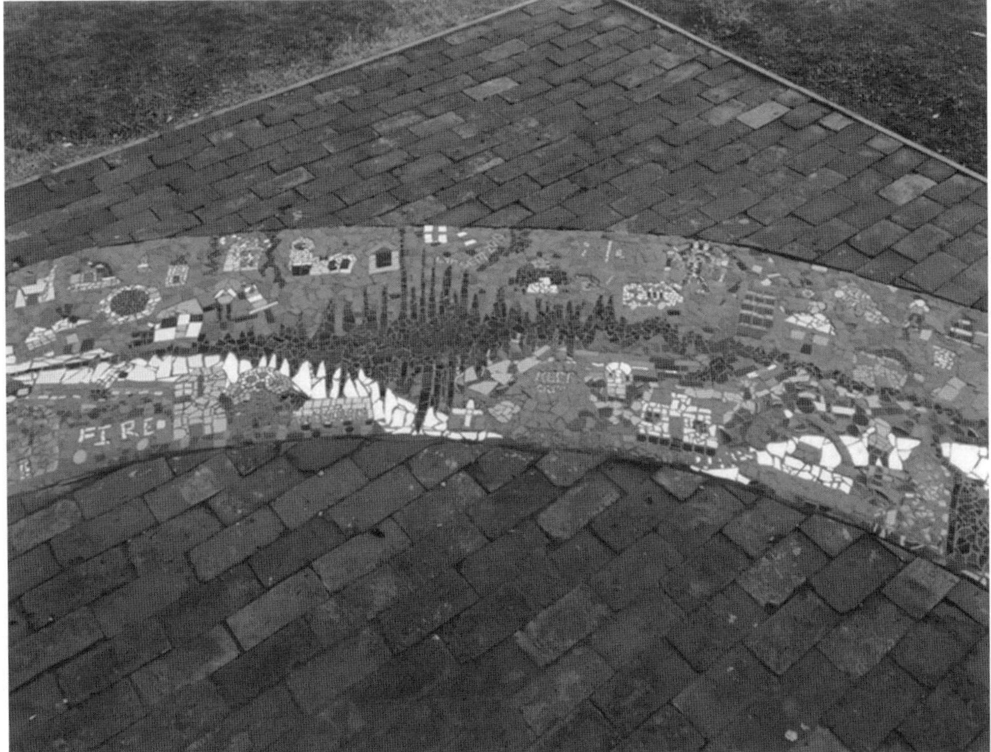

Figure 2: Aerial view of mosaic. Image: Carol Mutch and Sarah Yates, 2015.

earthquakes. This statement was spoken when the group of children and I walked the perimeter of the mosaic site and the inevitable queries surfaced as to whether the mosaic itself was safe from the aftershocks or more earthquakes. This statement can be read in the literal sense of the mosaic consisting of broken pieces in the form of broken tiles so any further earthquake-induced 'breakages' become null and void, or even impossible. However, a reflexive approach to research, in which the self-referencing mechanism of retelling the interview has the capacity to produce alternative readings, provides the space for a different and less literal interpretation of this statement to emerge (Davies 1999). To this end, this fragment of the chapter recalls another response to an earthquake that occurred over 250 years ago alongside the present statement about brokenness, and one person's answers to the implications of the shifting of the earth beneath his feet.

In 1755 the city of Lisbon suffered a devastating earthquake whose aftershocks were felt across Europe. According to Jones (2013), a lesser-known reaction to the disaster was from Immanuel Kant who, at this stage in the early phase of his career, set about writing three 'earthquake essays' with an aim to present the best available research at that time on their causes. While Jones challenges the overall efficacy of this research in terms of its relevance to contemporary understandings of earthquakes, she places the significance of the essays in the context of their continuing impact on Kant's wider philosophical thinking. The Lisbon earthquake, says Jones, 'continues to send tremors through Kant's later writing', specifically in relation to his developing notion of the 'sublime' (Jones 2013: 274). Jones goes on to define the Kantian sublime as the terror felt when one is confronted with either 'nature's apparently uncontainable infinity or by its awe-inspiring power' (Jones 2013: 274). The oft-quoted depiction of the sublime in nature from which Kant takes his inspiration is the dramatic mountain range or the thundering waterfall. This is for Kant a terrifying experience where the magnitude of the sublime encounter with nature is too big for the mind to synthesize in all its vast expansiveness, and instead we are left in a state of being that is, literally, awe-struck. In such an encounter the subject confronts that which is 'excessive for the imagination' and which, Kant says, is like 'an abyss in which the imagination is afraid to lose itself' (Kant, cited in Jones 2013: 274).

The terror Kant articulates through the notion of the sublime resonates with many of the children's statements about the anxiety and fear experienced during and after the earthquakes in Christchurch. However, the statement under analysis here, about the way the mosaic can escape destruction *because it's already broken*, can be reread in a more triumphant, even pleasurable way. The resilient psychological stance and the wilful defiance of adversity was a quality that was constantly reinforced throughout the conversations with the children. When the student articulated this positive statement about brokenness, it was met with resounding approval and agreement from the other students. While not wanting to belittle the terrifying aspects of experiencing a natural disaster, as these children certainly did, this more triumphant tenor that was struck by the students when talking of the resilience of the mosaic points to an added dimension to the Kantian sublime. 'The delight in the sublime does not so much involve positive pleasure as admiration or respect', Kant tells us. As such it 'merits the name of a negative pleasure' (Kant 1952: 495). In some interesting ways, it was this 'negative pleasure'—in surviving, in living through, in seeing the destruction and then witnessing the eventual reconstruction—that added such a vibrancy and vitality to the children's recollections, and the mosaic itself. Instead of interpreting the panel of the earthquake 'in motion' with the jet black image of the seismograph surrounded by the deep blood red as brutally violent, the students instead spoke of their pride in the black and red colours of the Canterbury rugby team.

To further develop this idea of the sublime as a 'negative' pleasure and the intriguing mix of defiance, pride, fear and triumph that the students so effectively conveyed during the interviews, we turn now to the mosaic as an affective artwork in its own right. While the Kantian version of the sublime would take a prominent place in the *Critique of Judgement* particularly, it is an appropriation by Lyotard of the sublime placed in the service of art that helps extend the discussion towards the affectivity of the mosaic. According to Lyotard, art derives its power from an encounter that involves 'magnitude, force, quantity in its purest state, a "presence" that exceeds what imaginative thought can grasp at once in a form' (Lyotard 1994: 53). Drawing on the Kantian notion of the sublime as an encounter beyond the synthesizing capacities of the mind, Lyotard instead focuses on the sublime encounter within art as involving sensorial affect that pierces daily reality and moves us in ways that are unique and site-specific. Like Kant, the sublime for Lyotard occurs when the encounter cannot be represented. Kant's awesome feat of nature, such as the mountain range or thundering waterfall, for Lyotard is transplanted to the shuddering affect one feels when confronted with a work of art. Rather than locate the sublime in nature like Kant, Lyotard instead locates the infinite dimension of the sublime in the most immediate and subtle sensations of a sensorial event. Such an event is singularly irreplaceable and infinitely unique. Lyotard explains the openness to nuance the sublime initiates in the following:

> a singular, incomparable quality—unforgettable and immediately forgotten—of the grain of a skin or a piece of wood, the fragrance of an aroma, the savour of a secretion or a piece of flesh, as well as a timbre or a nuance [...]. They all designate the event of a passion, a passability for which the mind will not have been prepared, which will have unsettled it and of which it conserves only the feeling—anguish and jubilation—of an obscure debt.
> (Lyotard 1991: 141)

In line with the mosaic as experienced as a sensorial event, throughout the day of interviews every student at some point spoke of their pride in the mosaic. This pride was intermingled with a sense of achievement at the completion of a project well done, but there was also a pervading sense from the students that the mosaic *belonged* to them. '*People can come here and spend time here and it's like our own place that we can share with others sort of thing*', one student explained. However, alongside this sense of belonging and ownership was the way another student spoke about the mosaic panels as if they were living entities that affected her by being both really interesting to look at and to spend time with, while also providing a sense of solidity and security. She explains:

I come here quite a lot, like after school and stuff like that. Like I've got this thing … after school today I'll come down and say 'see ya, see you on Monday'. Because I always come and see them after school. So I quite like it because I feel like it's home to me sometimes.

In a Lyotardian context, this student articulates the encounter with the mosaic as a work of art that draws on the 'negative pleasure' of the sublime that speaks to an inherent loneliness or solitariness that is awakened or nudged into being by the artwork. However, the student is also signalling an 'excess' to the mosaic that speaks to a presence that obliges her to say goodbye and to reassure the mosaic that she will be back 'on Monday' to wander about and soak in the different colours, images and feelings. By talking to the mosaic the student is tacitly acknowledging that the mosaic speaks to her, thus fulfilling the ethical dimension of the sublime encounter that demands a response, but carries with it the obligation to 'address

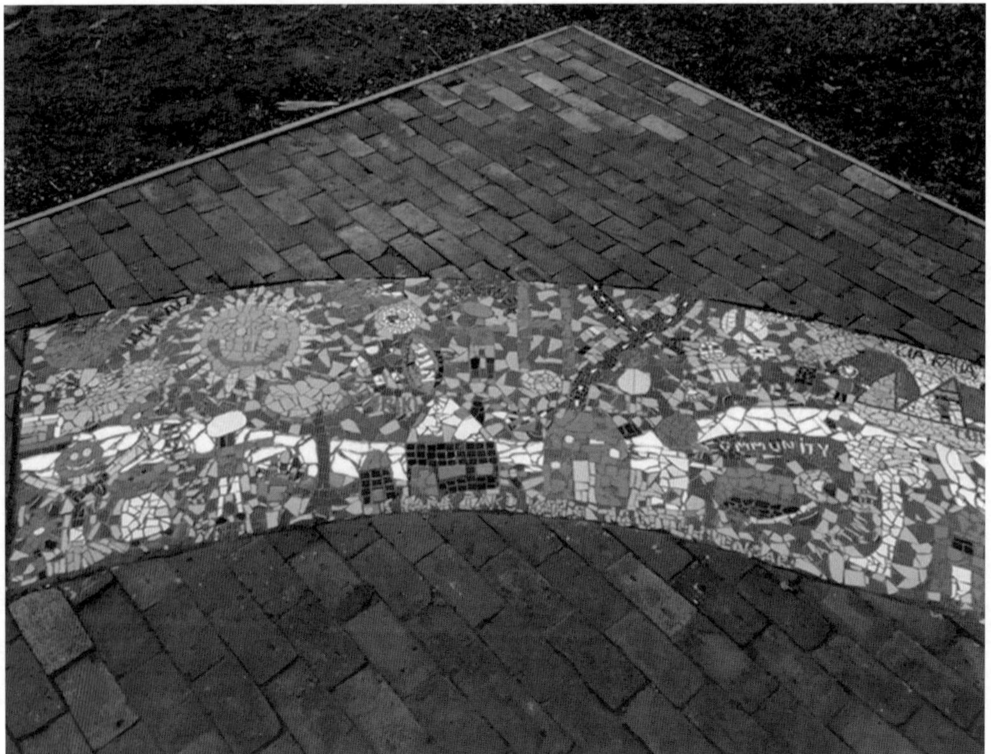

Figure 3: Close view of mosaic panel. Image: Carol Mutch and Sarah Yates, 2015.

and carry forward' (Lyotard 1997: 229). To return to the opening quote of this section, the already broken form of the mosaic, which is made up of lots of fragments, exists alongside an excess that shares with its interlocutor the resilience of being unable to be broken, or break, any further. To 'carry forward' is seen in the return of this student, and children from her school, to the mosaic every day to continue their interaction and conversations further.

Pieces of Memory

An alligator brushing his teeth by the swamp.

After a morning of interview groups of children, the school then organized individual students who had been involved with the mosaic from its inception to completion to come and speak to me. Like the group interviews, these individual interviews were conducted at the site of the mosaic. The very last student to be interviewed provided some of the most intriguing statements in relation to her memory of the earthquakes and the nostalgia she felt for a world and life that had been altered significantly and had perhaps even disappeared in the aftermath of the disaster. When asked at the top of the interview about her school history, it transpired that this student had moved to the school in Kaiapoi because the family had been forced to relocate to Kaiapoi from their badly damaged house in a nearby suburb. As we were standing looking at one of the panels in the mosaic the student recounted a favourite activity that belonged to the old house (and her life 'before') that was prompted by reflecting on the artwork:

> *I had good memories in that place. It was quite hard … like my mum's bedroom was right next to my bedroom and in the night when I used to start crying mum used to bring me into her room 'cos I missed her… And we used to lie in bed and mum used to put the torch on. And we had this roof and it had all these, like, decorations sort of things on it. And I always used to find this alligator! It looked like an alligator was brushing his teeth by the swamp. So that was my challenge. Whenever I'd go into mum's bed I'd see if I could see it.*

This activity for the student, even though it was prompted by night terrors, was recalled with fondness. The activity for this student involved the imagination where out of nowhere, mysterious animal-like forms with even more mysterious and incongruous habits would appear. A unique dimension to the mosaic as a school project was the way the children designed the layout and content from the very beginning, allowing for some life forms to appear on the banks of the Kaiapoi River in the 'future' panel that were indecipherable to the adult gaze. Standing in the middle of the space surrounded by the four mosaic panels, this student did not hesitate to articulate her creative desire to form shapes out of formless, thin air. This was a pleasurable thing for her to do, and as we continued to walk among the panels as we were talking, the student continued the activity recounted in the story by stopping to point out different tiles and shapes in the mosaic that related to other memories. A piece of broken pottery salvaged from the destroyed house was singled out; an unknown entity with the name of a 'crockfish', meandering on the border of the panel, was introduced to me.

Throughout this interview it became apparent that the mosaic itself served an important function in the preserving of small, and perhaps insignificant, fragments of the everyday that had disappeared and existed now only through the prompting of an artwork that was itself made of broken pieces of pottery, tiles and bricks, remembered in a previous time and context to the earthquakes and in different forms. Within Lyotard's lexicon, another dimension that is linked to art as a sublime and affective encounter is the testimony art provides to memory. For Lyotard, this testimony involves a lack of representation that bears witness to 'apparition over appearance. Yet, in appearance and through the means of appearance' (Lyotard 2004: 103). In some interesting and perhaps unintentional ways, the mosaic provides its own apparitions akin to the alligator brushing his teeth in the variety of images the children drew and created. To move a step further, perhaps these apparitions 'appear' through the broken tiles and smashed pottery in ways that testify to lives, memories and experiences of the past that are no longer represented in the present. Seen from this Lyotardian perspective, memory is hidden in the discontinuous pieces and fragments of pottery that appear in another form, and in doing so, add to the affective potentiality of the mosaic as a 'means of appearance' (Lyotard 2004: 103).

Related to the notions of appearance and memory is the extent to which the decision to create a mosaic at this school differed from other responses from schools towards the earthquakes. In the same interview, the student talked of how incredibly lucky she felt that she belonged to a school that was brave enough to attempt such a large project. Rather than a photographic record of the earthquakes and its effects, the school opted for a form of artwork that existed as far back as Ancient Greece. This also has resonance in Lyotard's analyses of art, in that unlike digitized technologies such as photography and the ubiquitous iPhone video, there is instead, a permanence and concreteness to the mosaic that means it cannot be easily deleted. For instance, in *The Postmodern Condition,* Lyotard (1984) talks of the way certain forms of knowledge and experience are under threat because of their inability to be put to use for productive means. As such, anything that cannot be quantifiable or turned into 'data' can disappear so that room can be made for new information. Accordingly, 'the pragmatics of scientific knowledge replaces traditional knowledge or knowledge based on revelation' (Lyotard 1984: 44). In an important way, this student and many other students articulated their delight that the mosaic would be there when they had moved on to high school and they would always be able to return:

Other schools have ... made like photo albums and dvd's. Our one is different. And it's permanent.

Hidden Desires and Meanings

A place to talk about boys.

Sitting on the wooden seat at the centre of the mosaic with one of the older girls, muddy cowboy boots and scuffed school shoes poking at the grouting between red bricks, there was a break in conversation as we silently meditated on the bright colours of the mosaic and the school vista in the distance. I turned to the student and commented how easy it was to be contemplative in this spot. The vibrant colours of the mosaic and the lush green of the playing field set against a luminous blue sky echoed the contrasting colours and energy of the mosaic tiles. The student agreed and began talking about how she engaged with the space alongside her friends away from the surveillance of adults as, among other things, *'a place to talk about boys'*. This hidden dimension of what the children spoke about away from listening adults hints at the absorption of this site into everyday realities where the artistic vibrancy of the mosaic space has become entangled with the dynamic and layered ebbs and flows of the lived lives and everyday realities of the children. The student gently elaborated her encounters with the mosaic space, her friends and their casual conversations in the following:

> *Well sometimes when my friends are here it starts off with boys and then it switches when we all just take the time to look at this. We all start cracking up laughing about those times we all did something funny here. And then those times back in the earthquake.*

This comment spans a temporal and emotional trajectory that charts a present engagement with the mosaic that involves hopes, dreams, desires and the hint of unknown futures. It also traces back to those times when the earthquakes occurred and in so doing encompasses the emotional maelstrom of terror and bewilderment, and the transition to acceptance and absorption of the disruption and event of the quakes into daily reality. This timeframe also includes the process of making the mosaic, where the students kneeled and sat together when they were placing the mosaic pieces made of their crockery from their own homes onto the demarcated spaces in the ground. As the story-telling portrayed by each mosaic panel became clearer to understand and articulate through the construction of images, the children chatted and made jokes so that their lived experience of making a work of art was infused through the artwork in ways where lives and art intermingled and conjoined. The student's statement above also points to the transition of living 'through' the artwork as construction and artistic process, to living 'on top' of the site. Next to the mosaic site is a wooden fitness structure from which the students would sit in pairs or small groups and look down, from above, onto the mosaic space. Taking the time to look, to contemplate, to remember the jokes and fun for the students also prompted reminders of the confusion and unease of the earthquakes, but in ways that made meaning for the children away from adult narrations and meaning-making processes of the quakes.

Recalling Lyotard's appropriation of the Kantian sublime, the children's interactions with the mosaic as a process of art making and construction through to an engagement with a completed artwork signify a shift from perceiving the ground as a site of terror into a space of wonder where images tell stories through dynamic and imaginative interactions with the space. For Lyotard, 'the inadequacy of images, as negative signs, attests to the immense power of Ideas' (Lyotard 1991: 91), and while the mosaic panels tell a story of the earthquake experience for the children, it also points to the inadequacy, or negativity of a stable and all-encompassing narrative that fits all stories, memories and interpretations of the earthquakes, the aftermath of the earthquakes, and the responses through art that the mosaic in this context symbolizes. As '*a place to talk about boys*', the site of the mosaic blends, glues and juxtaposes the fragments of memory in ways that animate the present.

Sublime Fright and Wicked Delight

A story without words.

The process of making the mosaic was a long one, involving many different steps that developed the competencies of the children to the point where completing the project could become a reality. The group of three photos tell a story of the complexities involved in developing the artistic skills of the students (see Figure 4). The first photo is a collection of drawings the first group of students made that involved a brainstorming of all the images that the children remembered as being important to the days of the earthquakes. There are fire trucks, ambulances and buildings that have partially collapsed. At the left-hand side of the first photo there is a pencil sketch of a small child crying. The child has no facial features, yet the gesture and positioning of the arms and the cradling of the face in the hands conveys very clearly a sense of agony and emotional turmoil. As one of the very first sessions with the children, this group of preliminary sketches provided the initial blueprint for the first mosaic panel, and many of these images, including the crying child, would be

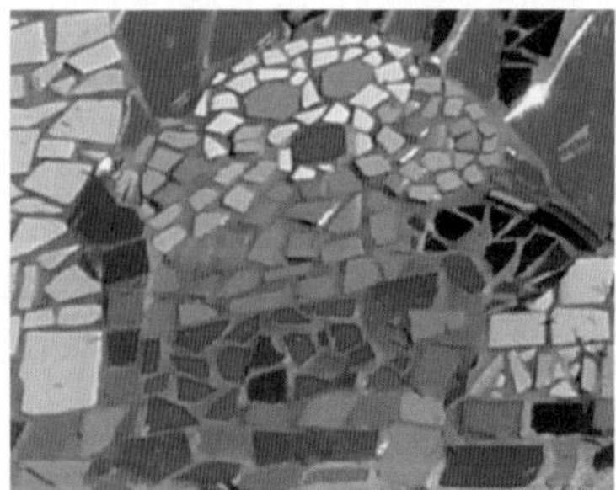
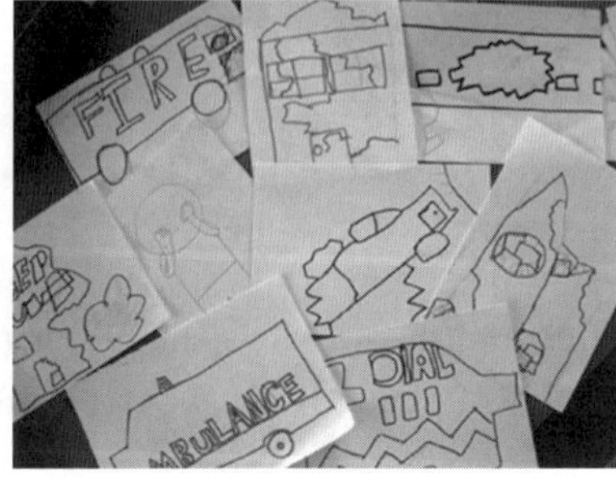

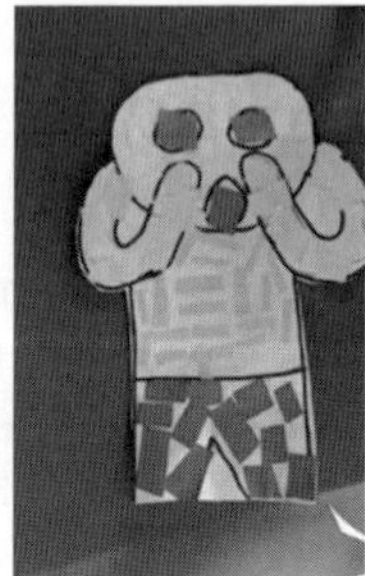

Figure 4: Close-up view of a mosaic panel. Image: Carol Mutch and Sarah Yates, 2015.

incorporated into the design of the mosaic. The second photo of this image is a later stage in the pedagogical process of teaching the students, and is a paper collage that prepared the students for the technical aspects of laying tiles. However, in this collage the small child now has bright blue eyes and a large red mouth that enhance the agonized but faceless previous sketch. The outline of the body and the bodily gestures are exactly the same, yet the child has been reworked and filled in with colour, thus making the anonymous child-figure somehow both more universal and more 'human'. The final image depicts the child in mosaic form, head slightly askew, eyes welling with blue tears and hands framing a mouth an oval shape of bright red horror. The emotional vibrancy of this image, and the development by different children over time to this vibrancy and energy in the different iterations of the image, echoes Edvard Munch's iconic *The Scream* (1893). Importantly the original title given by Munch was *The Scream of Nature* (*Der Schrei der Natur*), where the confrontation between inner human turmoil and the outward violent unpredictability of nature is depicted by a lone figure in the foreground surrounded by a swirling blood-red sky, face frozen in an expression of unmitigated horror as two figures in the background walk into the distance leaving the lone figure to suffocate in desolation and isolation in their wake.

The emotional intensification of the crying child that occurred in the process of transferring pencil sketch to completed mosaic signalled a direction the children spoke about in the interviews as we continued carousing the different panels. Speaking excitedly and passionately in a small group, one student pointed out the mosaic was 'a story without words'. The other children enthusiastically agreed, and each one added another statement in support:

> *It's just like a story of pictures without words!*
> *It's our picture book!*
> *It's our human picture book!*

The depiction of a 'story without words' when read through the development of the first sketches signalled more than simply an absence of words for the children, but also an 'excess' of feelings and imaginings that went further than the visual representations of the earthquakes. Just as each image developed towards a conceptual whole in the form of the completed mosaic, the narratives and collective articulations of the stories of the quakes also accumulated more emotional intensity as the fragments of different memories, crockery and images began to speak of things beyond what the children were prepared or even capable of saying. While the mosaic can be read as a series of troubling and sad perceptions and interpretations of the human cost of the earthquakes, there was also present in their interactions with the mosaic space an engagement that reached beyond the negative to something that resembled more of a 'wicked delight' that seemed to dwell and swirl in the emotional and physical fissures opened by the earthquakes. The exuberance with which the children recounted their stories as they skipped and jumped, giggled and squealed, ran and leapfrogged from one panel to the next, was filled with energy and joy; these were sad images and stories that spoke of very 'grown-up' and adult dimensions of loss and tragedy, but for the children, the mosaic site overflowed with potential to challenge dominant (adult) interpretations with their own interpretations. *This is our picture book* stakes a claim about owning the mosaic, but implicit within it is also the demarcation of the space away from the 'adult' anxieties and worries of the earthquakes and post-earthquake reactions. To quote Jones's interpretations of Kant's earthquake essays, the 'earthquake as abyssal event' (2013: 298) for the children was certainly present in terms of terror and catastrophe, but it was also entwined within the 'sublime shock' of this event, where it opened spaces for adventure, excitement and the spaces for 'wicked delight'.

Conclusion

I feel like it was made for me.

This discussion has placed different fragments of speech, memory, ideas and feelings of a group of children in an attempt to 'write' the mosaic in a way that echoed the artistic process the children undertook, when they committed to designing and making their own artwork. Lyotard's work on the Kantian sublime explores the 'negative pleasure' involved in an engagement with aesthetic experience. Through artistic expression and through the long process of making a significant work of art, the children interviewed for this project displayed a myriad of complex and often complicated responses to the trauma of the earthquake events. Not all of these responses, feelings and interactions with the mosaic space can be read as purely painful; in fact, the children displayed incredible amounts of resourcefulness, resilience and even pleasure during the long journey of making the mosaic and through their continuous interactions with the space in their everyday lives. Lyotard's interpretation of the Kantian sublime emphasizes its double-sided dimension that intermingles pleasure and pain in ways that produce the feeling that accompanies evocations of the 'unpresentable', as a lack of presentation, through art. This notion has been utilized here in two ways: the context of the unthinkable shock these children underwent in their lived experiences of the quakes and the continuing trauma of living on unstable ground; and also, importantly, in the creation of an artwork producing its own testimony to the Lyotardian aesthetic notion that through art, 'something happens rather than nothing' (Lyotard 1991: 90). Through art, the collective and individual memories of the quakes are embedded into the work in ways that bear witness to what cannot be articulated by the children, but are 'said' through images and artistic affect.

It is this point that pedagogical questions may be asked, particularly: what can we learn from the process? While this discussion is not advocating a 'scaling up' of this process to all communities who experience significant trauma, there are however some important pedagogical implications that can be drawn from the construction of this mosaic in Kaiapoi. Of particular significance is the pedagogical value conferred through the way that this type of artwork, in this instance a mosaic, is permanent. While photos and videos have their own form of life, the children spoke of their happiness with the solid 'concreteness' of the mosaic. In an age where digital images and recordings have become as instant and accessible as any hand-held phone or tablet, and are constantly under threat of 'deletion' as Lyotard observes, the tangible, touchable, static dimensions to the mosaic offered the children a space of continuity and stillness at a time when the ground they stood on, the buildings and life as they knew it were constantly shifting and moving. Another significant aspect to the creation of the artwork was the way in which children were at the very centre of every step of the process. While teachers, researchers, artists and many more adults were intricately involved, it was the children who led the design, who decided on the themes of each mosaic panel, and who smashed, sorted and laid the tiles and crockery to form the work. It has also been the children who continue to animate the artspace by playing, wondering, imagining and living their lives on top and in the spaces of the artwork. Crucially, this living is predominantly away from adults, allowing the site to be interpreted and engaged in ways that lie outside the remit of adult forms of meaning-making. This is a space that allows casual conversations about boys, about memories of times before the quakes, of quiet times for contemplation and rambunctious times for revelling in the joys of living. It is a space, according to one child, that feels *like it was made for me*.

Finally, as a work of art that memorializes a significant trauma in the lives of those who lived through the earthquakes, the mosaic at the heart of this project opened a space that, drawing on Kant and Lyotard, offered a passage where the moving earth and the concomitant shock involved in the earthquakes provided a 'sublime' encounter through art—an encounter not limited to horror and trauma. Instead, as the fragments of this paper attest, there was a promise provided through the artistic process and the completed artspace: they were imbued with the promise of transformation and shared adventures whereby the earthquakes have not been the defining event in these children's lives, but a shaking out and beginning of wonders and delight to come.

Acknowledgement

This chapter, with minor editorial alterations, is reprinted from the *International Journal of Disaster Risk Reduction*, 14: Part 2, Locke, K. and Yates, S., 'Fragments, Lyotard, and Earthquakes: A mosaic of memory and broken pieces', pp. 152–159 (December 2015), with permission from Elsevier.

References

Davies, C. A. (1999), *Reflexive Ethnography: A guide to researching selves and others*, New York: Routledge.

Deleuze, G. (1986), 'Life as a Work of Art', (trans. M. Joughin), in L. D. Kritzman (ed.), *Negotiation: Gilles Deleuze*, New York: Columbia University Press, pp. 94–101. (First published in German 1990.)

Jones, R. (2013), 'Adventures in the Abyss: Kant, Irigaray and earthquakes', *Symposium: Canadian journal for continental philosophy*, 17: 1, pp. 273–299.

Kant, I. (1952), 'The Critique of Judgement', (trans. J. C. Meredith), in J. M. Adler (ed.), *Kant: The Critique of Pure Reason, The Critique of Practical Reason and Other Ethical Treatises, The Critique of Judgement* (Vol. 42), Chicago: William Benton, *Encyclopaedia of Brittanica*.

Lyotard, J.-F. (2004), 'Scriptures: Diffracted traces', *Theory, Culture and Society*, 21: 1, pp. 101–105.

——— (1997), 'Music, Mutic', (trans. G. Van Den Abbeele), in J.-F. Lyotard, *Postmodern Fables*, Minneapolis: University of Minnesota Press, pp. 217–234. (First published in French 1993.)

——— (1994), *Lessons on the Analytic of the Sublime*, (trans. E. Rottenberg), Stanford: Stanford University Press. (First published in French 1991.)

——— (1991), *The Inhuman: Reflections on time*, (trans. G. Bennington and R. Bowlby), Stanford: Stanford University Press. (First published in French 1988.)

——— (1984), *The Postmodern Condition: A report on knowledge*, (trans. G. Bennington and B. Massumi), 10th ed., Manchester: Manchester University Press. (First published in French 1979.)

Mutch, C. (2014a), 'The Role of Schools in Disaster Preparedness, Response and Recovery: What can we learn from the literature?', *Pastoral Care in Education: An international journal of personal, social and emotional development*, 32: 1, pp. 5–22.

——— (2014b), 'The Role of Schools in Disaster Settings: Learning from the 2010–2011 New Zealand earthquakes', *International Journal of Educational Development*.

Mutch, C. and Gawith, E. (2014), 'The New Zealand Earthquakes and the Role of Schools in Engaging Children in Emotional Processing of Disaster Experiences', *Pastoral Care in Education: An international journal of personal, social and emotional development*, 32: 1, 54–67.

Section IV

Temporal City

Chapter 11

Feature 13: Suburban *Terrain Vague*

Anthony McInneny

Introduction

'Un-habited, un-safe and un-productive': Ignasi de Solà-Morales Rubió describes city spaces of abandoned industrial sites as Terrain Vague (Solà-Morales 1995: 120). He posits these spaces as the city's 'negative image as much as in the sense of criticism as in that of possible alternative' (1995: 120). For Solà-Morales, these strange places are signifiers of a constantly changing world that 'inevitably produces a permanent strangeness' and this 'loss of consistent principles corresponds ethically and aesthetically' in the formation of the divided individual of contemporary society (Solà-Morales 1995: 121).

Solà-Morales proposes that photography and performance manifest Terrain Vague in ways that are different from architecture and urbanism, which, he claims, violently transforms this estrangement into citizenship. Alternatively, time-based art preserves Terrain Vague in the 'uncontaminated magic of the obsolete' (Solà-Morales 1995: 123). Such sites of emptiness operate as both a network that is endemic to post-industrial cities, and specific urban places with a past that is evident in the residue of their formation.

James Meyer identifies the literal site in site-specific art as '[…] a place, and only there' (Meyer 2000: 26). This is in contrast to the concept of the functional site that may or may not be a physical place. By demanding a physical acuity of being present, site-specificity in a literal sense shifts the emphasis from the artwork to the viewer, from the institution of art to a place and a presence within a space and time. From this critique of the institution of art to that of society's broader structures, institutions and relations, the functional site in art is related to the construction of identity and the contingency of place—both operating as frames for art practice. Terrain Vague can be considered both as a functional site for art that frames an alternative to urban transformation, and as a series of specific sites in a literal sense of their history and current state of obsolescence.

The project in this chapter, Feature 13, investigates the suburban form of Terrain Vague by interweaving the functional with the literal site through performance and photography as temporalities of an art practice located in suburban public space. Firstly, through this art practice of spatial re-appropriations (Lefebvre 1991), I develop a typology of public spaces generated by, and specific to, the evolution of what Aiden Davison describes as the Suburban City (Davison 2005). Secondly, I discuss the cultural specificity of metropolitan Melbourne as a Suburban City, and the potential of the literal site for site-specific art to be indicative of the functional site of a suburban identity in relation to urban transformation. Thirdly, I document the development of Feature 13 as a temporary and temporal artwork in the unmarked suburban site of a demolished historic building. Shortly after the formal establishment of Melbourne in 1835, this building was constructed as the barracks of the Aboriginal Police of the Port Phillip District. The site is now situated at the suburban point of a non-urban area, known as a Green Wedge. This is one of twelve such areas designated in the 1970s to limit, or at least mitigate, the effects of a second period of sustained suburban expansion of Metropolitan Melbourne (1947–1971).

In the third period of suburban transformation commencing in 2000 (Victoria 2002), this art practice offers an alternative to the response of architecture and urbanism by way of incorporating the rhizomatic forces that shaped its current emptiness into a 'continuity that does not clarify' (Solà-Morales 1995: 123).

In conclusion, I will demonstrate how Solà-Morales' proposition that temporal art practice in Terrain Vague preserves a 'contradictory complicity' (Solà-Morales 1995: 123) in the productive logic of the city's transformation, and how this can be amplified silently in the collective imaginary of suburban public space.

Typology of Suburban Public Spaces

Originating in England in the late-eighteenth century and at the time of Australia's colonization, suburbs have continued to transform the place of cities. The suburban form was adopted in Australia as the urban and cultural system of its major city centres in the late-nineteenth century, and extensively reinforced and fundamentally transformed in the post-World War II (WWII) period (Davison 2005).

In the third sustained suburban transformation of metropolitan Melbourne (from 2000), I look for different forms of public art to manifest the paradox of nature's enculturation in suburban public space (Davison 2005). The context for this public art necessitates a differentiation of suburban from urban public space. Such differentiation may be manifested through forms and uses of public space. In this context, the importance given by Solà-Morales to art in relation to the urban typology of Terrain Vague provides a means of approaching the post-WWII suburban form through its use or obsolescence as a temporality.

Temporality is the subjective experience of the passing of time (Hoy 2009). Lewis Mumford's pre-WWII observation that '[…] suburbia is a collective effort to live a private life' (Mumford 1938: 472) places this temporality in a specific social and spatial context. Henri Lefebvre's concept of the re-appropriation of spaces that outlive their purpose (Lefebvre 1991) is both a method and means to investigate the implications of this collective 'private life' on the purpose of its public spaces. Similarly, James Meyer's description of the functional site (Meyer 2000), as the frame for art practices related to the construction of identity and the contingency of place, positions the built public spaces of the post-WWII suburban form as specific temporal sites that take a central role in this new urban identity.

The public art project presented in this chapter forms part of a wider investigation of suburban public space through practice-led research (McInneny 2014). The research traces the development of Aiden Davison's Suburban City (Davison 2005) and identifies the potential of three urban forms, which are in fact systems, as functional sites and frames for a practice of public art. These functional sites are: the freeway network; the car-based enclosed shopping centre as a suburban system; and the reserved non-urban land areas within metropolitan Melbourne called Green Wedges as a twice-cultured imagining of nature. Each of these forms was introduced, formed and transformed by post-WWII suburban development.

In his seminal survey of the history of suburbia, Robert Fishman notes that the massive suburban expansion of post-WWII Anglo-American urbanization '[...] represents not the culmination of the 200-year history of suburbia but rather its end' (Fishman 1987: 183). Metropolitan Melbourne doubled its physical size in the post-WWII period. In this chapter, this growth is considered as neither a culmination of two centuries of suburban inheritance nor its end. Rather, Melbourne's post-WWII expansion is explored as one in the same part of an urban transformation based in the suburbs. Through the public art project discussed here, I investigate the implications of this transformation within a literal site that is situated in the third of the three functional sites as identified in metropolitan Melbourne: the Green Wedge system. I propose and implement a temporary/temporal artwork to preserve the erased and neglected elements of an abandoned suburban public space.

Ignasi de Solà-Morales Rubió denotes abandoned urban spaces by the French term, Terrain Vague. In being 'vague', argues Solà-Morales, the terrain becomes both empty and unoccupied, and is thus free, available and unengaged (Solà-Morales 1995: 119–120). In the perception of the city, these voids hold a latent promise, 'as encounter, as the space of the possible, of expectation' (Solà-Morales 1995: 120). Terrain Vague can be characterized as a place where the past is more dominant than the present or the future. This type of place signifies the original estrangement from nature that is inherent in the urban condition and the urban citizen.

However, the 'urban' condition of the project, as presented here, is a condition of the 'suburban'—a shift that compounds this estrangement. The presence of nature, conserved, preserved and/or reconstructed is central to the culture of Australian suburban living, and it is this characteristic that masks the estrangement of urbanization during processes of suburban expansion. Henri Lefebvre writes of existing space:

[It] may outlive its original purpose and the raison d'être which determines its forms, functions and structures: it may thus in a sense become vacant, and susceptible to being diverted, re-appropriated and put to a use quite different from its initial one.

(Lefebvre 1991: 167)

Lefebvre's analysis of spatial re-appropriation as applied to architecture and urbanism was co-conceived through an art practice of disruptive acts, events or use of media and communications called 'situations' (Ross 1997) or 'détournements' (Sadler 1999).

Re-appropriations, situations and détournements were opposite to the recuperation of urban space, in that they highlighted through this new use a redundancy in the modernist design. Lefebvre saw great potential in these types of diversions to teach us about the production of space and the possible alternative social relations within and through the urban form as a network. However, Lefebvre concludes that these new uses simply called a temporary halt to the domination of space inherent in the processes of urbanization and the political economy of late capitalism.

Re-appropriation in art, as a fragmenting of singular meaning, holds the processes of urbanization as the functional site of social and political relations and identities. It does this in physical, urban locations, but only through, and for the brief cessation of the domination of space through urbanization.

Cultural Specificity of the Suburban City

Robert Fishman documents the origins of suburbia from England in the late-eighteenth century and the changing mode of economic production, transportation and urbanization at the beginning of the industrial revolution (Fishman 1987). Fishman points out that, unlike their European counterparts in France and Germany, the rising middle class of England abandoned their city centres through a form of living, which was based on a physical separation of the private life of the emerging nuclear family from the public lives of people in the industrial city. This separation of work and home, arising from a sexual division of labour, was achieved spatially and ideologically through the notion of the bucolic home where children were best isolated from the influence and squalor of the transforming city. Inheriting these ideological attempts at social stability, Australia was established as a penal colony at the time of the birth of suburbia in England. Terry Flew argues that since the late-nineteenth century Australian cities have been established as a series of planning experiments designed to avoid 'the problems of high-density urban living in Britain that had necessitated the transportation of people to Australia in the first place' (Flew 2010).

Contrary to the myth of Australia as a largely rural society, since at least the mid-nineteenth century it has been a highly urbanized society, but this urbanism has been, in fact, suburban (Lewis 1999). Aiden Davison (2005) defines metropolitan Melbourne in the state of Victoria, Australia, as a Suburban City 'where capitals developed suburbs before their centres were built up' (Davison 2005, citing Frost, Dingle and La Trobe 1993). Davison identifies two key periods of sustained suburban expansion and transformation throughout Melbourne's brief urban history. The first period is a consequence of a population increase of 77 per cent in the decade of 1881 to 1891, following the gold rush (1852 to the late 1860s), with no increase in the city centre's density. The second expansion was for a longer period from 1947 to 1971, associated with post-WWII prosperity, and a 92 per cent increase in population that saw marginal increases in city-centre populations (Frost, Dingle and La Trobe 1993). During these 25 years a second Melbourne was built, situated around the first suburban city (Rundell 1985). Such a rapid and disruptive transformation of the landscape led to a mitigating measure that aimed to preserve the suburban imaginary yet, paradoxically, contain sprawl. The 1970s saw the establishment of Green Wedges as designated non-urban areas (Melbourne Metropolitan Board of Works 1971). The Wedges were reserved within, or sliced into, metropolitan Melbourne from outside the first urban growth boundary established in 1954. It was not until 2002 that the Green Wedges were recognized formally in planning documents. The original intent of the Green Wedges was central to the urban planning framework entitled 'Melbourne 2030' (Victoria 2002), and central also to the collective imaginary of future suburban living. This framework was revised within three years of its release (Victoria 2005) in light of increased population growth projections for 2050. Subsequently, the Green Wedges are under constant threat from further suburbanization.

For Davison, the image and imagining of the suburbs of Australian cities distinguish them from those in England and North America. In Australia the suburbs are not 'locked between the city and the country', and as such they developed 'a more expansive imagination of time and space' (Davison 2005). However, this imagination avoids the pre-urban past specific to the establishment of Melbourne and the legal concept of *Terra Nullius*: land belonging to no one. Governor Arthur Phillips established the first convict settlement in Australia in 1788. However, it was the foundation of Melbourne in 1835 that began the history of what James Boyce calls the most extensive, vast and rapid seizing of any land in British colonial history (Boyce 2011). Boyce documents how this taking of land through the customary practice of effective occupation became the legal tenure for the dispossession of Aboriginal land across Australia. It was not until the late-twentieth century that Native Title abolished the legal fiction of *Terra Nullius*. Native Title is granted where it can be established that indigenous people have continuous and exclusive use of land, permanent settlement and systems of government. For the overwhelming number of indigenous people, their continuity and rights under Native Title were extinguished through effective colonial occupation.

The relationship between the establishment of Melbourne and a national dispossession is well known. Less known is the short-lived, mid-nineteenth-century experiment in the assimilation of Aboriginal people into the system of their dispossession. The physical site of the only architectural form that housed this experiment was demolished in 1964, but its location is the literal site of the project presented here. In colonial societies, dispossession is the first layer of estrangement upon which the urban form is conceived. In the case of Australian urbanism, two forms of distancing—firstly from place and then from nature—is compounded by the paradox of a society that is, and always has been, highly urbanized, but with a low urban density. Dispossession, absent architecture and nature as open public space represent the three distances of an urban estrangement that paradoxically hold a presence within the transformation of this Suburban City.

The Dandenong Police Paddocks Reserve is situated at the suburban tip of one of metropolitan Melbourne's 12 Green Wedges within an area of land known as the Southern Ranges. This reserve appears as an empty paddock rising from Stud Road on its western perimeter before expanding towards and enveloping a national park. New suburbs flank this wedge on both sides as it opens and extends to a re-established outer-eastern, urban boundary some 65 kilometres from the metropolitan Melbourne city centre. The Dandenong Police Paddocks Reserve, like Stud Road and the nearby Police Road, derives its names from the equestrian history of the area: this site was a stud farm for the Victorian Police of the late-nineteenth and early-twentieth centuries. It was so named in 1927. Before this date and the ubiquitous use of the car, police rode horses and the term 'police paddocks' designated any land used for the stabling and caring for police horses. Numerous sites across metropolitan Melbourne and Victoria are known as police paddocks, a term also used in other states of Australia. However, the site of the Dandenong Police Paddocks was established by an earlier mounted police force, unique in Victoria's history, which was stationed there for 12 years in the mid-nineteenth century.

In a nineteenth-century measure of distance, the site of the Dandenong Police Paddocks is one day's horse ride from the centre of the City of Melbourne (25 kilometres as the crow flies). This site contains the structural foundations of the nineteenth-century barracks of the mounted Aboriginal Police of the Port Phillip District who were known also as the Native Police Corps. Formed just two years after the official establishment of Melbourne in 1835, the Native Police Corps were in operation in four key formations between 1837 and 1853. Ostensibly created for the policing of outlaws during and after the formative years of the state of Victoria (Fels 1988), between 1842 and 1853, the Native Police Corps was based at what is now called the Dandenong Police Paddocks Reserve. A set of buildings and farmlands was built on the site by the Corps to house and sustain themselves and the white officers.

In 1990, a planning committee comprising of representatives of the Wurundjeri people (the traditional owners of the land), and municipal and state government authorities, commissioned an archaeological survey of the site of the Dandenong Police Paddocks Reserve (Rhodes 1990). Records of the archaeological survey note that: 'It is common "knowledge" that around 1964 that the Chief Engineer of the Dandenong Council bulldozed the barracks and other buildings in the Police Paddocks without knowledge or permission of the Council' (Rhodes 1990). The survey also states that 'reconstruction of buildings or other archaeological forms is not a desirable objective of the site management' (Rhodes 1990). The foundations of the historic buildings are overgrown and a rise in the groundcover is all that vaguely marks the footprint of the barracks. Two rows of poorly maintained trees now indicate what was once an avenue leading to other buildings constructed at a later date that were demolished along with the barracks. In 1994, the archaeological survey served as the basis for an unrealized master plan for the site based on the construction of an Aboriginal cultural centre and environmental education park.

In 2011, a call was made by the Victorian State Government for a public art commission to mark the contribution of indigenous people to the State of Victoria (Premier announces major public art commission 2011). The site for the public artwork could be anywhere in the State of Victoria and was to be nominated in the proposal of a creative team that was to be led by, or at least involve an indigenous person in a lead role. The proposals could be for temporary works.

In 2011, the Dandenong Police Paddocks Reserve looked just like a paddock. Its use was incidental and from all entry points it appeared to be just other open public space within a Green Wedge. Since 2005, I had been walking regularly in the Dandenong Police Paddocks Reserve. As the seed for what would become a larger research of suburban public space (McInneny 2014), I was monitoring the maintenance of the site of the demolished barracks through photography. As the only implemented aspect of the 1994 master plan, interpretative signage stood in an illegible state of disrepair, subject to vandalism, before it was subsequently removed around 2012. Marie Fels' authoritative examination of existing historical documents of the Aboriginal Police of the Port Phillip District (Fels 1988) offers a way to make evident abandoned sites that are now suburban and invisible, i.e. through what is documented, by whom, in what form and how this is circulated. I was involved as both a coordinator, in 2006, and as a participant, in 2010 and 2011, of walking tours of the site with scholars and indigenous experts. My interest lay in maintaining the site's emptiness as an artwork in order to explore its place in the suburban imaginary. To this end, I met with central representatives of the Dandenong Police Paddock Reserve 1994 master planning committee, and discussed this idea with indigenous writer and historian, Tony Birch, and with writer and locative media artist, Matt Blackwood. As a collaborative group we nominated the Dandenong Police Paddock Reserve for the Victorian Government's 2011 public art commission, offering the proposal for a locative media project under the working title of 'Storyspace'. The proposal was for indigenous and non-indigenous poets, writers, historians and artists to create works that would be composed with, and augmented by the knowledge that the audience had to be in the site of the Dandenong Police Paddocks Reserve to experience these works via mobile media. The proposal was unsuccessful, but I decided to pursue the idea by focusing on an unsolicited intervention in a specific site within the reserve. This would be for an uninitiated and possibly disinterested audience who were physically distanced from this place.

Feature 13

Two images exist that provide conflicting visual accounts of the form and orientation of the original barracks of the Native Police Corps. A single sketch of the site made in 1855 by the landscape painter, Eugene von Guérard provides detail of the context, the scale and the orientation of the cluster of buildings that included the barracks (see Figure 1). The second visual record is a photograph from the 1950s that shows a smaller building, but without other architectural references (see Figure 2). Both images situate the building in the same location, but each orientation and form is different from the other. Von Guérard's sketch establishes the orientation of the barracks through identifiable geographical references: Dandenong Creek in the foreground and the Dandenong mountain ranges in

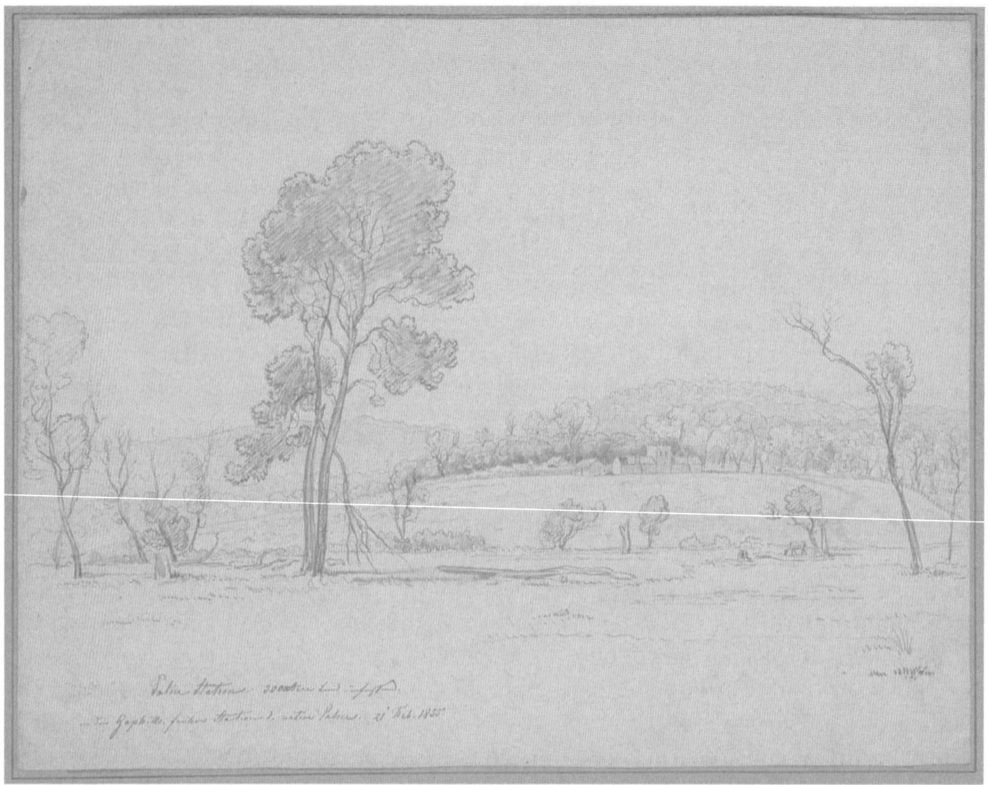

Figure 1: *Barrack Headquarters*, Eugene von Guérard, 1855. Image reproduced with permission from the State Library of New South Wales.

the background (see Figure 1). The photographic image establishes the orientation of the building by the avenue of trees in the background. These trees were planted after the making of the drawing by von Guérard (see Figure 2). The archaeological survey from 1990 that cites these records provides no conclusive evidence of which image is that of the barracks, and the issue remains unresolved without further archaeological investigation. The site of the two contradictory records of the building purported to be the barracks is identified in the survey as simply 'Feature 13'. In 2012, the site maintenance was at a minimum due to a scarcity of public funding to maintain public parks across Victoria and, in this case, the overgrowth was used as a method to protect what little remains of the footprint of the original structures in their abandoned state (see Figure 2).

The two visual records of a building in this site preserve two contradictory memories of the barracks not as lived-in buildings but as abandoned spaces. The barracks were abandoned by the collapse of the Corps in 1853. In von Guérard's sketch of 1855 can be seen the deteriorating state of the building's roof on the lower left side (see Figure 1). The photograph from the 1950s shows a different stone building in a crumbling and uninhabitable state of

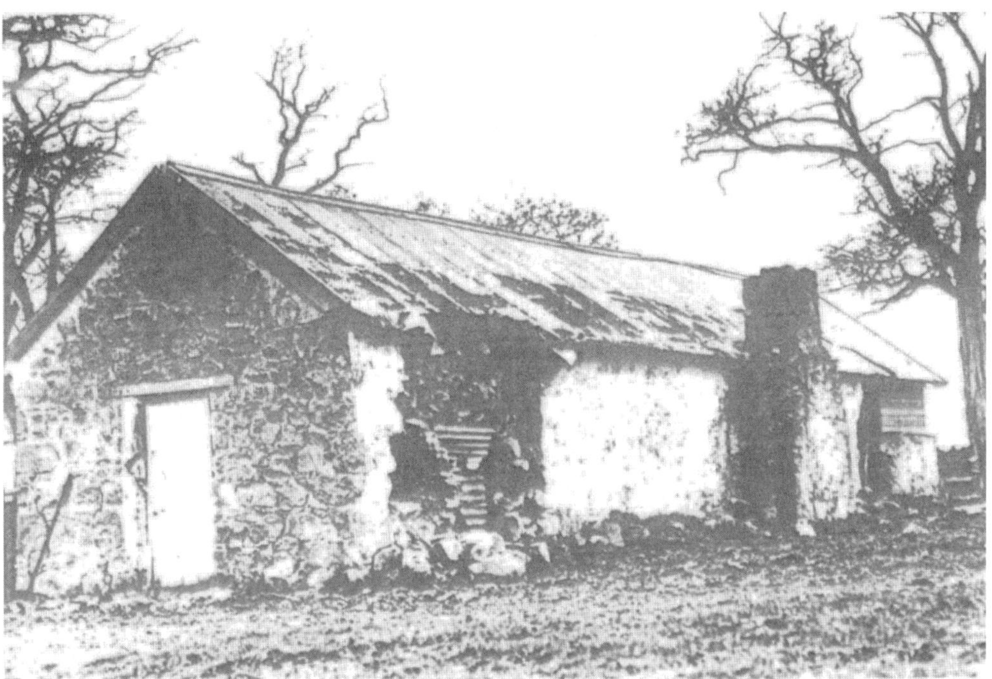

Figure 2: *Barracks of the Aboriginal Police of the Port Phillip District,* ca. 1950, Anon. Image reproduced with the permission of the Knox Historical Society.

disrepair (see Figure 2). A third record of the barracks preserves a contentious social space that no longer exists, but which held a possible alternative to black-and-white relations. In her historical account of the Aboriginal Police of the Port Phillip District, Marie Fels draws attention to a written record of an exchange within the barracks between indigenous police and their white commandant, Dana. In this account, Dana's 'learned dissertation' was received 'with great applause from both sides of the barracks room. The speaker left the chair amidst deafening cries of hear him, chair, turn him out, order etc.' (Fels 1988: 82). This exchange is noted by Fels, firstly for its demonstration of a collapse of social distance between white authority and black police; secondly, it is noted for the use of procedural terminology; and thirdly, it is noted because these specific aspects of the relationship warranted recording in the official logbook from where this account is taken.

Solà-Morales observes that our fascination with abandoned, empty urban spaces, and the spaces themselves, reflect our own insecurities and fears of being external to the urban system. This holds certain relevance to the Suburban City as a colonial concept and place. In discussions with representatives and members of the 1994 master planning committee, the key agency responsible for the upkeep of the reserve did not want anything in the park that would require maintenance. Nothing in the park became central to the art project as a way to maintain the physical site of the barracks in a state of emptiness, disrepair and distance. By default of circumstances, 'a continuity as opposed to clarity' (Solà-Morales 1995: 123) is possible in this site as one of the alternatives present at its point of urban origin. An expectancy of an alternative to the urban also resides within the place of a suburban public space such as the Green Wedge. In the promise of Terrain Vague, Solà-Morales argues for continuity of the world's strangeness as it confronts us. Such a continuity of estrangement 'should be undertaken from a contradictory complicity that would not shatter the perceptive elements which maintain its continuity in time and space' (Solà-Morales 1995: 123).

The suburban condition, as such, is not discussed by Solà-Morales. However, the suburban condition offers a frame to consider colonial settlement and Aboriginal dispossession through the functional site of the Green Wedges and the literal site of the demolished barracks as terrain vague. Solà-Morales suggests 'a casual unfolding of a particular proposal, which is superimposed on the already existing: repeated void on the void of the city: silent, artificial landscape touching the historical time of the city yet neither cancelling it nor imitating it' (Solà-Morales 1995: 123).

In context of this spatial, social, historical and political landscape, I created the work entitled, Feature 13. The work re-appropriates two elements of the site; it does so to maintain a condition of emptiness or invisibility. These elements are established through the physical and cultural remoteness of the audience from the unmarked site of an unknown structure in an open suburban public space. The first re-appropriation manifests in the performance of the construction and removal of a structure in the site of the demolished barracks. The second re-appropriation is via communication of a digital recording of this performance from specific sites related to both the site of the unmarked, demolished barracks, and the naming of the Dandenong Police Paddocks Reserves as a generic term for a type of suburban public space.

The first re-appropriation is of the footprint of the demolished barracks that is concealed by overgrowth. This is the location for the temporary installation of a structure that is an internally illuminated cube (see Figure 3). The structure is installed pre-sunrise and pre-sunset over the working days of a week and recorded in situ via a digital video recorder. Before the sun rises and after it sets the illuminated cube is visible publicly from Stud Road, about 500 metres away. A driver travelling along this Road would have been able to see the structure, but only when it is dark, when the physical site is inaccessible for the practical reasons of bush walking. The site of the former barracks is accessible only on foot, and after 15-minutes of walking into the paddock from an entrance with no indication of its location. If the driver were to return on foot, of a day, to find out what was the 'light on the hill', it would not be there and yet the same person would be unknowingly in the site of an unmarked building.

The temporary structure derives from three aspects of the history of the barrack in the site that denies or confuses its form: firstly, the demolition of the original building and the archaeological report's recommendation not to reconstruct it; secondly, the two contradictory visual records of the building's existence; and thirdly, the fact that the site can be located yet its foundations that could reveal its form remain overgrown to protect what little remains.

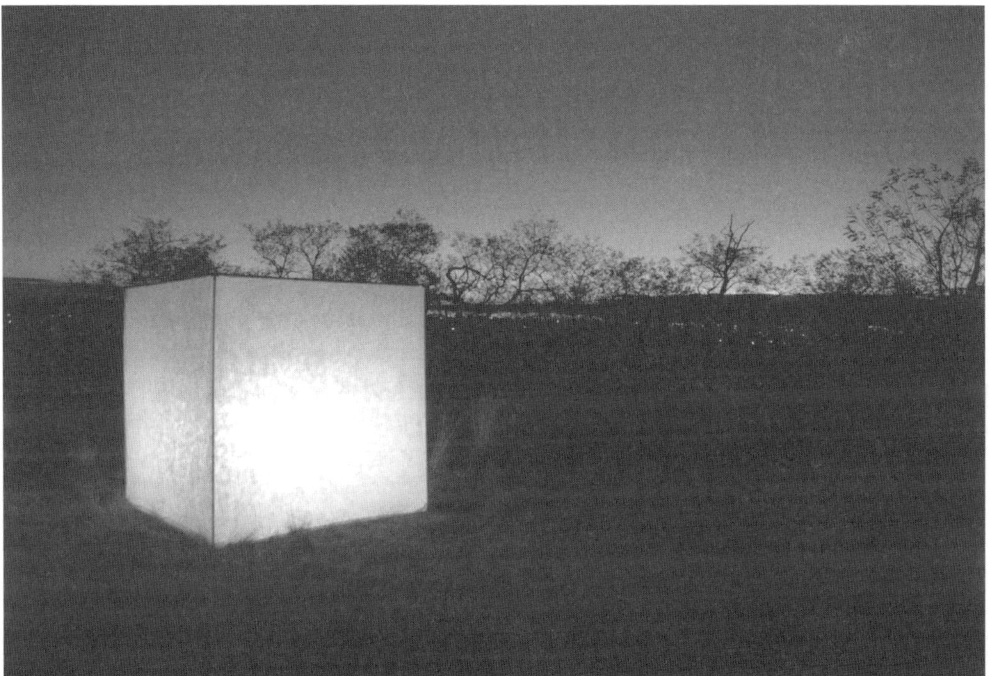

Figure 3: *Feature 13*, Installation view, Anthony McInneny, 2013. Aluminium frame, horticultural clothe, gas lantern. Dimensions 2.2m × 2.2m × 2.2m. Dandenong Police Paddocks Reserve, Rowville, Australia. Image: Anthony McInneny, 2013.

The structure of a cube represents the two possibilities and realities of the buildings purported to be the barracks: a cube appears the same when viewed from either of the vantages of the contradictory visual records. The demolition of the original barracks was, as far as the records intimate (Rhodes 1990), not a deliberate act to erase the history of the building, but an expedient and careless act of ridding the site of a dangerous structure. An equally dangerous site remains. Suspended overgrowth between the remaining strip footing foundations creates a continuous carpet across the absent floor marking the building's footprint. It is possible to imagine from this organic trapdoor the scale of the barracks, but not its form. The intention of Feature 13 is to mark this unremarked site through its undefined presence. This actual performance is to be experienced by commuters in their daily and weekly routine of driving to and from a place of work along the main, public north-south route of the outer eastern suburbs. In the week of the winter equinox, when this performance occurred, peak hour traffic travels in both the pre-dawn and early evening darkness.

The second re-appropriation is of the vantages derived from the visual records of the two buildings purported to be the barracks (Rhodes 1990). The contradictory views in these two images are clearly not of the same structure, and this can be ascertained from their respective contexts, orientations and forms. The perspective of von Guérard's drawing is established by reference and alignment of the Dandenong Creek in the foreground and the Dandenong Ranges in the background of this *plein air* study (see Figure 1). It is interesting to note that von Guérard was known for making composite or ideal landscape paintings from such sketches where he would combine elements of nature from one location and place them in another scene (Pullin 2007). From the perspective and landmarks of von Guérard's landscape sketch, it is possible to establish him as perhaps having been on the perimeter of the Dandenong Police Paddocks Reserve when he made this drawing. This position is now located in the Brady Road entrance to the reserve where there is 'way-finding' signage for the reserve, but not for the site of the demolished barracks. The perspective of the later photograph can be determined from the view of the avenue of trees in the background of that image (see Figure 2). While this building no longer exists, one of the trees in this image is still situated in the site. The unknown photographer from the 1950s was closer to his or her subject than von Guérard when taking the shot. This was in a slightly elevated position located in a west-south-westerly direction from the site of the barracks. Unlike von Guérard's sketch, where he may have added components and perspectives of a greater landscape, the photograph has a fidelity to location that is composed by the viewfinder and an optically identifiable horizon.

For reasons of differentiating the two mediums, views and methods of image making, I have traced the horizon through the view of the photograph to a point on the perimeter of Dandenong Police Paddock Reserve situated in Stud Road. These two differently derived points on the perimeter of the reserve are each locations for an anonymous QR code to be installed on existing signage (see Figure 4). The QR codes connect mobile devices to a recording of the installation that was in the site of the demolished barracks. It was possible to view this recording at any time, day or night, after the installation had been removed, but only from the site of the two QR codes. Standing at either of these sites and reading the existing and official signs that give no indication of the location or significance of the barracks of the Aboriginal Police of the Port Phillip District, the viewer is looking unknowingly in the direction of the demolished building(s) (see Figure 4). The cultural and temporal distance is twice amplified for the audience by the built and temporary structures no longer being there and in not knowing that they are not there. The QR codes download video content to a mobile device that is viewed from each of the two perspectives: a sun rises or sets behind an internally illuminated architectural form located in the abandoned site of the demolished barracks. Temporality as a subjective experience of the passing of time is witnessed as being present at either of these perspective points and watching the real-time video recording. The video content is static except for the representation of time in the arc of the rising or setting sun that bleaches or emphasizes the illumination emanating from the architectural form. The invisibility of aboriginality in the urban landscape, the effective occupation of this purported emptiness through urban settlement and the transformation incorporated in a suburban form that appears to not change are each manifest in this experience.

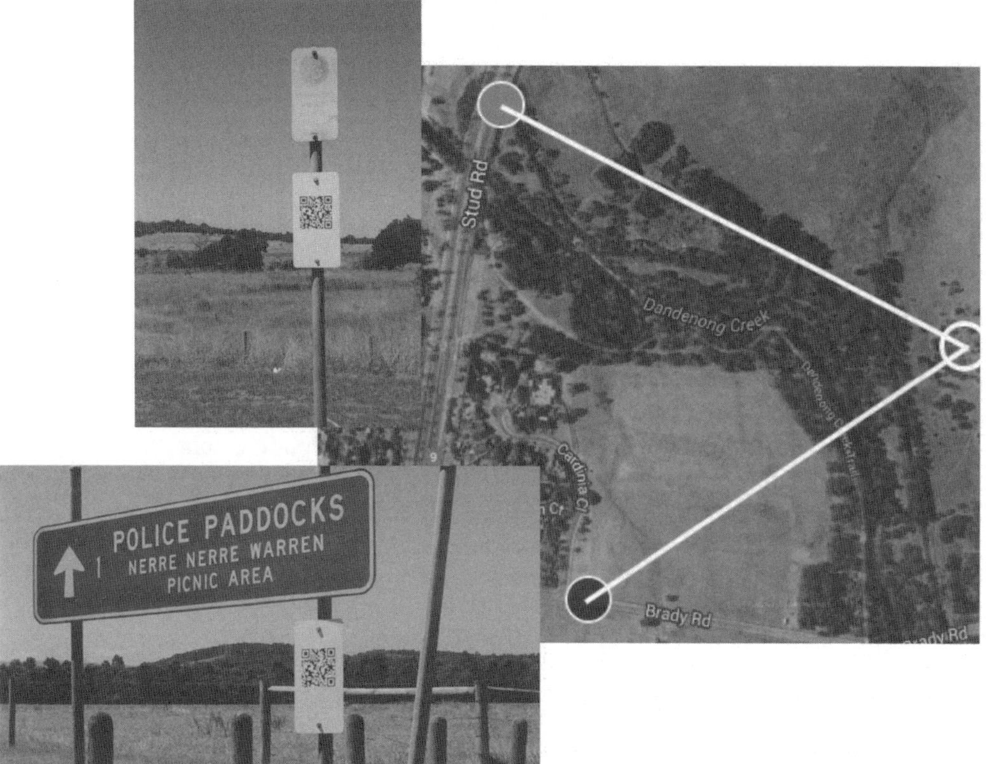

Figure 4: *Feature 13,* Locative media QR codes, Anthony McInneny, 2013. Stud Road and Brady Road, Police Paddocks Reserve, Rowville, Australia. Image: Anthony McInneny, 2013. Aerial photograph from Google Earth.

Concluding with Suburban Terrain Vague and Transformation

This conclusion brings together the main features of Suburban Terrain Vague and its relevance to transformation as a suburban condition.

Solà-Morales proposes that art in Terrain Vague preserves a 'contradictory complicity' (Solà-Morales 1995: 123) in the productive logic and urban estrangement of the city. This proposition holds a specific resonance in the continuing transformation of metropolitan Melbourne as a Suburban City. A double masking of urban estrangement exists in the suburban form and condition. Initially, this is based in the effective occupation of indigenous place through dispossession. Then, there is the underpinning of this irreconcilable antinomy in the expansion of the suburbs by the enculturation of nature's otherness as landscape. The demolished barracks of the Aboriginal Police of the Port Phillip District is a literal site of the first layer. As parts of the network of open suburban public spaces, the Southern Ranges' Green Wedge, which includes the Dandenong Police Paddock Reserve, is a functional site of the second layer. The two faces of this one disguise hold the urban and architectural project of the Suburban City, and its physical transformation through the idea of empty space, vacant space and continuing growth. Alternatively, the transformation of the suburban imaginary can be conceived through the site of the Dandenong Police Paddock Reserve as Suburban Terrain Vague. Through an art practice of re-appropriation and temporality, a specific site is brought together with the literal site of the suburbs, in the preservation of this complex space.

Performance affords a re-appropriation of space in and through the act of intervening as the possible, the expectative and the alternative of Terrain Vague. Photography represents and re-presents the temporality of this performance and of a previous and continuing available emptiness. Solà-Morales' proposition for such a preservation of terrain vague applies to its suburban counterpart as both a literal and functional site for art.

Art in Suburban Terrain Vague proposes an incorporation of the subdued suburban estrangement from place, nature and the urban itself to reveal the forces rather than forms that shape our suburban relations. Performance and photography, as strategies of re-appropriation, situations, détournements and site-specificity, create a temporality in Suburban Terrain Vague. These strategies amplify the invisibilities of temporality through our cultural and spatial distances. As such, in the suburban imaginary, the idea of nothing in the space is no longer possible.

References

Boyce, J. (2011), *1835: The Founding of Melbourne & the Conquest of Australia*, Melbourne: Black Inc.

Davison, A. (2005), 'Australian Suburban Imaginaries of Nature: Towards a prospective history', *Australian Humanities Review*, 37, <http://www.australianhumanitiesreview.org/archive/Issue-December-2005/davison.html>. Accessed 1 September 2015.

Fels, M. (1988), *Good Men and True: The Aboriginal Police of the Port Phillip District 1837–1853*, Melbourne: Melbourne University Press.

Fishman, R. (1987), *Bourgeois Utopia: The rise and fall of suburbia*, New York: Basic Books.

Flew, T. (2010), 'Globalization, Suburbanization and the Creative Workforce: Findings from Australian suburban communities', *Spaces and Flows conference*, UCLA, Los Angeles, CA, USA, 4–5 December 2010, <http://www.academia.edu/386940/Globalization_Suburbanization_and_the_Creative_Workforce_Findings_from_Australian_Suburban_Communities>. Accessed 1 September 2015.

Frost, L., Dingle, T. and La Trobe, U. (1993), *Sustaining Suburbia: An historical perspective on Australia's urban growth*, Melbourne: Dept. of Economic History, La Trobe University.

Hoy, D. C. (2009), *The Time of Our Lives: A critical history of temporality*, Boston: MIT Press.

Lefebvre, H. (1991), *The Production of Space*, (trans. Donald Nicholson-Smith), Oxford: Wiley-Blackwell. (First published in French 1974.)

Lewis, M. (1999), *Suburban Backlash: The battle for the world's most liveable city*, Melbourne: Blooming Books.

McInneny, A. (2014), 'Latent Space: Temporary art and suburban public space', unpublished PhD thesis, RMIT University Australia.

Melbourne Metropolitan Board of Works (1971), 'Planning Policies for the Metropolitan Planning Region', Melbourne.

Meyer, J. (2000), 'The Functional Site; or, the Transformation of Site-specificity', in E. Suderberg (ed.), *Space, Site, Intervention: Situating installation art*, Minneapolis: University of Minnesota, pp. 23–37.

Mumford, L. (1938), *The Culture of Cities*, New York: Harcourt, Brace and Company.

Pullin, V. R. (2007), 'Eugene von Guerard and the Science of Landscape Painting', unpublished PhD thesis, School of Culture and Communication, The University of Melbourne.

Rhodes, D. (1990), 'The Dandenong Police Paddocks. An Archaeological Survey. Volume 1–3', Department of Conservation and Environment, Occasional Report Series No. 25, Melbourne.

Ross, K. (1997), 'Henri Lefebvre on the Situationist International', Interview conducted and translated 1983, *October*, 79, Winter, <http://www.notbored.org/lefebvre-interview.html>. Accessed 1 September 2015.

Rundell, G. (1985), 'Melbourne Anti-freeway Protests', *Urban Policy and Research*, 3: 4, Melbourne: Swinburne University of Technology, pp. 11–21.

Sadler, S. (1999), *The Situationist City*, Boston: MIT Press.

Solà-Morales, I. (1995), 'Terrain Vague', in C. Davison (ed.), *Anyplace, Anyone Corporation*, New York/Cambridge: MIT Press, pp. 118–123.

Victoria, Department of Infrastructure (2005), 'Melbourne 2030: A planning update', Melbourne @ 5 million, <http://www.dtpli.vic.gov.au/planning/plans-and-policies/planning-for-melbourne/melbournes-strategic-planning-history/melbourne-2030-a-planning-update-melbourne-@-5-million>. Accessed 1 September 2015.

—— (2002), 'Melbourne 2030 Planning for Sustainable Growth', <http://www.dtpli.vic.gov.au/__data/assets/pdf_file/0005/228299/2030_complete.pdf>. Accessed 1 September 2015.

Victoria Government (2011), 'Premier Announces Major Public Art Commission 2011', <http://creative.vic.gov.au/News/News/Archive/Media_Releases/2011/Premier_announces_major_public_art_commission>. Accessed 1 September 2015.

Chapter 12

Beyond the Tarmac: Temporality and the roadside art of Melbourne

Ashley Perry

Introduction

The aim of this chapter is to examine site-specific public artworks situated within the geography of two extensive motorways, the EastLink Tollway and the Peninsula Link Freeway, positioned on the South Eastern edges of metropolitan Melbourne. Specifically, it explores how two prominent artworks may transform the physical spaces and temporal experiences of 'drive time'. Transformation becomes possible by establishing an array of relational, affective and momentary attachments that are assembled and enacted between motorists, in their vehicles, and these roadside objects. The planning, design, construction and governing of both Tollway and Freeway have reinforced the 'historic link between economic liberalism and automobility' (Davison 2004: 243) as a feature of Melbourne's transportation system. The re-activation of land usage on the peri-urban fringe of the city has sought to accommodate expanding commercial industries and changes in individual lifestyle and consumption practices by a growing suburban population that rely upon mass motoring on a daily basis.

Sited in a prominent position along the Tollway roadside is Callum Morton's (Australia) evocative artwork, *Hotel* (2008). A scaled model of a multi-storey hotel the artwork simultaneously embodies imaginative, generic and symbolic notions of both the local and global characteristics of contemporary cities. Equally, at the point where the Peninsula Link passes over the EastLink Tollway, at a major interchange between the two roads, is Louise Paramor's (Australia) public sculpture *Panorama Station* (2012). The large-scale assemblage of brightly coloured and found plastic objects establishes an imaginative and fictional form, possibly related to the space of industry or some type of advanced machine.

By focusing on the relationships established by motorists' encounters with these two distinctive artworks, this chapter investigates the spatial, temporal and aesthetic characteristics suggested by these artworks. Further, it seeks to demonstrate how site-specific public art may produce a transformative effect on the geographies of outer Melbourne, and also on the motorists, who travel through these semi-private landscapes.

Automobilities

In recent times social scientists have sought to account for the diverse, complex and interdependent nature of movement and flow within globalizing processes by investigating a range of physical, informational, visual, imaginative and virtual movements that define contemporary social life. Writing in *Sociology Beyond Societies* (2000), John Urry argues that the movement of 'peoples, objects, images, [capital] and information travel [...] produce and reproduce social life and cultural forms' (2000: 49). This (re)production occurs through modalities relating to the contemporary experience of time, space, dwelling and citizenship. Urry investigates these corporeal, informational, imaginative and virtual mobilities through concepts of 'metaphor and process' (2000: 49). He suggests that:

> [...] some of the material transformations that are remaking the 'social', especially those diverse mobilities that, through multiple senses, imaginative travel, movements of images and information, virtuality and physical movement, are materially constructing the 'social as society' into the 'social as mobility'.
>
> (Urry 2000: 2)

More recently there is the emergence of a 'new mobilities paradigm' or 'mobility turn' (Hannam, Sheller and Urry 2006; Sheller and Urry 2006; Creswell 2010). This new condition is gaining considerable attention and traction within the social sciences. As a nascent field of 'mobilities research', academics such as Peter Adey (2006, 2004) and Mike Crang (2002, 2001) investigate new forms, different styles, hidden sites and increased levels of mobility. They consider ways of thinking and theorizing that foreground the mobility of people, ideas, places and things as a geographical fact that lies at the centre of constellations of power, the creation of identities and the microgeographies of everyday life (Creswell 2010).

Such research into automobility engages with the multiple interlocking dimensions of the car and the broader machinic complex it constitutes (Urry 2004, 2000; Böhm et al. 2006). In attempting to account for the complexities of the 'car-system' and the hybrid figure of the 'car-driver' (Sheller and Urry 2000) in context of the ways in which contemporary social life is shaped and organized, a notable focus of automobility studies situates the socio-spatial and material investigations of motorways. The urban geographer Peter Merriman, for example, examines the critical sociologies and geographies of driving in terms of site-specific encounters, with an emphasis on:

> [...] the ways in which subjectivities, materialities and spatialities associated with driving emerge through the folding and placing of the spaces and materialities of cars, bodies, roads and surroundings (with a variety of thoughts, atmospheres, senses and presences) into dynamic, contingent topological assemblages.
>
> (Merriman 2004: 146)

Additional studies within the automobilities' field include the multifaceted exploration of driving within motorway landscapes, as in Tim Edensor's 'Defamiliarizing the Mundane Roadscape' (2003) and Iain Borden's 'Driving' (2010). Both Edensor and Borden critique the notion that the environments of the car are dystopian, featureless and desensitized spaces and that driving is a purely automatic behaviour. A typical example of this characterization is located in Marc Augé's concept of 'non-place' and the notion that drivers experience feelings of detachment, distraction and boredom in contemporary places and non-places. This includes spaces of 'supermodernity' such as airports and motorways, which function 'like palimpsests' constantly being 'rewritten' (Augé 1995: 79).

This discussion seeks to account for the complex relationships to place, specific sites and moments of travel that may be encountered through driving. It does this by investigating the EastLink Tollway and the Peninsula Link Freeway as temporal, material and imagined routes that become central to the formation of identities and the production of meaningful attachments for motorists. In particular, the discussion focuses on the 'affective and imaginative connections' (Edensor 2003: 152) that may occur between the presence of public artworks and motorists who are experiencing an array of embodied and engaging sensations within what Edensor calls, the 'complex topographies of apprehension and association' (2003: 152) attributable to roads.

The proposition underpinning this discussion is that the artworks located along the Tollway and the Freeway assist in re-configuring an experience of urban time and space, while re-asserting concepts of place. This is where Augé's non-place is put to the test via recognition of new forms of relational experiences. An underlying theme running through this investigation relates to the centrality of car-led mobility in urban life, identified specifically in this discussion as the urban life of Melbourne. The characteristically animated and embodied experience of driving calls for consideration to be given to the 'specific feelings which arise from momentary associations and attachments that are integral to the ongoing [and] performative constructions of places' (Merriman 2006: 77). Such feelings and associations envelop motorists travelling on the EastLink Tollway and the Peninsula Link Freeway, and may affect their encounters with public art along these road corridors, but they are not limited to these specific locations. The associations as experienced by motorists may occur on other motorways in other urban settings.

Motorway Driving

A significant amount of research addresses the role and powerful effects of the car-system in relation to contemporary urban life (Sheller and Urry 2006, 2000). This focus has been supplemented recently by considerations of the conditions, experiences and pleasures of driving within cities. Iain Borden suggests:

Through driving—a continual and restless mobile interaction with cities, architecture and landscape—the human subject emerges as someone who has experienced one of the most distinctive and ubiquitous conditions of the modern world, and who has become, as a result, a different kind of person.

(Borden 2010: 120)

Borden's research, with its focus on urban environments, examines the affective qualities of driving in terms of sensory, cognitive and embodied experiences while questioning 'the various pleasures involved in different kinds of driving, at different speeds and in different kinds of spatial landscapes' (Borden 2010: 100). Borden sets out to reappraise the relationship between driving and the urban environment. He suggests that the material conditions of urban architecture when experienced through the mobile and animated activity of driving are responsible for unlocking a range of social and cultural meanings as well as powerful emotions from the motorist. The material conditions and physical sensations related to the practice and experience of Tollway and Freeway driving may be characterized as non-sterile, embodied and pleasurable. Motorists ensconced within a 'mobile semi-privatized capsule' (Urry 2000: 190) engage in a series of physical and mental skills that are reinforced by an implicit connectedness to the passing spatial landscape.

At the commencement of their investigation into automobility, Sheller and Urry described the motorway as a site of 'pure mobility within which car-drivers are insulated [...]' (Sheller and Urry 2000: 746). This negative connotation of motorway spaces as solitary and alienated environments with motorists enveloped in high-speed travel derives from theories of Paul Virilio and Jean Baudrillard. Sean Cubitt suggests that for Virilio the motorway remains 'the scene of picnolepsia, the suspended consciousness of auto-pilot driving' (1999: 140), where the car becomes 'a device which isolates the driver from the world' (1999: 139), and 'a device for immobilization and subjection' (1999: 140). Such a configuration encompasses a roadscape effectively 'smeared across the windscreen, devoid of detail, no longer a world of objects but a landscape flattened into a perpetual and undifferentiated present' (Cubitt 2001: 62). Baudrillard posits that driving at high speeds reduces 'the world to two-dimensionality, to an image, stripping away its relief and its historicity' (1996: 70). Definitively labelled in terms of Augé's 'non-places', the spatial conditions of such motorways are characterized alternatively as 'abstract' (Lefebvre 1991) and 'placeless' (Relph 1976; Casey 1993). This characterization is reinforced by the familiar trope of the single-occupant driver speeding programmatically to-and-from work along what Edensor casts as 'unstimulating and desocialised' auto-routes or passages (2003: 152).

On the other hand, Peter Merriman, in *Driving Spaces* (2007), argues for the potential of such urban typologies to afford a wider spectrum of experience. In his cultural-historical investigations of the landscape of England's M1 Motorway, Merriman counters the malign positioning of travelling by car on the motorway. As Merriman suggests:

The practice of driving or being a passenger in particular cars, travelling to and from particular places, along particular stretches of motorway, provokes a range of emotions, thoughts and sensations: from feelings of anxiety or excitement about being in motorway traffic, to emotions surrounding one's departure and arrival at another place.

(Merriman 2007: 218)

His less dystopian positioning of the experience, practice and performance of driving, located within 'the diverse "scapes" associated with car travel' (Merriman 2006: 75), resonate with journeying by car along the EastLink Tollway. A car trip along the EastLink Tollway or the Peninsula Link Freeway exposes motorists to fleeting and/or sustained moments of stimulation and reverie. In this state, imaginative, visually diverting and existential thoughts may arise: daydreams, musings and opinions as well as physical sensations and feelings. Deriving from the high-speed encounters between the two routes, the motorist and the roadside environment amplify the driving experience. Additionally, there is an uncovering of a series of 'topologies and multiple, heterogeneous "placings"' (Merriman 2004: 154) along the elaborately conceived, designed and engineered motorways. Strategically positioned, site-specific public art thus augments the 'multiple sensualities, materialities, topographies and psychogeographies' (Edensor 2003: 152) encountered on the Tollway and the Freeway.

Link Geographies

It was in 2008 that the dual, six-lane, EastLink Tollway opened up a new arterial passage linking inner city Melbourne to its outer Eastern and South Eastern suburbs. Characteristic of neo-liberal forces of privatization that position the city as 'a decentralized metropolis where relatively few journeys [are] capable of being made by public transport' (Davison 2004: 252), the Tollway is designed as an urban infrastructure system to 'meet the transportation needs of the new world of electronic communication, information-based industries and just-in-time-technology, and of a workforce increasingly geared to part-time, casual and mobile employment' (Davison 2004: 252). Its route extends across an interstitial space that slices through established suburbs, passes by new outer-urban housing developments and across a collection of other sites such as golf courses, scrap and timber yards, electrical substations, water treatment facilities, market gardens, wetlands and grasslands, and commercial and industrial parks. As with many of the city's major arterial roads the EastLink Tollway is aligned to a significant creek line, reinforcing the arterial form of Melbourne's road transportation network.

The EastLink Tollway was conceived initially during a period of urban expansion marked by freeway building in the early-1960s. For the duration of its construction period (commencing in March 2005), the Tollway represented Australia's largest and one of the most expensive infrastructure projects. Since its inception the Tollway has underperformed financially, yet it has been lauded for its complex architectural design, engineering characteristics and timely construction. An initial review of the Tollway by architectural critic, Dimity Reed demonstrates an example of its positive local reception. Reed observes:

To drive along EastLink is to experience the city as through a film clip. You move from dense residential areas to open landscapes and big skies, on through industrial landscapes, back to parklands and outer-suburban developments, and then on through market gardens beneath more big skies.

(Reed 2008: 70)

Reed's impression of the road as it passes along an unerring trajectory through 13 outer-metropolitan suburbs equally reflects and invokes the kinaesthetic nature and experience of high-speed car travel along the Tollway. Her comments are also suggestive of the possibility, for motorists journeying along the route, of 'sight, senses, intellect, landscape, meaning, artistic creativity and the human body' to be 'potentially reconfigured' (Borden 2010: 109). In this reconfiguration lies the potential for relational assemblages.

At the beginning of 2013, the opening of the toll-free Peninsula Link Freeway established a new two-lane, dual carriageway enabling motorists to travel from central Melbourne, via existing arterial roads, freeways or the EastLink Tollway—while bypassing the large City of Frankston—in order to access the Southern end of the Mornington Peninsula. The Freeway, in a similar vein to the EastLink Tollway, was conceived first during the 1960s, with the EastLink Tollway operator ConnectEast offering in 2006 to build the freeway upon completion of its user-pays motorway. By 2010, the Victorian State Government had established a Public Private Partnership (PPP) by Linking Melbourne Authority (LMA) with a private contractor who built the 27-kilometre road at a substantial cost to taxpayers. The route retains many of the architectural design features, engineering performance and aesthetic traits of the EastLink Tollway.

Together, the EastLink Tollway and the Peninsula Link Freeway encompass built characteristics that enhance a road terrain of vibrant and diverse geographies, and equally possess the ability to facilitate a sense of 'strangeness, newness and disconnectedness' (Borden 2010: 108). This sense may occur at various times of the day and night. In many instances these relational assemblages and sensibilities are governed by the temporal conditions on the roads including traffic volumes and movements. They encompass both fleeting moments or sustained periods of thought and embodied sensation that may lead to the onset for motorists of 'immanence, nostalgia and anticipation' (Edensor 2003: 154). This assessment extends towards Edensor's belief that:

[…] the linearity of the road […] dissolves as monuments, signs, and surprises form a skein of overlapping features, enveloping the motorway in a web of associations. This is a topography of possible sights and destinations that reference other spaces and times because motorways are spaces of material, imaginative, and social flows.

(Edensor 2003: 156)

When travelling by car along the EastLink Tollway or the Peninsula Link Freeway motorists encounter ideas, feelings and sensations available through the temporal logic, spatial organization and material conditions on and off the road. The positioning of many multi-scaled artworks within the modulating geography of both roads offers the potential to trigger in the motorist any number of 'memories, sensations, desires, fantasies, interpretations, stories and bits of knowledge' (Edensor 2003: 166). Tactile non-human objects, signs, surfaces and textures are embedded within the varying natural and built forms of the roadscapes. Sculptured road barriers oscillate between the extensive plantings of trees, shrubs and grasses along the roadside. The spectacular design features are essential components of the Tollway and the Freeway's capacity to forge a dynamic and engaging sense of place for motorists.

Car travel along these routes offers the potential for drivers and passengers to 'become enfolded within [the] externalities' (Thrift 1999: 296) of the road-scapes. A process of aesthetic integration between the two routes informs the built structures and multifaceted surfaces of the roads. Various materials feature across both routeways, including brightly coloured metal cladding on footbridges, transparent orange and green-tinted road barriers, as well as disruptive-patterned concrete walls.

The program of roadside artworks represents a tangible link to the 'visual regime of the motorway[s]', where exist the 'constant oscillation from the detail to the territorial, from the local to the global' (Borden 2010: 114). The presence of *Hotel* and *Panorama Station* amplifies this juxtaposition through individual and collective experiences of the passing landscape. The experience offers multiple opportunities for motorists to apprehend and consider 'a host of intertextual and interpractical spaces, places, eras and occasions' (Edensor 2003: 153). The landscape is imbued with 'many stories [from] pre-settlement through to the making of orchards, market gardens, industry and new housing' (Reed 2008: 70). Thus, not only objects and sensations, but also histories of place become alive.

The EastLink Tollway's and the Peninsula Link Freeway's program of public artworks remain configured in diverse and spectacular forms. The artworks are positioned at various points and in the line-of-sight of motorists travelling in either direction along both the inbound and outbound trajectories of the two roads. They have the capacity to engage an array of audiences in ways that are suggestive of a desire to offer a more expansive, intensive and non-standard preoccupation with art objects beyond the institutional spaces of the art gallery (Kwon 2004).

Site-specific Public Artworks

It is the large artworks that command the greatest attention of motorists due to their prominent positioning on the Tollway and the Freeway roadside. When travelling South along the route of the EastLink Tollway the first visible sculpture adjacent to the northbound carriageway is James Angus' (Australia) *Ellipsoidal Freeway Sculpture* (2008). Formed by a painted fiberglass and steel framework, with 24 white, green and blue modular ellipsoids, from one to three metres in diameter, the work is 36 metres long, five metres high and six metres wide. Its formal abstract qualities constantly modulate depending upon the direction and speed of encounter with the artwork. From the perspective of a moving car the colours of *Ellipsoidal Freeway Structure* blur and warp slightly, its form establishing an affective albeit brief moment of visual spectacle for the passing motorist. Further south along the Tollway and adjacent to the southbound carriageway is another sculpture, Emily Floyd's (Australia) *Public Art Strategy* (2008). Standing 13 metres in height, this painted steel blackbird, with a seven-and-a-half metre wingspan featuring a worm-like object at its base, produces a spectacular form, drawing immediate attention to the roadside positioning of the Tollway.

The Southern-most sculpture adjacent to the northbound carriageway is Simeon Nelson's (Australia) *Desiring Machine* (2008). Resembling a fallen tree or electrical tower, the metal structure is made from galvanized steel plate, 36 metres long, nine metres high and eight metres wide. It is suggestive of a future calamity. Resonating with themes of decay, equally abstract and ornamental, it exhibits a structural logic not easily identifiable from a passing car.

Then, placed between *Public Art Strategy* and *Desiring Machine* is Callum Morton's previously mentioned *Hotel*. This is arguably the most visible and iconic artwork, given its size, scale and position along the route, as well as the international status of its creator. Of the artwork, Dimity Reed writes:

In concrete, it stands to the west of the road on a site that hints at dereliction. Hotel is writ large across the upper façade, above rows of windows and a doorway. It is quite extraordinary in the way it ambiguously invites you in, while somehow hinting that there is no in. This is Hitchcock on the film clip.

(Reed 2008: 70)

At the interchange between the EastLink Tollway and Peninsula Link Freeway stands Louise Paramor's *Panorama Station*, a permanent artwork dominating the intersecting routes; it was commissioned under an arrangement known as the Peninsula Link Sculpture Commission. This 25-year commissioning arrangement establishes *Panorama Station* as a single, permanent, commissioned artwork along with the addition of two semi-permanent artworks provided through the biennial Southern Way McClelland Commission. This long-term commitment ensures many new artworks will be displayed along the Peninsula Freeway's route. The inaugural commissions include Dean Colls' (Australia) *Australis: The King is dead, long live the King* (2012), a large-scale ram's head, created with a patina of rust-coloured corten steel; and Phil Price's (New Zealand) *The Tree of Life* (2012) a tall, glistening, wind-activated, kinetic sculpture fabricated from stainless steel.

Within the landscapes of the Tollway and the Freeway all of the artworks have the potential to activate the possibility for conscious and imaginative interpretation whereby the passing motorist may engage, feel, concoct, reflect upon and/or dismiss the relationship between the artwork and the geography. Following Merriman's argument, the artworks may be considered as affective markers of place that assist in the re-imagining of the Tollway and the Freeway as road spaces. Beyond utilitarian purpose, they contain dynamic, contingent and topological assemblages of cars, bodies and varied surroundings embedded with thoughts, atmospheres, senses, presences and feelings (Merriman 2004), either distinctly non-utilitarian or banal. Another way to think about the EastLink Tollway and the Peninsula Link Freeway, amplifying Reed's observation, is in cinematic terms, which Borden describes as '[…] framing, sequencing, editing, unusual juxtapositions and montage, changing pace, unexplained events and sights and so on […] induced by the speeding kinematic nature of driving' (Borden 2010: 108–109).

Travel on both routes does not preclude other multisensory and embodied conditions such as the affective qualities of speed/motion and sound both within and beyond the interior of the car. It also includes the sensual transference of feeling between the control of the car and physical texture of the road surface. The built environment of the Tollway and the Freeway comprising multi-level interchanges, bridges and flyovers, tolling gantries (in the case of EastLink) and electronic signs, footbridges and roadside protective barriers where light reflects upon and refracts across the artificial surfaces as well as the multiple moments afforded by on and off ramps to enter and exit the route, all feed into '[…] a complex series of flows and matrices that connect spaces, times, representation, and sensations' (Edensor 2003: 154). For Reed, the variance in the EastLink Tollway's material conditions is 'dramatized by a curve of the road, by the slope or detail of a wall, by a swathe of mass plantings, a bridge, a tunnel or a sculpture' (2008: 70). This theatricality also becomes apparent when passing *Hotel* or *Panorma Station* on the Peninsula Link Freeway, with its uncanny ability to suggest momentarily that it is something more than an elaborate installation of sculpture.

Typical perceptions by motorists encountering the artworks of the Tollway or Freeway, for the first time, encapsulate notions of novelty, while those road users passing the forms on a regular basis are able to identify with them as familiar and arguably reassuring components of the journey. In many ways they offer motorists 'points of orientation […] to which the […] imagination may extend as a sort of virtual travel' (Edensor 2003: 159). While activating imagination via apprehension the artworks inevitably leave traces of their aesthetic qualities with the motorist. Via aesthetic perceptions and the fixing of bearings, all of the public artworks located throughout the landscape of the EastLink Tollway and the Peninsula Link Freeway assist in establishing the conditions for a 'complex, associational, and folded geography' (Edensor 2003: 156). Interwoven into the fabric of the roadside environment, they elicit traces of ideas, memories and events along with the other permanent and semi-permanent surroundings of the Tollway and Freeway such as petrol stations, advertising billboards, or broken-down vehicles.

Hotel and Panorama Station

In her recent survey of Callum Morton's career, *Call Me Mr. In-Between*, Linda Michael suggests that his 'highly ambivalent objects […] animate the tensions between art and life, history and the present, and make us look again at the ubiquitous structures we see but

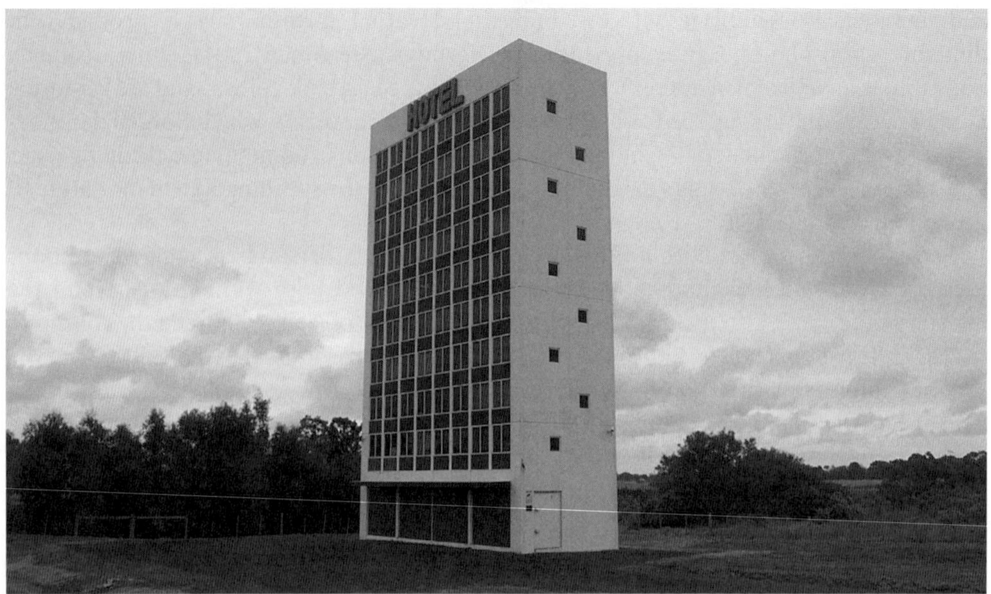

Figure 1: Callum Morton, *Hotel*, 2008, installation, EastLink Tollway Melbourne. Image: Ashley Perry, 2015.

rarely notice' (2011: 3). Situated in an unlikely context and exhibiting a slightly altered and unfamiliar architectural quality, *Hotel* offers a particularly good example of Morton's concerns with ambivalence (see Figure 1). His site-orientated, or arguably, context-specific public artwork invites motorists to gaze upon its deliberately odd scale, and its slightly unconvincing prefabricated quality. As Michael notes:

Fakery, mimicry and automation are used to comic effect, deflecting our anxiety about the life they hint at behind his walls and surfaces. Through his mastery of inference and implication, dumb staring turns into imagining and wondering. Everything is not alright in Morton's world, *our* world, and the viewer is asked to take the uncertainty on.

(Michael 2011: 3; emphasis added)

Morton reinforces the strangeness of his work:

Hotel continues the development of what amounts to a parallel built universe that I have been constructing alongside the real world for a number of years. In this world things appear in unlikely contexts in oddly de-scaled and altered form, as if they have been pushed down a portal from the recent past and popped out mistakenly in this time and place. *Hotel* appears as a piece of roadside architecture, only there are no other buildings for miles and you can't get in.

(Morton 2007)

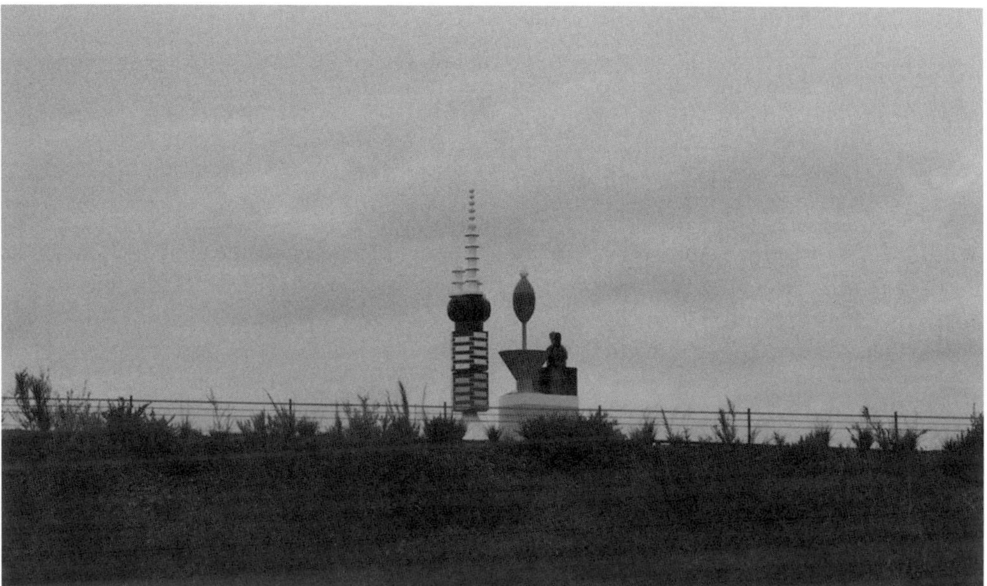

Figure 2: Louise Paramor, *Panorama Station*, 2012, installation, Peninsula Link Freeway Melbourne. Image: Ashley Perry, 2015.

The unique qualities of *Hotel* coupled with the site-specific conditions attributed to its roadside position assist in problematizing the status and position of Morton as its creator. Although the artwork contains 'traditional aesthetic values such as originality, authenticity, and uniqueness' (Kwon 2004: 31), motorists encountering the artwork have no opportunity to identify its author. Stopping and parking in front of the artwork is strictly prohibited. Thus, via the temporal nature of the encounter, Morton, an internationally recognized artist, is recast not as author but as 'a silent manager/director' (Kwon 2004: 31). Yet this process does not impact upon the site-specificity of the public artwork, nor to its boundedness with the Tollway landscape.

Additionally, the visually engaging aspects of Louise Paramor's *Panorama Station*—17 metres at its highest point and 11 metres wide at its base—positioned strategically on top of an overpass at the Tollway and Freeway interchange also calls into question the role of its creator. Art advisor and consultant, Fiona McIntosh describes *Panorama Station* as:

[…] an over the top extrapolation of Paramor's previous works—assembling bits and pieces of found plastic detritus to create alien structures. Panorama Station feels familiar because the component shapes resemble all too familiar stuff, albeit scaled up. Is that a giant ping-pong ball resting on top?

(McIntosh 2014)

Paramor characterizes the assembled nature of her work in these terms:

> The artwork blurs the lines between sculpture, architecture and machinery and thus infers a direct affinity with the ways of the road, while the overall skyward thrust of the piece inspires a feeling of buoyancy and optimism.
>
> (Paramor 2014)

Within the geography of the Tollway or the Freeway, regardless of the ability of motorists to identify with accuracy the author of the public artwork, Callum Morton and Louise Paramor remain central to their creation, and they are equally the 'progenitor of meaning' (Kwon 2004: 51):

> What is prized most of all in site-specific art is still the singularity and authenticity that the presence of the artist seems to guarantee, not only in terms of the presumed unrepeatability of the work but in the presence of the artist also endows places with a 'unique' distinction.
>
> (Kwon 2004: 53)

A tension exists between the position of the motorist as a casual viewer of the artworks and the artist as a privileged figure within a cohort of professionals responsible for the planning, operation and governance of the Tollway and Freeway. The bearing and signification of Morton's *Hotel* and Paramor's *Panorama Station* within the geography of both Tollway and Freeway links ultimately to the artworks' association with motorists and to the 'flow of experience that moves inward and outward folding together places, people, stories, performances, and sensations over time' (Edensor 2003: 167). There remains at work a temporal condition that is enacting an associative identification process between artworks, motorists, sensations and motorways.

Conclusion

The foregoing investigation has shown that site-specific public artworks have the capacity to enliven mobile practices and temporal experiences for motorists. The site of research, the EastLink Tollway and the Peninsula Link Freeway on the South Eastern edges of Melbourne, allows the identification of specific practices, while enabling a general picture to emerge. Although based upon the logic of contemporary neo-liberalism the Tollway and the Freeway provide the capacity for complex, and affective, relational assemblages to occur between a range of various site-specific public artworks and the passing motorist. These assemblages assist in transforming the temporal, spatial and material qualities of the outer urban environments and landscapes across which motorists traverse, and in which they temporally and temporarily exist.

The collection of dynamic public artworks seemingly scattered, but strategically placed along the edges of both roads remain central to the co-production, animation and performance of these relatively new places and sites of Melbourne's outer urban geography. The artworks assist in the production of a different form of drive time; they establish the possibility for an imaginative driving experience that significantly counters popular and negative assumptions about the banal affects and mundane spaces of motorway driving. Feelings of erasure and indifference, when travelling on the EastLink Tollway or the Peninsula Link Freeway, may be resisted actively by these encounters. The strategically positioned public artworks serve to activate sensorial and richly relational engagements for motorists, who may then inhabit temporalities and spatialities directly connected to their daily suburban experience of Melbourne.

References

Adey, P. (2006), 'If Mobility is Everything then it is Nothing: Towards a relational politics of (im)mobilities', *Mobilities*, 1, pp. 75–94.

——— (2004), 'Surveillance at the Airport: Surveilling mobility/mobilising surveillance', *Environment and Planning A*, 36, pp. 1365–1380.

Augé, M. (1995), *Non-Places: Introduction to an anthropology of supermodernity*, London: Verso.

Baudrillard, J. (1996), *The System of Objects*, London: Verso.

Böhm, S., Jones, C., Land, C. and Paterson, M. (eds) (2006), 'Introduction: Impossibilities of automobility', in S. Böhm, C. Jones, C. Land and M. Patterson (eds), *Against Automobility*, Oxford: Blackwell, pp. 3–16.

Borden, I. (2010), 'Driving', in M. Beaumont and G. Dart (eds), *Restless Cities*, London: Verso, pp. 99–121.

Casey, E. S. (1993), *Getting Back Into Place: Towards a renewed understanding of the place-world*, Bloomington: Indiana University Press.

Crang, M. (2002), 'Between Places: Producing hubs, flows, and networks', *Environment and Planning A*, 34, pp. 569–574.

——— (2001), 'Rhythms of the City: Temporalised space and motion', in J. May and N. Thrift (eds), *TimeSpace: Geographies of temporality*, London: Routledge.

Creswell, T. (2010), 'Mobilities I: Catching up', *Progress In Human Geography*, 35, pp. 550–558.

Cubitt, S. (2001), *Simulation and Social Theory*, London: Sage.

——— (1999), 'Virilio and New Media', *Theory, Culture & Society*, 16, pp. 127–142.

Davison, G. (2004), *Car Wars*, Sydney: Allen & Unwin.

Edensor, T. (2003), 'Defamiliarizing the Mundane Roadspace', *Space & Culture*, 6, pp. 151–168.

Hannam, K., Sheller, M. and Urry, J. (2006), 'Mobilities, Immobilities and Moorings', *Mobilities*, 1, pp. 1–22.

Kwon, M. (2004), *One Place After Another*, Cambridge: MIT Press.

Lefebvre, H. (1991), *The Production of Space*, (trans. D. Nicholson-Smith), Oxford: Blackwell. (First published in French 1974.)

McIntosh, F. (2014), 'From the Fast Lane: Public sculpture along the freeways of Melbourne', *Fiona McIntosh Art Advisory and Consultancy Services*, <http://www.fionamcintoshart.com.au/from-the-fast-lane-public-sculpture-along-the-freeways-of-melbourne/>. Accessed 5 July 2015.

Merriman, P. (2007), *Driving Spaces*, Oxford: Blackwell.

—— (2006), 'Mirror, Signal, Manoeuvre: Assembling and governing the motorway driver in late 1950s Britain', in S. Böhm, C. Jones, C. Land and M. Patterson (eds), *Against Automobility*, Oxford: Blackwell, pp. 75–92.

—— (2004), 'Driving Places: Marc Augé, non-places, and the geographies of England's M1 motorway', *Theory, Culture, Society*, 21, pp. 145–167.

Michael, L. (ed.) (2011), 'Call Me Mr. In-Between', in L. Michael (ed.), *Callum Morton: In Memoriam*, Melbourne: Heide Museum of Modern Art, pp. 2–51.

Morton, C. (2007), *Hotel*, Melbourne: ConnectEast Group.

Paramor (2014), *Louise Paramor*, <http://www.louiseparamor.com/index.html>. Accessed 5 July 2015.

Reed, D. (2008), 'EastLink Motorway', *Landscape Architecture Australia*, 120, pp. 68–74.

Relph, E. (1976), *Place and Placelessness*, London: Pion.

Sheller, M. and Urry, J. (2006), 'The New Mobilities Paradigm', *Environment & Planning A*, 38, pp. 207–226.

—— (2000), 'The City and the Car', *International Journal of Urban and Regional Research*, 24, pp. 737–757.

Thrift, N. (1999), 'Steps to an Ecology of Place', in R. J. Johnston, P. J. Taylor and M. J. Watts (eds), *Human Geography Today*, Cambridge, UK: Polity, pp. 295–322.

Urry, J. (2004), 'The System of Automobility', *Theory, Culture, Society*, 21, pp. 25–39.

—— (2000), *Sociology Beyond Societies*, London: Routledge.

Chapter 13

Walking the Post-Quake City: (Re)making place in Ōtautahi Christchurch

Barbara Garrie

History begins at ground level, with footsteps.

(de Certeau 1985: 129)

Introduction

When the earthquake of 22 February 2011 struck Ōtautahi, Christchurch, New Zealand, at 12.50pm, I was working at the Arts Centre on the Western fringe of the CBD. The shaking was violent and the complex was soon evacuated. Somewhat bewildered, I made my way home by foot. I lived close by—on Montreal Street—so the journey was usually a quick one: a short cut across the Arts Centre Quad, past the Christchurch Art Gallery and on up through Cranmer Square. On this occasion, however, I couldn't follow my usual route. Instead, I followed the Avon River along Park Terrace in an attempt to keep my distance from dangerously broken buildings. The footpath along this stretch of river was badly cracked and parts of the riverbank had slumped into the flowing water, taking trees with it. I rounded the final corner onto Salisbury and Victoria streets where the windows of office buildings had smashed, sending glass across the roads. As the aftershocks continued, I sat outside on Montreal Street near my apartment with a group of other tenants. One of my abiding memories of those few hours, sitting there waiting, is the image of thousands of people who, like me, were making their way out of the city centre by foot. People poured out of the CBD along its main arteries. Many of the main roads through the city were blocked by debris, others were severely damaged, and so people walked.[1]

Five years on from the initial quake events, Christchurch is a transitional city in the process of being rebuilt. Within this transforming landscape, art has played an important role in questioning how we might come to know the city again, and how we might re-establish our urban identity. Indeed, in the post-quake city, practices of walking have garnered some significant currency within the creative sector. Since 2013 in particular, Christchurch has been the site of a variety of processions, tours and trails that have sought to re-engage people with the urban sphere and to act as forms of cultural activism.[2] In this post-disaster context, the commonplace act of walking can be read as a tactic that allows individuals to humanize the monumental effects of the quakes, and to negotiate the past, present and future of the city.

This chapter addresses two such art projects, which share a common interest in documenting and imaginatively performing the experience of post-quake Christchurch through processes of walking. Bookending the period between the onset of the major quakes, and the writing of this chapter, are Tim Veling's photographic project *Orientation* (2011), and Chris Cottrell's and Susie Pratt's audio guide, *With Fluidity* (2015). Both works take the central city—a symbolic site in the construction of collective civic identity—as their primary focus and are structured around two key features that have become significant within the post-quake rhetoric: the city cordon and the Ōtākaro Avon River. In their different ways, the cordon and the river represent boundaries that have mediated experiences of the inner city and have marked its transforming limits or frontiers. As such, these sites have become increasingly political, operating as indicators of the contested direction of the rebuild and discontent with the earthquake response.

However, these sites have also become poignant reference points as spaces where memories of Christchurch are conjured and brought into the present. Despite problematic claims that post-quake Christchurch presents a 'blank canvas' (Sutton 2014) on which to build, the city remains inscribed with meanings (Blundell 2014). *Orientation* and *With Fluidity* draw on memories of the pre-disaster city in a way that considers how the past may influence or inform the future. It is through the embodied act of walking that these distant temporal moments—past and future—converge in the present.

A City in Transition

While the quake of February 2011 was the most significant of the seismic events to shake Christchurch, the earthquake sequence began six months earlier. On 4 September 2010, the city woke to a 7.1 magnitude quake, which struck at 4.37am. There was considerable damage to a number of inner-city buildings, but remarkably there was no loss of life and within weeks the city centre was largely accessible for business as usual. The earthquake of 22 February 2011 was much more significant. Hitting at 12.51pm, this quake measured only 6.3 on the Richter scale but it was shallower and considerably more violent than the September event. As a result of this earthquake, Christchurch suffered widespread devastation, particularly in the central city and eastern suburbs. The death toll rose to 185, and many more were injured or displaced.

Although New Zealand is a seismically active landmass, Christchurch was not considered to be in a high-risk earthquake region. Nonetheless, the city and the surrounding Canterbury region experienced one of the country's largest recorded natural disasters. Most were unprepared for the consequences of such an event. In the aftermath of the 2011 quake, residents of Christchurch were faced with the task of getting to know the city again, rebuilding communities and learning how to adapt to what was popularly referred to as 'the new normal'. Cities are by their very nature constantly transforming systems, but the changes wrought on Christchurch have radically altered the city in a much more rapid and dramatic way, presenting significant disruptions to urban life.

Since the first quakes, Christchurch has cultivated an identity as the 'Transitional City'; an identity that has been grown through the experimental initiatives of creative community groups. Post-quake organizations such as Gap Filler, The Festival of Transitional Architecture (FESTA) and Life in Vacant Spaces (LIVS) have embraced the opportunity to produce temporary projects with, as Gap Filler assert, the intention to 'innovate, lead and nurture people and ideas; [and contribute] to conversations about city-making and urbanism in the 21st century' (Gap Filler 2015). The longer-term implications of these ventures are articulated by FESTA, for whom the term 'transitional' describes projects that 'not only offer immediate renewal but also inform and influence the long-term "permanent" recovery of the city' (FESTA 2015). The attitudes reflected by groups such as these have led, as Linda-Jean Kenix observes, to 'public space in Christchurch [becoming] explicitly participatory' (Kenix 2015).

However, the buoyancy and perhaps utopianism that marked early responses to the post-quake city and the potential of the rebuild has waned, as the authors of *Once in a Lifetime* note: 'In late 2013, the editors of this book felt that what had been a fairly widespread optimism about the rebuild—for both the official plans and the unofficial activities and developments—was steadily wearing away' (Bennett et al. 2014: 23). In particular, the City Blueprint—a proposed template for the redevelopment of the CBD—released by the Christchurch Central Development Unit (CCDU) in 2012 has proved to be a controversial, even polarizing document that has raised many concerns about the course of Christchurch's reconstruction.

The Practice of Walking

As both an aesthetic undertaking and a political strategy, walking has a long history within urban discourses. More than simply a means of moving between locations, walking is a practice imbued with cultural resonances that underscore social, economic, environmental and psychological experiences of the city. Urban geographies are defined not only in terms of their spatial or material conditions but also as ideologically constructed sites. Thinkers such as Walter Benjamin (1999), Michel de Certeau (1985, 1984) and Henri Lefebvre (2004) have been instructive in suggesting how urban space is produced—and contested—through our interactions with it. Walking also has a well-established lineage as a trope employed by artists to examine and challenge the systems of knowledge and power that operate within city spaces (O'Rourke 2013). From the wanderings of the nineteenth-century *flâneur* (Baudelaire 1995; Benjamin 1983) to the dérive of the Situationist International (Debord 1994) and more contemporary engagements with social practice in public space, artists have used the practice of walking in various ways to both embed and disrupt the political legibility of the cityscape.

Walking by its nature is as much a temporal as a spatial activity. The practice of walking might in some ways be seen as antithetical to the zeitgeist of the modern city, a space increasingly characterized by the fast pace of everyday living. However, this emphasis on speed and more fluid urban mobilities (for example, the kind of quick transportation of cars and trains) has also resulted, conversely, in a concern for modes of locomotion that offer a different temporal experience of urban space. Walking by its nature is of course as much a temporal activity as it is spatial. During the 1950s and 1960s Debord stressed the movements of the dérive as 'the projection onto space of a temporal experience, and vice versa' (Kaufmann 2006: 109). This is further elucidated by a number of recent writers (May and Thrift 2011; Massey 2005; Rendell 2009) who have argued for the 'reassertion of time in spatial practice' (Rendell 2009). Time of course is not apolitical and certainly, as Frederica Gatta and Maria Palumbo have suggested, 'the more we are technically able to move around the city, and the world, using transport systems (avoiding walking), the more walking became either a choice or a necessity by default, characterizing a political view or social condition' (Gatta and Palumbo 2014: 245).

This spatial-temporal nexus, and its political implications, has particular saliency in the post-quake situation. In Christchurch, the earthquakes highlighted the complex network of connections that define our sense of place and certainly worked to underscore the temporal nature of our relationship with the city, and the land more broadly. Notions of time and space have been thrown into sharp relief by the often-discordant experiences precipitated by the earthquake events. Indeed, the post-disaster city has been characterized by conflicting temporalities in which time appears to have been both slowed down and sped up, and where past, present and future have become contested sites. The most destructive of the quakes in February 2011 lasted only 24 seconds yet the city will be in the process of reconstruction for many years to come. The speed at which a single building can be dropped to the ground in the process of clearing a site contrasts with the slow recovery response in the east of the city and the lengthy periods of time that many have had to wait to receive insurance payouts, both of which have been much criticized. The proliferation of temporary community projects around the city or the time spent negotiating road works as infrastructure is repaired equally speak to different forms of temporal experience extending out from the initial quake events.

Orientation

In the immediate 2011 post-quake period, photographer Tim Veling began a project that sought to come to terms with the ruined urban landscape of the city. *Orientation* (2011) was the outcome of Veling's wanderings around the newly established, city-centre cordon, which encircled Christchurch's inner sanctum. A state of civil emergency was quickly announced following the February quake and a fence patrolled by New Zealand Defence Force personnel was established to lock down the heart of the city. This procedure of 'making safe' rendered parts of the city off limits, a state that extended into the following years until the last vestiges of the cordon were finally removed in mid-2013. During this time images of the Central City Red Zone (the official name given to the restricted area of the central city) were streamed via social media, newspapers and television, but for all bar a few demolition and construction workers, and city officials, the once public space at the centre of Christchurch was rendered 'other'. With the loss or injury of numerous landmarks in the vicinity of the city centre, the cordon became a new object around and in relation to which members of the community have had to reorient themselves.

Tracing the perimeter of the cordon, *Orientation* pictures the changed urban landscape; tape, fences, cracked paths, building support structures, warning signs and emptied sites are quotidian fragments of everyday life in a spectacular environment. Yet the cordon also figures here as a sign of the stratification of power in the city (Garrie and Ibbotson 2015). The raising of the cordon made the authority of local council and civil defence abundantly clear, despite the fact that many residents of the city felt entitled to access properties and possessions confined behind the enforced cordon boundary line. Even as the cordon was adjusted and incrementally pulled back, the sense of disenfranchisement initially exemplified by the cordon fence was replaced by dissatisfaction with the top-down attitude of the rebuild, a view that was widely expressed in the media. By tracking the line of the cordon while photographing the city, Veling might be seen, paradoxically, to have at once affirmed the newly imposed border by not transgressing its boundary and to have made a personal act of defiance by scrupulously walking that same contour.

The cordon images are presented within the context of an elegant but modest artist's book (see Figure 1). Each image is initially hidden, framed by two details placed on facing pages: a map of the central city on which the location of the picture is marked and an enlarged detail taken from within the photograph itself. Opening out the right-hand leaf reveals the full photograph so that map and photo are visible together. In this way a kind of memory game

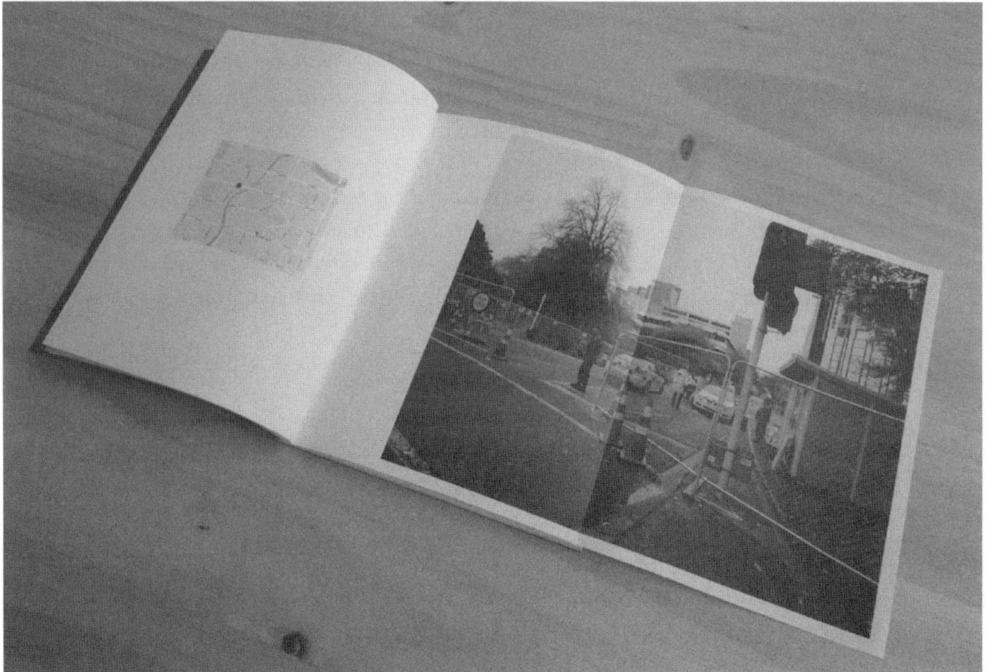

Figure 1: Tim Veling, *Orientation*, 2011, Christchurch: Al-les Press, n.p. Image courtesy of the artist.

takes place within the pages of the book, one that reflects the experience of moving around the post-quake city. In many respects the earthquakes rendered the city of Christchurch uncanny; once familiar streetscapes became strange and unhomely. Arto Haapala suggests that it is in fact through the play of strangeness and familiarity that we make sense of the world around us (Haapala 2005). In making ourselves at home in a particular place we establish connections— to buildings, spaces, people etc.—that allow us to develop a sense of familiarity and belonging. We see or experience these markers in our everyday inhabitation of that place, and through these repeated habitual actions we locate ourselves in relation to them. According to Haapala, when familiarity is ruptured by an encounter with the new then we begin to look afresh.

Veling's photographs speak to such a paradoxical sense of placement and displacement. In one sense *Orientation* was an intensely personal endeavour; as a citizen of Christchurch, his project can be understood as part of the artist's own process of coming to terms with the effects of the earthquake. Yet, this series of works also operates as a reflection of the shared trauma of the earthquakes, echoing the experiences of many other city-dwellers. The sense of displacement triggered by the quakes, as Veling's work suggests, has engendered collective processes of disorientation and reorientation within the built environment. The profound changes to the built environment, to which Veling bears witness, demonstrate the importance of urban knowledge in our ability to navigate the social and physical space of the city. Wayfinding, to use Tim Ingold's term, 'is cultivated by moving along paths that lead around, towards or away from places' (Ingold 2000: 229–230). When paths, as well as landmarks that signpost these routes, are suddenly transfigured or disappear altogether, then urban mobility becomes a more problematic practice. Walking the new urban frontier becomes a way of garnering new knowledge about the city in an attempt to make it familiar again; Veling's images represent the performance of making familiar, of defining new paths and identifying alternate marker points.

Memory is key to this procedure of reorientation; new spatial knowledges are committed to memory, while recollections of the city past are called to mind through the process of re-inscription. Readers of *Orientation* mirror the artist in this negotiation of past and present as they move through the pages of the book, comparing photographs to their map location and seeking out those details extracted from within the larger picture. The book therefore sets up an embodied encounter with the photographic images that relies on the presentness of the viewer or reader. Gennifer Weisenfeld writes: 'By underscoring the present temporal position of the viewer, who embodies the potential to act in the future, photographs communicate a sense of immanence while reinforcing a sense of distance' (Weisenfeld 2012: 6). Certainly in *Orientation* this tension between past, present and future is palpable. Veling's photographs are compelling in echoing the forms of the pre-quake city but, even for those who have never known Christchurch, they also operate as potent signposts of an urban space opening out to a future of radical transformations, no matter how uncertain these shifts may have been in 2011.

The immanence or presentness of the photograph that Weisenfeld describes can also be apprehended by way of other sensory affects that the photographs elicit. *Orientation* finds resonance not only as a visual record of a particular moment in Christchurch's history but as the product of the artist's active gestures in the city, which communicate the textures of the damaged urban environment and the visceral experience of the landscape. Memory, sound, the effects of weather, the feel of materials underfoot, all contribute to the way in which the city is apprehended and acted upon (Tonkiss 2003; Ingold 2011; Lorimer 2011). Veling's photographs convey something of the corporeal experience of walking in a space of ruination by rendering the city as both a visual phenomenon and a terrain composed of other forms of sensation that mediate perceptions, for example the awkward feeling of walking on uneven ground, the sound of wind flicking through ribbons of plastic tape, or the odd silence of roads bereft of cars (see Figure 2). The 'material excess' (Edensor 2008: 134) of the post-disaster city, in which objects are disorganized and dislocated from their usual context—a fallen tree, pile of bricks, road cones and portaloos on the street—also precipitates a different way of walking in the city where, as Edensor puts it, 'a mindful, preoccupied mode of movement is engendered by the need to manoeuver, but we may also suddenly become aware of bodily strain, the texture of the immediate surroundings and the eruptions of memory' (Edensor 2008: 134).

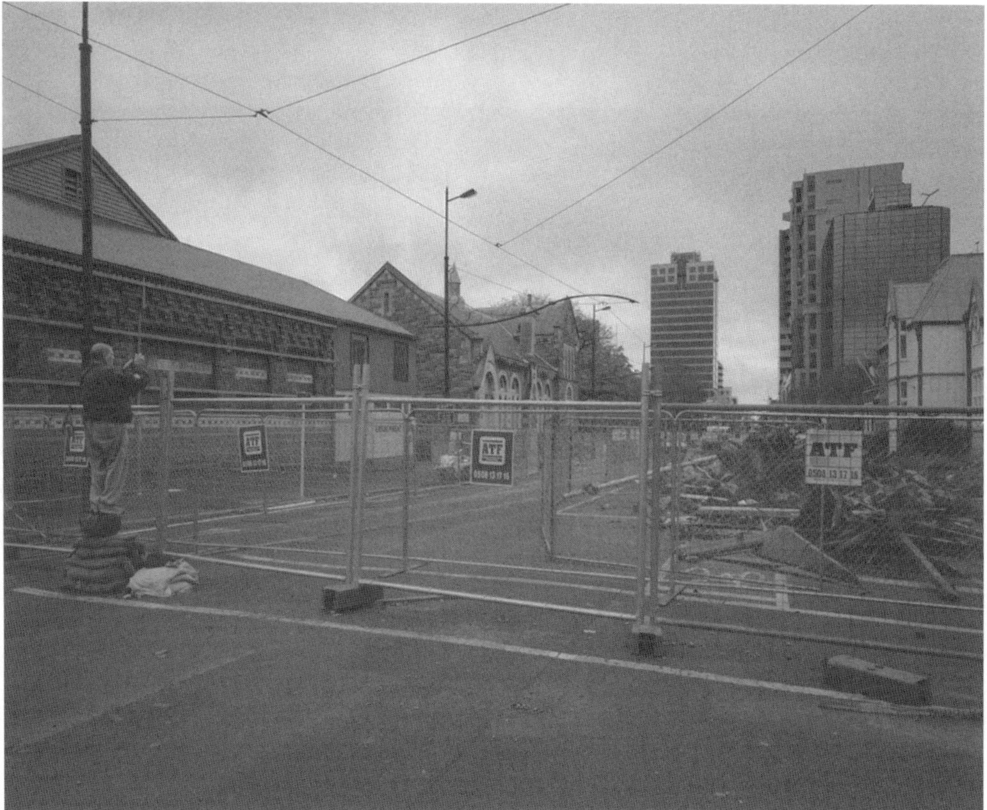

Figure 2: Tim Veling, *Orientation,* 2011, Christchurch: Al-les Press, n.p. Image courtesy of the artists

With Fluidity

Embodied investment in the urban landscape is also an essential part of Chris Cottrell's and Susie Pratt's audio walk, *With Fluidity*. The pilot version of the project was unveiled in July 2015, loaded as a 14-minute file to soundcloud and made available via the website of local art project space The Physics Room. Beginning at Victoria Square, *With Fluidity* takes listeners on a journey that meanders alongside the Ōtākaro Avon River. A series of instructions, voiced by the artists themselves, provides direction: 'take a seat on the bench', 'turn into the park', 'walk down to the river's edge' (see Figure 3). These directions are then punctuated by periods of walking in which the footsteps of the artists can be heard and the ambient sounds of birds, traffic or running water are audible in the background. A commentary providing fragments of historical narrative and personal reflection is also interspersed throughout the track. Accompanying the recording and walking tour is a small risograph-printed artist's book, which features a simplified schematic map of the inner city with the winding line of the river running through it. Within the pages of the book the artists pose a series of questions: 'How do the river and the city choreograph each other? What turns is the city making?' (Cottrell and Pratt 2015).

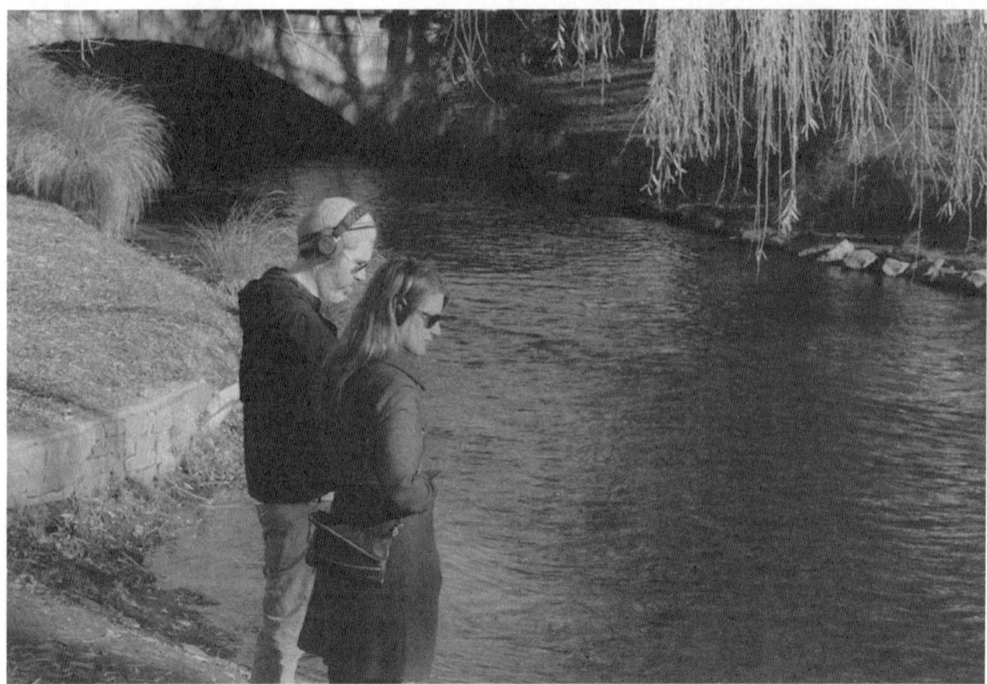

Figure 3: Audio walk participants at the edge of the Ōtākaro Avon River. Chris Cottrell and Susie Pratt, *With Fluidity* 2015, two channel audio walk, 14.07 minutes. Image courtesy of the artist.

The Ōtākaro Avon, which is central to this work, is a significant natural feature that has strong connections to the civic identity of Christchurch. The river provided a wealth of resources to early Māori settled in the area and after European settlement it continued to provide rich sustenance to the burgeoning community. Indeed, along with the troubled Christ Church Cathedral, the stylized form of the river remains an integral motif in the Christchurch City Council logo (Galloway 2014).[3] Within the post-quake City Blueprint, the river has been positioned as a significant part of the overall re-shaping of the central city. Establishment of the Te Papa Ōtākaro/Avon River precinct has already begun with an ongoing riverbank regeneration project and will include a proposed art trail taking the form of a 'large-scale public art project that has the identity of the river at its heart' (CCDU 2015).

However, despite the bountiful history of Ōtākaro and its significance as a symbol of the city, the river, as Cottrell and Pratt point out, was also implicated as an agent in the destruction caused by the recent earthquakes, particularly in terms of the widespread effects of liquefaction. The land upon which Christchurch now sits was largely a flat area of swamp during the mid-nineteenth century when the origins of the contemporary city began to be constructed (Rice and Scharfe 2008). Over subsequent decades the wetlands were drained so that building of the city could continue and the network of tributaries within the swamps were reformed into two primary waterways: the Ōtākaro Avon and the Heathcote rivers.

The history of this relationship between the land and the built city is one that surfaces in *With Fluidity* as a means of drawing the past into the present and asserting the temporal dimensions of the lived landscape. The artists narrate anecdotes about the river and recite geographical information: 'A Scottish man named this river after a river that flowed through his grandfather's land' (3: 33); 'You didn't used to be able to see the Cathedral from here. There was an old cinema, there was a couple of old cinema's actually. Two old cinema's standing in the way' (5: 23); 'They called them Ō Roto Repo, swamp dwellers. Later the land was no longer safe to live on. Removal of properties in this area was compulsory' (6: 34); 'She looked down from the hills and saw a swamp: raupo, flax, channels of water' (8: 37). These details do not unravel in a linear sequence, however. Historical accounts, personal memories of the pre-quake city and reflections on the current urban landscape are woven together in a way that compresses and layers the temporal dimensions of the city; the experience of the present is therefore read through a rendering of the past.

This effect of layering is enhanced further in the sections of audio in which only the sound of the artists' footsteps can be heard as they traverse streets and riverbank. In the process of undertaking their own walks, participants of *With Fluidity* echo the recording as their own bodies in motion produce ambulatory noises. Again, there is a confluence of past and present, brought into being through embodied encounters with the environment, which signifies the role of the body in creating and propagating cultural memory. Like Veling's photographs, the recorded footsteps act as an index of what has been and these ghostings, reiterated by the movements of the contemporary walker/listener, present a profoundly important sense of continuity in the midst of substantial change.

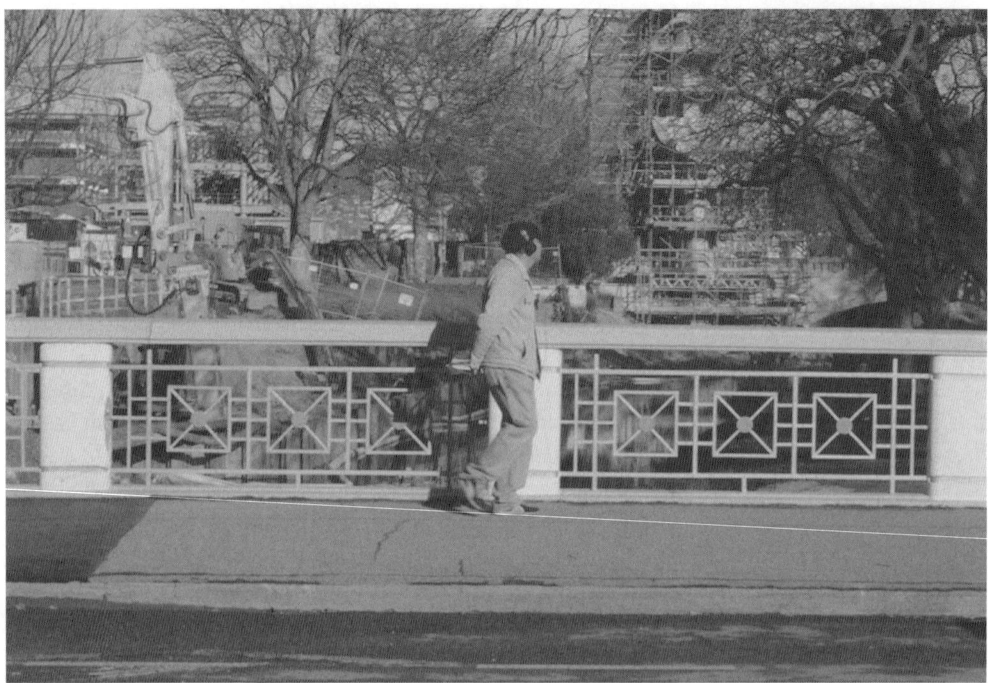

Figure 4: Audio walk participant crossing the Ōtākaro Avon River at the Hereford Street bridge. Chris Cottrell and Susie Pratt, *With Fluidity* 2015, two channel audio walk, 14.07 minutes. Image courtesy of the artists.

Looking forward, Cottrell and Pratt identify the river as an alternative model for thinking about how the city of Christchurch might be redefined, post-quake (see Figure 4). In *With Fluidity* the river is conceived of as a form that is always in motion, something unpredictable and difficult to control. The mutable character of the river reflects the organic way in which cities grow, generally over long periods of time, and in many ways reflects a sense of the diversity or plurality of communities that constitute urban spaces. In Christchurch, however, this open process of city-making has given way to a much more programmatic development led by the Canterbury Earthquake Recovery Authority (CERA), which attempts to rationalize and rigorously manage the rebuild. The development of new 'precincts' is a good example of this. Anchor projects in the rebuild include an Innovation Precinct, Justice and Emergency Precinct and Performing Arts Precinct. This model has also been mapped onto the river with the establishment of the Te Papa Ōtākaro /Avon River Precinct, which at least in principle represents an attempt to contain or regulate the river.

With Fluidity can therefore be seen as offering a counter to the much-disputed siloing of the city and the bureaucratic systems at play in the reconstruction process. Moving against the geometry of the manmade city grid, the river weaves its way through and around the intersecting roadways that mark out the inner city and becomes emblematic of the potential for more creative approaches to the rebuild. The audio tour similarly provides a compelling example of how walking can make us more sensitive to the world and can provide space for reflection. While the artists certainly take an authoritative role in directing the *With Fluidity* walk, their commentary appears thoughtfully to provoke listeners/walkers to take notice of the environment around them and to acknowledge the multiple histories and meanings already rooted in these places. That indigenous histories emerge strongly from *With Fluidity*, for instance, is a critical example of how Christchurch, often described as the most English of New Zealand cities, might reframe its identity.

Conclusion

The changes that have taken place in Christchurch have raised significant questions about how urban space is constituted and how a future city might be adequately constructed in a way that remembers its past and acknowledges the experiences of its inhabitants. Along with a range of other post-quake initiatives, works such as Veling's *Orientation* and Cottrell's and Pratt's *With Fluidity* have been important in engaging with these issues and informing discussion about the unfolding city rebuild.

In the period following the initial quakes, communities in the city were faced with the difficult task of getting to know their altered urban environment again and beginning the process of reasserting their belonging within the city—a process that was complicated by the ongoing sequences of aftershocks. Five years later, the transitional city now looks further ahead but the rebuild continues to court fraught debate. The adoption of walking as a creative means of responding to the material and political situation of the city has its own logic for, as Gatta and Palumbo have argued, 'moving on a terrain is a first step towards interrogating the context of a transforming place' (Gatta and Palumbo 2014: 249). And as they continue, 'the urban walker is not just experiencing the transformation of a concrete process that modifies spaces, but also a continuous re-articulation of an image of the city's future' (Gatta and Palumbo 2014: 260). Certainly the projects on which I have focused in this chapter spell out, through the act of walking, the entwined nature of the city's spatial and temporal dynamics, and the entangled nature of the past, present and future identities of Christchurch.

References

Baudelaire, C. (1995), 'The Painter of Modern Life', in J. Mayne, *The Painter of Modern Life and Other Essays*, (trans. J. Mayne), London: Phaidon Press, pp. 1–41. (First published in French 1863.)

Benjamin, W. (1999), *The Arcades Project*, (trans. H. Eiland and K. McLaughlin), Cambridge and London: Harvard University Press. (First published in German 1982.)

—— (1983), *Charles Baudelaire: A lyric poet in the era of high capitalism*, (trans. H. Zoyn), London: Verso. (First published in German 1969.)

Bennett, B., Dann, J., Johnson, E. and Reynolds, R. (eds) (2014), 'Introduction', in B. Bennett, J. Dann, E. Johnson and R. Reynolds, *Once in a Lifetime: City-building after disaster in Christchurch*, Christchurch: Freerange Press, pp. 18–26.

Blundell, S. (2014), 'Resisting Erasure in Christchurch', in B. Bennett, J. Dann, E. Johnson and R. Reynolds (eds), *Once in a Lifetime: City-building after disaster in Christchurch*, Christchurch: Freerange Press, pp. 45–51.

Certeau, M. de (1985), 'Practices of Space', in M. Blonsky (ed.), *On Signs*, Baltimore: The Johns Hopkins University Press, pp. 122–145. (First published in French 1980.)

——— (1984), *The Practice of Everyday Life*, (trans. S. Rendall), Berkeley: University of California Press. (First published in French 1980.)

Christchurch Central Development Unit (CCDU) (2015), 'Ōtākaro Art by the River: A cultural drawcard for the city', <https://ccdu.govt.nz/projects-and-precincts/te-papa-otakaro-avon-river-precinct/otakaro-art-by-the-river>. Accessed 5 August 2015.

Cottrell, C. and Pratt, S. (2015), *With Fluidity*, Christchurch: Ilam Press.

Debord, G. (1994), *The Society of the Spectacle*, (trans. D. Nicholson Smith), New York: Zone Books. (First published in French 1967.)

Edensor, T. (2008), 'Walking Through Ruins', in T. Ingold and J. Vergunst (eds), *Ways of Walking: Ethnography and practice on foot*, Farnham: Ashgate, pp. 123–142.

Festival of Transitional Architecture (FESTA) (2015), <http://festa.org.nz/about/>. Accessed 15 May 2015.

Gap Filler (2015), <http://www.gapfiller.org.nz/about/>. Accessed 15 May 2015.

Galloway, M. (2014), 'A Message and a Messanger', in B. Bennett, J. Dann, E. Johnson and R. Reynolds (eds), *Once in a Lifetime: City-building after disaster in Christchurch*, Christchurch: Freerange Press, pp. 112–121.

Garrie, B. and Ibbotson, R. (2015), 'Things Change: Objects and transition in post-quake Christchurch', in CRASSH (Centre for Research in the Arts, Social Sciences and Humanities), *Objects in Motion: Material culture in transition*, Cambridge, 18–20 June.

Gatta, F. and Palumbo, M. A. (2014), 'Walking Through Urban Transformation: Fieldwork in the northeast of Paris', in E. Brown and T. Shortell (eds), *Walking in the European City: Quotidian mobility and urban ethnography*, Farnham, UK: Ashgate Publishing, pp. 245–262.

Haapala, A. (2005), 'On the Aesthetics of the Everyday: Familiarity, strangeness and the meaning of place', in A. Light and J. M. Smith (eds), *The Aesthetics of Everyday Life*, New York: Columbia University Press, pp. 39–55.

Ingold, T. (2011), *Being Alive: Essays on movement, knowledge and description*, Abingdon, Oxon and New York: Routledge.

——— (2000), *The Perception of the Environment: Essays on livelihood, dwelling and skill*, Abingdon, Oxon and New York: Routledge.

Kaufmann, V. (2006), *Guy Debord: Revolution in the service of poetry*, (trans. R. Bononno), Minneapolis: University of Minnesota Press. (First published in French 2001.)

Kenix, L. (2015), 'From Prim to Punk: The successfully altered marketing of Christchurch City post-disaster', *Global Review of Research in Tourism, Hospitality and Leisure Management*, 1:2, pp. 299–317, <http://globalbizresearch.org/files/v537_grrthlm_linda-jean-kenix-187305.pdf>.

Lefebvre, H. (2004), *Rhythmanalysis: Space, time and everyday life*, (trans. S. Elden and G. Moore), London: Continuum. (First published in French 1992.)

Lorimer, H. (2011), 'Walking: New forms and spaces for studies of pedestrianism', in T. Cresswell and P. Merriman (eds), *Geographies of Mobilities: Practices, spaces, subjects*, Surrey and Burlington: Ashgate Publishing, pp. 19–34.

Massey, D. (2005), *For Space*, London and Thousand Oaks, CA: Sage.

May, J. and Thrift, N. (eds) (2011), *TimeSpace: Geographies of temporality*, Abingdon, Oxon and New York: Routledge.

O'Rourke, K. (2013), *Walking and Mapping: Artists as cartographers*, Cambridge and London: The MIT Press.

Rendell, J. (2009), '(the re-assertion of time) into Critical Spatial Practice', One Day Sculpture Project keynote lecture, pp. 1–23, <http://onedaysculpture.org.nz/_symposium/jane%20rendell%20formatted.pdf>. Accessed 20 May 2015.

Rice, G. and Scharfe, J. (2008), *Christchurch Changing: An illustrated history*, 2nd ed., Christchurch: Canterbury University Press.

Sutton, R. (2014), 'A Blank Canvas for New Beginnings', in B. Bennett, J. Dann, E. Johnson and R. Reynolds (eds), *Once in a Lifetime: City-building after disaster in Christchurch*, Christchurch: Freerange Press, pp. 52–58.

Tonkiss, F. (2003), 'Aural Postcards: Sound, memory and the city', in M. Bull and L. Black (eds), *Auditory Cultures Reader*, New York: Berg, pp. 303–309.

Weisenfeld, G. (2012), *Imaging Disaster: Tokyo and the visual culture of Japan's great earthquake of 1923*, Berkeley and Los Angeles: University of California Press.

Notes

1   While this chapter focuses on the practice of walking, it is important to acknowledge that pedestrianism is not a universally accessible mode of locomotion. Those for whom mobility impairments prevent walking by foot might experience urban space in quite different ways.

2   Other examples of walks, tours and trails in post-quake Christchurch include: *Rebuild Tour* (2012–ongoing) operated by Red Bus; *Two Attempts* (2013) by Paul Paul, a walking project produced during The Social caravan residency; Free Theatre's *Canterbury Tales* (2013), a processional performance presented as part of FESTA 2013; Gap Filler's Central City Audio Tour (2013); *Whakapapa Project* (2014), a treasure hunt highlighting significant Māori sites, initiated by Regan Stokes as part of FESTA 2014.

3   At the time of writing, the future of the Christ Church Cathedral remains uncertain. In 2012 the Church Property Trustees elected to demolish the partially damaged building. Following opposition and court action from the Great Christchurch Building Trust, it was announced in September 2015 that an independent government-appointed consultant would be drafted to assist in negotiating plans for the future of the Cathedral. In December 2015 mediator Miriam Dean QC found that the building could be either restored or replaced. In response, the Church Property Trust has agreed to investigate the safety and cost issues involved in restoring the Cathedral.

Section V

Creative City

Chapter 14

Listening to the City

Kristen Sharp

Introduction

The acoustic encounters of place in recent examples of sonic practice demonstrate the important role of contemporary art in responding to the variable nature of urban space. *The Library by Soundpocket*, a Hong Kong-based sound art organization, which has created an online public library of urban site-specific sound recordings generated by a range of artists and amateurs, and *Stereopublic: Crowdsourcing the Quiet*, an Australian-funded initiative that creates a soundscape of 'quiet' places from cities around the world, are useful examples of how art constructs social, material and aesthetic encounters with the city. By existing as both site-specific and localized recordings, from *somewhere*, and as downloadable files accessible from the Internet, *anywhere*, they provide useful approaches to understanding experiences of urban place as *trans*located. Although the projects are based on site-specific recordings, there is no intention they be experienced in situ, unlike most examples of site-specific art practice. That is, the work and listening practices engaged by *The Library* and *Stereopublic* are mutable and fluid; they have the capacity to move across locations and to create new and unexpected encounters with urban place for listeners. These soundscapes emphasize the city as a symbolic space, an embodied space activated through listening, and as a social space activated through online communities of listeners.

The significance of the experience mediated by *The Library* and *Stereopublic* is based on the juxtaposition between the place represented in the work and the place in which the work is encountered. This is achieved through the production and reception of the work. These two places do not remain separate and distinct in the listening process; rather, they blend together hermeneutically and acoustically to forge a new sense of place. The experience of place is represented directly through the sounds recorded by the artist and composer. It is mediated through the choices of the recorder (or 'earwitness') and composer in selecting what sounds to draw attention to. The work is further mediated through the listening context (a different place) when accessed online. The place of reception, in which those sounds are listened to, is usually an entirely unrelated place. For example, listening to 'Street' by Fiona Lee (2013), a Soundpocket listed recording of Hong Kong, on a mobile phone while walking to work in Melbourne, Australia, juxtaposes the locale of Hong Kong with that of Melbourne. The two places cannot sit in isolation—they are experienced together through the work because ambient sound always bleeds through headphones and other listening devices. This juxtaposition of place can create a sense of disjuncture; also it can expand the experience of place through the layering of sound. This is not entirely different from existing practices of listening with mobile mp3 players. Choice of music tracks and volume can be used to 'compose' an experience of place. Sound can be used to block out or enhance the existing soundscape through which the listener is moving. In the case of *Soundpocket* and *Stereopublic*, however, the sound being listened to differs from the usual music scenario because it comprises site-specific recordings. It is the relationship between site-specificity and its displacement into another locale, facilitated through the Internet, which provides new understandings of soundscapes and the meaning of place in a contemporary urban context. Drawing from soundscape studies, cultural geography, anthropology and media studies this chapter explores how place can be understood as *trans*located. This is undertaken through an examination of two contemporary sound art projects. Translocated in this sense relates to how artworks, based on soundscapes, can move across sites, blending together to create something more than just a document or representation of place.

Place in Urban Geography and Art

The meaning of place comprises more than geographic location or material context (such as the walls of a house, or the digital features of a website); meaning is also generated through emotional and symbolic (including imaginative) senses (Cresswell 2015). While place can be mapped as a point in space, and often comprises some form of material structure (visual, sonic, haptic or olfactory), it is also formed through social relations. In Henri Lefebrve's (1991) terms spaces are 'lived'. For many cultural and urban geographers, it is precisely how a sense of place and meaning is generated that is important to an understanding of not only urban geographies, but also social geographies. This sense of place is never exclusively one or the other, for example the material can carry emotional meaning and vice versa; rather they are interrelated components in understanding the meaning of place.

Doreen Massey (1994) refers to places as 'stories so far', referring not only to the emotional and symbolic relations of place but also their plural identities. The meaning of place is not static, nor frozen in time, rather it is formed in the processes of change. Importantly, Massey highlights how place is not hermetically sealed; it does not have a clearly delineated inside and outside. What is meant by this conceptualization is that place is formed through flows—movements, connections and networks across space and time. It is a site of constantly shifting meanings. Massey highlights how, in a global context, the meaning of place emphasizes this porosity. Under the fluid processes of globalization, place is not becoming more homogenous, but rather its uniqueness is reproducing. Place, in this global sense, can be considered an open site.

Artists have contributed to such an open understanding of place through various urban representations—a re-imagining of place in art (Grierson and Sharp 2013). From the traditions of landscape imagery/practice in art (Cosgrove 1998; Tufnell 2006; Wells 2011) to soundscape practices in art (LaBelle 2006), art provides a vital tool to examine how cities may be experienced as social, cultural and aesthetic places. Artists exploring the relationships between place and representation are exemplified in the history of landscape painting and photography, and by the Land Artists of the 1950s and 1960s, such as Robert Smithson's *Site* and *Nonsite* works. For Smithson the Site is the place encountered in the landscape—the original site; and Nonsite is a form of analogy to this place in the form of material exemplars and references (such as dirt, rocks, maps, mirrors and text), which are exhibited in the gallery (Tufnell 2006: 29). Audiences encounter the site through the Nonsite. What is significant and relevant for this discussion is that the Nonsite creates an affective encounter for the audience, but 'they ultimately refer to something that is elsewhere; another place and a past experience', which is the Site (Tufnell 2006: 29). It is the complex dialectic between site and nonsite that is a useful way to consider the works of *Soundpocket* and *Stereopublic*. Like Smithson's works both projects require an original (physical) place that is recorded and composed (re-presented) by the artist in situ. This sound work is then listened to in a separate location.

The dialogue between actual place and the image or material object, as represented, is also explored through phenomenological approaches. Artists such as Richard Long and Hamish Fulton are well-known practitioners of walking as an art practice. While they might exhibit residues of their works in galleries—photos, text or sound—these exhibits are considered 'memory aides' (Wells 2011: 288) of the walking experience. That is, they are not literal documents because the full sensory experience of the (solitary) walk cannot be replicated through representation. They argue that the artwork is the walk itself. Thus the remnants exhibited, 'testify to the experience of walkers' (Wells 2011: 288). Importantly, Liz Wells argues that the images and recordings of the walk are also 'not about *place* in itself so much as about the *experience* of place' (Wells 2011: 288). This is a critical point when considering the relationship between a recording or re-presentation of an experience and the initial experience itself. Here the critical difference is between works, such as Bernd and Hilla Becher's images of industrial objects and landscapes from the late 1950s as 'topographic', focusing on observation of place and its surface features, and works by Long and Fulton that are about more than just surface features but also about affect and the journey of walking. Long and Fulton's practices move beyond the representation of place as visual or sensory and acknowledge the role of art in forming place, in creating the 'experience of place'. Thus, as art forms and frames social, political and aesthetic encounters, it is a form of 'spatial practice' (Lefebvre 1991). The meaning of place as practised experience, and one that is fluid and porous in Massey's sense rather than bounded, is necessary for an understanding of the dynamic activated by *The Library* and *Stereopublic*.

Sound and Place

The dominant form of cultural and aesthetic representation and practice of the city tends to be visual. Yet when the spaces of the city are encountered in actuality, it is not only through the eyes, but also the ears, mouth, nose and hands that a sense of place comes into being.

There is increasing recognition of multisensory approaches as a critical element in cultural geography, anthropology, media studies, cultural studies and urban studies (Cox, Irving and Wright 2016). These approaches recognize that the city is experienced in and through the body. Urban soundscapes connect or disconnect bodies to place (Bull 2007), mediating the experience of place.

Sound can be used to compose physical, emotional, imaginative and material journeys through the city. A choice of quiet or loud listening or the type of material listened to can be based on a myriad of factors, not the least of which may be the locale in which the listening takes place. Mobile technologies, such as mp3 players facilitate greater flexibility in experiencing urban soundscapes. Smartphones and mp3 players create different ways to construct soundscapes as listeners move through the city. The technologies can block out or enhance the external sounds of those places (Bull 2013: 8). While the Sony Walkman is an early version of a contemporary personal mobile and digital sound technology, what is significantly different about contemporary digital mobile sound technologies, is they do not just play/record sound but they can be connected to online applications and users.

Users can re-make experiences of place according to their chosen sound. Thus, the meaning of place is mutable to those experiences. This effectively extends the possibilities of experiencing 'places' that one is physically and imaginatively 'in' at any given time. Even the physical terrain can be altered. For example, the rhythm of ones walking or pace may be determined by the type of sound listened to, in which case, the topography of place—smooth, bumpy, fractured—may alter. As Michael Bull argues, '[Sound] is used to actively recreate and reconfigure the spaces of experience. Through the power of sound the world becomes intimate, known and possessed' (Bull 2013: 15).

By activating a uniquely aural experience of cities, urban sound-based projects, such as *The Library by Soundpocket* and *Stereopublic*, offer a critical alternative to the visually dominant forms of capturing and reproducing urban experience and how place is known.

The Library by Soundpocket and *Stereopublic*

The Library by Soundpocket, Hong Kong is an online library/database open to the public for uploading any sound files related to recordings of the city.[1] The database works as an online sound map. It is a semi-curated social platform, which aims to encourage public participation in recording the changing sonic scape of Hong Kong and its urban development.

The Library is a community-orientated project that focuses largely on local (Hong Kong) sonic topographies, with some extension to international sites (Taiwan). It brings together professional artists/composers and amateurs. One of the core aims of the project is to encourage social as much as sonic awareness: listening 'as a way of being and being with others' (The Library, About Us). As Elaine Ho describes, 'The role of the library [...] never needed to be about the "we" of being together *per se*; it can be understood rather as a being "in common" that happens over and across time' (Ho 2013). This is a way of being together, of connecting, which is facilitated in and through the immateriality and quick-time mobility of the Internet. Due to the emphasis on community building, the website is only one branch of activity for *The Library*. They also facilitate community workshops on sound recording, active listening and artist talks, and they commission artistic and curatorial responses to the existing works in the collection.

Stereopublic: Crowdsourcing the Quiet is an online participatory art project that utilizes current smartphone applications and geotagging to create an online collection of 'quiet' urban spaces from around the world.[2] Their tagline is 'crowdsourcing the quiet'. Australian sound artist, Jason Sweeney has created *Stereopublic* as a new approach to acoustic ecology (influenced by R. M. Schafer's socio-political critique of contemporary urban development and as a form of pathology creating 'sick cities' through noise pollution in his *World Soundscape Project* starting in the 1970s). Sweeney aims to promote a sonic health by encouraging 'earwitnesses' to record quiet spots in the city on their mobile phones and upload these to his web application. Sweeney then re-composes these recordings into sound-art works, and makes them available on an interactive global sound map.

Both projects aim for public participation, although *Stereopublic* is more heavily curated than *The Library*. However, what is significant about both works, beyond their collaborative processes, is the ways in which they engage their various publics, and the relationships between the recordings posted and the original sites. The projects are dependent on a form of documentation of sonic environments of specific local sites—requiring physical audio recordings, which are identified by using GPS technology on smartphones. These recordings can be accessed and listened to anywhere, thereby creating a complex interaction between site and place. Place in this context comprises not just the site recorded, but also the listening environment in which the piece is listened to. Whether this is across the world or even in the same city:

> As these words continue to be written, I meander through 'Day and Night' and 'Hubbub' and find myself in Hong Kong again. It feels somehow ridiculous to listen to these sounds through the computer when I could simply go outside. But it is precisely that these recordings are not, as one may think, about going elsewhere. While they certainly may be of a previous time, or a place we've never been, such presencing made aware to us by the hands and ears of another is exactly the form of embodiment that precipitates the certitude of *nowness*, *hereness* and the *being-with*. These sounds carry with them another form of immediacy, where immediacy becomes flow, and sound occurs not only over the passage of time but *is* the passage of time.
>
> (Ho 2013)

The spatio-temporal relationships created by *The Library* are not only about what is contained in the downloaded sound pieces, but also about how the pieces are encountered in real time and the other sounds they interact with. The mix between the real-time sound of the environment where the piece is listened to and the actual recording creates sonically, complex inter-compositions. For instance, listening to the sounds of Hong Kong International Airport in 'Paper Airplane' (2013) by Rika Wong, while riding a tram in Melbourne, intersperses the sounds listened to online with the ambient offline sound. When using a computer to access the online works, there are additional sounds generated by navigating through digital space (the computer keyboard and clicking of the mouse): sounds that are different from the barely audible finger swiping of smartphone technologies. Elaine Ho refers to this as a form of 'quietness', likening it to the physical sounds encountered in quiet spaces, like libraries, where the quietness consists of incidental sound—turning of pages, shuffling of feet and papers or gentle corporeal eruptions. It is the sound of the 'whole' that gives The Library its 'quietness', as a distinct space (Ho 2013). That is, it is a form of focused listening, training the ears. The concept of quietness permeates both projects, albeit in distinct ways, and brings into focus how place is experienced through ambient sound as much as directed listening.

The distinct space of quietness is situated according to specific socio-cultural contexts. For example, *The Library's* recordings around protests in Hong Kong, 'Give Way' by Choi Tsui-Lin, 2012, or *Stereopublic's* sourcing of 'quiet' locales and recording them. This unique situating of the work reinforces that the interpretation of *trans*location as a smoothing over of the unique socio-cultural topographies of place should be critically avoided. Furthermore, specificity is not erased through the simultaneity of place, that of represented place and the listening context, but rather it is extended. As Massey argues in interpreting a global sense of place as an open site that is constantly changing, places are not homogenous.

The mobility of place actualized in the art projects readily facilitates an imaginative construction of place, a third-place to borrow a term from Homi Bhabha (1994), which is neither of one place or another but a hybrid of the two. Arjun Appadurai (1996) usefully interprets the mobility of ideas and images as a 'landscapes of images', facilitated through the contemporary 'mediascapes' and 'ideoscapes', which for Appadurai constitute the contemporary experience of 'imagined worlds' (after Benedict Anderson) of cultural globalization (Appadurai 1996: 35). For contemporary practitioners, art that moves physically and imaginatively across such 'scapes'—as it circulates globally through exhibitions, art fairs, education, and analogue and digital publications—is now part of a common experience and expectation. As Terry Smith reminds, art is *of* and *from* the world (Smith 2011). This type of multiplicity of identity is foregrounded increasingly as art forges spaces of encounter and exchange—spaces in which cultural difference, local identities and global connectivities are being formed.

The Library and *Stereopublic* also generate dialogues between local sites, which not only create new sonic relationships between places, but also set up transnational social communities of listeners, as an outcome of the specifically social nature of these participatory projects. This community culture is part of the popularity of socially engaged art practices more generally (Bishop 2012, 2006; Kester 2011, 2004), but also the 'participatory turn' (Burgess and Green 2009) in online networked media, which emphasizes 'vernacular creativity' (Burgess 2007). The ever-present and visible (and aural) nature of contemporary communication technologies, particularly mobile technologies, is emphasizing increasingly how much our social connectivity is mediated through these technologies (Bull 2013: 3). Also there is an emphasis on how this, in turn, changes our sense of what public space is. Online spaces require an expansive and less fixed definition of public, of the crowd and of the audience as intimate publics (Hjorth, King and Kataoka 2014), as people are able to forge and maintain connectivities across physical distances previously held as barriers to such sustaining relationships. Critical questions arise when considering the audience for these works. The nature of the Internet is such that it would be rare for someone to stumble across the works while searching online. So, while they do open up the potential for broader audiences translocally, they are still, arguably, quite limited in terms of the audiences accessing them.

Stereopublic borrows from R. M. Schafer in a focused selection of determining what are noisy and quiet spaces and the impacts of these on living in cities, but it also departs from Schafer's politics of reproduction. Schafer was highly critical of what he termed 'schizophonia', a split between the original sound and its electroacoustical reproduction and broadcast (Schafer 1969). He was an advocate for contextualized listening, rather than practices and technologies, which enable sound to be decontextualized, or placed 'out of socket' (Schafer 1994; see also Thompson 2002). But, as Ari Kelman (2010) argues, it is the sonic and cultural context in which sound is encountered that is meaningful, including recorded sound. It is the 'interplay of contexts', which become important for investigation, because the relationships and negotiations between sound, context and listening are where the production of meaning occurs (Kelman 2010: 177–178). The works from *The Library* and *Stereopublic* arise from specific, targeted recordings of place and are therefore mediated through the socio-political and cultural lens of the person making the recording. When listened to, the choice of work and the locale in which they are listened to are also mediated through the socio-cultural context of the listener and of place. As Kelman points out:

> To study sound means to attend to background noise not as something to be tuned out or silenced, but as a critical component of acoustic phenomena, and making informed distinctions about sound is a social process in which context plays a crucial role.
>
> (Kelman 2010: 178)

In *Stereopublic*, for instance, there is an unusual sense of play established between emphasizing the site specificity of the recording, such as descriptive GPS coordinates and other geographic details, and the ways in which they get displaced through the composing process. The composer, Jason Sweeney may not be intimately familiar with all the locales presented, so they exist through his re-imagining of place. For example, 'Quiet Space 816' is based on a recording by Marc St Pierre, in Vancouver Canada (St Pierre's role identified as 'earwitness'), which is then re-composed by Sweeney into a soundwork and posted on the

Steopublic website (Sweeney and St Pierre, n.d.). In a similar way, *The Library* is based on site-specific recordings and yet many of the titles of works and clustering of works tend to be open-ended and less focused on prescriptive descriptions of site. For example, 'Give Way', a recording of a political protest gathering in Hong Kong, does not provide specific detail as to the protest or the broader context of site, just a general description of the event recorded. This movement between specificity and generality is also evident in the type of technology being used to record sound.

The majority of technologies for the works posted in *The Library* and *Stereopublic* appear to be hand-held recording devices, such as mobile smartphones, which tend to focus on ambient noise in space rather than on specific sounds. That is, they are more of a general snapshot of a wide-ranging sense of a place rather than a detailed investigation. The sense of specific and deliberate soundscapes is sacrificed for something more random: whatever sounds are in the foreground or distance. It is a less specific approach to composition that appears to remove decision, rather than drawing attention to the decisions that field recording involves. 'Kit's Beach Soundwalk' (1989) by Hildegard Westerkamp, one of the members of Schafer's World Forum for Acoustic Ecology (WFAE), foregrounds listening and the role of the recorder in amplifying or de-emphasizing elements within a soundscape. The ease of use for the types of technologies encouraged by *Stereopublic* and *The Library* means that the number of producers making the works can increase as they do not require specialized equipment or training, and thus foster the more open and community-focused approach of the projects. It also means that a more generalized use of ambient recording arguably becomes the norm.

The Library and *Stereopublic* offer an alternative to popular visual and text-based technologies of place evident in online social media forms such as SMS, Instagram, Vimeo and Facebook. These applications can be used to create visual markers of identity and place. For example, Instagram provides a way to mark personal presences in place evidenced through the current proliferation of the online 'selfie' image propagated through smartphones. Selfies function as digital postcards, albeit with a much broader audience base, operating as indexical markers of place: 'I am here', or 'I did this'.

While *Stereopublic* and *The Library* heavily emphasize a sonic approach to place, this is not at the exclusion of the visual. A critical characteristic of online and digital technologies is that they do not just enable sound to be listened to, but they connect to the visual. The screens on sound-enabled mobile devices are rarely blank. Both projects also utilize highly crafted visual presentations to present the compositions and to facilitate navigation through the works. In the case of *Stereopublic*, a series of blotches of black ink-like effects (or coffee cup stains) populate a map of the world to identify the locale of the sound compositions. *The Library* uses a very specific typographic and colour palette and a series of collective headings as signposts that emphasize a non-linear approach to the works. *The Library* is bi-lingual and provides detailed information not only of artist, title, date and locale, but also of the method of recording and a short statement about the work.

Conclusion

Sonic-based art projects, such as *The Library* and *Stereopublic*, broaden how we understand the representation and experience of place mediated through contemporary digital technologies. The projects foreground the multisensory ways the material, social and symbolic dimensions of place may be experienced.

The sonic relationships of place created in these projects respond to and represent specific places. But they are more than this. The method by which they can be accessed from anywhere and at anytime, due to the nature of mobile technologies, such as mobile smartphones, make them a part of how real-time place is experienced. This creates an intertwining of local and global spaces, in which art can be not only a representation of the transformations of an urban place, but also part of the space of transforming how we understand places more generally.

References

Appadurai, A. (1996), *Modernity at Large: Cultural dimensions of globalization*, Minneapolis: University of Minnesota Press.

Bhabha, H. K. (1994), *The Location of Culture*, Oxon: Routledge.

Bishop, C. (2012), *Artificial Hells: Participatory art and the politics of spectatorship*, London: Verso.

—— (2006), *Participation*, London: Whitechapel.

Bull, M. (2013), 'General Introduction', in M. Bull (ed.), *Sound Studies*, London and New York: Routledge, pp. 1–22.

—— (2007), *Sound Moves: iPod Culture and urban experience*, London: Routledge.

Burgess, J. (2007), 'Vernacular Creativity and New Media', unpublished PhD thesis, Queensland: University of Technology.

Burgess, J. and Green, J. (2009), *YouTube: Online video and participatory culture*, Cambridge: Polity.

Choi Tsui-Lin (2012), 'Give Way', <http://www.thelibrarybysoundpocket.org.hk/main/protest-抗爭/?post_type=listen>. Accessed 13 August 2015.

Cosgrove, D. E. (1998), *Social Formation and Symbolic Landscape*, Madison: University of Wisconsin Press.

Cox, R., Irving, A. and Wright, C. (2016), *Beyond Text: Critical practices and sensory anthropology*, Manchester: Manchester University Press.

Cresswell, T. A. (2015), *Place: An introduction*, Hoboken: Wiley Blackwell.

Grierson, E. and Sharp, K. (2013), *Re-imagining the City: Art, globalization and urban spaces*, Bristol: Intellect Books.

Hjorth, L., King, N. and Kataoka, M. (eds) (2014), *Art in the Asia-Pacific: Intimate publics*, New York: Routledge, pp. 91–104.

Ho, E. (2013),' The Library Reviewed', <http://www.thelibrarybysoundpocket.org.hk/media/The-Library_reviewed-by-Elaine-W-Ho1.pdf>. Accessed 13 August 2015.

Kelman, A. Y. (2010), 'Rethinking the Soundscape: A critical genealogy of a key term in sound studies', *The Senses and Society*, 5, pp. 212–234.

Kester, G. (2011), *The One and the Many: Contemporary collaborative art in a global context*, Durham and London: Duke University Press.

———— (2004), *Conversation Pieces: Community and communication in modern art*, Berkeley: University of California Press.

Labelle, B. (2006), *Background Noise: Perspectives on sound art*, New York: Continuum International.

Lee, F. (2013), 'Street', <http://www.thelibrarybysoundpocket.org.hk/tag/morning/>. Accessed 13 August 2015.

Lefebvre, H. (1991), *Production of Space*, Oxford: Blackwell. (First published in French 1974.)

Massey, D. (1994), *Space, Place and Gender*, Oxford: Polity.

Schafer, R. M. (1994), *The Soundscape: Our sonic environment and the tuning of the world*, Rochester: Destiny Books.

———— (1969), *The New Soundscape: A handbook for the modern music teacher*, Don Milles: BMI Canada Limited.

Smith, T. (2001), *Contemporary Art World Currents*, London: Laurence King.

Sweeney, J. and St Pierre, M. (n.d.), 'Quiet Space 816', <http://www.stereopublic.net/map/#quiet-space/816>. Accessed 13 August 2015.

Thompson, E. A. (2002), *The Soundscape of Modernity: Architectural acoustics and the culture of listening in America, 1900–1933*, Cambridge and London: MIT Press.

The Library by Soundpocket (2015), 'About Us', <http://www.thelibrarybysoundpocket.org.hk/project_info_page/about-us/>. Accessed 13 August 2015.

Tufnell, B. (2006), *Land Art*, London: Tate.

Wells, L. (2011), *Land Matters: Landscape photography, culture and identity*, London and New York: I.B. Tauris.

Wong, R. (2013), 'Paper Airplane', <http://www.thelibrarybysoundpocket.org.hk/main/transportation/?post_type=listen>. Accessed 13 August 2015.

Notes

1 *The Library by Soundpocket*, Hong Kong <www.thelibrarybysoundpocket.org.hk/>.
2 *Stereopublic: Crowdsourcing the Quiet* <www.stereopublic.net>.

Chapter 15

Applying the Creative City: Curating art in urban spaces

Tammy Wong Hulbert

Introduction

Since the 1990s urban authorities are rethinking cities as potentially creative spaces in attempts to re-imagine and transform uses of urban spaces. As a knowledge-based economy replaces a manufacturing and industrial based one, there is increasing focus by policy-makers and city planners on local people and their creative potential for shaping cities and building the economy. Literature such as *The Creative City* (Landry 2000) has been influential in encouraging urban authorities to apply creative thinking more effectively and open-mindedly towards the planning of city communities. As a result, city planning now incorporates an array of arts including the work of artists, architecture, urban design and planning, and creative approaches to community events, in interpretive, expressive and innovative responses to place.

The transformative power of artistic and creative works occurring in everyday urban environments can be significant. In recent years there have been innovations in the public art arena, with many state and local governments introducing programs, policies and schemes to fund public art initiatives. Such enterprises are opening up the practices of public art to a more diverse group of artists, while introducing new materials and approaches to working in the urban public sphere. The increased interest in new approaches to public art programs is reflective of a more globalized, and conceptually orientated, contemporary art practice, with artists looking actively at ways of engaging in and with their urban environments.

Recently, major Australian cities such as Melbourne and Sydney have been influenced by creative city concepts. Urban planners look to creative communities of architects, landscape architects and artists to re-imagine urban spaces as sites that engage public audiences. Artists have been involved in taking on the role of publicly interpreting, expressing and giving meaning to public spaces. This approach is evidenced in the laneway spaces of central Melbourne, which were cast as dormant and abandoned spaces in the late 1980s to 1990s. During this decade, the work of local street artists occupied warehouses and their adjoining laneways; occupations that led to recognition of creative capacity by the local city authority. Taking a collaborative community-based approach, urban planners have worked with local communities to further activate these spaces through social, creative and artistic methods. Gradually changes occurred, with once abandoned spaces becoming iconic tourist sites. This process demonstrates how the artistic interpretation of place can imbue sites with meaning, connect with communities and have far-reaching benefits in broader society.

In considering the theme of the transformative power of re-imagining the city as a creative space, this chapter considers an alternative model of exhibition practice of 'curating the city' as a methodology for applying creative city concepts. Currently, city inhabitants may experience a range of art in public space practices, which are diverse in the way they are formed. In the past, art in the public sphere was mostly the domain of sculptors and muralists, and often the artworks were designed or commissioned to commemorate a particular person or public event. Well-recognized public sculptures in London's Trafalgar Square or outside Victoria's State Library in Melbourne demonstrate this point. However, as social perceptions of the role of creativity and the arts change, the arts play a more significant role in the urban experience, and consequently a wider variety of expressions can be seen in public urban spaces: street-art works, ephemeral art projects, site-specific art practices and projects commissioned by both government and private sectors.

This discussion considers the reframing of the city as a curatable space. It offers an alternative model of publicly based exhibition practices by focusing on re-imagining urban space as a site for expressing, viewing, exploring, engaging and interpreting artistic intentions and interactions. The discussion investigates why, in delivering this ideal, the encouragement of the creative city through re-imagining the city as a curated space, should be considered as an alternative model to that of 'the museuology'. The argument focuses on an approach that is centred on the historical city as a site for artistic exploration, curating as a method of re-imbuing the sacred in urban society, re-imagining the city as a site for exhibition, and viewing the curated city as a more accessible and democratic model of exhibition practices suitable for the twenty-first-century city.

The City as a Site for Exploration

If we begin to view the city as a curated space, we come to understand the city as a site for visual exploration. Since the late nineteenth century, planners following trends from European modernism have treated the city as a site for observation, investigation and experience. Before the turn of the twentieth century, the French author and poet, Charles Baudelaire depicted the character of urban life through Monsieur G. in his essay, *The Painter of Modern Life* (1964). Monsieur G. was a sophisticated gentleman who walked the city to observe and experience it, a man passionate about being amidst the action of urban life. Monsieur G. is described by Baudelaire as a *flâneur*, a French term translated as a stroller (Macey 2000: 131). In his essay, Baudelaire describes Monsieur G. as follows:

His passion and his profession are to become one flesh with the crowd. For the perfect *flâneur*, for the passionate spectator, it is an immense joy to set up house in the heart of the multitude, amid the ebb and flow of movement, in the midst of the fugitive and the infinite. To be away from home and yet to feel oneself everywhere at home; to see the world, to be at the centre of the world, and yet to remain hidden from the world—

such pleasures of those independent, passionate, impartial natures which tongue can but clumsily define.

(Baudelaire 1964: 9)

In the nineteenth century, Baudelaire's depiction of the *flâneur* became a metaphor for transforming urban conditions. It was a reflection of Paris becoming a modern city through its restructuring, manifesting in Haussmann's great boulevards and the changing social life of the working classes. Time for leisure and consumerism were being depicted increasingly by artists of the time such as Manet and the French Impressionists. Baudelaire's *flâneur* gained much influence in academic, artistic and literary circles as he describes how cities were becoming orientated increasingly towards the growth of the public sphere, where individuals were able to feel increasingly comfortable in the public environment. Writers concerned with spatial theorization, including critic and philosopher Walter Benjamin, regarded the *flâneur* as a metaphor for the conditions of mid-nineteenth-century, Parisian city life, which was changing as a result of industry and consumerism born from the industrial revolution. Benjamin's study *Passengenwerk* (written between 1927 and 1940), an incomplete study published posthumously, investigated the Paris arcades of the nineteenth century as thoroughfares for the luxury goods trade, prostitution and gambling. Benjamin argued they represented the beginning traits of modernist consumerist culture of commodity fetishism and alienation in society.

In the contemporary, globalized, urban world, the concept of the *flâneur* or *flâneuse* as a person who strolls to observe and explore the city remains relevant as cities look to ways to reinvent themselves as sites of discovery and exploration. In an age of creative and cultural tourism, cultural industries are built upon tourist participation in the act of voyeurism of 'the other'. As we grapple with identities in the complexity of globalizing cities dominated by consumerism, we look towards concepts of artistic and cultural interpretation to give renewed meaning to place.

As urban environments of the twenty-first century become increasingly complex ecosystems, access to culture is viewed as an urban human right. UNESCO's 'World Charter for Human Rights to the City', inspired by Henri Lefebvre's writings in *Le Droit a la Ville / The Right to the City*, in 1968, states that it recognizes:

human rights to housing, social security, work, an adequate standard of living, leisure, information, organisation and free association, food and water, freedom from dispossession, participation and self-expression, health, education, culture, privacy and security, a safe and healthy environment.

(UNESCO 2010)

Therefore, in the contemporary urban environment, access to culture, where the majority of the world's population live, deserves attention. This chapter offers a framework to consider how arts and cultural activity can become more accessible in cities.

Curating the Sacred in Urban Life

Today, the term 'curator' is broad in its application; its general definition refers to a custodian of a museum or collection. Over time the definition has expanded to incorporate a multitude of meanings. This includes an expanded interpretation that curators are responsible for the management, expertise, interpretation and exhibition of a collection, usually in the institutional context. In the visual arts the term 'curator' has become loaded with many connotations, suggesting the voice of authority, particularly with the rise of the popularity of the freelance visual arts curator of the late-twentieth-century, a role perceived in recent times as one of authority in the international contemporary art world.

In the twenty-first century, with the acceleration of globalization in the visual arts, the curator is seen as a creator of exhibitions and is perceived as holding a position of status and power. Art historian, Malcolm Gee comments in *Art Criticism Since 1900* that the visual arts became aligned with innovation in conceptual thought throughout the twentieth century. Artists responded to the rapidly changing conditions of contemporary society, and curators became aligned with the rise of experimental art of the 1960s. This alignment of the visual arts to innovation positioned the visual arts curator as possessing the foresight to predict new directions in innovation, thus reinforcing the perception of the curator as occupying a position of authority (Gee 1993: 3). Since the 1960s, the rise of the international biennale model of exhibition, and notably with the success of major biennales such as Venice, has taken the curator to the centre of international attention and acclaim. Swiss Curator, Harold Szeeman (1933–2005), was the original visual arts curator who famously claimed independence from the institutions when he resigned as Director of the Kunsthalle Bern in 1969. As Director, Szeeman began to gain a reputation for his experimental contemporary art exhibitions, particularly after he curated *Live in Your Head: When Attitudes become Form* (1969). The exhibition caused conflict and division about the direction of the museum in the art community, which eventually led to his resignation. Following this episode, Szeeman proclaimed himself as an *Ausstellungsmacher*, a maker of exhibitions, leading to a career of freelance curation. Later he was involved in introducing 'Aperto' in 1980, an exhibition of emerging art at the Venice Biennale. From the 1980s onwards, Szeeman's exhibition occurred in non-traditional spaces such as a private apartment, gymnasium and a theatre (Ulrich-Obrist 2008: 80). The breaking away of curators from the institutions can be compared to artists in mid-nineteenth-century Paris. Then the avant-garde refused the publicly endorsed power of the Salon via their *Salon des Refusés* exhibitions.

This current perspective on the visual arts curator represents only one model of curating, which is dominated by the connotation of curating as a position of status held by an individual. In curating urban sites as a shared space of community, it seems more appropriate that curating is viewed as a shared process. This change of emphasis turns the focus back towards the artwork, thus treating the experience of art as a communal practice. In the world of art, in the public sphere, there is a tendency for local government authorities (in Australia, dominating as commissioners of public art) to shy away from the term 'curator', as the term has become associated with the individual voice of authority. This shift away from the perceived voice of authority echoes attitudes expressed by prominent literary critic, Roland Barthes in his essay, *The Death of the Author* (1967), in which he critiqued the authority of the voice of the author with the birth of the reader. At that time, meanings were becoming democratic as the author or artist's autonomous role in meaning-making practices was being questioned. This is also consistent with changes in cultural and economic monopolies in the late 1960s to 1970s, and consistent with the 1968 civil demonstrations in Paris, where over one million French workers were on strike, and students occupied the campus at the University of Nanterre to protest for democracy in a social revolt against traditional systems that were seen to be out of reach of everyday realities.

In the case of the museums, the death of the curator was exchanged with the birth of the audience. As government authorities in Australia commission a large percentage of public art, the voice of the curator implies an authorial voice in contrast to the voice of the people and this points to reasons why the term 'curator' has been deemed inappropriate for use. Currently, a majority of public art is commissioned by local government and is selected by a panel of citizens and stakeholders. The process attempts to be democratic in approach by including a larger selection of people in the decision-making process. This process has impacted upon the management of public art in local government areas of Australian cities, leading to the development of unique processes of selection that reflect the voices of a larger section of the community, representing the shared nature of urban spaces and the birth of the audience. The elitist affiliation of the term 'curator' sits in a difficult position with government authorities due to the museum's responsibility of representing the entire community with its diverse and often competing views and self-interests.

On the other side of curating, through the consultation process of government structures are the actions of unsanctioned street artists, independent artists who make and exhibit their work in the public sphere without gaining official permission. Such artists create work in a spontaneous and often illegal manner, thus ignoring the process of consultation, and claiming territory through the evidence of their marks.

Moving away from the terms used in the contemporary art world affiliated with the experimental art scene, this research positions the term 'curator' by considering the word's origins. The etymology of 'curate' shows the origins of the word from Latin, 'cura' meaning 'care', in reference to a 'vicar, rector or parish priest', the 'carer of souls' referred to as the 'curate'. The current meaning of the term, 'to select, organize, and look after the items in a collection or exhibition', can be dated to around the late-nineteenth century, but definitions related to the religious role of curating can be dated earlier with origins in medieval Latin (AD 600–1500), the term 'curatus' becoming commonly used in middle English (AD 1150– 1470) (Merriam-Webster 2009). Thomas Moore, psychotherapist and author of *Care of the Soul,* refers to the role of the curate in the religious sense and examines the role of spirituality in the everyday.

The role of the curate, as he was called, was to provide a religious context for the larger turning points in life and also to maintain the affectional ties of family, marriage, and community. We can be the curates or curators of our own souls, an idea that implies an inner priesthood and a personal religion. To undertake this restoration of soul means we have to make spirituality a more serious part of everyday life.

(Moore 1992: 8)

With this original context in mind, the sacred origins of curating reminds us of the spiritual and sacred origins of the context of the care of objects, and how the meaning has expanded to incorporate the museological world, as early collections of significant artefacts would have belonged to the highest authority of the time (the Church, the state, imperial or aristocratic dynasties in the western and eastern context). In a contemporary society that is predominantly secular (particularly in Australia), curating the city could be considered an alternative model to finding a place for the spiritual in urban society. It may offer the possibility of seeking spirituality in a more individual sense through the re-enchantment of urban spaces. Influential, nineteenth-century, German philosopher, G. W. F. Hegel put forward the proposition in his *Lecture on Aesthetics* in 1886 that art represented the spiritual. Hegel is mentioned here in context of the arts and their alignment with the spiritual in the natural progression and universalizing of 'man' through history to a utopian endpoint:

The divinity is identified with nature itself; but this gross worship cannot last. Instead of seeing the absolute in real objects, man conceives it as a distinct and universal being; he seizes, though very imperfectly, the relation which unites the invisible principle to the objects of nature; he fashions an image, a symbol destined to represent it. Art is then the interpreter of religious ideas.

(Hegel, cited in Marxism Archive 2011: para 1)

Thus, in Hegel's thesis, art is related to a naturalistic view of the human being in its universally applied progression that brings together nature, divinity, man and reason. This idealized philosophical position has been much contested via writings by Frederich Nietzsche, Martin Heidegger, Jacques Derrida and other twentieth-century continental philosophers. Their writings deal with ontological and epistemological questions, and are concerned with how to show the workings of art, aesthetics and reason in terms that can take account of the complexities and specificities of a contemporary world.

If we consider spirituality as affecting the spirit, then curating urban spaces would come to represent the redistribution of our spiritual lives throughout urban life. As proposed by Hegel, the relationship between art and the spiritual is a perspective that has existed in many ancient civilizations and can be traced universally in terms of idealist philosophy. This view is also coherent with the philosophical writings of Immanuel Kant and his universal principles of right and morality, also much contested by the twentieth-century continental philosophers noted above.

Looking towards non-Eurocentric cultural perspectives of humans and their relationship towards their environment, we can also see that, in traditional Chinese philosophy, the spiritual aspects of urban inhabitance form the bedrock of ways of understanding people in relation to their physical environments. In particular, the philosophy of *Feng Shui* refers to the spiritual approach applied to the design of cities. This is a practice found in ancient Chinese cities, built according to the spiritual guidance of *Feng Shui,* which guides how a city should be planned according to a system of laws around the natural landscape of the surrounding area in relation to flow of energy (qi). In major cities such as Hong Kong, *Feng Shui* is still an influential practice in the design and consideration of urban planning. The term refers to the philosophy of spiritual guidance according to the environment, each separate character meaning 'wind' and 'water' referring to a spiritual balance between these elements in the environment and dates back as early as *Zang Shu* / The Book of the Burial in c. 276–324 (Guo Pu 2004). This example provides evidence that we should consider the wisdom of past civilizations in finding a place for the spiritual in contemporary urban life. The process of the curation of visual arts in urban spaces could be viewed as a shared sacred process, a way of connecting urban communities to the broader sense of the spiritual and thus re-imbuing meaning in place. Rather than being situated in an idealist position, this can be a highly contemporary viewpoint when it is integrated with the actual complexities of global conditions, and when it takes account of these complex configurations in on-the-ground practices of the public sphere.

The contemporary meaning of the word 'curator' has expanded to mean not only a carer of a collection, but also one who is responsible for specialized knowledge of a particular collection. Such care is undertaken through research and the development of exhibitions, usually in an institutional museological context. As proposed by Moore, in order to restore soul in contemporary society, the sacred needs to be a serious part of the everyday. If we view the arts as a tool for expressing the sacred, then they call to be re-imagined as holding the capacity for re-integration into everyday life. The proposition here is that viewing urban life from this perspective would allow the sacred to re-enter the everyday experience of the urban condition. In terms of specificity, and not as a universal principle, and in recognizing and valuing the complexity of the twenty-first century, this perspective has the capacity to reinvigorate the sacred within configurations of social, cultural, political and economic spaces. This complexity forms the ecosystem of which we are a part.

The City Museum or the Museum City?

Callum Storrie, curator, exhibition designer and author of *The Delirious Museum* (2006) proposes that by 'shifting the perception from the collection and the container [...] it is possible to re-evaluate the relationship between museum and city in terms of a shared experience' (Storrie 2006: 2). Storrie proposes that instead of seeing ourselves as the individual observer investigating the city, we now become part of a community of shared urban experiences. Through investigation of our urban environments we are able to reconnect with the curatorial narratives of each city's museums, as they inform us of a shared story of place. The concept of community is significant for this research as the curation of public spaces advocates ways of reconnecting communities to shared public places through the addition of meaning and narration of place. Reconnecting individuals to public urban spaces is a way of encouraging a sense of belonging in urban societies, and being part of a strengthened community.

Within urban space, existing and shared curatorial narratives are embedded in the environment and often expressed as art in public space works. If we, as urban dwellers, are able to alter our lens to view the city from the perspective of these collective histories, we would experience the city as a site for artistic and cultural exploration, a city as a curated space. These narratives of urban spaces have existed in parallel to the world of the museology; and museological institutions represent only one perspective.

This discussion frames the city as a curated space rather than as a museum. Such framing of the city implies the incorporation of the historical legacy of the museology while, at the same time, proposing the site of the curated city as a model of exhibition that is ever-changing, shaped by the ebbs and flows of the city and urban community. Increasingly, we are becoming a local and global society that is more connected virtually, allowing more flexibility in where we work, learn, communicate and play. But this also potentially changes the function of urban spaces and how we use public space, and how we can become more isolated. In a society that is becoming dominated increasingly by alienating virtual experiences, it becomes necessary to refocus attention to the physical spaces of the city, to reframe these physical spaces within a curatorial framework. Reframing the city as a curated space provides a vehicle for individuals to physically reconnect and re-engage with public urban spaces by finding shared meaning in place, and thereby creating a sense of belonging in the polis.

Museums, Democracy and Access to Culture

In considering the role of curators and museums, curators were traditionally viewed as the gatekeepers of culture. Culture, as defined earlier, refers to the shared values and practices of particular groups. In Australia, museums have become recently more accessible to the public, as society has become increasingly democratic. Distributed democracy refers to the notion that resources may be coordinated to be available to the broad mass of a population, thus favouring a social equality model of public governance, an ideal many societies advocate and work towards. While this ideal may be followed in Australian society, it is evident that this is not the case in all societies: hence the global situation of displaced people, forced migration, hatred, violence, starvation and loss of cultural histories. Museums as cultural institutions also work increasingly towards a distributed model; they are no longer operating primarily as infrastructure to house collections; their roles have diversified immensely. Today they are also vehicles for educating the public, reflecting the movement towards a more equal society in terms of access to knowledge (Hudson 1975: 10).

As public art has always been publicly accessible and has contributed a similar role in educating publics predominantly about public history, public art has been consistently a form of art for the public. Storrie argues in *The Delirious Museum* that the most democratic society should have free museum admission. He argues that public culture should be accessible and that museums should be an extension of the streets (Storrie 2006: 2). By extending Storrie's concept of the museum and urban space as one fluid entity, this gives rise to the proposition that the curated space of the city acts as a democratic form of exhibition by offering free access to public exhibitions of artistic expression. Then entry to the museum would not be based on a financial transaction, but rather on the individuals being able to re-imagine themselves as audience, opening their mind to the possibility that urban spaces may be viewed as sites for individual expression of artists, as well as for the engagement of public history, as part of a shared urban experience.

The Existing City as a Curated Space in the Global Age

In context of the history of city growth and development, visual arts activity has existed consistently in the public sphere, albeit in different and varying forms. However, the city may not have been conceptualized as a curated space. By articulating the city as a curated space, a site for sensory investigation, this framework attempts to re-enchant the commuter, the pedestrian or the tourist within urban spaces to see urban spaces beyond the functional. This reframing allows an interpretation of the city as a space of meaningful engagement, with capacity to activate creative, cultural and personal expressions. US-based art critic and author of *The Re-enchantment of Art* (1991), Suzi Gablik argues that the role of visual arts under the modernist paradigm needs radical reframing. She makes a convincing case that artists 'are trying to make the transition from Eurocentric, patriarchal thinking and the "dominator" model of culture toward an aesthetics of interconnectedness, social responsibility and ecological attunement' (Gablik 1991: 22). This reveals a more globalized approach to artistic practices, working appropriately with the curated city model. Urban planning theorist, Leonnie Sandercock (1997) also reflects this focus on a total reframing of urban consciousness in urban planning by recognizing the culturally diverse nature of city communities, as a response to the renewed conditions of globalization.

Gablik argues for 'a resonant environment' as a move away from the 'confrontational, oppositional mind of modernism' (Gablik 1991: 169). Gablik urges that the role of artists needs to be more socially integrated in the age of sustainable development of cities. Such renewed and connected role of the arts in society would enable a re-enchantment of urban populations for not only the arts, but also the urban environment.

Suzanne Lacy, artist and author of *Mapping the Terrain: New genre public art* (1995) retraces the changes of approaches to public art from historical artefacts placed in the park to artists re-imagining urban spaces as a new form of exhibition space.

> One version of history, then, begins with the demise of what Judith Baca calls the 'cannon in the park' idea of public art—display of sculptures glorifying a version of national history that excluded large segments of the population. The cannon in the park was encroached upon by the world of high art in the sixties, when the outdoors, particularly in urban areas, came to be seen as new exhibition space for art previously found in galleries, museums and private collections […] The ability for art to enhance public spaces such as plazas, parks and corporate head quarters was quickly recognized as a way to revitalize inner cities, which were beginning to collapse under the burden of increasing social problems. Art in public spaces was seen as a means of reclaiming and humanising the urban environment.
>
> (Lacy 1995: 21)

Lacy suggests that, as the socio-political environment changed throughout the twentieth century and turned towards advocacy for increased equality in the distribution of resources, public art practices also evolved to reflect changing attitudes. The opening up of society, led by the avant-garde artists of the 1960s, influenced a wider variation of artwork in public spaces. With the change in attitude towards art practices, artists looked at ways of working in the public sphere, and by doing so took ownership of contested space of the urban environment.

In the age of globalization, the treatment of cities as planned environments has become recognized increasingly by urban planners and local governments, as 'placemaking' is positioned in the strategic design of urban environments. The emergence of the cultural tourism industry as an effect of economic and cultural globalization encourages city planners to enhance and create unique qualities in their urban spaces. Not only are urban planners seeing this as beneficial in terms of cultural tourism, but they are also seeing the benefits of access to public culture in cities as a way of creating a stronger and more socially cohesive society (Sandercock 1997). As for cities becoming a 'global city', increasingly competitive and emerging cities use citywide exhibitions such as biennales as a strategy for drawing attention to urban culture on a global stage through the spectacle of contemporary art. The Shanghai Biennale, which emerged in the late 1990s, was a successful international art exhibition that showcased innovative, contemporary, Chinese and international art. The exhibition emerged with the rise of Shanghai as an international financial hub (Barrett 2001: 203). Local Shanghai authorities see this as a way of enhancing the image of their city by aligning it with innovative artistic production and signifying that they are open-minded and creative in approach. This aligns with the ideals promoted by creative city literature.

The 1960s was a period of significant social transformation and this was reflected in the ways artists changed their attitudes towards making art. Avant-garde artists under post-war conditions sought to break down the paradigm of authority, expressing this through their conceptual processes. In the public art realm, artists challenged traditional Eurocentric forms of public art by creating works that represented excluded communities to reclaim urban public spaces in cities for these groups. As a response to the civil rights movement in the United States, *The Wall of Respect* (1967) was a ground-breaking public mural in Chicago, depicting African American heroes of the arts. It was painted collaboratively by a group of African American artists Sylvia Abernathy, Elliot Hunter, Wadsworth Jarrell, Barbara Janes-Hogu, Carolyn Lawrence, Norman Parish and William Walker. The work questioned the dominance of Eurocentric artists represented in American museums and reclaimed a public urban space for the voice of the African American community. Considered controversial at the time, the work challenged accepted social norms of community representation.

Heightened awareness of social health and cultural awareness of the post-colonial age led to activation of various forms of public practice in attempts to implement approaches to rebuilding relationships between individuals and communities. This can be seen in examples such as Newcastle Gateshead, UK, a city where the activation of arts and cultural activity has led to the revitalization of this former industrial town (Ward 2002). Although the actions of the avant-garde has opened ways of redefining the role of artists in urban life, the tensions still exist between local communities, artists, public art practices and the use of public urban spaces. Different community sectors hold competing visions of how public spaces should be used. In the renewed condition of global capitalism, urban space is viewed as valuable economic space, and artists in the public sphere continue to work in this contested space. Not only are individual artists competing with the voices of authority, they are also competing with the widely accepted view of urban space as a commercial commodity (Lefebvre 1991).

Conclusion

This chapter proposes that the curation of urban spaces could be considered as an alternative model of exhibition practices to the museological model and a way of applying the creative city concept. Today, creativity and the arts have become more valued in society. As a result, imaginative public art plays an important role in how urban spaces are experienced: this may include street-art works, ephemeral art projects, site-specific art practices and projects commissioned by both government and private sectors, and are not mutually exclusive.

By framing the curation of practices of contemporary artists in urban spaces, potentials arise for communities to re-engage with urban spaces through the reading of meaning into place, and thereby gaining new connections and relationships to public sites. Through a discussion on the historical artistic engagement with the city, and the sacred role that the curation of art may play in urban spaces, this chapter argues that re-imagining the city as a curated space could, potentially, offer a more accessible and democratic model of exhibition practices suitable for individual cities and their citizens of the twenty-first century and beyond.

References

Barrett, D. (2001), '2000 Shanghai Biennale: A day-by day eyewitness account', in H. Wu (ed.), *Chinese Art at the Crossroads,* Hong Kong: Timezone 8, pp. 223–244.

Barthes, R. (1967), *The Death of the Author,* <http://www.deathoftheauthor.com>. Accessed 2 June 2015.

Baudelaire, C. (1964), *The Painter of the Modern Life and Other Essays,* (trans. J. Mayne), London: Phaidon. (First published in French 1863.)

Benjamin, W. (2002), *The Arcades Project,* (trans. H. E. K. McLaughlin), Cambridge: The Belknap Press of Harvard University. (First published in German 1982.)

'Curator' (2009), *Merriam-Webster Dictionary,* <http://www.merriamwebster.com/dictionary/curator>. Accessed 1 May 2016.

Gablik, S. (1991), *The Re-enchantment of Art,* London: Thames and Hudson.

Gee, M. E. (1993), *Art Criticism since 1900,* Manchester: Manchester University Press.

Guo, P. (2004), *The Book of Burial (Zang Shu),* (trans. by J. Zhang), London: Edwin Mellen Press. (First published in Chinese c. AD 276–324.)

Hudson, K. (1975), *A Social History of Museums: What the visitors thought,* London: Macmillan.

Macey, D. (2000), *Dictionary of Critical Theory,* London: Penguin.

Marxism Archive (2011), *Hegel—Lectures on Aesthetics 1886,* <http://www.marxists.org/reference/archive/hegel/works/ae/ch03.htm#29>. Accessed 17 June 2015.

Lacy, S. (1995), *Mapping the Terrain: New genre public art,* Seattle: Bay Press.

Landry, C. (2008), *The Creative City: A toolkit for urban innovators,* 2nd ed., London: Earthscan Publications.

Lefebvre, H. (1991), *The Production of Space,* (trans. D. Nicholson-Smith), Oxford: Blackwell. (First published in French 1974.)

Lefebvre, H., Kofman, E. and Lebas, E. (1996), *Writings on Cities,* Oxford: Blackwell.

Moore, T. (1992), *Care of the Soul,* London: Piatkus Books.

Sandercock, L. (1997), *Towards Cosmopolis: Planning for multicultural cities,* New York: John Wiley.

Storrie, C. (2006), *The Delirious Museum,* London: I.B Tauris.

Ulrich-Obrist, H. E. (ed.) (2008), *A Brief History of Curating,* Zurich: Les Presses du reel.

UNESCO (2010), 'Urban Policies and the Right to the City', <http://unesdoc.unesco.org/images/0017/001780/178090e.pdf>. Accessed 22 June 2015.

Ward, D. (2002), 'Forget Paris and London, Newcastle is a creative city to match Kabul and Tijuana', *The Guardian,* 2 September, <http://www.guardian.co.uk/society/2002/sep/02/communities.arts1>. Accessed 10 December 2015.

Wolff, J. (1985), 'The Invisible flâneuse: Women and the literature of modernity', *Theory, Culture & Society,* <http://www.fll.vt.edu/Johnson/431405paristexts/wolff.pdf>. Accessed 15 June 2015.

Chapter 16

The Poetic City: Old songs left beneath the arches

Nicholas Lyon Gresson

Introduction

Walking the city, seeking the city, relating to things, no hierarchies, this is the way of writing, coming to know the tracing of it all. Michel de Certeau (1984) talked about the walker as a tactical being, navigating and way-finding at will. By taking short cuts, denying official maps or instructive devices, there may be a transformative process in action. But who is transforming whom? Is the city transforming the walker or walker transforming the city? This is but one of the thoughts running through this discussion.

In this chapter I am an artist writing about my own project. But the hunger of an artist as poet is necessarily subsumed; the person is removed from the poetry. Do we ever see Shelley's everyday life in his words of poetry? T. S. Eliot in *The Hollow Men* (1959 [1925]) and Nietzsche in *Thus Spoke Zarathustra* (2003) are not consumed with self-reflection; theirs is a wider commentary on the state of being human, writing from their time and place. Eliot's Hollow Men may have been the effigies burned on Guy Fawkes, but beyond that they speak of the empty state of being human in a post-World War I world: *'We are the hollow men /We are the stuffed men /Leaning together /Headpiece stuffed with straw. Alas!'* (Eliot 1959); and maybe Nietzsche meant exactly that with his succinct *'God is dead!'* (Nietzsche 2003).

The words take the power, and through the words the subject becomes manifest. The words are always around the corner, and the next corner for the taking; it takes time and relentless pursuing and crafted containment. This discussion shines a torch light on the mid-nineteenth-century French poet, Charles Baudelaire, in all his 'unsound' contradistinctive glory; and imposes the difficulty of taking on the motif of the *flâneur* (stroller) today. But wandering off, slipping off the mapped agenda, I come back to walk the plane of the city.

Characterizing Baudelaire

What of the city? It is the age, it is the time, it is now; but in its DNA lies the expressions of the past. Thinking of T. S. Eliot, Cyril Connolly writing as Palinurus, said, '[w]orks of art which survive must all be indebted to the spirit of their age' (Connolly 1984: 120), and to that can be applied the city; maybe the city has a work of art power. As a walker in the city we must resist the temptation to catch up, too easily, on the *flâneur* and Baudelaire, and find an easy identification there, through the many roles that Baudelaire could alight upon. Baudelaire belongs implicitly to the spirit of his age, that is, mid-nineteenth-century Paris:

> [A] time when a city was narrow, unhealthy, insufficient, but picturesque, varied, charming, full of memories [...] going for a stroll was not something that tired you out, it was a delight. It gave birth to that eminently Parisienne compromise between laziness and activity known as *flânerie*!
>
> (Victorien Sardou 1866, cited in White 2001: 37–38)

This was the time of the disappearing decadence, the lively, unrepentant eroticism, the sweeping up of horseshit by the broom of modernity through Haussmann's 1853, massive renovation and remodelling of the city. Baudelaire engaged enigmatically with the best and the worst of it, with the despair and the repair: he has joined into it, consenting to his own damnation in a poetic search for his dream of and in the city; his posturing is like a moth to a flame. Of Baudelaire, French literary critic and dramatist, Jules Lemaître wrote, in 1895:

> 'One confronts a work full of artifice and intentional contradictions [...] even as he gives the crassest description of the bleakest details of reality, he indulges in a spiritualism which greatly distracts us from the immediate impression that things make upon us. [...] He curses "progress" yet he enjoys the special flavour which this industry has given today's life. [...] the specifically Baudelairean is the constant combination of two opposite modes of reaction [...] one could call it a past and a present mode. A masterpiece of the will [...] the latest innovation in the sphere of emotional life'.[1] To present this attitude as a great achievement of the will was in Baudelaire's spirit.
>
> (Benjamin 1973: 94)

Twenty-first-century Melbourne or Auckland or London or Christchurch are not mid-nineteenth-century Paris, and Baudelaire's poetry does not match today's repertoires, today's cast of importunating desires and loaded politics of identity and human rightfulness—where global freedom pre-empts the advent of paradise, where anywhere is better than here, in our hurried steps away from anguish.

The 'special constellation in which greatness and indolence meet in human beings [...] governed Baudelaire's life. He deciphered it and called it "modernism". [...] Modernism turns out to be his doom' (Benjamin 1973: 95–96). The decadence of Paris in Baudelaire's *Les Fleurs du mal* resonates with its times, and with the poet's melancholy spirit:

Je pense à la négresse, amaigrie et phtisique,
Piétinant dans la boue, et cherchant, l'œil hagard,
Les cocotiers absents de la superbe Afrique
Derrière la muraille immense du brouillard;

I think of the lean consumptive negress trudging through the mud, with her haggard eyes peering in vain through the huge wall of fog for the absent palm-trees of her noble Africa;

(Baudelaire 2014: 200)

To compare the city of today with Baudelaire's Paris may lack legitimacy; convenient comparisons with anything *flâneur*-ish call for examination. We do not have the church adjacent to the doss-houses of the *Rue de la Charbonnière*, the rag pickers, the parasols, lost youth *sur les trottoirs*, the refuse-barges skidding and sliding on the Seine, the secret significance, the urban crotch in your face. Poetry demands that you do not instrumentalize strangeness. That old '*merveilleux* belongs to the nineteenth-century past. That strangeness is necessary as an ingredient of beauty and what proportion of violence is best suited to creative emotion' (Connolly 1984: 125).

Yes, in psychiatry today Freudian intrapsychics are often tactfully avoided and discredited—aggression emasculated by outside, professional denials and displacements of the advent of violence in the human psyche. But '[u]gliness, cruelty, self-destruction, terror, are included in the Baudelairian concept of beauty' (Peyre 1964: 10). Does it do us any harm?

The *flâneur* has moved on and his last heroic act may be his disappearance. Once with incalculable indifference and a magic eye, he observed the rising bourgeoisie, the *bohème*, the untidiness, the insouciant high-class woman with her pretty shoes and bodices, the prostitute with her torn, irregular skirt, the stray cat cowering. 'The *flâneur* is the creation of Paris' (Benjamin 1929, cited in White 2001: 46). '[…] Benjamin explains, the *flâneur* is in search of experience, not knowledge. Most experience ends up interpreted as—and replaced by—knowledge, but for the *flâneur* the experience remains somehow pure, useless, raw' (White 2001: 47). The *flâneur* picks and chooses as he will, aside or astride the absinthe, and at his loss of kinship with the hero, the *flâneur* could take and leave without questioning what his senses might have told him.

Of all the experiences which made his life what it was, Baudelaire singled out his having been jostled by the crowd as the decisive, unique experience. The lustre of a crowd with a motion and a soul of its own, the glitter that had bedazzled the *flâneur*, had dimmed for him. […] Baudelaire battled the crowd—with the impotent rage of someone fighting the rain or the wind.

(Benjamin 1973: 154)

His poetic thoughts jostled, modernism jostled him; his city was destined to change in the changing means of production. 'Baudelaire was perhaps the first performance artist in history. At least he was one of the first to live out his aesthetics, to make his home décor, his clothes, even his way of moving, consistent with his poetry' (White 2001: 126). Baudelaire has awakened us to the tempo of his times—and our times.

Old Songs left Beneath the Arches

Today we are all consumers of the city: signs dominate; advertising boards shout what you want, the soaps you must use, the cars that will signal prosperity, the travel that will lure with an exotic inoculation. We are all implicated in the dislocation via economic and ideological globalization. 'So much for all that –' (Gresson 2015: 25).

Via poetics we may elicit truth-obligations beyond the macro-politics of urban governmentality and put a positive spin on the 'faultlines' as the *flâneur* was able to do in nineteenth-century Paris. Today we are in a compression of space-time; and satellites map our every move. Hélène Cixous has inscribed with pertinence:

> When an event arrives which evicts us from ourselves, we do not know how to 'live'. But we must. Thus we are launched into a space-time whose coordinates are all different from those we have always been accustomed to. In addition, these violent situations are always new. Always. At no moment can a previous bereavement serve as a model. It is, frightfully, all new.
>
> (Cixous, cited in Merewether 2006: 045)

There is a different means of production. If there is a hero today it is the celebrity; if there is a cultural custodian today it is the economic advocates who market a collective consumption of fiction-proliferating lifestyle promises. There is another music; the hum and covenant of economic progress, the motor shielded from sight. This city is not Paris of the mid-nineteenth century; not the rise of iron and gas lighting. The epoch has changed. Says Foucault: 'We are in the epoch of simultaneity: we are in the epoch of juxtaposition, the epoch of the near and far, of the side-by-side, of the dispersed' (Foucault 1984)—so I walk across the city, catching 'inesteemable' moments, the lived reality of it all, the chairs that are put out on the footpaths, the chairs that are brought in. There is no chessboard of moves, no instrumental strategy here.

Perhaps we need to accord Baudelaire with the last *flâneur*—the hero-becoming-dandy, seamlessly abandoned to idleness in the 'secure harbour' (Benjamin 1973: 96). Why try to maintain that *virtue of freedom*? If it was an ideal then, now it is anchoritic; but no *flâneur* would say freedom was an ideal; it belonged to its time, the time of modernity. The *flâneur* had a very specific meaning for the city and for its times. Why impugne the pungency of our times?

My impulse is not of the *flâneur,* not of Baudelaire's Paris, nor *La Belle Epoch,* not reflecting the visions of an F. Scott Fitzgerald and his angst-ridden Zelda—but I did catch a tail end of such bohemian life in 1964 London, New York and Buenos Aires, and undeniably it mattered; but Henry Millar mattered just as much because he could never be matched or repeated. My poetry comes today from walking the city as an ordinary citizen in the business of everyday life; in de Certeau's terms, a tactical act rather than a Baudelairean strategy.

The *flâneur* of Paris, poetic strategist *par excellence*, revelled in the authentic edginess and legitimate statement of a city's implosion, a society's implosion. To the *flâneur* is accorded the strategic act of walking the arcades, described by a Paris Guide as 'a new contrivance of industrial luxury [...], glass-covered, marble-floored passages [...] such an arcade is a city, indeed a world, in miniature' (Benjamin 1973: 158). Walking this world, the *flâneur* was not a badge of authority or meaningfulness. We would not find Frederico García Lorca's bucolic, mysterious gypsy here, and Oscar Wilde showed how precarious it all was. Wilde kept his best poetry to the very end when he had stopped being the dandy, and that impulse to transgress had run out.

Jostling the Moment

My tactics find moments of observation now, stopping the city's 'history' through the interventions of words and fullstops; the poem nudges a point in time, time held, a beginning again—not altogether different from photography's mein. In the poem, *Old Songs* it is the Yarra not the Seine; it is Melbourne or Christchurch of the twenty-first century not elsewhere:

> you think of things down by the river
> the weight of the city in your wake
> the way things pass or stick
> like wet shoes from last week's rain.

(Gresson 2013a: 30)

Commonality is no longer to be despised; Parisienne migrants from Africa are no longer peering from a blighted absence in nobilized exhortations. The poet is walking, but is a collector of images, not the collector of despair or meaning anticipating angst, exoticisim, eroticism or sites of exalted penance. Here the poet endorses the moment.

> But the little girl with braces
> is getting used to her glasses
> today's focus routine tears
> maybe her culture will cross-reference
> I don't expect so.
>
> See the proliferating helmets making deals
> with who knows what God
> the strollers strolling
> the rowers sweeping the waters
> fast-food papers floating
> old hearts walking past conflict
> young breasts beating

the old beggar buggered by torment
wowsers left laughing
as the long day slips by and night presses.

(Gresson 2013a: 30–31)

It is the opening of a moment. In *Old Songs* the river is flowing; boats that pass shall pass by again; bridges that cross, do just that:

Today bridges are bridges
air is air
and the bridge is above me
the river steps take me down
the river steps take me up.

And maybe that's what the plan is all about
old songs left beneath the arches.

(Gresson 2013a: 31)

The poet is tactically stopping the moment to grasp (through just words) the hovering eternal recurrence, which per Nietzsche, would be considered more as an *internal personally-felt, snagging, recurrence*, an act of responsibility to the self and relationships with others. Foucault would enter here and irresistibly say:

We are at a moment, I believe, when our experience of the world is less that of a long life developing through time than that of a network that connects points and intersects with its own skein […] an ensemble of relations.

(Foucault 1984)

Creative City

Does a poetic network of moments mean the city is inherently creative? To say the city is 'creative' is perhaps a suitable label for entrepreneurship. What is needed is a pragmatic recognition of the creative city in the role and rhyme of economic pressures and forces. The so-called old venal parts of London and New York have been removed out of sight, renovated beyond recognition over the past five decades. The café is no longer a nucleus of philosophical or fermenting discourse; my Ninth Street Diner in Hoboken, New Jersey is now sterile; no more Allen Ginsberg there, that HOWL is gone.[2] Now jeans are parked parallel on handy chairs; designer bag and belt sitting next to designer belt and bag; so much is gentrified. Carnaby Street in the Soho district, for example, from the Mods and Hippies of the late 1960s to present day, epitomizes the economization of a bohemian past transmogrifying into a well-packaged future; a benign salutation of a past held *in memoriam*, trading on an iconoclast reputation: a commodified substitution. Can this be called a 'creative city'? It is certainly a creativity commodified around the café latte: any threshold to get the city on a global map.

In spite of age and experience, I do not have an ownership of any poem about walking grey New York streets in winter, or the narrow Brighton footpaths in summer, or the ancient, frozen, paving stones of Beijing's Forbidden City, nor do I snag the terror that hangs over Tiananmen Square. But to my mind the poetic city exists there as much as anywhere; it depends on our living language—a language that can shine in front of us. In Melbourne, Christchurch and Auckland—these three cities being my customary cathexes brewed over many years—there is something of a poetic city rather than a creative city imbuing the poetry, coming from my observations while walking and thinking there. In *Melbourne Morning* (Gresson 2011a: 125) the gaunt winter branches permit the sun access:

> Yes, it is like Christchurch
> A morning in Melbourne,
> The gaunt winter branches making spaces
> The sun releasing us from the bondage of cold
> Lets the light probe places
> Polishes the wide streets
> Stretches buildings.

City life and outdoor eating hold their place:

> Even the area of Hoddle and Victoria
> Becomes a place of grace.
>
> And the carpet of roadside tables in Lygon
> Catch happier patrons.

(Gresson 2011a: 125)

But whatever the reason or season the city will be reinventing itself in spite of any strategic plans or urban indoctrinations to hold the glass and sun index in place. Like a poem the city will have its own tactic:

> And slowly spring will come
> And paint upon the streets, café awnings, bridges,
> Trams and people
> A veneer of hope.

(Gresson 2011a: 125)

By the 1990s the creative city was envisioned as a rationalized entity for economic growth. However, the earth's destructive powers can vent their fury on the stability of a city and alter this in a moment. Christchurch was decimated by the earthquake of 22 February 2011:

My eyes feel so cold today
Still, still a beautiful solemn spin of the tide.

And while the music played
and the seas were glass at Sumner
and the southerly kept at arm's length from the sea
and Bexley's best boys slept at school
urged, the mountains moved
old hanging stones slipped
clouds and buildings swayed
feet fought in hollow halls
and on a rock bend
the stones and wings of time crumbling
and all over gutted word and store and dust flew
the human rain closed in a city's flock.

(Gresson 2011b: 149)

From the 6.3 earthquake in Christchurch 185 people died and thousands of chimneys toppled, the jolt coming from a 15 kilometre-long fault line beneath the Port Hills, shallow, and only 10 kilometres from the city. The earlier earthquake of September 2010 was stronger at 7.1, but the damage and fatalities were less. Older brick and stone buildings weakened by the 2010 quake capitulated in the 2012 quake: heritage buildings, the founding Anglican Christchurch Cathedral, the Catholic Cathedral, the Provincial Council Chambers and Lyttelton Timeball Station; and over a quarter of the city's buildings damaged beyond redemption.

And out of the falling an untenable transition
a city jolted fell apart in the middle
and from her edges too saw asphalt wave and crack
homes trekked and safe old footpaths held shards of glass
as wild screams the thick air heard and wore.
How long deep hands were tied
how long deep cries were waiting
the façade of a thousand souls crumbling.

(Gresson 2011b: 149)

Rock cliffs of Sumner split and collapsed leaving homes clinging precariously. Grey liquefaction squeezed and spat through cracks in the ground and the oozing mud and silt engulfed streets, sections, houses, as pipes burst and water and sewerage gushed.

So was knitted a filthy burning
tables, pipes and signs silent

no mercy in time's tides and schemes;
and beneath it all slanted bleeding bleached
those left buried too long there
to see their lover's eyes sparkling like a star.

Time tethered not time held.

Will it ever be laid out for us more lucid
this remorseless time?
And I shall be a stranger in my sleep
spreading down a quilt of prayers.

(Gresson 2011b: 150)

The City of Christchurch was flung into a national state of emergency, the central business district a no-go zone as people left the city by the thousands, and parliament legislated for recovery.[3] Then comes the rebuilding, and a city is forced into reconsideration. By August 2012, a city strategy was declared to establish not a 'creative city' out of the rubble, but an accessible city, a liveable city, a green city, a vibrant city of noise, entertainment and hospitality.[4]

Gifts of the City

Perhaps it is in the tactical extinction of self-ness that one finds the gift of and from the city, and by time, from history itself. The self-qua-self ceases to exist: we may even meet the stranger in ourselves. Why should we assume to know the gift when it is given? The gifts of the city extend beyond vision. You walk the city as a stranger and the footpaths and disrupted signs define your fields of perception. A cat on a park bench could invite you to sit down; the noise of music playing from an impromptu bar may invite recognition; a stranger's churlish call to share a drink may embolden a new conversation. Coffee from a ship's container, as in post-earthquake Christchurch, in an unrecognizable Cashel Street, may engender new music, new sound; that very dislocation may be the gift of the eternal recurrence. One day by the Yarra in Melbourne:

So I am watching the little sparrow
chirping on the back of a chair
as I suck on my iced-coffee straw and listen
and wonder what antennae he had cranked up.

And by a brown river
the doors of the food-hall
opened and shut
shut and opened
and often for no reason—you know what I mean.

But the sun shone and the girls strode
they seem to know what they're about
and the seagulls just seagulled
swooping and squawking
and some shadows slid and concrete set.

So I scraped the chocolate out—and the cream
and with the last sip he came back and chirped again.

Then a big broad white shirt squatted and
squashed the place he had perched on
that's how it goes.

(Gresson 2013b: 32)

The city gave me this: a city sparrow perched on the back of a chair. There lies the hospitality of a gift.

I will write it down with smoke and cigarettes and discarded dreams
and like so
by dint of
it goes like
well—like with smoke and cigarettes.

(Gresson 2013b: 32)

Conclusion

On such a subject unusually difficult to encapsulate with contributory worth, this discussion has worked between the poetic voice and the explanatory voice. It has not been a question of giving evidence as such, but allowing the contribution of the poetic in life and city. Perhaps, as a poet, I can be lean on the logic of analytical philosophers, but if an internal logic of diffuseness and difference has been raised by the consciousness of the poetic then so be it.

Whether or not this has been transformative is another matter. Perceptions of the city will always vary. Here I have introduced the notion that the city is an inherently poetic space, and perhaps the transformative lies equally between the space of the city, the time of the city and the tactical mind space of a walker. It is a question of who defines whom. Could it be a poetic fusion? Do we dare leave out the cat or the sparrow or the barges on the Seine? Will it ever be decided?

References

Baudelaire, C. (2014), *Baudelaire: The complete verse*, 2nd ed. (trans. Francis Scarfe), London: Anvil Press Poetry. (First published in French 1863.)

Benjamin, W. (1973), *Charles Baudelaire: A Lyric poet in the era of high capitalism*, (trans. Harry Zohn), London: NLB. (First published in German in 1969.)

Certeau, M. de (1984), *The Practice of Everyday Life*, (trans. Steven Rendall), Oakland: University of California Press. (First published in French 1980.)

Connolly, C. (1984), *The Unquiet Grave: A word cycle by Palinurus*, Harmondsworth: Penguin Books. (First published 1944.)

Eliot, T. S. (1959), 'The Hollow Men' 1925, in *Collected Poems* 1909–1935, Glasgow: University Press, pp. 85–90. (First published 1936.)

Foucault, M. (1984), 'Of Other Spaces: Utopias and heterotopias', *Architecture, Mouvement, Continuité 5*, (trans. Jay Miskowiec), pp. 46–49. (First published in French 1967.) <http://web.mit.edu/allanmc/www/foucault1.pdf>. Accessed 4 November 2015.

Ginsberg, A. (1956), *Howl and Other Poems*, San Francisco: Pocket Poet Series, City Light Books.

Gresson, N. L. (2015), *A Gathering*, Melbourne: Arcadia, Australian Scholarly Publishing.

—— (2013a), 'Old Songs', in *Walking With Time*, Melbourne: Arcadia, Australian Scholarly Publishing, pp. 30–31.

—— (2013b), 'The Sparrow', in *Walking With Time*, Melbourne: Arcadia, Australian Scholarly Publishing, p. 32.

—— (2011a), 'Melbourne Morning', in E. Grierson (ed.), *A Life in Poetry: Nicholas Lyon Gresson*, Melbourne: Arcadia, Australian Scholarly Publishing, p. 125.

—— (2011b), 'Earthquake 22.2.2011', in E. Grierson (ed.), *A Life in Poetry: Nicholas Lyon Gresson*, Melbourne: Arcadia, Australian Scholarly Publishing, pp. 149–150.

Merewether, C. (2006), 'Taking Place: Acts of survival for a time to come', in *2006 Biennale of Sydney: Zones of contact*, Sydney: Biennale of Sydney, pp. 45–60.

Nietzsche, F. (2003), *Thus Spoke Zarathustra*, (trans. R. J. Hollingdale), London: Penguin Books. (First published in German 1883–1891.)

Peyre, H. (1964), 'Charles Baudelaire', in S. Burnshaw (ed.), *The Poem Itself: 150 poems translated and analysed*, Harmondsworth, Middlesex, UK: Pelican Books (Penguin), pp. 10–19. (First published in USA 1960.)

White, E. (2001), *The Flâneur: A stroll through the paradoxes of Paris*, New York and London: Bloomsbury Publishing.

Notes

1 Jules Lemaître, *Les contemporains*, Paris, 1895, pp. 29ff, in W. Benjamin (1973 n. 81).

2 'Howl' is a 1955 poem by Allen Ginsberg, first published in his collection, *Howl and Other Poems* (1956), dedicated to Carl Solomon and introduced by William Carlos Williams.

'Howl' was considered as one of the defining works of the 'Beat Generation'. Its publication led to an obscenity charge against the publisher, defended with the help of American Civil Liberties Union (ACLU).

3 *Canterbury Earthquake Recovery Act 2011* (NZ).

4 The Christchurch Central Recovery Plan <https://ccdu.govt.nz/the-plan>. Accessed 4 November 2015.

Author Bionotes

Professor William Cartwright AM has an international reputation in cartography. In recognition of his significant service to cartography and geospatial science, he received the honour of AM (Member of the Order of Australia). Professor of Cartography in the School of Science at RMIT University, his major research interest is the application of integrated media to cartography and the exploration of different metaphorical approaches to the depiction of geographical information. William is well published in his field.

Dr Barbara Garrie is Lecturer in Contemporary Art in the Department of Art History and Theory at the University of Canterbury, New Zealand. She has a specialist interest in contemporary photography, and the field of artists' publishing. Recently her research has also been concerned with the role of contemporary art practices in the post-quake city. She is currently working on an edited volume with colleague Dr Rosie Ibbotson, which critically reflects on art and material culture in post-quake Christchurch (forthcoming, Canterbury University Press).

Professor Paul Gough is Pro Vice-Chancellor and Vice-President of RMIT University. A painter, broadcaster and writer he has exhibited internationally and is represented in the permanent collection of the Imperial War Museum, London, the Canadian War Museum, Ottawa, and the National War Memorial, New Zealand. In addition to roles in national and international higher education, his research covers art history, cultural geography and heritage studies. He has published a monograph on Stanley Spencer: *Journey to Burghclere* (2006); *A Terrible Beauty: British Artists in the First World War* (2010) and *Your Loving Friend*, the edited correspondence between Stanley Spencer and Desmond Chute (2011); and books on the street artist *Banksy* (2012) and on the painters, John and Paul Nash (2014).

Nicholas Lyon Gresson QSM is an independent writer and poet in New Zealand, with interests in law, justice, poetry and photography. He has worked as a legal investigator and *amicus curiae* in legal cases in New Zealand. To honour his public work against crime and assistance with those in mental health, he was awarded a Queen's Service Medal for public services in 1999. His poetry is published in three collections: *A Life in Poetry* (2011), *Walking with Time* (2013) and *A Gathering* (2015) (Australian Scholarly Publishing). A fourth book of poetry is underway and an auto-ethnography embracing the judicial histories of his family.

Professor Elizabeth M. Grierson has been an academic leader and researcher with RMIT University Melbourne for 11 years. She is a Life Fellow of Royal Society of Arts (UK), and is well qualified with a PhD in Education (Auckland); Juris Doctor, Distinction (RMIT); MA, 1st Cl Hons, (Auckland); and Graduate Diplomas in law and education. She is editor of *ACCESS* journal. Authored and edited books include *De-Signing Design* (2015); *Re-Imagining the City* (2013); *Supervising Practices for Postgraduate Research in Art, Architecture and Design* (2012); *Designing Sound for Health and Wellbeing* (2012); *A Skilled Hand and Cultivated Mind* (2012, 2008); *Creative Arts Research* (2009); *Thinking through Practice* (2007); *The Arts in Education* (2003). Elizabeth is an Australian and New Zealand lawyer.

Fiona Hillary is a Lecturer in Art in Public Space at RMIT School of Art. She is the Curator/Producer of *Urban Laboratory* at the Centre for Art, Society and Transformation. She is a public artist, collaborating on temporary investigative projects, and a permanent work in Noble Park for the City of Greater Dandenong. Fiona's research interests are in collaborative practice, socially engaged art practice and temporary installations. Fiona is a PhD candidate at Deakin University, researching the role of temporary public art practices in re-imagining futures. She co-authored 'Empty-Nursery Blue: On atmosphere, meaning and methodology in Melbourne street art' in *Public Art Dialogue* (2014).

Dr Geoff Hogg is Director of CAST, Centre for Art, Society and Transformation, RMIT University, Melbourne. Geoff holds a PhD (RMIT) in the expanded field of art in public space, and has an international reputation in this field as both an artist and educator. Publications include *Outer Site: International art in public space RMIT* (co-ed., McCulloch and McCulloch 2010). He has an international reputation in his field and has led over 80 major Art in Public Space projects both in Australia and overseas.

Dr Tammy Wong Hulbert has worked as an artist, arts editor and curator in Beijing, Sydney and Melbourne and trained as an artist and arts manager at College of Fine Art, University of New South Wales. Her PhD research, 'The City as a Curated Space' was a study repositioning contemporary art in public urban space under the framework of the curated city. She continues to work on research in this field and is a casual academic in Art Theory and Arts Management at RMIT and Melbourne universities.

Dr Kirsten Locke is a philosopher of education at the Faculty of Education, University of Auckland, whose work is primarily informed by continental philosophy and aesthetic theory and practice. Kirsten's research interests are in the area of affective pedagogy and the educational function of aesthetic experience to the spaces of education. Kirsten has published internationally and is currently writing a book under contract with Springer on affective pedagogy that focuses on the pedagogical value in the aesthetic theories of Jean-François Lyotard.

Dr Maggie McCormick is head of the Master of Arts (Art in Public Space), and a key researcher in the Centre for Art Society and Transformation (CAST) at RMIT University. Working between Australia, Asia, Europe and South America, Maggie's research focuses on the changing nature of urban consciousness and its evidence in contemporary art practice. Maggie holds a PhD, 'The Transient City: Mapping urban consciousness through contemporary art practice' (University of Melbourne 2009). Recent publications are *SkypeLab: Transcontinental faces and spaces* (Eichinger and McCormick 2016); 'The Transient City: The city as urbaness' in *Re-Imagining the City* (Grierson and Sharp 2013); 'Urban Practice and the Public Turn' in *Asia Pacific Journal of Arts and Cultural Management* (2012).

Clare McCracken is a mixed-media artist and PhD candidate at RMIT University, researching methodologies of participatory art in the age of hyper mobility. Investigating place and identity through narrative, images and installations, she creates works for public space, theatres and galleries. Clare has permanent works installed beside the Eastlink Freeway, Melbourne and in the Post Office Hotel, Richmond. Her work is included in the State Library of Victoria's permanent collection and numerous private collections.

Dr Anthony McInneny is a visual artist and academic as conjoint fellow at the University of Newcastle (Australia), guest professor at Universidad Mayor (Chile) and Pontificia Universidad Católica de Chile and member of the RMIT Centre for Art, Society and Transformation (CAST). McInneny holds a PhD (architecture), *Latent Space, Temporary Art and Suburban Public Space, 2014*. His research concerns Henri Lefebvre's concept of spatial practice through James Meyer's analysis of the functional and literal site in art. He is interested in the contemporary forms and uses of the street, the plaza and the park. He is currently living and working in Santiago, Chile.

Dr Grace McQuilten is a Vice-Chancellor's Research Fellow at RMIT University. Her PhD explored the relationship between art, design and consumer culture. She is an art historian, artist, curator and writer, working across the fields of contemporary art, design, social enterprise and community development. She published *Art in Consumer Culture* (Ashgate 2011) and *Art as Enterprise: Social and economic engagement in contemporary art* (IB Tauris 2015), co-authored with Anthony White.

Dr Keely Macarow is an Associate Professor and Deputy Head of Research and Innovation in the School of Art, RMIT University. Her PhD (University of Melbourne) is titled, 'Disturbance: Bodies, disease, art'. Keely has worked as a producer, artist, curator and researcher for film, video, performance sound and exhibition projects, presented in Australia, Europe and the United States. Her research is focused on socially engaged art.

Roger Nelson is an art historian and independent curator based in Phnom Penh, and a PhD candidate at the University of Melbourne researching modern and contemporary

Cambodian art. His writing on Southeast Asian art is published in magazines including *ArtAsiaPacific,* and journals, *Contemporaneity: Historical Presence in Visual Culture; Stedelijk Studies;* and *Udaya: Journal of Khmer Studies.* He has curated projects in Australia, Cambodia, Singapore, Thailand and Vietnam.

Jodi Newcombe is a curator and creative producer specializing in artistic responses to environmental challenges. She is director of Carbon Arts, an organization working to facilitate an increased role for artists in generating awareness and action on climate change. An environmental engineer and economist by training with an international career in consulting to business and government, Jodi is committed to multidisciplinary and creative approaches to progressing a low-carbon future. Jodi is a PhD candidate with Creative Industries, Queensland University of Technology.

Dr Ashley Perry is affiliated with the School of Media and Communication at RMIT University. He holds a PhD, 'Car-tographies: A critical visual analysis of three Melbourne autoscapes' (RMIT 2014). Ashley's research interests are inter-disciplinary, spanning the fields of mobilities studies, cinema studies and public art research. In 2013, he published a chapter in *Re-Imagining the City: Art, globalization and urban spaces* (Grierson and Sharp, Intellect), examining the role of site-specific artworks situated along the EastLink Tollway corridor in outer-suburban Melbourne.

Professor Jane Rendell is Vice Dean of Research and Professor of Architecture and Art at the Bartlett School of Architecture, University College London. She is a writer, art critic and architectural historian/theorist/designer, whose work explores interdisciplinary intersections between architecture, art, feminism and psychoanalysis. Authored books include *Spaces of Transition* (2016); *Site-Writing* (2010); *Art and Architecture* (2006); *The Pursuit of Pleasure* (2002); co-edited books are *Pattern* (2007); *Critical Architecture* (2007); *Spatial Imagination* (2005); *The Unknown City* (2001); *Intersections* (2000); *Gender, Space, Architecture* (1999); and *Strangely Familiar* (1995).

Dr Kristen Sharp is Senior Lecturer in Art History and Theory at RMIT School of Art. Her research focuses on contemporary art and urban space, collaborative practices in transnational art projects and contemporary Asian art. Kristen was a Chief Investigator on a three-year, Australian Research Council Linkage Project *Spatial Dialogues: Public art and climate change,* in Melbourne, Shanghai and Tokyo. Recent publications: *Screen Ecologies: Art, media and the environment in the Asia-Pacific* (co-author, MIT 2016); *Re-imagining the City: Art, globalization and urban spaces* (co-ed, Intellect 2013); *Outer Site: International art in public space RMIT* (co-ed, McCulloch and McCulloch 2010). She co-curated 'The Sonic City' for Liquid Architecture sound art festival; and was an International Visiting Researcher at Musashino Art University, Tokyo (2012).

Sarah Yates is an artist and social activist working for Greenpeace Australia and New Zealand as a researcher and Oceans intern, and who participated in the Rainbow Warrior 'Save the Reef' tour in North Queensland. Sarah was project leader for the building of the mosaic that is the focus of this chapter. She is committed to exploring the social value of public art and its pedagogical implications in post-disaster research.